AUTO RACING

Memorabilia and Price Guide

Mark Allen Baker

Published by

krause publications

700 E. State Street • Iola, WI 54990-0001
Telephone: 715/445-2214

Please call or write for our free catalog of automotive publications. Our toll-free
number to place an order or obtain a free catalog is 800-258-0929 or please use
our regular business telephone 715-445-2214 for editorial comment
and further information.

Library of Congress Catalog Number: 95-82424
ISBN: 0-87341-437-3
Printed in the United States of America

Dedication

To Thomas and Nancy Allen, my uncle and aunt, and Tommy, Jr. and Kelly, my cousins.

Also in memory of Sherman and Margaret Allen.

Contents

Acknowledgments

Foremost, I would like to thank everyone at Krause Publications for their continued confidence and support of this project, especially Mark K. Larson, Deborah Faupel, Pat Klug, Bob Lemke, Hugh McAloon, Chris Williams, and Marge Larson.

The following people and organizations have contributed to the information and photography presented in this book. My sincerest and heartfelt appreciation for your gratitude and permission to use the material:

Public Affairs Department - Ford Motor Company - Ford Quality Care Racing - Dick Trickle, Team Lowe's Racing - Sports Marketing Enterprises - Denise W. Michaux - Brett Bodine - Junior Johnson, Exide Batteries Racing Team- Exide Motorsports - Geoff Bodine, Pennzoil Racing - Bahari' Racing - Michael Waltrip - Cohn & Wolf - Drew Brown, Ernie Irvan Fan Club - Selena King, Alumax Indy Car Race Team - Alumax Aluminum - Rick Shaffer- Stefan Johansson - Tony Bettenhausen, Ricky Craven Fan Club, Du Pont Motorsports - Performance PR Plus - Kimberly O'Brien - Jeff Gordon - Rick Hendrick, Hardee's Racing - Bob Boyles - Greg Sacks, Troy Beebe, The Ertl Company Inc. - Robert W. Eager, Mattel Inc. - Diane L. Kapantzos, Bobby Labonte Fan Club, Cruz Pedregon Motorsports - McDonald's Racing Team - Cruz Pedregon - Cory McClenathan - Jim Yates, Gene M. Snow Enterprises Inc. - Gene Snow, STP Products Inc. - Bobby Hamilton - Richard Petty, Skoal Racing - U.S. Tobacco Motorsports - Jay Wells - Rick Mast, Pennzoil Racing - Hall Racing - Jim Hall - Gil de Ferran, Diamond Ridge Motorsports - Peggy Schrock - Meineke Racing Team - Steve Grissom, Indy Car, Jasper Motorsports - Bobby Hillin, Camp & Associates Inc. - Larry M. Camp - Interstate Batteries Motorsports - Bobby Labonte, Simpson Products, Pioneer Drag Racing Team - Tom Hoover, Maxx Race Cards - Jill Santuccio, Cotter Communications - David Hart - Western Auto Racing - Shelly Anderson, King Sports Inc. - Kirk Weeks - Quaker State Racing - Hut Stricklin - Kenny Bernstein, Smokin' Joe's Racing - Rob Goodman - Jim Head - Gordie Bonin, Hormel Foods - Spam Racing - Lake Speed, National Sprint Car Hall of Fame - Thomas J. Schmeh, Roush Racing - Stephanie Smith - Ted Musgrave, Entertainment Marketing Corp. - Tide Racing - Ricky Rudd, D-R Racing Enterprises - Anna Marie Malfitana - Tim Fedewa, Motorsports Hall of Fame - Barbara Flis, Sabco Racing - Jon Sands - Kyle Petty, Kmart Texaco Havoline Racing - Newman/Haas Racing - Michael Knight - Michael Andretti - Paul Tracy, Rahal Hogan - Bobby Rahal - Raul Boesel, Kodak Film Racing - Sterling Marlin, Stavola Brothers Racing - Ketta Allen - Jeff Burton, Forsythe Racing - Thomas Soltis - Teo Fabi, Don Garlits Museum of Drag Racing, Hooters Racing, Creasy Family Racing - Gary Bolger, Fred Lorenzen - Autodreamers, International Motorsports Hall of Fame - Don Naman, PPG Indy Car World Series - Carol M. Wilkins, Phoenix Network - Kenny Koretsky, Muhleman Marketing Inc. - Bob Hice - Ricky Craven, Project Indy - Andreas Leberle - Hubert Stromberger, Team Menard - Andy Card - Arie Luyendyk - Scott Brayton, Galles Racing - Adrian Fernandez, Elliott Museum & Souvenir Centre Inc. - Cindy K. Elliott, Indy Regency Racing Eurosport - Lesley Incandela, American International Motorsports - Tammy Oberhofer - Connie Kalitta - Scott Kalitta, Kellogg's Company - Jennie Donohue - Kellogg's Racing - Terry Labonte - Rick Hendrick, Miller Brewing Company - Marc Abel - Rusty Wallace, Hooters Racing - Jill Horton - Elton Sawyer, Al Hofmann, Dale Earnhardt Fan Club, Chesrown Racing, Inc - Cathy Carelli - Rick Carelli, Bobby Allison Motorsports Team, Inc. - Derrike Cope, NHRA, Valvoline Racing - Joe Amato Racing - Donna Bresnahan, Elliott Hardy promotions - Bill Elliott, Keystone Marketing Co - Gigi D'Antonio - Tommy Houston - Mike Wallace, The Source International Inc. - Teddi Smith - Ward Burton, Dover Downs, Mid-Ohio Sports Car Course - Michelle Gajoch, Portland International Raceway, The Milwaukee Mile - Dave Austin, Bristol International Raceway, Grand Prix of Cleveland - Denny Young - IMG Motorsports, New Hampshire International Speedway - Lorraine Faford, Molson Indy - Jerry Priddle - Edelman Houston Group, Charlotte Motorsports Inc. - Charlotte Motor Speedway -

Eddie Gossage, Atlanta Motor Speedway, Sears Point Raceway, North Carolina Motor Speedway, Toyota Grand Prix of Long Beach, Bob Laycock (deceased), Annette Combs - Indianapolis Motor Speedway Hall of Fame Museum.

To R. J. Reynolds Tobacco Co., PPG Industries Inc. Automotive Products, and Anheuser-Busch Inc., whose dedication, commitment, and support of auto racing is appreciated by every fan of the sport.

To Alison M. Long for your love, support, and belief that what once was, can be again. It can, we can, and we will. I love you!

To my parents, Mr. and Mrs. Ford W. Baker, thank you for always being there when I need you.

To Jeffrey Baker, Tracey and Haysam Rachid, Matthew and Jennifer Baker, I miss you all dearly.

Finally, to Aaron, Elizabeth, and Rebecca (R. J.) Baker. The last few months have been hard on us all. Remember you are always in my thoughts and prayers. With this book maybe Indianapolis won't feel so very far away. I love all of you so very much and I am so very proud to be your father.

Introduction

As you look at the sport of auto racing, look deep inside to all the wonderful elements that make it work. It doesn't take you long to figure out that it is actually one big family. From the long hours of set-up time put in by race teams to the seemingly endless commitment by sponsors, each person involved in the sport is a critical element to its success and a member of its family. Understanding what it takes to trust in the professionalism and skills of the driver in front of you as you draft him at 185 mph is a feeling few of us have ever had. It is part of the sport and its family. Not to mention the level of confidence it takes to get in a car and know that you can drive it as hard as you want because you trust in each and every member of your race team, your family. Auto racing is one of the only sports where as a fan, you also feel a part of the family. Why? The answer is simple—because you are. The crews, track employees, sponsors, team owners, and drivers all need each other and especially need you. What makes auto racing different from baseball, football, and basketball is that its stars, people like Dale Earnhardt, Mark Martin, Rusty Wallace, and Jeff Gordon, know, appreciate, and understand how much the sport relies on you, the fan, while the stars of the other sports do not. This is why Mark Martin spends hours after his victory at Watkins Glen signing autographs for free. When was the last time you saw Dennis Rodman sign autographs for hours after a big Chicago Bulls win?

As racing fans we love the sport, the thrill of Rusty Wallace drafting Dale Earnhardt into a corner at Talladega, or watching the masterful cornering through a chicane by Jacques Villeneuve, or the

Fans wait for hours in the grueling heat for driver autographs

From cleaning the windshield to tightening lug nuts, it doesn't take long to realize racing is a family (The car featured is Ted Musgrave's The Family Channel Ford #16.)

anticipation of the "Christmas Tree" lights as Scott Kalitta apprehensively sits on the starting line next to Kenny Bernstein. As racing fans we identify most with the drivers. The longevity of a racing fan's loyalty to his favorite driver probably surpasses the length of most marriages. As loyal fans we are not afraid to adorn ourselves in applicable driver apparel as an example of our commitment.

As a way to show how much I appreciated the material that was provided me for this book by race teams, sponsors, and track officials, I thought I would give them this introduction as forum for expression. As a fan you too will enjoy some of the quotes, all of which are contained in press kits or media guides that many of you have never had an opportunity to read.

In Their Own Words – Racing in 1995

"We just have to keep doing what we're doing. We're finishing races, and that's very important. But we go out to win. When we don't win, we're disappointed."

– Jeff Gordon

"The Kid is good. The light switch is on this year. I know him real good, and I can tell it's his time. When he's switched on like this, he's hard to turn off."

– Ray Evernham, crew chief for Jeff Gordon

"If it doesn't happen this year, it'll happen next year. Hopefully, we're going to be around for a long time. Time is on my side."

– Jeff Gordon

"Sometimes you can take a team, make a change in its leadership, alter the car's paint job and turn the whole program around. Well, we've just done that."

– Kyle Petty

Kenny Bernstein, "Mr. 300," has been a prominent figure in both NHRA Funny Car and Top Fuel drag racing for many years. He also owned Indy Car and NASCAR racing teams in recent years, but has since sold both to concentrate on returning his Top Fuel team to victory lane on a regular basis. Early in 1996 he scored a victory on the NHRA trail in his Budweiser-backed dragster and is a threat to win the Top Fuel championship. (Photo courtesy of King Sports, Inc.)

"I enjoy the people in racing, for the most part, more than the people in Hollywood. There's a lot of 'bull' in racing, but it's fun, put-on 'bull.' Nobody takes themselves seriously while doing it. That's what makes it fun."

– Paul Newman, Newman/Haas Racing Team

"It definitely seems different, not racing against dad. My whole career in Indy Cars, he's been there, too. He's still there at the races, but it's definitely different."

– Michael Andretti, speaking about his father, retired racing champion Mario Andretti

"The fun, the only real fun, in racing is winning. If you win, Sunday night is fun and it might even carry over to Monday morning. Then it's work again."

– Carl Haas, Newman/Haas Racing Team

"It seemed like everybody … everybody … said 'yeah, yeah, sure you can … sure you can,' and when we put the big numbers on the board at Rockingham we were able to open their eyes and shut their mouths."

– Rusty Wallace

"I think Raul (Boesel) has a finesse, a sense of what he likes in a car that is similar to mine."

– Bobby Rahal

"He (Joe Gibbs) keeps calling me his quarterback and I get a kick out of that. Next to racing, professional football is my favorite sport."

– Cruz Pedregon

"Short tracks have been good for me over my racing career and I know Bristol is going to be a good challenge for us. It can be really tough. It's so fast, anything can happen really quick. There's hardly any time for a reaction, and you can get caught up in something real quick."

– Ricky Craven

"I feel we've gotten to this position in Winston Cup racing in a short time. But I've had a lot of good people helping me. I doggone sure didn't do it on my own."

– Ward Burton

"A TV reporter asked me shortly after it was announced that I'd be driving for Richard (Petty), 'Why are you going to such an unstable team?' I answered, 'It won't be unstable anymore.'"

– Bobby Hamilton

"We got a Funny Car that thinks it's a Top Fuel dragster, and we're not telling it otherwise."

– John Force

"In another sixteen seasons, I'll be as old as Harry Gant was when he retired last year and we raced against each other for the 1979 Winston Cup Rookie-of-the-Year title."
– Terry Labonte

"The drivers are a lot more aggressive now than they have ever been in the history of racing. You are cramming so many good cars into the race track and expecting every team to be successful. It's just a sign of the times."
– Michael Waltrip

"We would all be heroes now if not for the bad luck. I know I've said that before, but it's the truth. If we can just shake the bad luck, we'll be there. Believe me."
– Rick Mast

"Driving a Top Fuel car has no equal on the planet. Nothing compares to the adrenaline rush you get in a Top Fuel dragster. It's an absolute rocket ship ride every time down the track."
– Jim Head

"Late in the race, having to deal with No. 3 (Earnhardt), I knew it wasn't something I would enjoy. Our cars always seem to come together, especially in the old days. I didn't know what to expect. But he raced us hard and raced us clean. He crowded us a little bit in three and four, but didn't give us any cheap shots."
– Ricky Rudd

"It's tough to beat experience, and that's what I really need. Look at Earnhardt. He's won 65 races, and I've only been in 73 races. He's raced in almost 500 Winston Cup races, so that's giving up a lot of experience."
– Bobby Labonte

"The more there are strikes and stuff in sports, the more people relate to us. I'm happy to be able to do a job I enjoy. I understand their side. They only have so many years to play. But people don't want to hear that. They don't want to hear somebody telling them how tough it is. They want to enjoy the game."
– Jeff Burton

History of Indy Car Racing and Championship Auto Racing Teams

Although auto racing historians have tried to pinpoint when Indy Car, or AAA, championship racing actually started, a consensus has yet to be reached. Some state that the first AAA national championship actually occurred as early as 1902; others feel it may have been as late as 1916. Whatever the case, Indy Car racing stands as the longest continually scheduled major motorsport championship in the world.[1]

The American Automobile Association (AAA) began sanctioning major races in 1904, although the first American automobile race actually took place in 1895. The country's single biggest and most prestigious motor race of the year was the Vanderbilt Cup. This race was run on open roads and was organized by the AAA from 1904 to 1916. A rival organization, the Automobile Club of America, also sanctioned an event called the American Grand Prize road race. This event was sanctioned by the ACA from 1908 to 1916.

Using a surface of crushed rock and tar, the Indianapolis Motor Speedway was opened in 1909. The world of purpose-built speedways began to unfold, and this was met with some skepticism whether such venues could compete against road races. In 1911 the first Indianapolis 500-mile race took place. The original track surface had been replaced by more than three million paving bricks, thus coining the nickname "The Brickyard." Using a locally-built Marmon Wasp, Ray Harroun averaged 74.59 mph on his way to victory in the first Indy 500. It took him six hours, forty-two minutes, and eight seconds.

In 1909, *Motor Age* magazine's editorial staff began selecting their "national driving champion." Using lists of all types of AAA races, two officials from the organization created a mythical series of championships from 1909 to 1920, but the idea was discarded by higher representatives. Years later, proof of the idea was rediscovered by AAA officials who since have credited Val Haresnape and Arthur Means for their keen approach to a racing championship. The first year in which the AAA nominated specific races to stand as rounds of a national championship has been traced to 1916. The success of "The Brickyard" set forth a wave of high banked "board tracks" to be built around the United States. The years 1915 and 1916 saw no fewer than eight of these tracks built of pine boards and by the end of the next decade over twenty had been added. The early speedways acted as the core of the AAA's early national championships.

---

1. Indy Car racing progression of organization:

AAA	1904-1955
USAC	1955-1979
CART	1979-1991
Indy Car	1991-date

The first national title awarded by the AAA in 1916 went to an Englishman, Dario Resta. He won not only the inaugural national championship, but also the Indianapolis 500. Resta captured the checkered flag at "The Brickyard" having run only 300 miles, the only time the race was ever scheduled to run less than the now traditional 500.

World wars would twice impact auto racing, first in 1917 and 1918, followed by 1942 through 1945. The second championship, awarded in 1920, is believed to have been won by Gaston Chevrolet; however, some historians argue that it was Tommy Milton. It was Chevrolet who drove one of his own Frontenacs to victory at Indianapolis and, according to newspaper accounts, to a national title awarded at the end of 1920.

The "Roaring Twenties" were good to auto racing, as record crowds came out to watch many of the major events. They witnessed fleets of American-built Millers battle Duesenbergs, with race records falling like checkered flags. With so many advances in racing technology, especially supercharging, the 100 mph mark was first topped at Indy in 1919 and increased ten percent six years later. Board track records also fell, some seeing speeds of 140 mph. New heroes called race car drivers emerged. Ralph De Palma, Earl Cooper, Ralph Mulford, Jimmy Murphy, and Tommy Milton soon developed a following of spectators who watched in awe of their skills during the sport's "Golden Age."

The Depression saw both the disappearance of jobs and maintenance-intensive board tracks. In order for racing to survive it had to be brought under some cost guidelines. The stock-block engine formula was introduced as such an effort. Unfortunately the sport would still take a beating, as only three AAA national championship races were run. Most races were now taking place on dirt horse tracks, a prelude to a recipe that would serve both the AAA and USAC national championship racing for decades.

Driver Rene Thomas and his unidentified riding mechanic (right) used this Delage speedster to win the 1914 Indianapolis 500. The lack of safety equipment available to racers of this era is evident in this photo and explains why many prewar drivers had brief careers behind the wheel. (Photo courtesy of the Indianapolis Motor Speedway)

14

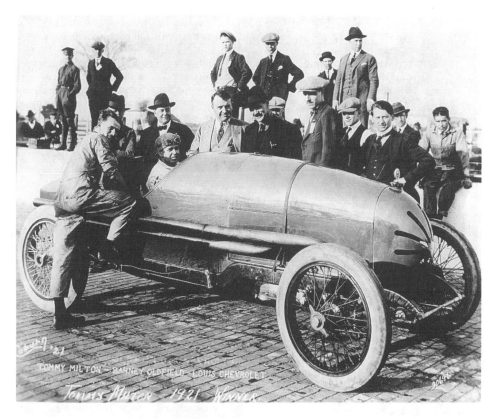

This lineup represents a Who's Who of early auto racing luminaries. The 1921 Indy 500 winner Tommy Milton is shown in the cockpit of the victorious Frontenac Eight. Standing to the right of Milton is "The Father of Speed" Barney Oldfield and to his right is Milton's car owner Louis Chevrolet. Louis' brother Gaston won the previous year's Indy 500 and controversy exists among racing historians whether he (Gaston Chevrolet) or Tommy Milton was awarded the national (AAA) racing title for 1920. (Photo courtesy of the Indianapolis Motor Speedway)

The Vanderbilt Cup was resurrected in 1936 and 1937, bolstering a tattered AAA championship with two road course races at Roosevelt Field on New York's Long Island. Two European champions, Tazio Nuvolari (Alfa Romeo) and Bernd Rosemeyer (Auto Union), had their names added to record books by winning the races. While at Indianapolis, the last two years of the decade belonged to Wilbur Shaw. Driving in a Maserati Grand Prix car, Shaw scored two consecutive Indy 500 victories.

Indianapolis faced another challenge after World War II, as former air ace and owner Eddie Rickenbacker sought to sell the Speedway. Former champion Wilbur Shaw feared that the land would be sold to real estate developers and the property subdivided. Shaw sought out someone who would continue with the racing tradition at the Speedway. He was lucky enough to find a wealthy Indiana businessman, who was also a sportsman, by the name of Anton "Tony" Hulman, Jr. to buy the site.

Hulman asked Shaw to serve as the general manager of the track and the great race was revived in 1946. Prewar car eligibility remained the same to insure a competitive field. Ted Horn, who finished third at Indy in 1946, was a consistent and competitive element in all six of the circuit's races, earning him the first postwar series championship.

Many elements of racing were slow to change after the war. There still remained two distinct types of competition. Outside of Indianapolis, every other race on the circuit took place on dirt oval tracks. This meant that in order for a driver to be competitive, he must develop his skills on both surfaces.

The varied surfaces led many car owners to build special creations just for Indianapolis. Offenhauser-powered cars dominated the surface at Indy, as lighter, front-wheel-drive vehicles became the rage. The Blue Crown Spark Plug Specials of Lou Moore finished 1-2 in 1947 and 1948, won in 1949, and finished second in 1950. Lighter, conventional rear-wheel-drive cars used on multiple surfaces

Events run for the prestigious Vanderbilt Cup were revived in 1936 and 1937 and were staged as part of the national (AAA) championship trail. This program cover depicts the 1937 road course event at Roosevelt Raceway won by Bernd Rosemeyer in his Auto Union.

dominated racing from 1950 to 1952, but they too would fall prey to technology.

In 1952, the first "roadster" emerged from creator Frank Kurtis and it had an immediate impact on the racing community. To allow for the drive shaft to pass beside the driver instead of beneath him, a wider chassis was featured in the design. To reduce the car's center of gravity, as well as the frontal area, the inline four-cylinder Offenhauser engine was tilted. As a result, the car could go through turns 10-15 mph faster than conventional designs, but it was totally inadequate for dirt tracks.

The Kurtis roadster led some of the 1952 Indy 500 before a steering arm broke. The following two years, however, it won the prestigious race. The national championships the same years were won in conventional upright dirt cars driven by Sam Hanks and Jimmy Bryan.

In 1955, A. J. Watson began to make significant developments to the Kurtis design. Watson was the chief mechanic that year as Bob Sweikert won the Indy 500. Watson-built entries would win at Indianapolis in 1956 and then dominate from 1959 to 1964.

New drivers were emerging, like Bettenhausen, Ward, and Foyt, who exhibited exceptional skills while becoming extremely popular with race fans. The AAA stopped

Bill Holland won the Indianapolis 500 in 1949 behind the wheel of the potent Blue Crown Spark Plug Special shod with Firestone tires. The Blue Crown cars dominated the Indianapolis Motor Speedway in the late 1940s. (Photo courtesy of the Indianapolis Motor Speedway)

16

Formula One world driving champion Jim Clark ran "The Brickyard" in 1964 (finishing second) and 1965 (victory). Clark's Ford-powered Lotus utilized monocoque construction that linked body and chassis and reduced weight while adding rigidity. Clark dominated the 1965 Indianapolis 500, leading 190 of 200 laps and averaging a then-record 150 mph pace for the 500 miles.

History in the making at the 1977 Indianapolis 500. This Lightning Offenhauser was driven by Janet Guthrie, the first woman to race at "The Brickyard."

sanctioning races after the 1955 season. To conduct the Indy Car series the United States Auto Club (USAC) was created. The organization began to add more events on paved surfaces such as Darlington, Milwaukee, Phoenix, and Trenton.

In 1963, English car owner and designer Colin Chapman was approached by Dan Gurney about the possibility of both forces joining together for an assault at "The Brickyard." The previous year on the Formula One circuit, Chapman had perfected a rear-engined chassis design and "lay down" driving position with his Lotus 25. For the Indianapolis 500 he agreed to race a modified version of the Lotus 25 powered by an engine from his new partner, the Ford Motor Company.

The new Lotus featured a lower center of gravity, which increased corner speeds over the conventional roadsters. To add rigidity and reduce weight, the car utilized monocoque construction and fabricated sheet metal instead of welded tubes. The monocoque construction was borrowed from the aviation industry, in which the chassis and body were one and the same.

In addition to Gurney running at Indy, Chapman also asked his regular number one driver Jim Clark. Gurney qualified twelfth and struggled to finish seventh, while Clark qualified fifth and finished second with an extraordinary performance. Clark would win at Milwaukee in August and also capture the Formula One Championship. In 1965, Clark along with Lotus sealed the fate of the Offy roadster by leading 190 of 200 laps at Indianapolis. Clark also became the first driver to average over 150 mph for the duration of the race.

The early 1960s belonged to A. J. Foyt, who dominated the circuit, winning the 1960, 1961, 1963, and 1964 Indy Car Championships. In 1964 he set a circuit record by winning ten of thirteen races at an unbelievable .769 season winning percentage.

An Italian immigrant named Mario Andretti challenged Foyt for the crown in 1965 and won in his first full Indy Car season. Using an imitation of Clark's Lotus called a Hawk-Ford, Andretti became the first driver to win the championship with a rear-engined car. He also won the first road race on the Indy circuit since the Vanderbilt Cup. The 150-mile race was held at the Indianapolis Raceway Park and proved to flatter Andretti's skills perfectly.

Turbochargers, tires, and turbine cars were some of the elements that would affect Indy Car racing during the end of the 1960s. Turbochargers made a comeback, tires got wider while Goodyear and Dunlop battled Firestone, and a Ken Wallis-designed STP Turbine car dominated at Indy in 1967. Mario Andretti captured his second straight series championship in 1966 and nearly a third in 1967. A. J. Foyt won his third Indy 500 in 1967 and the season championship in a circuit that now included twenty-one races.

In 1968, Bobby Unser became the first turbocharged winner in Indianapolis history and narrowly captured the championship from Mario Andretti after a long grueling season that included twenty-eight races.[2] Andretti finally found himself in "Victory Lane" at Indianapolis in 1969. It was a strong season for the driver, who won nine of twenty-four races en route to his third championship. The season also marked the first appearance of wings on Indy Cars. Wings work to improve cornering capabilities, enhance traction, and maintain a balanced vehicle.

Wedge-shaped McLarens found their way from Europe to the United States in 1971. The design was the first to feature the now-universal side radiator arrangement. It opened everyone's eyes when it took the two top spots on the starting grid at "The Brickyard." Al Unser successfully defended his title at Indy, but couldn't overtake the powerful performance of teammate Joe Leonard in the point standings. For Leonard it would be the first of two straight titles.

With no mechanical similarities to paved races, resulting in excessive costs to car owners, dirt races were removed from the Indy Car Championship for the first time in 1971. Logic had finally prevailed, as over the years the two forms of racing had grown so far apart that not even the engines were the same.

The next decade would find increased fervor in the Indy Car series. In 1972 the first official 200 mph Indy car qualifying lap was turned by Jerry Grant in Gurney's Eagle-Offy. In 1977 A. J. Foyt became the first four-time winner at Indianapolis. The parts news of the decade centered around tires, as Goodyear became the sole supplier to Indy Car from 1975 to 1994. As many as forty-four tires are allowed for 500-mile events (short ovals and road courses are limited to twenty-eight), at a cost of $1,200 per set. One car can use more than $150,000 worth of rubber during the season.

Prior to 1976, turbocharged Offenhauser engines dominated Indy Car racing. They were followed by a Cosworth DFX V-8 engine. Al Unser, equipped with Cosworth power, became the first and only driver to win three Indy Car 500-mile races in the same season. The following year the Cosworth won eight of fourteen races and an amazing all but one race from 1979-1986. Such was the defeat of the Offy.

Costs continued to escalate while purse did not, creating dissension among Indy Car owners. The owners, who had only one position on the twenty-one-member USAC board, wanted greater participation in their own destiny. When it was clear that would not be the case, eighteen Indy car owners

2.   The turbine of the turbocharger, powered by exhaust gases, powers a compressor which compresses the intake air and forces it into the intake manifold, resulting in much more efficient engine operation and a substantial increase in horsepower.

met and decided to create their own organization and run their own events. On November 25, 1978, Championship Auto Racing Teams, Inc. and the Indy Car World Series was born.

The group headed by President U. E. "Pat" Patrick was determined to be more responsive to the needs of those in and around the sport. They were confident that through increased visibility and marketing they could increase revenues while controlling costs.

The first event staged by the newly formed group was a 150-mile race at Phoenix International Raceway. In front of a national network television audience, Gordon Johncock narrowly escaped Rick Mears for the victory. The success of the first event was a prelude to what was to follow. The group staged thirteen races and included the results of the Indianapolis 500 in the final point standings. In his first full season of Indy Car competition, Rick Mears won three races and compiled enough points to win the first Auto Racing Teams Championship. Later that same year, a milestone announcement took place as PPG Industries announced it would be the title sponsor for the 1980 Indy Car World Series.

As the decade came to a close, more and more racing teams were experimenting with "ground effects." Jim Hall, known for pioneering aerodynamic down force with wings, teamed with designer John Barnard in 1980 to produce the **Chaparral 2K**. The goal of the design was to create a low-pressure area underneath the car by modifying its bottom design so that it seemed to be "sucked" to the pavement. Combined with wings on the front and rear of the car, these under-car tunnels create down force, permitting the vehicle to corner at greater speeds. With each passing year, technology such as "ground effects" continued to improve any weaknesses in Indy Car designs.

Johnny Rutherford impressively won the 1980 PPG Indy Car World Series Championship by compiling five wins in twelve starts. Meanwhile, competition and race revenues consistently increased. Rick Mears put together back-to-back titles in 1981 and 1982, while Al Unser edged Teo Fabi by five points to win in 1983. The always impressive Mario Andretti took his fourth championship in 1984. Nepotism reigned in 1985 as Al Unser beat his son Al Unser, Jr. by only one point to grab the title. A new rivalry developed on the circuit between Bobby Rahal and Michael Andretti. Both these talented drivers exhibited tremendous track skills and remarkable consistency. Rahal registered back-to-back championships in 1986 and 1987, narrowly escaping his nemesis. A new engine, the Chevrolet Ilmor, emerged in 1988. It would dominate during the next four seasons, capturing all but three races.

Jim Crawford, driving the Quaker State/King Motorsports entry owned by drag racing legend Kenny Bernstein, competed in the 1991 Indianapolis 500 using a Buick V-6 stock block power plant that was capable of producing 800 horsepower.

To emphasize the highly competitive nature of Indy Car racing, six different drivers would win the PPG World Series Championship over the next six years. Danny Sullivan, Emerson Fittipaldi, Al Unser, Jr., Michael Andretti, Bobby Rahal, and Nigel Mansell each took the spotlight in a sport that now featured four different types of tracks. From superspeedways (long ovals greater than one mile) to short ovals, or from temporary road courses (such as downtown streets) to permanent road courses, each of these unique settings tests a different set of driver skills.

Purses continued to climb as the end of the decade edged closer. Many of the goals set forth by the Championship Auto Racing Teams, Inc. were coming to fruition and the organization was strong enough to modify its structure if the organizers felt it was required. The Detroit Grand Prix became the first and only Indy Car event with a $1 million purse in 1989, but the following year would see five others. An overseas event was added in 1991, as the schedule included the Gold Coast Indy Car Grand Prix in Surfers Paradise, Australia. The year also marked the first time since 1959 that the first six races were won by different winners.

"Indy Car" was officially introduced as the new "brand name" for the sport in 1992. The new name replaced the former acronym CART (Championship Auto Racing Teams), which remained as the governing body of all events in the PPG Indy Car World Series except the Indianapolis 500.

Another engine development occurred as Ford introduced its first factory-entered engines in twenty-one years, built by Cosworth. It proved to be everything the manufacturer claimed by winning five out of sixteen races. Unlike the vintage days of auto racing in which one engine/chassis combination usually dominated, drivers now had several quality alternatives.

During the next three years new rules were implemented to control costs, increase competition and safety, and maintain policy consistency. One such rule was the three-year "rollover" promoter contract that allowed for improved planning. The circuit also added a new event, the New England 200 at New Hampshire Int. Speedway, which was the first of its kind since 1928.

In 1993 many new names were frequenting the top of the results. One such name was Nigel Mansell, the reigning Formula One champion, who became the first rookie in history to win the championship. The British driver also tied Paul Tracy for the most wins in the season (five). Other drivers such as Robby Gordon, Scott Goodyear, Stefan Johansson, and Raul Boesel began to establish themselves on the circuit.

The organization continued to evolve structurally as control of the group reverted to the team owners holding the twenty-four franchise shares. New strategies were implemented to take the sport into the next century.

Al Unser, Jr. captured his second PPG Championship in 1994. Driving in his inaugural season for Marlboro Team Penske, he won eight races including the Indianapolis 500. Penske teammate Emerson Fittipaldi also put together a fine season to finish second in PPG Cup standings. The team also used a Mercedes-Benz all-new 209 cubic inch pushrod engine at "The Brickyard."

The Rahal-Hogan team debuted a Honda offering to the circuit in 1994 and Rookie of the Year honors went to a young driver by the name of Jacques Villeneuve. Villeneuve would rock the circuit in 1995 by capturing a very early PPG Cup Championship.

History of NASCAR and the Winston Cup Series

The world's fastest growing professional sport began during the post World War II era as an attempt to add some organization to a group of men and machines who just couldn't be separated. The vision of NASCAR's founder Bill France, Sr. was to organize all of the quality stock car teams and build it into a national and international unit.

France called the first organizational meeting on December 14, 1947 in Daytona Beach, Florida. Even though NASCAR wasn't formally incorporated until February 21, 1948, the group sanctioned its first race six days prior on Daytona's beach course. The Ford modified No. "22" car driven by Red Byron won the race. Jim Roper won the first race of the Grand National division the following year at Charlotte, NC.

Ushering in the speedway era, Darlington Raceway played host to the inaugural Southern 500 on September 4, 1950, a race won by Johnny Mantz. In 1952 NASCAR launched its Speedway division of Indianapolis-type cars, using American-made block engines. Buck Baker won the first title in a division that was very popular with fans despite its short history.

Expansion hit NASCAR in 1954 as ten West Coast tracks were brought into the circuit. The following year another division made its debut as NASCAR merged with SAFE, a Midwestern racing

The "Fabulous Hudson Hornet" was the scourge of early 1950s NASCAR racing. (Above) Eventual 1952 race winner Marshall Teague enters the straightaway in his 1952 Hornet while (below) Dick Rathmann #120 (1951 Hornet) battles Tim Flock #91 (1951 Hornet) through a corner on the original Daytona Beach, Florida, oval that utilized part of Highway A1A, as well as the beach. The 1958 beach race was the final event on the sand as the 2-1/2-mile Daytona International Speedway opened in February 1959. (Photo courtesy of the Phil Hall Collection)

Early action at the 2-1/2-mile Daytona International Speedway has Bunkie Blackburn (#42 Petty Enterprises Plymouth) leading eventual winner Fireball Roberts (#22 Pontiac) during the 1962 Daytona 500. Sadly, Roberts would succumb to injuries received in a racing crash two years later. (Photo courtesy of the Daytona International Speedway)

organization. Don Oldenberg became the first champion in the convertible division. That same year Herb Thomas won his third Southern 500, becoming the first man to do so.

One of the most important elements in NASCAR's growing popularity was beach racing. It dated back to 1930 and had been with the organization since its inception. It came to an end in February of 1958 as Paul Goldsmith drove to victory in the last race held on Daytona sand. It would not by any means, however, mark the end to racing in Daytona, as the giant International Speedway opened in February of 1959. After three days of studying the photo finish, Lee Petty was determined the winner of the inaugural Daytona 500. In addition to his victory at Daytona, the talented Petty also picked up his unprecedented third Grand National Championship.

In 1960 NASCAR added two gems to its arsenal, the Atlanta International Raceway and Charlotte Motor Speedway, both of which added enormous strength to the organization's schedule. Network television added fuel to the fire of NASCAR popularity when ABC's "Wide World of Sports" program aired The Firecracker 250 at Daytona International Speedway for the first time.

A mark in single-season winnings was set in 1963 as Grand National driver Fred Lorenzen topped the $100,000 level. Ned Jarrett won his second national championship in 1965, having previously won in 1961. It was a year that would mark new developments in safety, most notably the Firestone Racesafe fuel cell bladder that diminished many drivers' concerns of fire. The following year the Goodyear Tire & Rubber Company introduced a safety inner liner tire in a move to minimize the effects of high-speed blowouts.

Richard Petty was busy constructing his racing legacy as he added a second win at the Daytona 500 in 1966. Little did he know the following year he would accomplish the greatest individual season on record. Petty captured an amazing twenty-seven wins, including ten consecutive and a second Grand National Championship. The talented and aggressive driver was virtually unbeatable.

David Pearson put together a solid performance in 1968 by scoring sixteen victories in forty-eight starts and winning his second national driving title in three years. The following year, driving a Holman-Moody Ford, he was again unstoppable en route to becoming the second man to win three Grand National driving championships. The decade would add one more superspeedway before ending. A 2.66-mile track called the Alabama International Motor Speedway opened at Talladega.

Entering the next decade, NASCAR could be evaluated with one word, "potential." There seemed to be no end in sight to its popularity and strength. Although 1970 provided many milestones, such as Buddy Baker's 200 mph closed course mark at Alabama and the last Grand National race on dirt in September at Raleigh, it will be forever remembered as the year R. J. Reynolds Tobacco Company joined forces with NASCAR as the series sponsor. It was the largest commitment to the sport by a non-automotive related company and a relationship that would only solidify over time.

Now a popular racing analyst, Buddy Baker campaigned this Dodge Charger 500 during the 1969 NASCAR season. The following year Baker established a blistering 200 mph closed course speed record at the 2-1/2-mile Talladega (Alabama) Speedway.

NASCAR claimed its first driving millionaire in 1971, and its third three-time champion, Richard Petty. The forever enduring and accomplished driver would break the mark he tied with both his dad and David Pearson the following year by capturing an unprecedented fourth Winston Cup Championship. While Petty was still adding to his legendary status, another was stepping down. Bill France retired in 1972 as president of NASCAR and was succeeded by his son Bill France, Jr.

The year 1973 marked the Silver Anniversary of NASCAR. David Pearson put together an incredible season, winning eleven of the eighteen races he entered. Pearson was also named the Amer-

Although Richard Petty (#43) has always been the "King" of NASCAR stock car racing, Cale Yarborough (#11) was the dominant driver in the 1976-1978 seasons as he scored three consecutive NASCAR championships while driving for legendary car owner Junior Johnson. Johnson retired from NASCAR racing at the end of the 1995 season after forty years in the sport as both driver and car owner. (Photo courtesy of the Phil Hall Collection)

A potent force on the circuit since day one of his NASCAR career, Dale Earnhardt won rookie honors in 1979 and backed that up with a NASCAR championship the following year. "The Man in Black" in 1996 is chasing a record eighth NASCAR championship. Here he takes in the spoils of victory at the April 4, 1982, Rebel 500 at the Darlington Raceway in South Carolina.

ican driver of the Year, the fourth NASCAR driver in five years to win the illustrious award. Pearson, along with Cale Yarborough and Richard Petty, dominated again in 1974, but it was "King Richard" who would finally win his fifth NASCAR Winston Cup Championship in a very close battle. The following year Petty would repeat the performance, as there continued to be no end to his outstanding racing skills.

The following three years belonged to Cale Yarborough, as he put together three consecutive NASCAR Winston Cup Championships. David Pearson put together a solid season in 1976 and became the first two-time winner of the coveted American Driver of the Year award. That same year Buddy Baker became the first driver to finish a 500-mile race in less than three hours. In 1977 the NASCAR modified division saw Jerry Cook pick up his unprecedented sixth national championship. In retrospect, these years were a tribute to Cale Yarborough, the first NASCAR competitor to win over $500,000 in a single season.

The 1979 Daytona 500 became the first 500-mile race to be telecast live in its entirety by CBS. It was during the same season that saw Richard Petty win his seventh NASCAR Winston Cup title. "King Richard" edged Darrell Waltrip by

"Awesome Bill from Dawsonville" (Georgia), NASCAR champion Bill Elliott poses with the Winston Cup Series show car at the December 2, 1988, NASCAR awards banquet held at the Waldorf Astoria in New York City. Elliott practically owns the Most Popular Driver award, as voted annually by racing fans, and now drives the McDonald's Ford Thunderbird #94.

just eleven points. The 1979 Rookie of the Year honors went to Dale Earnhardt, who would turn around and win the 1980 Winston Cup Championship, the first driver ever to do so. During a 31-race season, Darrell Waltrip captured the 1981 NASCAR Winston Cup Championship while setting a single season earnings record.

Bobby Allison won his first NASCAR Winston Cup Championship in 1983 during a season that saw twelve different drivers win thirty NASCAR Winston Cup events. The R. J. Reynolds Tobacco Company continued its outstanding relationship with NASCAR by increasing its funding of the Winston Cup Series in a variety of ways during the decade. As such, during the 1985 season it was possible for the first time in motorsports history to have two drivers surpass the $1 million mark in winnings. Bill Elliott won the inaugural Winston Million, which was a $1 million bonus offered by R. J. Reynolds for any driver winning three of four major races. Darrell Waltrip also surpassed the $1 million mark on his way to his third NASCAR Winston Cup Championship.

The following two years belonged to "The Intimidator," who captured two consecutive Winston Cup Championships. Dale Earnhardt won five of twenty-nine races in 1986, and eleven of twenty-nine races in 1987. During the 1987 season alone he had twenty-one Top 5 finishes, while topping the $2 million earnings mark. There was absolutely no doubt after the 1987 season that Dale Earnhardt would be a force in Winston Cup racing from this point on.

Bill Elliott captured his first Winston Cup Championship in 1988, barely holding off a fine driver from St. Louis named Rusty Wallace. Wallace came back in 1989 to take his first Winston Cup title, but it was not without a battle as he edged Dale Earnhardt by just twelve points, the second closest battle in history. Earnhardt was back full force in 1990. "The Intimidator" won nine of twenty-nine races, with eighteen Top 5 finishes. In 1990 Earnhardt became the second driver in NASCAR history to win the prestigious title more than three times—the other of course being Richard Petty. Like Petty, Earnhardt's ability never seems to diminish. The following year he won again.

Also in 1991, Bobby Labonte, brother of 1984 NASCAR Winston Cup champion Terry Labonte, captured the NASCAR Busch Series Championship for the first time. Alan Kulwicki won his first NASCAR Winston Cup title in 1992 during the closest championship ever. The year also marked the end of Richard Petty's magnificent career. The most financially successful driver in NASCAR Winston Cup history retired following the final race of the season.

The next two years belonged to a racer who is leaving behind his own legacy, Dale Earnhardt. Earnhardt won six of thirty races in 1993 and four of thirty-one races in 1994. During both seasons he combined for an amazing thirty-seven Top 5 finishes. He now stands beside Richard Petty with a record seven titles.

In 1994 a NASCAR event was held at the famed Indianapolis Motor Speedway for the first time. The inaugural Brickyard 400 was won by a youthful Jeff Gordon in front of the largest crowd ever to see a NASCAR Winston Cup race. Gordon, the 1993 Winston Cup Rookie of the Year had seven Top 5 finishes and established himself as a key Winston Cup contender. Gordon came back solid in 1995 and edged in points the forever competitive Dale Earnhardt to capture his first NASCAR Winston Cup Championship.

The 1992 NASCAR championship battle went down to the final event at Atlanta Motor Speedway with Alan Kulwicki (#7) besting Bill Elliott (#11) by a mere ten points at season's end. Tragically, Kulwicki would not be able to defend his crown as he was killed in a plane crash in April 1993 en route to a race in Bristol, Tennessee.

Former NHRA Pro Stock Champion Bob Glidden campaigning a 1986 Ford Thunderbird a decade ago while carrying the #1 designation that goes with being champion. Glidden recently underwent heart surgery and is back on the NHRA Pro Stock trail in a Ford Probe Pro Stock car.

A Brief History of and Introduction to NHRA Winston Drag Racing

Under the guidance of Wally Parks, the roots of NHRA drag racing started to grow on the back roads and dry lake beds of Southern California more than four decades ago. It was the vision Parks and those around him that made NHRA drag racing one of the world's most popular and successful forms of motorsports. What led to the organization's birth in 1951 continues to be the foundation of NHRA's existence—educate the general public about the sport and adopt and maintain strict safety standards.

John "Brute" Force is a many-time champion of NHRA's Funny Car division, but is better known as a true "character" of motorsports who loves to mug for the camera and tell it like it is. Here he tells TNN's drag racing analyst Steven Evans how it was.

NHRA Board Chairman Wally Parks and his new organization established guidelines for organized drag racing. They standardized the quarter-mile as the measure of performance and created a firm framework that would oversee the safety of the sport.

Servicemen returning from World War II were drawn to the sport because of its excitement and found it to be a natural outlet for their mechanical inclinations. The news of this new form of auto racing spread swiftly across America, while the NHRA worked diligently on a nationwide schedule of events. Meanwhile, auto makers, intrigued by what they were seeing, rushed to introduce the most powerful engines they could build.

The Sixties saw drag racing mushroom in its popularity, while Detroit auto makers focused on performance in an era that would eventually be known for its "muscle cars." NHRA kept pace with the changes, established a technical services department, and even opened up divisional offices in seven geographic regions.

Even more races would be added in the decade to follow and the NHRA teamed up with Winston in 1975 to create a championship points fund. This new system would draw even more fans and provide the drivers with purses that exceeded $1 million per season.

The organization now boasts a membership of 80,000, 136 member tracks, more than 26,000 licensed competitors and more than 3,800 member-track events. The circuit of eighteen NHRA Winston Drag Racing events was given comprehensive media coverage in 1994, with the 1995 television package including nearly eighty hours of programming and all nineteen series events.

NHRA-style drag racing events and exhibitions have now been presented in more than twenty foreign countries and innovative Youth and Education programs can now assist young people in career guidance as it relates to the sport. A new generation of stadium-style "supertracks" is evolving as drag racing's media exposure continues to increase and draw more and more fans. The NHRA Winston Drag Racing Series now attracts 6.5 million fans with no end in sight to its popularity.

Introduction to Drag Racing

Of the three types of racing covered in this book, collectors are probably least familiar with this form. Drag racing is an acceleration contest between two cars racing down a straight-line quarter-mile course. The event is made up of a series of individual two-car races called eliminations. Cars are divided into a variety of classes that govern engine size, type of fuel, vehicle weight, allowable modifications, and aerodynamics.

A "Christmas Tree" is a set of lights used at the starting line, with a 0.4-second interval between the flash of all the amber lights and the flash of the green light in the "pro start" system. (This differs in handicap racing.) Any time a driver leaves the line before the green, a red light is illuminated to signal a foul and the offending driver is disqualified.

The total time it takes to go from the starting line to the finish line is called the elapsed time. Elapsed time doesn't begin until the car moves, so sometimes a driver can win despite a slower elapsed time than his opponent because he had a quicker reaction time to the green light. Handicap racing allows for slower cars to compete on an equal basis by altering the starting procedure to allow for the difference. National records are kept for elapsed time and speed in all classes.

The NHRA reviews all the mechanical differences in the cars competing in the sport and then accounts for not only them, but also for the ability of the drivers. Before the 1995 season the organization had established 220 individual classifications. These classifications are grouped into basic eliminator categories, complemented by a less structured program of elapsed time handicap brackets. Regulations for the twelve basic eliminator categories are strictly governed by the NHRA, while such is not the case with guidelines at many local tracks. These twelve categories are: Top Fuel, Funny Car, Pro Stock, Pro Stock Motorcycle, Top Alcohol Dragster, Top Alcohol Funny Car, Competition, Super Stock, Stock, Super Comp, Super Gas, and Super Street.

Top Fuel, Funny Car, Pro Stock, and Pro Stock Motorcycle comprise the four professional categories of NHRA competition. In addition to the two alcohol and three "Super" categories, these four categories feature a single type of race car or motorcycle. A wide variety of racing machines can be showcased in the other categories and equalized with the handicap systems.

Drag racing's top-of-the-line category is Top Fuel, in which 5,500-horsepower, nitromethane-burning dragsters can reach speeds of over 300 mph. The super-accelerating fuel-injected, custom-built, 500 cubic inch engines are mounted behind the driver. Entering the 1995 season, the quickest and fastest runs were 4.690 seconds and 314.46 mph. So fast are these vehicles that two parachutes

The Top Fuel cars of the NHRA burn nitromethane fuel and keep spectators sitting on the edge of their bleacher seats, watching every pass as the Top Fuelers' power and deafening noise make for quite a show. Violent engine explosions due to nitromethane's volatility are commonplace in this division.

are activated manually as the car's primary braking system to slow the 2,000 pound minimally weighted vehicles.

The short-wheelbased Funny Cars, with their fiberglass replica production car body, have engines that are identical to those that power the Top Fuel machines with one notable difference—they are located in front of the driver. These machines are also capable of elapsed times under five seconds and top speeds of 300 mph. Entering the 1995 season, the quickest and fastest speeds in a Funny Car were 4.939 seconds and 303.95 mph respectively for these vehicles that can not exceed 2,275 pounds.

Pro Stock cars at first glance resemble typical street cars, but feature extensive engine modifications, sophisticated chassis and suspension development, a maximum 500 cubic inch engine displacement, and a minimum weight of 2,350 pounds. Two-door coupes or sedans are used but the car must be 1990 or newer. Pro Stock cars all use carburetors, burn gasoline as fuel, have conquered the seven second elapsed time mark, and have attained speeds just under 200 mph.

To put speed in perspective with regard to NHRA drag racing, consider the following: a Top Fuel dragster leaves the starting line with a force nearly five times that of gravity, identical to that of the Space Shuttle when it lifts off the launching pad. This is faster acceleration than a jumbo jet, a fighter jet, or a Formula One race car.

A real crowd-pleasing aspect on NHRA's Funny Car division is the "burn out" done before a race pass down the quarter mile. This is done to heat up the rear tires for better traction. Here "240" Gordie Bonin melts his slicks at a 1995 NHRA meet at Firebird Raceway in Phoenix, Arizona. (Photo courtesy of Smokin' Joe's Racing)

PPG Indy Car World Series Speedways and Races

The Indianapolis 500: A Chronology

As this book went to press, the battle for "control" of Indy Car racing's future still raged on between the franchise owners of Championship Auto Racing Teams (CART) and Tony George, head of Indianapolis Motor Speedway and founder/organizer of the upstart Indy Racing League. This conflict has spurred CART to schedule a "boycott" race, the U.S. 500 at Michigan International Speedway, directly against the Indianapolis 500 on May 26, 1996.

With neither side willing to back down and legal battles among participants brewing in court (chiefly A. J. Foyt's lawsuit against CART), what the future of Indy Car racing will hold is anyone's guess at this point.

PPG Indy Car World Series Speedways and Races

The following speedways and races are organized chronologically according to the Indy Car racing season.

* Records are through the 1994 season

Marlboro Grand Prix of Miami

Miami Motorsports
1110 Brickell Ave., No. 206
Miami, FL 33131
303-379-5660

Australian FAI Indy Car Grand Prix

Indy Car Australia
Level 5
64 Marine Parade
Southport, QLD 4217
61-75-88-6800

The closed 2.795-mile temporary road course has a very demanding combination of five straight sections linked by chicanes to give sixteen turns. For a Grand Prix course it has a real race track feel due to its layout. Practice begins at 9 a.m. Saturday, with qualifying ending by 1:30 p.m. Warm-ups on Sunday begin at 9:00 a.m. and the race begins at 1:00 p.m. The final chicane on the back straight is a very exciting place to watch the race. Grandstand seating, which has the best view, is very limited.

Emerson Fittipaldi, Nigel Mansell, and both John and Michael Andretti have won at Surfers Paradise. Mansell, who has captured two poles here, also holds both the single lap record (106.053 mph) and race record (97.284 mph).

Collector's Note: Since this race began in 1991, the distance represents the real challenge in acquiring a collection of tickets and programs.

Slick 50 200

Phoenix International Raceway
P.O. Box 13088
Phoenix, AZ 85002
602-252-3833

Phoenix International Raceway is a one-mile oval located in a beautiful desert setting outside of Phoenix, Arizona. The one-mile oval features eleven-degree banking on Turns 1 and 2, while Turns 3 and 4 have nine-degree banking. Air turbulence from other cars is the greatest concern of drivers, who find each lap featuring a different set of driving conditions. Although many prefer to watch the race from Turn 1, Turns 3 and 4 can often be faster and much more interesting.

This event began in 1964, with A. J. Foyt winning its inaugural race at a speed of 107.536 mph. Al Unser served up the first back-to-back wins here in 1969 and 1970. The mid-1970s found Gordon Johncock and Johnny Rutherford putting on some nice driving exhibitions on their way to numerous victories. Tom Sneva won three consecutive fall races from 1980 to 1982, and Rick Mears went back-to-back in 1989 and 1990. Paul Tracy set a new single lap speed record in 1994 at 176.266 mph.

Collector's Note: Although teams stay all over town, the Wigwam (Litchfield) and Holiday Inn (West) are two of the more popular spots to run into your favorite driver. After the race, head to the paddock instead of fighting the traffic, as some drivers hang around there at the end of their day.

Toyota Grand Prix of Long Beach

Grand Prix Association of Long Beach
3000 Pacific Avenue
Long Beach, CA 90806
310-981-2600

The Long Beach 1.59-mile temporary road course features two long straights joined by a series of turns at each end. Often considered the most festive event on the circuit, it is also one of the "majors," like Indy, Detroit, Toronto, Michigan, and Laguna Seca. Celebrating its twenty-second year in 1996, more than 200,000 racing enthusiasts will gather along Shoreline Drive under the bright California sun to enjoy three great days of racing.

The Inaugural event, held in April of 1984, was won by Mario Andretti at a speed of 82.898 mph. He would then win two out of the next three races, surrendering only to his son Michael in 1986. The race would then be dominated by Al Unser, Jr., who put together a very impressive four consecutive victories from 1988 to 1991. "Little Al" would win once again in 1994 by setting a course record average speed of 99.283 mph.

Bosch Spark Plug Grand Prix

Nazareth Speedway
P.O. Drawer F
Hwy. 191
Nazareth, PA 18064
610-759-8000

The Nazareth Speedway is a one-mile tri-oval that features a single-file Turn 1, a fast Turn 2 with a downhill exit, and a blind Turn 3 with an uphill exit. Although its uniqueness is intriguing, its drawback is that you can't see the whole track from any one place.

Emerson Fittipaldi won back-to-back races at Nazareth in 1989 and 1990. He also holds the single lap speed record set in 1994 at 185.60 mph. The race, which dates back to 1987, has also been won by Michael Andretti, Danny Sullivan, Arie Luyendyk, Bobby Rahal, Nigel Mansell, and Paul Tracy. Andretti won the inaugural race in 1987 and has taken two poles at the event.

Indianapolis 500

Indianapolis Motor Speedway
P.O. Box 24152
Speedway, Indiana 46224
317-481-8500

The most famous race track in the world, this rectangular-shaped Speedway is two and one-half miles around with four turns banked at nine degrees. The Indianapolis 500 is the world's largest single-day sports event, with crowds of nearly a half million people.

Roberto Guerrero set both a single lap record (232.618 mph) and a four lap record (232.482 mph) in 1992, while Arie Luyendyk set the race record at 185.981 mph when he won the prestigious event in 1990.

Many teams arrive a month in advance to prepare for this very special race, for to win here can insure yourself of racing immortality. The race track is closed from the last day of qualifications until the Thursday of race weekend when cars can make final pre-race runs around the track.

If you want a collecting challenge, try putting together a set of programs, tickets, or winner's autographs from this auto racing event. It will indeed challenge both your commitment to the task and your wallet, as many items are not only difficult to find but expensive to purchase.

Miller Genuine Draft 200

The Milwaukee Mile
7722 W. Greenfield Ave.
West Allis, WI 53214
414-453-5761

The Milwaukee Mile is a one-mile oval with nine-degree banking in all four turns. The Wisconsin State Fair track is rich in racing history, as some of the greatest drivers of all time have driven on the track. Often described as wide, flat, and bumpy, the track is particularly hard on tires.

This very nostalgic event dates back to 1933 and has been won by virtually every big name in motorsports. Al Unser, A. J. Foyt, Bobby Unser, Tom Sneva, and both Mario and Michael Andretti have won the race at least four times. The great Rodger Ward has won this event seven times, twice back-to-back. Raul Boesel holds the single lap speed record of 165.752 mph, while the 200-mile race record is held by Michael Andretti, who drove to victory at 138.031 mph in 1992.

Indy Car 1995 at The Milwaukee Mile© (Photo courtesy of The Milwaukee Mile©)

Collector's Note: Autograph seekers are best to try hotel lobbies and restaurants, especially those along Moorland Road in nearby Brookfield. With so many former winners, the event has played a major role in the careers of many. Memorabilia from Tom Sneva's string of three consecutive wins (1982-1984) makes a nice ticket and program series.

ITT Automotive Detroit Grand Prix

Motor Marketing International of Detroit, Inc.
300 River Place
Suite 4000
Detroit, MI 48207

The same man who designed New York's Central Park also created Belle Isle Park in Detroit, Michigan. The beautiful setting along the water is reminiscent of the classic circuits of Europe. The event takes place on a 2.1-mile temporary road course that was shortened in 1992.

Michael Andretti has sat on the pole four times, and won in 1990. He also holds the single lap record on the old course (88.721 mph), as well as its race record of 84.902 mph. Paul Tracy set a new course record when he won in 1994 at a speed of 86.245 mph. Emerson Fittipaldi has won twice at the raceway—the inaugural race in 1989 and again in 1991.

Budweiser/ G.I. Joe's 200

Portland International Raceway
Global Events Group
4242 SE Milwaukee
Portland, OR 97202
503-232-3000

This nine-turn road circuit is demanding on fuel, as drivers work the two long straights very hard. Three 180-degree turns link the straights on this municipally owned track. Built on the former loca-tion of Vanport, which was wiped out by a flood in 1948, the first Rose Cup races were held in 1961.

The raceway attracts approximately 350,000 spectators to 135 annual events and is in use nearly every day of the year. It facilitates a wide spectrum of users from driving schools to Indy Cars.

This 1.95-mile road course has attracted a variety of outstanding Indy Car drivers to its event, which dates back to 1984. But it is the name Andretti that has become so familiar. Mario Andretti won back-to-back races here in 1985 and 1986, and Michael put together a series of three consecutive victories from 1990 to 1992. Michael Andretti's win in 1991 was at a record speed of 115.208 mph for that distance. Of the various single lap records, it's Emerson Fittipaldi's 1991 speed of 122.470 that has been so very impressive.

Texaco/Havoline 200

Road America
N7390 Highway 67
Elkhart Lake, WI 53020
414-892-4576

Constructed in the mid 1950s, this four-mile track is one of the longest and fastest circuits in the United States. Its fast straights and tight turns make fuel consumption an important factor.

Both Emerson Fittipaldi and Mario Andretti have won this event three times. Mario and Michael Andretti have both accomplished back-to-back victories. Michael Andretti set the race record in 1991 running at a speed of 126.205 mph on his way to his second victory. In recent years Paul Tracy has run this course extremely well, capturing three consecutive poles from 1992 to 1994, and winning the race in 1993.

Molson Indy Toronto

Molson Indy
Exhibition Place
Exhibition Stadium
Gate 9, 4th Floor
Toronto, Ontario
Canada M6K 3C3
416-260-9800

This 1.78-mile run through the streets of Toronto and along beautiful Lakeshore Boulevard is well liked by the drivers because of its smooth wide surfaces.

This temporary road course event dates back to 1986, when Bobby Rahal won the inaugural event at the speed of 87.414 mph. Michael Andretti has won four times in Toronto and put back-to-back victories together in 1991 and 1992. Andretti's victory in 1991 was won at a speed of 99.143 mph, the highest in the short history of the event. In 1994 Robby Gordon managed a single lap record of 110.191 mph.

Molson Indy Toronto (Photo courtesy of Edelman Houston Group/Molson Indy)

Collector's Note: All collectors are encouraged to head to the Molson Indy Marketplace (east of Exhibition Stadium, south of the Molson Export Bridge) and sample the wide variety of the latest motor racing souvenirs and novelties.

Collectors should also remember that there are three specialty passes that provide spectators with access to areas tickets do not: 3-Day VIP Pit Walk-thru Pass ($25), gold ticket holders only, limited pit lane access; 3-Day Snap-on Tools Indy Car Garage Pass ($15), all gold tickets include this MUST pass for autograph collectors; and 3-Day Super Photo Pass ($160), the only way to go for photographs and a great way to view the race.

With the event dating back to only 1986, it's still very possible to put a nice collection of memorabilia away from this event. All of Michael Andretti's wins, especially the back-to-backs, make a nice collectible series.

Medic Drug Grand Prix of Cleveland

Burke Lakefront Airport
Motormarketing International of Cleveland, Inc.
One Erieview Plaza
Suite 1300
Cleveland, Ohio 44114
216-781-3500

Burke Lakefront Airport, located next to Lake Erie, is the site of this 2.369-mile, ten-turn temporary road course. The circuit, which combines two runways and a taxiway, is one of the fastest road courses on the Indy Car schedule. From the grandstands spectators can view most of the circuit while watching the cars achieve 140 mph lap averages.

Both Emerson Fittipaldi and Danny Sullivan have won three times at Cleveland. Paul Tracy holds the single lap record (144.139 mph) at the current course length, while Al Unser, Jr. turned the course on his way to victory in 1994 at a speed of 138.026 mph.

Collector's Note: The race dates back to only 1982, so putting together a collection of tickets and programs shouldn't be an exhaustive task for racing memorabilia collectors.

Marlboro 500

Michigan International Speedway
12626 US 12
Brooklyn, MI 49230-9068
517-592-6666

This is one of three such circuits owned by Roger Penske, and he immediately paved it after his purchase to make it one of the fastest tracks in the series. The two-mile Superspeedway features eighteen-degree banked turns with straights at both five and twelve degrees.

This race dates back to October of 1968 when the inaugural event was won by Ronnie Bucknum at a speed of 163.043 mph. Since then some of the biggest names have won here including A. J. Foyt, Gordon Johncock, Johnny Rutherford, and Rick Mears. Both Bobby Unser and Mario Andretti have managed back-to-back wins here during the same season at different distances, with Andretti setting a new course single lap record in 1993 at 234.275 mph.

During its history, the race has been held at a variety of distances from 126 miles to its current 500 miles. Al Unser, Jr. set a new 500-mile speed record with his win in 1990. "Little Al" flew around the oval at an average speed of 189.727 mph.

Collector's Note: Race memorabilia from the inaugural event in 1968 can sometimes be elusive, as can some of the early programs and tickets. Both back-to-back wins make a nice series to commemorate. Collectors remember that the Speedway began the multiple race format here in 1973 and kept it until 1986.

Miller Genuine Draft 200

Mid-Ohio Sports Car Course
Steam Corners Road
P.O. Box 3108
Lexington, OH 44904
419-884-4000

Les Griebling opened Mid-Ohio Sports Car Course in 1962. It was refurbished by the Trueman family in the mid-eighties, and began to emerge as a premier facility. The now 2.25-mile road course, with its intriguing layout, is rather narrow with sections requiring very quick cornering.

Johnny Rutherford won the first Indy Car race held at Mid-Ohio in a Cosworth/Chaparral at a speed of 88.601 mph. Al Unser, Jr. set a new single lap speed record in 1994 at 119.517 mph. Emerson Fittipaldi, who has won the event three times, set the race record in 1992 at 107.352 mph.

Bobby Rahal, Michael Andretti, and Emerson Fittipaldi have all put together back-to-back victories at the Mid-Ohio Sports Car Course. Teo Fabi has also won the event twice, once from the pole.

Collector's Note: With this Indy Car event dating back to only 1980, it's still possible for collectors to put together a complete collection of tickets, posters, and programs. There was no race in 1981 and 1982, so there are two you won't have to worry about, but finding memorabilia from the 1980 race could take some time.

Official event merchandise is available at the Mid-Ohio souvenir stands or you can order these items by calling 614-793-4613. Items that were available for this year's event included T-Shirt ($15), Hat ($14), Ribbed T-Shirt ($20), Poster ($5), and Souvenir Program ($5).

New England 200

New Hampshire International Speedway
1122 Rte. 106 North
P.O. Box 7888
Loudon, NH 03301
603-783-4744

This beautiful one-mile oval features tight twelve-degree turns over a smooth racing surface. This event was first hosted in 1992, with the inaugural winner being Bobby Rahal at a speed of 133.621 mph, a track record.

Nigel Mansell won in 1993, and Al Unser, Jr. in 1994. Emerson Fittipaldi set the single lap speed record at 175.091 mph in 1994 and captured the pole that year as well.

Collector's Note: Although a relatively new race has little collecting challenge, it certainly offers beginners a cost effective and comfortable place to begin their Indy Car collections.

Molson Indy Vancouver

Concord Pacific Place
Molson Indy Vancouver
765 Pacific Blvd. South
Vancouver, British Columbia
Canada V6B 4Y9
604-684-4639

This 1.677-mile temporary road course features nine turns around downtown's British Columbia Place stadium. It is known for its very narrow lanes and limited passing availability.

This event began in 1986 as Bobby Rahal drove to victory at a speed of 87.414 mph. Since that point, Michael Andretti has won half of the following eight races. Andretti even managed back-to-back victories in 1991 and 1992, and holds two race records at different distances. Robby Gordon set a single lap speed record of 110.191 mph in 1994.

Collector's Note: In addition to Andretti collectors enjoying the memorabilia from this course, Al Unser, Jr. collectors can add two victory programs and tickets to their "Little Al" collection.

Toyota Grand Prix of Monterey

Laguna Seca Raceway
1021 Monterey Hwy. 68
Salinas, CA 93908
408-648-5111

Located in the foothills of California's Monterey Peninsula, this 2.214-mile road course somewhat mimics the format at the Mid-Ohio Sports Car Course. The track was built in 1956, replacing the former Pebble Beach course. Known for its elevations, this eleven-turn course is picturesque in its surroundings.

This event began in 1983, with Teo Fabi winning its inaugural race at a speed of 106.943 mph. Following Fabi, Bobby Rahal amassed four consecutive wins all in excess of 112 mph. Danny Sullivan would follow Rahal, picking up two of the next three races. Michael Andretti then put back-to-back victories together in 1991 and 1992. Paul Tracy repeated Andretti's feat in 1993 and 1994. While taking the checkered flag in 1994, Tracy managed to set a single lap speed record of 113.768 mph. Prior to 1989 the course was only 1.9 miles.

Collector's Note: For Rahal fans, putting together a series of programs or tickets from his four consecutive wins here is a must. Andretti and Tracy fans can set their sights on the back-to-back series and compile some nice Laguna Seca Raceway memorabilia. Autograph hounds are forewarned that the paddock attracts huge crowds, making your task much more difficult. Collectors should be sure to drop by the Souvenir Store, next to the Expo Area by the lake.

The Indianapolis 500: A Chronology

The significance of this event, auto racing's premier race, and its associated memorabilia necessitates a race chronology. A value guide for programs and pit badges has also been provided for collectors. An occasional "Collector's Note" offers additional information about specific race memorabilia.
* Note: Pins with cardboard "Race Day Backups," add $15.00

1911

The first Indianapolis 500 was held on Tuesday, May 30, 1911. The red Fiat of David Bruce-Brown's led for much of the race, but it was Ray Harroun (#32) in his yellow Marmon Wasp who finished first to become the event's first winner. Harroun, who had designed the Marmon (chassis) Wasp, actually came out of retirement to win the race and upon its conclusion retired once again. The sleek tailed, yellow with black trim Wasp was appropriately named and finished at a winning speed of 74.602 mph. Pace Car: Carl Fisher (inventor of the rolling start behind a pace car), Stoddard-Dayton .

Program: $1,650

1912

Although it was Joe Dawson (#8) riding in his National that finally took the checkered flag, the race had been dominated by Ralph De Palma (#4). De Palma's Mercedes drove a rod through the crankcase in the 198th lap, forcing him out of the race. Having led since the third lap, a disappointed De Palma then found himself pushing his car over a mile and into the pits. Dawson's winning speed was 78.72 mph. Pace Car: Carl Fisher, Stutz Roadster.

Program: $1,375

1913

Jules Goux, winner of the 1913 Great Indianapolis Classic, and his DOHC Peugeot

Utilizing a revolutionary new design, Frenchman Jules Goux (#16) drove his DOHC Peugeot to victory at a speed of 75.93 mph. A frustrated Bill Endicott (#33), driving in his Case, became the first driver in race history to drop out after one lap. Pace Car: Carl Fisher, Stoddard-Dayton.

Program: $1,375

Collector's Note: The program from the race features an illustration of two cars racing around a corner of the track. The illustration is centered on the cover within a graphic design that is flanked by two of the speedway's logos. The program, which has a white background, reads as follows from top to bottom: "Official Program," "INDIANAPOLIS," "MOTOR SPEEDWAY" (red ink), logo, "PROGRAM 10¢" (black ink), "IMS" (blue ink), illustration, "IMS" (blue ink), "The GREATEST RACE COURSE," "IN THE WORLD" (black ink), "MAY 30, 1913" (black ink). The program, which is highly sought by collectors, is not an easy acquisition and often difficult to find in higher grade conditions.

1914

Using Delage and Peugeot machines, the top four finishers in the race were all European: Rene Thomas (#16), Arthur Duray (#14), Albert Guyot (#10), and Jules Goux (#6). Thomas's 2,300 lb. Delage won the race at 82.47 mph. The race is often remembered for the slang expression "to pull a real Gilhooley," as Ray Gilhooley flipped his Isotta after forty-one laps. Pace Car: Carl Fisher, Stoddard-Dayton.

Program: $1,225

1915

The relentless Ralph De Palma (#2) fiercely battled Dario Resta's Peugeot (#3) the entire race to win his first Indy 500. De Palma completed the race despite having the same problem he had in 1912—putting a rod through the crankcase. A crowd of 60,000 spectators watched De Palma crawl to victory on three cylinders at a speed of 89.84 mph. Pace Car: Carl Fisher, Packard.

Program: $1,125

1916

With the war in Europe paramount in everyone's mind, racing took a back seat to global affairs. The race, with its smallest ever starting field (twenty-one), was shortened to 300 miles (500 kilometers) out of respect for those at

An illustration depicting Rene Thomas' victory on May 30, 1914

war. Dario Resta (#17), in the same Peugeot he had used in 1915, dominated the race and captured his first Indy victory at a speed of 84 mph. The race at Indianapolis had always eluded Resta, who at the time of his victory had won just about every race he had entered. Considered one of the greatest drivers of his era, he would die tragically at Brooklands in 1924 when his Sunbeam blew a tire. Pace Car: Frank E. Smith, Premier.

Program: $1,000

1917-1918

The race was not held due to World War I.

1919

The 1919 Indianapolis 500 is best remembered as the first race with qualifying times exceeding 100 mph. Using a prewar Peugeot owned by the Speedway, Howdy Wilcox (#3) drove to victory at 88.05 mph. The race was marred by tragic crashes as three men were killed and two more critically injured. Pace Car: Jesse Vincent, Packard V-12.

Program: $950

Official program for the May 31, 1919 race

1920

Ralph De Palma, who would compile an astounding 613 leading career laps—a mark eventually broken by Al Unser in 1988—dominated the race. On Lap 187, De Palma's Ballot caught fire and had to be put out. He hobbled around the track on four cylinders and the field, led by Gaston Chevrolet, quickly passed him by. Chevrolet won the race in his Monroe at 88.62 mph. Pace Car: Barney Oldfield, Marmon 34.

Program: $950

1921

Tommy Milton (#2), who was chosen as a substitute for Gaston Chevrolet, won the 1921 Indy at a speed of 89.62 mph. Gaston had been killed during a race at the board track in Beverly Hills. Milton was driving one of two Frontenacs sponsored by designer and builder Louis Chevrolet. The other Frontenac, driven by Ralph Mulford (#8), finished ninth. Ralph De Palma (#4) led most of the race, but was unable to correct his bad luck. He thrust a rod through his engine block on Lap 112 and finished

Back in 1920 fifteen cents could buy you the official program for the Indianapolis Motor Speedway race

twelfth. This was the first radio broadcast of the Indianapolis 500 by Chicago station WGN. Pace Car: Harry Stutz, H.S.C. Series 6.

Program: $900

1922

The 1922 Indianapolis 500 was won for the first time by the pole sitter. Jimmy Murphy (#35), who was already known to many having won the 1921 French Grand Prix, took the victory at 94.48 mph. He put a new Miller I-8/181 cu. in. engine in his old Duesenberg chassis and qualified ahead of the field at 100.5 mph. Eight of the top ten finishers had a Duesenberg I-8 chassis. Pace Car: Barney Oldfield, National.

Program: $900

1923

A 1923 rule change allowed for new single-seaters to enter the field. On-board mechanics were no longer necessary due to the increased reliability of the automobiles. Tommy Milton (#1) became the first two-time Indianapolis winner as he drove his Miller to victory at 90.95 mph. It was the first win for the Miller I-8/121 cu. in. engine on a Miller chassis, a combination that would dominate American racing until the end of the decade. Milton's victory also marked the second consecutive year that the pole sitter was victorious at Indy. Pace Car: Fred Duesenberg, Duesenberg Model A.

Program: $825

1924

The driving team of Lora L. Corum and Joe Boyer took their Duesenberg (#15) to victory at 98.23 mph. Of the twenty-two cars in the field, fourteen were Miller (63.6%), while only four (18%) chose to drive a Duesenberg. The aggressive style of Boyer allowed him to sweep past the three fastest Millers, driven by Earl Cooper (#8), Jimmy Murphy (#2), and Harry Hartz (#4). Pace Car: Louis Pettijohn, Cole Master Model V-8.

Program: $800

1925

Outpacing the Miller dominated field, a Duesenberg once again crossed the finish line first. Peter De Paolo (#12) , Ralph De Palma's nephew, became the first winning driver to finish above 100 mph with a speed of 101.13 mph. Second place finisher Dave Lewis (#1) became the first front-drive Miller I-8 in the 500. The famous Indianapolis "pagoda" at the start/finish line burned the morning after the race and was later replaced by a more modern rendition. Pace Car: Eddie Rickenbacker, Rickenbacker 8.

Program: $725

1926

The Miller I-8 cars, now at the 1.5 liter formula (91 cubic inch), dominated the race. Frank Lockhart (#15), a substitute driver who

The 1925 program for the 13th International Sweepstakes at Indy is worth $725

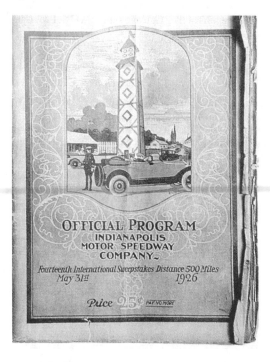

Official program for the May 31, 1926, Fourteenth International Sweepstakes Distance 500 Miles

had never raced on a paved track, drove his Miller to victory at 95.904 mph. The race was stopped at 400 miles because of rain. Pace Car: Louis Chevrolet, Chrysler Imperial Model 80.

Program: $675

Collector's Note: The white program from the race features an illustration of a car in the foreground with the track in the background. The two-color (orange and black) graphic illustration appears inside a simple border surrounded by ornate white lines. The program reads as follows from top to bottom, below the illustration: "OFFICIAL PROGRAM," "INDIANAPOLIS," "MOTOR SPEEDWAY," "COMPANY," "Fourteenth International Sweepstakes Distance 500," "May 31st" (same line) "1926," "Price" "25¢" (orange ink) "PAY NO MORE." All text is in black ink except where indicated. This program can be elusive to collectors, especially in higher grade conditions. Many of the programs have water stains due to the rain. Additionally, a shorter race typically means less time to sell programs.

1927

The intuitive and naturally talented Frank Lockhart, the 1926 Indy winner, dominated the race. Then in the 121st lap, with speeds hitting all-time highs, Lockhart broke a connecting rod in his Miller. The race was finally won by George Souders (#32), who managed to keep his car in the race while so many of the faster cars died out. Of the field of thirty-three automobiles, only ten finished the 200 laps. Souders, in a Duesenberg, finished at 97.545 mph. Pace Car: Willard Rader, LaSalle 303.

Program: $725

Collector's Note: The white program from the race features a sharp two-color (orange and black) graphic illustration of a man holding an automobile above a silhouetted horizon of factories. The program reads as follows from top to bottom: "OFFICIAL PROGRAM" (an Indianapolis Motor Speedway Co. logo appears centered behind both words), to the left of the graphic, "15th" (orange ink), "INTERNATIONAL," "SWEEPSTAKES," "500 MILES," beneath the graphic, "MAY 30th," "1927," at the bottom of the program on the same line, "PRICE 25¢" (inverted text on black graphic), "PAY NO MORE."

Official program for the 15th International Sweepstakes 500 Miles. Note 25 cent price.

1928

Only five out of a field of twenty-nine drivers chose to race in an automobile other than a Miller. Louie Meyer (#14) won the 1928 Indy at a speed of 99.482 mph. Meyer had trailed Leon Duray (#4) and Jimmy Gleason (#39), both of whom dropped out of the race. It was Gleason's own mechanic, pouring water on the magneto instead of the radiator during a pit in Lap195, that forced the Duesenberg I-8 out of the race. Pace Car: Joe Dawson, Marmon Model "78."

Program: $600

1929

Louis Meyer (#1) came back to Indy in 1929 and gave an outstanding performance. As fate would have it, Meyer, who had led most of the race, stalled during his last pit stop. Ray Keech (#2), in a Miller originally built for Frank Lockhart, took advantage of Meyer's seven-minute pit and raced on to victory at a speed of 97.585 mph. Lockhart was killed instantly on April 25, 1928, when he crashed during an attempt to set a land speed record at Daytona. Pace Car: George Hunt, Studebaker President.

Program: $525

1930

New rules were drawn up by the AAA Contest Board for the 1930 season. The Great Depression made it impossible for most to afford the expensive ($15,000) Miller 91 engines. The new rules, quickly labeled the "junk" formula, were considered a step backwards. It now made it possible for competitive Speedway cars to be built for about $1,500. A maximum engine size of 366 cubic inches (6.0 liters) and a minimum weight of 1,750 lbs., were just some of the new rules. Riding mechanics were back and sitting in a variety of modified passenger and race cars. Pole sitter Billy Arnold (#4) led all but the first two laps and took the victory at 100.488 mph. Arnold drove a Miller I-8 (152 cu. in.) on a Summers chassis. Pace Car: E. L. Cord, Cord L-29 Cabriolet.

Program: $525

Collector's Note: The two-stubbed ticket from this race features an illustration of an Indy car in the center of the main ticket portion. The ticket was printed with black and magenta ink on a light magenta paper stock. The very top of the main ticket portion reads "FRIDAY 1930 (large) MAY 30" on the same line in inverted text on a black banner. I have seen a few "printer proofs," which have no printed seating assignment on the ticket, for sale in the market.

A few red, white, and blue photographer passes have changed hands over the years in the racing market. These passes, which are worth more if they include the original red, white, and blue cloth that attached to the top of the pass, are extremely attractive with an interesting die-cut shape. The red and blue ink is printed on a white cardboard stock. At the top center of the pass is the Speedway's logo. Below the logo reads: "18th INT'L 500 MILE" (inverted text in a red banner), followed underneath by "SWEEP" (left side) "STAKES" (right side) in red ink. The pass was "NOT GOOD FOR GATE ADMISSION," which is printed in a small banner using inverted text near the bottom of the pass.

1931

Billy Arnold (#1) came out strong and took the lead on Lap 7. A mere thirty-seven laps from victory, Arnold crashed after his rear axle broke. Although both he and his mechanic were not injured, a wheel from his car was recovered outside the speedway. Lou Schneider (#23), who had started thirteenth, took the victory at 96.629 mph. Pace Car: Willard Rader, Cadillac 370.

Program: $450   Pit Badge (Celluloid Pin): $2,250

A photo pass (upper left) and a team manager pass (upper right) for the 500 Mile Race held May 30, 1932. A general admission ticket (left) for the 5/30/32 race. (Photos courtesy of the Indianapolis Motor Speedway Hall of Fame Museum)

1932

Fred Frame (#34), driving a Miller I-8 (182 cu. in.) on a Wetteroth chassis, won the 1932 Indy 500 at a speed of 104.144 mph. His teammate, Billy Arnold (#5), was involved in a collision and forced out of the race after fifty-nine laps. Pace Car: Edsel Ford, Lincoln KB Sports Roadster.

Program: $450

Collector's Note: A few single-stubbed, full "GENERAL ADMISSION" tickets from this race have surfaced in recent years in the racing memorabilia market. The two-color (dark blue and orange ink) general admission tickets are printed on yellow stock and feature a graphic of three racing cars. The top of the main portion of the ticket reads: "20th INTERNATIONAL," "500," "MILE SWEEPSTAKES." A portion of one of the racing cars is also printed at the bottom of the "RAIN CHECK" stub.

The "REAR OF PIT" passes issued for this race are vertical in format and printed on a red cardboard stock. It is a two-stubbed pass, a postponement (Gateman's stub) check, followed by a rain check. The top of the pass reads "TWENTIETH" (inverted text), "INTERNATIONAL," then printed inside a square as inverted text, "500," "MILE," "SWEEPSTAKE," then beneath the square in a rectangle is printed as inverted text "1932." These passes differ from the team passes, which were round and much more colorful.

1933

Louie Meyer (#36), who had won the race in 1928, took his Miller to victory at 104.162 mph. As Meyer drove into Victory Lane, he became the first driver to receive a bottle of milk, now an Indy tradition. The race was marred by controversy, first by a drivers' strike, then a reduced purse, and finally by the death of five men. Pace Car: Byron Foy, Chrysler Imperial Custom 8.

Program: $400

1934

"Wild Bill" Cummings (#7), on now restricted amounts of oil and gas, raced to victory in his Mill-er at 104.863 mph. Mauri Rose (#9), also in a Miller, finished a mere twenty-seven seconds behind Cummings. Pace Car: Willard Rader, LaSalle Series 350.

Program: $400

1935

Fred Offenhauser purchased the rights to a four cylinder engine that was being built by Harry Miller, and formed the Offenhauser Engineering Company. Aided by Leo Goossen and Louie Meyer, the team created one of the finest engines ever and delivered it to the market at $2,000. Kelly Petillo (#5) drove the Offy I-4 (260 cu. in.) engine to victory at a speed of 106.240 mph. Wilbur Shaw (#14), also in an Offy I-4 (220 cu. in.), nearly caught Petillo but finished second for the second time in three years. Pace Car: Harry Mack, Ford 48 Convertible.

Program: $400

1936

Using a car he built himself, Louie Meyer (#8) won the Indianapolis 500 for the third time at a speed of 109.069 mph. Wilbur Shaw (#3) and Babe Stapp (#21) battled at the beginning of the race, but both Offy-powered cars fell prey to problems. With the Depression coming to a close and Speed-way improvements now in place, a new era at Indy was about to begin. Pace Car: Tommy Milton, Packard 120 Convertible, the first pace car ever presented to the race winner.

Program: $340

1937

The turns on the track were redesigned and widened in 1936, making the Speedway much safer. Then in 1937 the turns and the short chutes were repaved with asphalt. By 1940 the only brick remaining at "The Brickyard" was now at the front straight, where it was left for sentimental reasons. In 1937 superchargers were allowed back for the first time in eight years and gasoline, actually high-octane aviation fuel, was required to be in its original state. In previous races crew chiefs had often combined various explosive chemicals in hopes of improving performance. In a close race, Wilbur Shaw (#6) drove his sleek Offy I-4 on a custom built chassis to victory at 113.58 mph. Pace Car: Ralph De Palma, LaSalle Series 37-50 Roadster.

Program: $330

Collector's Note: Memorabilia from this race is extremely popular with Indy collectors. Celebrating its silver anniversary, the 1937 Indianapolis 500 used the theme in the design of many of the items used for the race. The silver and blue program includes two graphics (blue ink) of the track and one graphic (blue ink) of a race car in a silver center horizontal banner. A large horizontal silver banner at the top of the program features "Silver Anniversary" (blue ink) written in large scripted text. A graphic of a band leader also appears at the bottom left of the program just above the price.

The two-color (red and silver ink, red string) 1937 Season Pass also includes reference to the anniversary. The pass reads as follows from top to bottom: "19 (single-hole punch) 37," "Indianapolis" (scripted inverted text in silver banner), "MOTOR SPEEDWAY CORP.," "SEASON," "TRACK PASS," "Silver Anniversary 500 MILE RACE," "IMS" "CORP."

1938

Floyd Roberts (#23), a successful Sprint car driver, took the checkered flag at 117.2 mph. Roberts, driving a Miller I-4 on a Wetteroth chassis, started at the pole and led for most of the race. Of the thirty-three drivers starting the race, only five would finish. Pace Car: Stuart Baits, Hudson 112.

Program: $225   Pit Badge (Bronze Pin): $2,500

Collector's Note: The single-color (green, green string) 1938 Official Race Day passes are simple in design and not overly attractive. User identification, such as "EMPLOYEE," is printed in red ink on two designated areas. The pass reads as follows from top to bottom: "IMS" (single-hole punch above the M), "CORP.," "Indianapolis" (scripted text), "MOTOR SPEEDWAY," "CORP.," "26th INTERNATIONAL 500 MI Sweepstakes," (designated area for identification), "NOT GOOD FOR GATE ADMISSION," (designated area for identification), "Race Day," "OFFICIAL," MAY 30TH.," "1938" (printed to the right of the last three lines of text in green ink).

The Reserved Seat ticket design for the 1938 Indy 500 features on the main ticket portion a race car taking the checkered flag. The two-color ticket (red and green ink) is printed on a pink stock. Gate and Section designations are printed in red ink, while the Row and Seat designations are printed in green ink. A facsimile signature of Eddie Rickenbacker appears near the bottom of the main ticket portion.

1939

Tragedy surrounded the running of the 1939 Indy 500, as the race claimed the life of 1938 winner Floyd Roberts (#1). Roberts was involved in a multicar accident that also seriously injured Chet Miller (#3). Louie Meyer (#45) battled with Wilbur Shaw (#2) until Lap198, when Meyer crashed and was thrown from his car. Shaw, in a Maserati I-8, cruised to victory at 115.03 mph. Pace Car: Charles Chayne, Buick Roadmaster.

Program: $225   Pit Badge (Bronze Pin): $2,750

1940

Wilbur Shaw (#1) won the Memorial Day Classic for the second consecutive year, becoming the first Indy driver to accomplish the feat. It was Shaw's third Indy victory and he completed the feat using the same car he had used in 1939 at a speed of 114.27 mph. The race had run fifty laps under caution due to rain. Rex Mays (#33), Mauri Rose (#7), and Ted Horn (#3) all finished after Shaw, who proved just too quick for his rivals. Ted Horn was in the midst of compiling the best finishing record of any driver who raced at Indy. In nine races at "The Brickyard" (1936-1948), Horn would complete 1,799 laps out of a possible 1,800. Pace Car: Harry Hartz, Studebaker Champion.

Program: $225   Pit Badge (Bronze Pin): $1,750

Collector's Note: The two-color (red and black ink) 1940 Official Program features an outstanding illustration of a race car on the cover. The attractive program is simple in design, yet very appealing to collectors. Many of the programs found in the market have water stains due to the rain, thus making it difficult to find in higher grade conditions. The program reads as follows from top to bottom: In red ink - "TWENTY - EIGHTH," "INTERNATIONAL," "500 MILE RACE" (top right corner), underneath the graphic, "OFFICIAL PROGRAM" - black ink with red drop shadow, using inverted text inside a red block, "25¢," "PAY NO MORE," "MAY 30 - 1940," "INDIANAPOLIS MOTOR SPEEDWAY CORP." in black ink.

1941

A defective wheel sent Wilbur Shaw (#2) into the wall on Lap 152. Once again Shaw had dominated an Indy race, but this time he would not repeat his victory. Car owner Lou Moore replaced Floyd Davis with Mauri Rose, who had dropped out of the race with his Maserati at Lap 60. Moore was confident that Rose, who had started at the pole, could find his way to victory. In an Offy I-4 (270 cu. in.) with a Wetteroth chassis, Rose won the race at a speed of 115.11 mph. Pace Car: A. B. Couture, Chrysler Newport.

Program: $175   Pit Badge (Bronze Pin): $1,500

1942-45

The race was not held due to World War II. Anton "Tony" Hulman, Jr. purchased the Indianapolis Motor Speedway from Eddie Rickenbacker for $700,000 in 1945. The track was in poor condition after the war and in desperate need of repair. Wilbur Shaw became President and General Manager of the Speedway in 1945. Shaw would hold both positions until a tragic plane crash would claim his life on October 30, 1954. Following Shaw's death, Hulman became President and chose Sam Hanks as his Director of Racing.

1946

The AAA (American Automobile Association) quickly prepared the Indianapolis Motor Speedway for what would be its first postwar race. Many old cars were dusted off and tuned up for a race that saw only nine out of a field of thirty-three cars finish. George Robson (#16) took the checkered flag in a Sparks I-6 on an Adams chassis at a speed of 114.82 mph. Rookie Jimmy Jackson (#61) finished a mere thirty-four seconds behind. Pace Car: Henry Ford II, Lincoln Continental Cabriolet.

Program: $60   Pit Badge (Bronze Pin): $3,450

1947

Although the FIA (Federation de l'Automobile), the governing body of international racing, opted for Formula One, the AAA remained steadfast to the prewar rules—3.0 liter supercharged or 4.5 liter unsupercharged cars. In a race run with no weight restrictions, Mauri Rose (#27) would cross the finish line first at 116.338 mph. Rookie Bill Holland (#16), also in one of Lou Moore's famous Blue Crown Specials, led most of the race but slowed under instructions by his team leader. Pace Car: George Mason, Nash Ambassador.

Program: $60   Pit Badge (Silver Pin): $1,700
                           Pit Badge (Bronze Pin): $850

An Indianapolis 500 bronze pit pass/badge from 1948

1948

For the second straight year Lou Moore's front-wheel drive Offy I-4's (270 cu. in.) finished both first and second. Duke Nolan (#54), in a Novi V-8, gave the team a run for the money and had he not fallen prey to a refueling mistake, probably would have won the race. An extra pit stop by Nolan allowed Mauri Rose (#3) to win the race at 119.81 mph. Only seven out of a field of thirty-three cars finished the race. Pace Car: Wilbur Shaw, Chevrolet Stylemaster.

Program:	$60	Pit Badge (Silver Pin):	$300
		Pit Badge (Bronze Pin):	$250

Collector's Note: The two-color (green and blue ink on white paper stock) 1948 Official Program features a graphic of a race car speeding across the top of the cover. The bottom half of the program cover reads as follows from top to bottom: "Official," "PROGRAM," "32nd 500 Mile Race," inside a checkered flag near the bottom left reads: "50¢," "PAY NO MORE," to the right of the flag reads, "MAY," "31," "1948" (green ink), and at the bottom inside a horizontal white banner, "INDIANAPOLIS MOTOR SPEEDWAY CORPORATION" (blue ink).

1949

The 1949 Indy race was once again dominated by Lou Moore's team of fuel-efficient Blue Crowns. The updated Offy I-4s, now designed by the Meyer-Drake team (1946), dominated the field of thirty-three (only 32 actually started). An astounding 87.5% of the field ran on Offy engines, most at 270 cu. in. Bill Holland (#7) crossed the finish line first at a speed of 121.327 mph. Rookie Johnny Parsons (#12) finished second after qualifying at the highest speed (132.9 mph). Pace Car: Wilbur Shaw, Oldsmobile "88."

Program:	$60	Pit Badge (Silver Pin):	$450
		Pit Badge (Bronze Pin):	$235

Collector's Note: The three-color (red, blue, and black ink on white paper stock) 1949 Official Program features a graphic of a race car speeding across the top of the cover, taking a very large checkered flag. The program cover is similar in design to the previous year's. The bottom half of the program cover reads as follows from top to bottom: "OFFICIAL," "PROGRAM," "33rd. 500 Mile Race," inside a white circle near the bottom left reads: "50¢," "PAY NO," " MORE" (red ink), to the right of the circle reads, "MAY," "30," "1949" (white), between the text is a horizontal banner, "INDIANAPOLIS MOTOR SPEEDWAY CORPORATION" (blue ink on light blue).

1950

Using the same car he ran in 1949, Johnny Parsons (#1) drove his Kurtis to victory at a speed of 124 mph. Frank Kurtis, the most successful of five postwar Indy car builders, beat out the Emil Deidt front-wheel drive Blue Crown cars. Nearly half of the Indy starters were driving a form of Kurtis cars, and only one without an Offy I-4 engine. After 345 miles, the race was stopped because of rain. Pace Car: Benson Ford, Mercury Convertible.

Program:	$50	Pit Badge (Silver Pin):	$340
		Pit Badge (Bronze Pin):	$175

1951

Lee Wallard (#99), in a very quick Kurtis/Offy, won the race at a speed of 126.24 mph. The lighter and smoother Kurtis cars finished in the top three positions. The race marked the end of Mauri Rose's career, when he decided to retire following an accident. The now traditional front-engine/rear-drive Offy powered cars were being refined and churning out faster and faster speeds with minimal changes. From Stu Hilburn's fuel injection system to Conze disc brakes, the precision in Indy car construction was constantly improving. Pace Car: Dave Wallace, Chrysler New Yorker.

Program:	$50	Pit Badge (Silver Pin):	$275
		Pit Badge (Bronze Pin):	$175

1952

Bill Vukovich (#26) dominated the race until a crash after 191 laps. It was a young Troy Ruttman (#98) who took the checkered flag at 128.92 mph. It is not Ruttman's win, however, that is the most significant event of this race, but the entry of a diesel-powered car driven by Freddie Agabashian. The huge (401 cu. in.) inline-6 was designed for trucks and fitted with a turbo-charger—the first ever to run at the Speedway. Equipped with 50 hp more than an Offy, the diesel maximized fuel efficiency but lacked a streamlined design. Although the car started at the pole, it failed to finish the race. It was this entry that would mark the beginning of the "Roadster" at Indianapolis. Pace Car: W. C. Newberg, Dodge Royal 500 Convertible.

Program:	$50	Pit Badge (Silver Pin):	$275
		Pit Badge (Bronze Pin):	$175

Collector's Note: The three-color (green, yellow, and black ink) 1952 OFFICIAL PROGRAM cover features an illustration of two race cars speeding across the finish line, taking a very large checkered flag, with the grandstands in the background. The bottom program cover reads as follows from top to bottom: "OFFICIAL," "PROGRAM," "36th 500 MILE RACE," "May 30, 1952" (yellow ink) - above the grandstand, below the graphic "50¢ Pay No More ... INDIANAPOLIS MOTOR SPEEDWAY CORPORATION" (yellow ink against green).

1953

Bill Vukovich (#14) once again dominated an Indy race, but unlike the 1952 race, he would cross the finish line first at a speed of 128.74 mph. On an extremely hot track, the pole sitter Vukovich led for all but five laps of the race. Vukovich's winning combination was a Kurtis chassis (KK500A) and an Offenhauser engine (Offy I-4/ 270 cu. in.), a combination similar to all but eleven entries in the field. The magic of the Kurtis roadster centered around placing more than half of the car's weight to the left side. The cen-

The official program for the 37th 500-Mile Race held May 30, 1953

49

trifugal force of Indy's high-speed left-hand corners transferred nearly 400 lbs. of weight to the right-hand side of a vehicle at current raceway speeds. The Kurtis design tilted the engine to the right, equaling the weight, improving traction and creating more uniform tire wear. Pace Car: William Ford, Ford Sunliner.

| Program: | $45 | Pit Badge (Silver Pin): | $225 |
| | | Pit Badge (Bronze Pin): | $125 |

Collector's Note: The three-color (red, yellow, and black ink) 1953 OFFICIAL Program cover features a modern Speedway illustration in the background, with a two-color graphic of a race car in the foreground. Above the illustration reads: "50¢ PAY NO MORE," "OFFICIAL" (white), "Program" (yellow ink), below the graphics reads, "37th 500-MILE RACE ... MAY 30, 1953," "INDIANAPOLIS * MOTOR * SPEEDWAY * CORPORATION" (white).

1954

The 1954 Indy would be remembered as the best-running field in the race's history. Only two cars (Johnny Parsons and Bill Homeier) would fail to complete at least half of the race. The Art Cross Bardahl Special car (#45) would also set an Indy record for the most drivers (five) in a single car. At a speed of 130.84 mph. Bill Vukovich (#14) won the race for the second consecutive time, despite starting nineteenth due to mechanical troubles in qualifying. Pace Car: W. C. Newberg, Dodge Royal 500 Convertible.

| Program: | $45 | Pit Badge (Silver Pin): | $200 |
| | | Pit Badge (Bronze Pin): | $110 |

1955

Tragedy struck on Lap 57 when Bill Vukovich (#4), who was once again leading the 500, was killed after slamming into a four-car wreck begun by Rodger Ward (#27). Bob Sweikert (#6) eventually won the race at a speed of 128.2 mph. Sweikert won the race in a Kurtis KK500C prepared by a young builder by the name of A. J. Watson. Pace Car: Thomas Keating, Chevrolet Bel Air.

| Program: | $45 | Pit Badge (Silver Pin): | $200 |
| | | Pit Badge (Bronze Pin): | $100 |

1956

The Watson Era officially began in 1956 when Pat Flaherty (#8) drove his race car to victory at a speed of 128.49 mph. It was the second year in a row that John Zink owned a car in the winner's circle. It was a race marred by both accidents and minor flooding, but once again Indy had a winner who was also the pole sitter. Pace Car: Irvin Woolson, DeSoto Fireflite/Adventurer.

| Program: | $40 | Pit Badge (Silver Pin): | $200 |
| | | Pit Badge (Bronze Pin): | $95 |

1957

The displacement limit was reduced to 256 cubic inches (4.2 liters) in 1957 by the newly formed USAC. The change led to the "Watson" Offy 252, a mere 10 hp less than the 270, but with an added 800 rpm's. By altering construction materials Meyer-Drake was even able to reduce the Offy 252 down to 355 lbs. Sam Hanks (#9) won the race at a speed of 135.6 mph in a "laydown" roadster prepared

A circa 1955 Firestone Indy 500 tie tack given only to the officials of the race

by George Salih. Salih's roadster was a reworked Offy laid almost horizontal (72 degrees) with a cowl that was only twenty-one inches off the ground. Pace Car: F. C. Reith, Mercury Turnpike Cruiser.

Program:	$40	Pit Badge (Silver Pin):	$185
		Pit Badge (Bronze Pin):	$90

1958

The 1958 Indy 500 is best remembered as the worst multicar accident at the Speedway up until that time. On the first lap Ed Elisan (#5) and Dick Rathmann (#97), both in the first row, touched and started a chain reaction of crashes. Eight cars ended up beyond repair and forced out of the race. Pat O'Connor (#4), who had finished eighth the previous year, was fatally injured. With four of the top five contenders out of the race, Jimmy Bryan (#1) drove to victory in the same car Sam Hanks used to win in 1957. A twenty-three-year-old youngster named A. J. Foyt, in his first Indy race, finished sixteenth. Pace Car: Sam Hanks, Pontiac Bonneville.

Program:	$40	Pit Badge (Silver Pin):	$175
		Pit Badge (Bronze Pin):	$90

1959

Pat Flaherty (#64), Johnny Thomson (#3), Jim Rathmann (#16), and Rodger Ward (#5) battled the majority of the race. In an exciting finish, both drivers in matching Watson roadsters, Ward would edge Rathmann by only twenty-two seconds . For Rodger Ward, in his first season driving for Bob Wilke and A. J. Watson, it would be a very special year winning both the Indianapolis 500 and the USAC National Championship. Pace Car: Sam Hanks, Buick Electra 225.

Program:	$35	Pit Badge Silver Pin):	$185
		Pit Badge (Bronze Pin):	$95

A 1959 silver pit badge   *A 1959 bronze pit badge*

1960

The 1960 Indy would mirror the previous year, only this time it was Jim Rathmann (#4) taking the checkered flag before second place finisher Rodger Ward (#1). Both drivers battled competitively until three laps before the end, when Ward's tire wear required that he reduce speed in order to finish. Pace Car: Sam Hanks, Oldsmobile "98."

Program:	$35	Pit Badge (Silver Pin):	$125
		Pit Badge (Bronze Pin):	$65

1961

Celebrating the "Golden Anniversary 500" a field of thirty-three cars entered the race, but only ten would finish. In a race that most historians consider Indy's finest, A. J. Foyt (#1) chased Eddie Sachs (#12) until, with three laps remaining, Sachs would have to pit. Foyt then took the lead and the victory at a speed of 139.13 mph. The competitive race had twenty lead changes by seven different drivers. Although often

The official program for the 50th Anniversary of the "500"

remembered as Foyt's first win, it was a well-known Australian race entrant by the name of Jack Brabham in a Cooper/Climax that many can trace as a significant event in the race's history. The sleek Cooper, with its engine behind the driver, was a statement to the decline of the Offy roadster. Although Brabham finished ninth, he did so in a 260 hp, 2.7-liter (168 cu. in.) engine that could reach speeds of 150 mph on straights and 145 mph through corners. Pace Car: Sam Hanks, Ford Thunderbird.

Program:	$40
Pit Badge (Golden Anniversary):	$145

Collector's Note: The multi-colored 1961 OFFICIAL PROGRAM features seven racing flags mounted above the logo of the Indianapolis Motor Speedway. The fiftieth year program is attractive in its design and popular with collectors. The program reads as follows from top to bottom: "THE 500th (black over the "00") ANNIVERSARY" (white with the exception of the last "0" in 500 which is in gold ink), "1911," "1961" - flanking the center graphic, "OFFICIAL PROGRAM * 50¢" (white), "MAY 30, 1961" (black ink).

1962

Parnelli Jones became the first pole sitter to qualify at 150 mph in his Watson roadster. The race, however, would belong to the Leader Card 500 Roadster team who would finish first and second. Rodger Ward (#3) would take the victory at a speed of 140.29 mph. Hot-rodder Mickey Thompson showed up with a mid-engine car with a Buick V-8. The car was driven by Dan Gurney and although it qualified eighth, it would finish in twentieth place. Pace Car: Sam Hanks, Studebaker Lark Daytona.

Program:	$30	Pit Badge (Silver Pin):	$115
		Pit Badge (Bronze Pin):	$60

1963

Parnelli Jones (#98), paying little attention to the "mid-engine revolution," qualified first and finished first. Jimmy Clark (#92), a Formula One star, made an impact when he finished second in a Lotus powered by a Ford V-8 (256 cu. in.). Mickey Thompson showed up with three ultra-light "skates" designed by Lotus' John Crosthwaite. The aerodynamic "skates" were designed around aluminum small block Chevrolet V-8s (255 cu. in.) that were 200 lbs. lighter than Brabham's Cooper. Just thirty-three inches high to the top of the roll bar, these rear engine cars were the first to utilize twelve-inch "wide oval" tires. Pace Car: Sam Hanks, Chrysler 300J Convertible.

Program:	$30	Pit Badge (Silver Pin):	$115
		Pit Badge (Bronze Pin):	$60

1964

During Lap 2 of the 1964 race, one of the worst accidents in Speedway history occurred, claiming the lives of both Eddie Sachs and Dave MacDonald. MacDonald, in one of Thompson's "skates" that had been criticized for its instability, hit the wall of Turn 4 and burst into flames. The accident set off a chain reaction that eventually destroyed seven cars. Following a very somber restart, both Jimmy Clark (#6) and Parnelli Jones (#98) would lead the race until unfortunate circumstances forced them out of the race. Still driving his Watson roadster, A. J. Foyt went on to win his second Indy 500 at a speed of 147.35 mph. Pace Car: Benson Ford, Ford Mustang Convertible.

Program:	$40	Pit Badge (Silver Pin):	$115
		Pit Badge (Bronze Pin):	$60

1965

The 1965 Indy 500 belonged to Jimmy Clark (#82), as did the five Grand Prix that followed, at a speed of 150.68 mph, the first 150 mph race average in 500 history. In addition to winning at Indy, Clark would also claim his second World Championship and eventually claim twenty-five Grand Prix victories before he was killed at Hockenheim on April 7, 1968. The race solidified Ford's four-cam V-8 engine by finishing first through fourth. Rookie driver Mario Andretti (#12) finished third for his Auto Technics team. Worth noting is that this race was covered by the ABC television network for the first time. Pace Car: P.N. Buckminster, Plymouth Sports Fury.

Program:	$25	Pit Badge (Silver Pin):	$110
		Pit Badge (Bronze Pin):	$55

1966

The 1966 Indianapolis 500 was slowed by an eleven-car accident at the start and eventually gained momentum after another crash on Lap 5. Graham Hill became the first Indy "rookie" to win since George Souders in 1927. It would be Hill's first win, and last at Indianapolis, in a career that included 176 Grand Prix and an unprecedented five wins at Monaco. Hill retired from active driving in 1975 and was killed on November 25 of the same year when he crashed his private plane in bad weather. Hill's teammate Jackie Stewart had led much of the race, but lost oil pressure with only ten laps remaining. The race also marked the last 500 for legendary driver Rodger Ward (#26). Pace Car: Benson Ford, Mercury Comet Cyclone GT.

Program:	$25	Pit Badge (Silver Pin):	$110
		Pit Badge (Bronze Pin):	$50

1967

For 196 laps Parnelli Jones dominated the race in his STP gas-turbine. In an event that lasted two days due to a postponement because of rain, only one driver—the winner—actually completed 200 laps. When Jones was forced out of the race because of mechanical problems, A. J. Foyt assumed the lead. On his final lap Foyt faced a four-car accident that sent a billowing cloud of white smoke across the track. As if guided by instinct alone, Foyt found his way through the cloud to take the checkered flag at 151.20 mph. Pace Car: Mauri Rose, Chevrolet Camaro SS.

Program:	$35	Pit Badge (Silver Pin):	$110
		Pit Badge (Bronze Pin):	$50

1968

Joe Leonard (#60), driving one of Andy Granatelli's gas-turbines, qualified for the pole position at 171.59 mph. Leading the race and under a caution with just nine laps to go, Leonard stalled his car in a "flame-out" while taking the green flag. Bobby Unser (#3), in a turbo Offy, flew by Leonard and on to victory at a speed of 152.88 mph. Wings, or inverted airfoils, first appeared on Formula One cars in 1968 and helped improve "downforce." Although they also created aerodynamic drag, their use on Grand Prix courses was obvious, but their value at Indy was still unclear. Pace Car: William Ford, Ford Torino GT.

Program:	$25	Pit Badge (Silver Pin):	$110
		Pit Badge (Bronze Pin):	$50

1969

USAC essentially froze the racing rules at Indianapolis in 1969. European designers now dominated racing worldwide with their mid-engine cars. The next decade would see the dominance of a single winged-wedge design by McLaren's Gordon Coppuck. Racing on a freshly resurfaced track, the 1969 Indy would be the first victory for Andy Granatelli's Hawk. Despite crashing during qualifying, the STP Oil Treatment team managed to resurrect Mario Andretti's (#2) four-wheel drive Lotus and carry it to victory at a speed of 156.86 mph. USAC rules and Formula One rules were now so similar that it became possible to race the same car on either side of the Atlantic. Pace Car: Jim Rathmann, Chevrolet Camaro SS Convertible.

Program:	$20	Pit Badge (Silver Pin):	$110
		Pit Badge (Bronze Pin):	$50

A ticket from the 53rd International Indy 500 (Photo courtesy of the Indianapolis Motor Speedway Hall of Fame Museum)

1970

Despite some economic hard times, the Indianapolis 500 remained the biggest and richest race, with the 1970 purse now over $1 million. Al Unser (#2) started on the pole, dominated the race, and finished first at a speed of 155.74 mph. Unser led a total of 190 laps in a race that was redelayed and restarted on the first lap because of an accident. It was a belated birthday gift for Unser, who had turned thirty-one years of age the day before the race. Pace Car: Rodger Ward, Oldsmobile 442.

Program:	$20	Pit Badge (Silver Pin):	$100
		Pit Badge (Bronze Pin):	$45

1971

On Saturday, May 29, 1971, Al Unser (#1) took the checkered flag for the second consecutive year at a speed of 157.73 mph. Unser took charge during the second half of the race and out-raced pole starter Peter Revson (#86) in his McLaren M16. Pace Car: Eldon Palmer, Dodge Challenger.

Program:	$20	Pit Badge (Silver Pin):	$100
		Pit Badge (Bronze Pin):	$45
		Pit Badge (Bronze/NATO):	$550

The May 29, 1971, official program with "awards over one million dollars"

1972

Mark Donohue (#66) began the race in the front row after qualifying third and won the race at a speed of 162.96 mph. Donohue, in his McLaren/Offy I-4 (159 cu. in.), was able to take advantage of a fueling mistake by Jerry Grant (#48). Donohue's teammate Gary Bettenhausen (#7) had led the race for 138 laps. The McLarens and similar Eagles were responsible for the incredible qualifying speed increase of 25 mph during only a three-year time period (1970-1972). Pace Car: Jim Rathmann, Hurst/Olds Cutlass.

Program:	$15	Pit Badge (Silver Pin):	$90
		Pit Badge (Bronze Pin):	$45

1973

Gordon Johncock (#20) in his Eagle/Offy won the rain-delayed Indy at a speed of 159 mph after completing only 133 laps. Two race days were rained out before the race was finally run. In one of Speedway's most dismal and tragic races, both Art Pollard and Swede Savage were killed. Many will

The 1973 two-stub ticket featuring Mark Donohue and his McLaren (Photo courtesy of the Indianapolis Motor Speedway Hall of Fame Museum)

55

never forget the view of Salt Walther's #77 car sliding upside-down across the track at the beginning of the race with him still in it. Pace Car: Jim Rathmann, Cadillac Eldorado.

| Program: | $15 | Pit Badge (Silver Pin): | $90 |
| | | Pit Badge (Bronze Pin): | $45 |

Collector's Note: The multi-colored two-stub ticket features both a portrait of Mark Donohue and a picture of him with his McLaren on the main ticket portion. What better way to salute an Indy Champion than to put his picture on the following year's ticket. The "GATEMAN'S STUB" is to the left of the main ticket portion, while the "RAIN CHECK" detaches from the right.

1974

In 1974 USAC demanded a switch to a maximum of forty-gallon fuel tanks carried on the left side of the car. This now meant that the 500-mile race would require at least six pit stops. The change naturally affected driving strategy and tire design. Since a tire could be changed during a refueling, it was not necessary for the tires to last as long. The change led to the development of tires with greater adhesion and thus faster speeds. Johnny Rutherford (#3), in a McLaren/Offy, won the 1974 Indianapolis 500 at a speed of 158.58 mph. Rutherford battled pole sitter A. J. Foyt (#14) briefly before Foyt fell prey to a broken pump after 142 laps. Pace Car: Jim Rathmann, Hurst/Oldsmobile Cutlass W30.

| Program: | $15 | Pit Badge (Silver Pin): | $90 |
| | | Pit Badge (Bronze Pin): | $45 |

1975

An abrupt rainstorm caused the race to be halted after 174 laps. A battle ensued between A. J. Foyt (#14), Johnny Rutherford (#2), and Bobby Unser (#48), but it was Unser who was leading when the race was stopped. Unser, in Dan Gurney's Eagle/Offy I-4 (159 cu. in.), won at a speed of 149.21 mph. Goodyear become the sole supplier of Indy tires, as well as for many other races, replacing Firestone. In a tribute to the growing efforts to improve Indy car safety, Tom Sneva (#68) suffered a horrible crash that virtually broke his car in half, yet he walked away with only minor injuries. Pace Car: James Garner, Buick Century Custom.

| Program: | $15 | Pit Badge (Silver Pin): | $90 |
| | | Pit Badge (Bronze Pin): | $45 |

A ticket from the May 30, 1976, Indy 500 (Photo courtesy of the Indianapolis Motor Speedway Hall of Fame Museum)

1976

The 1976 Indianapolis 500 is remembered most as the shortest in race history. The "500" was shortened due to rain for the third time in four years, at the 255 mile mark. Johnny Rutherford (#2), in his dominant McLaren, won the race at a speed of 149.21 mph. Pace Car: Marty Robbins, Buick Century V-6 Turbo.

| Program: | $15 | Pit Badge (Silver Pin): | $90 |
| | | Pit Badge (Bronze Pin): | $45 |

1977

The 1977 Indy will always be remembered as one of the finest at "The Brickyard." Records fell like autumn leaves, as A. J. Foyt (#14) became the first driver to win the race four times. Foyt, using his own V-8 on a Coyote chassis, won the race at a speed of 161.33 mph. Janet Guthrie (#27), who dropped out of the race after twenty-seven laps, became the first woman to qualify and run in the 500. Tom Sneva also added his name to Indy history, becoming the first driver to lap the track at 200 mph. Sneva's accomplishment, in a Cosworth DFX V-8 (158 cu. in.), would be a prelude to future Indys. By the end of the decade the Cosworth DFX ruled both Formula One and Indy, eventually winning ten 500s. The engine had a superb design, precise fuel-injection, and although small, it was very durable. Pace Car: James Garner, Oldsmobile Delta 88 Royale.

| Program: | $35 | Pit Badge (Silver Pin): | $85 |
| | | Pit Badge (Bronze Pin): | $45 |

1978

Another banner year at Indianapolis, as Tom Sneva (#1) became the first driver to qualify at over 200 mph. Despite the accomplishment, Sneva would finish second for the second year in a row. Al Unser (#2) would take the checkered flag for his third time at Indy, this time at a speed of 161.36 mph. Unser's Lola/Cosworth, owned by Jim Hall of Chaparral, overcame the Penske racing team's Cosworth. Janet Guthrie (#51), the first woman to ever race at Indy, also became the first to finish—in ninth position. Pace Car: Jim Rathmann, Chevrolet Corvette.

A 1978 silver pit badge

| Program: | $15 | Pit Badge (Silver Pin): | $85 |
| | | Pit Badge (Bronze Pin): | $45 |

1979

Mario Andretti's 1978 Formula One Championship was acknowledged at Indy in 1979 as a full aerodynamic Chaparral 2K, and Penske PC-7 virtually copied the successful Lotus design. A driver now sat up between the front wheels, followed by the fuel cell, engine, and transaxle. Inverted airfoils now occupied the entire space between the wheels, essentially gluing the car to the track. Both Unsers, Al (#2) and Bobby (#12), dominated part of the 1979 race, but it was pole sitter Rick Mears (#9) who finally took the checkered flag at a speed of 158.89 mph. The forever competitive A. J. Foyt (#14) finished second. Pace Car: Jackie Stewart, Ford Mustang.

| Program: | $15 | Pit Badge (Silver Pin): | $85 |
| | | Pit Badge (Bronze Pin): | $45 |

1980

The 1980 Indianapolis 500 belonged to pole sitter Johnny Rutherford (#4), who dominated the race and finished first at a speed of 142.86 mph. Rutherford, driving in a Chaparral/Cosworth owned by Jim Hall, became only the sixth three-time winner. The "Texas Team" of Rutherford and Hall also picked up their first National Championship. Worth noting was the performance of Tom Sneva, who after starting the race in last position (33), managed to finish second. Pace Car: Johnny Parsons, Sr., Pontiac Trans Am.

| Program: | $15 | Pit Badge Silver Pin): | $80 |
| | | Pit Badge (Bronze Pin): | $40 |

1981

The 1981 Indianapolis 500 finished in controversy, as pole sitter Bobby Unser (#3) took the checkered flag just ahead of Mario Andretti (#40) at a speed of 139.02 mph. Unser was then penalized a lap for exiting the pits incorrectly, leaving Andretti the winner. However, the controversy didn't end, and after a review found that Andretti had also exited the pits incorrectly. Unser was declared the winner, but fined $40,000. Bobby Unser, nephew of Al Unser, Jr., then retired at the top. Holding numerous Indy Car records, he is considered one of the best racing drivers of all time. Pace Car: Duke Nalon, Buick Regal.

| Program: | $15 | Pit Badge (Silver Pin): | $80 |
| | | Pit Badge (Bronze Pin): | $40 |

1982

The 1982 Indy 500 is best remembered as the closet finish ever, and a race of brotherly love. Gordon Johncock's STP Wildcat/Cosworth edged Rick Mears' Penske/Cosworth by a "mere" 0.16 seconds. Mario Andretti (#40), who qualified fourth, rammed Kevin Cogan (#4) at the start, ironically putting the teammates of both top two finishers out of the race. It was one of the most bizarre looking crashes at the beginning of an Indy race, with Cogan inexplicably turning his vehicle into the car to his right. One-third of the entire field of drivers were brothers competing against each other—Indy nepotism at its finest. Pace Car: Jim Rathmann, Chevrolet Camaro Z-28.

A ticket from the 66th Indianapolis 500 held May 30, 1982 (Photo courtesy of the Indianapolis Motor Speedway Hall of Fame Museum)

| Program: | $20 | Pit Badge (Silver Pin): | $80 |
| | | Pit Badge (Bronze Pin): | $40 |

1983

Although he had dominated and impressed many during qualification runs over the past decade, Tom Sneva (#5) had never won an Indy 500. That all changed in 1983 as Sneva, in a March/Cosworth (161 cu. in.), finished at a speed of 162.11 mph. Finishing only 11.1 seconds ahead of Al Unser (#7), Sneva was able to hold on despite some nice blocking by Al, Jr., who was assisting his father. Worth noting was a rookie who qualified at the pole, Teo Fabi (#33). Pace Car: Duke Nalon, Buick Riviera.

Program:	$15	Pit Badge (Silver Pin):	$80
		Pit Badge (Bronze Pin):	$40

1984

The March/Cosworth field dominated the race and finished in the top fourteen positions. Rick Mears (#6), who had battled Tom Sneva (#1) for most of the race, crossed the finish line first at a record- breaking speed of 163.61 mph. Rookie Roberto Guerrero (#9) finished second in an outstanding performance. Mears was on his way to another Championship when he brutally crashed at Montreal, nearly severing both of his feet. In a triumph of human spirit, he came back in 1985 and ran five races. Pace Car: John Callies, Pontiac Fiero.

Program:	$15	Pit Badge (Silver Pin):	$75
		Pit Badge (Bronze Pin):	$40

1985

The 1985 Indy is most remembered as the year lucky Danny Sullivan (#5), while battling Mario Andretti (#3) at over 200 mph, spun his car 360 degrees without incident and regained his composure to win the race. At the finish line it was Sullivan by 2.4 seconds over Andretti at a winning speed of 152.98 mph. Pace Car: James Garner, Oldsmobile Calais 500.

Program:	$15	Pit Badge (Silver Pin):	$75
		Pit Badge (Bronze Pin):	$40

1986

Under a yellow flag with only a handful of laps remaining in the race, Kevin Cogan (#7) was narrowly leading Bobby Rahal (#3) and Rick Mears (#4). When the field was given a green, temporary drag racers Rahal and Mears let it all out for the lead. Rahal grabbed the front and won the race at a speed of 170.72 mph. The Truesports racing team cherished their first Indy victory and the significance it would have for well-liked car owner Jim Trueman, who would die of cancer just two weeks later. Pace Car: Chuck Yeager, Chevrolet Corvette Roadster.

Program:	$15	Pit Badge (Silver Pin):	$75
		Pit Badge (Bronze Pin):	$40

1987

If Hollywood scriptwriters wanted to pen a story about the Indianapolis 500, the 1987 race might just be a worthy subject. Al Unser, originally without a ride in 1987, substituted for Penske team driver Danny Ongais who had crashed during practice. If beginning the race in twentieth position wasn't enough of a challenge for Unser, add to it that he was driving a show car and the story really starts to get intriguing. On the first lap Unser barely escapes tragedy when Josele Garza (#55), who had started in the twenty-fifth position, spins wildly in front of him. Slowly moving up in position, Unser (#25) goes unnoticed for much of the race, but finally claims the lead with just a few laps to go and wins the race at a speed of 162.17 mph. The finish was not without excitement, however. Roberto Guerrero (#4), who had an excellent shot at winning the race, stalled his car twice during a pit stop near the end of the race and finished second. Pace Car: Carroll Shelby, Chrysler LeBaron.

Program:	$12	Pit Badge (Silver Pin):	$75
		Pit Badge (Bronze Pin):	$40

1988

The 1988 Indy 500 should have been called "The Penske Pole," as it was the only time that one team had qualified one-two-three at "The Brickyard." Not a lot would change at the end as Rick Mears (#5) was still first and Al Unser (#1) third. Only Danny Sullivan (#9) missed the finish line photograph. Mears in his dominate new Chevy V-8 held off all challengers at a finishing speed of 144.8 mph. The lighter Chevy engine was very similar to a Cosworth, as two former Cosworth engineers built it, but it had superior acceleration. Seven onboard ABC television cameras mounted on four different cars captured much of the excitement for a large home viewing audience. Pace Car: Chuck Yeager, Oldsmobile Cutlass Supreme.

| Program: | $12 | Pit Badge (Silver Pin): | $75 |
| | | Pit Badge (Bronze Pin): | $40 |

1989

The year 1989 belonged to Emerson Fittipaldi, who would win the CART PPG/Indy Car World Series and the Indianapolis 500. Fittipaldi (#20) started in the front row and stayed there, leading the race nearly 80% of the time. He finished at a speed of 167.58 mph and escaped a potentially tragic collision with Al Unser, Jr. (#2) with only two laps to go. Pace Car: Bobby Unser, Pontiac Trans Am.

| Program: | $12 | Pit Badge (Silver Pin): | $75 |
| | | Pit Badge (Bronze Pin): | $40 |

1990

Emerson Fittipaldi (#1) again dominated in his Penske Chevy and caught everyone's attention when he qualified at an average speed and new track record of 225.30 mph. Unfortunately Fittipaldi's faster speeds did little for his tires and he eventually was forced to make an extra pit stop. Arie Luyendyk (#30) and Bobby Rahal (#18) battled for Fittipaldi's lead, with Luyendyk the winner at a speed of 185.98 mph, a track record. Pace Car: Jim Perkins, Chevrolet Beretta Convertible.

| Program: | $10 | Pit Badge (Silver Pin): | $70 |
| | | Pit Badge (Bronze Pin): | $40 |

1991

Rick Mears took the checkered flag in his Penske/Chevrolet at a speed of 176.45 mph. Rick Mears, who always seems at home in the pole position, would log a career fifteen Indy Car wins from that position.

| Program: | $10 | Pit Badge (Silver Pin): | $70 |
| | | Pit Badge (Bronze Pin): | $40 |

1992

In one of the slowest Indy races in years, Al Unser, Jr. finished first in his Galmer/Chevrolet A at a speed of 134.47 mph. Unser's first Indy win would also be the closest in track history, 0.043 seconds over Scott Goodyear.

| Program: | $10 | Pit Badge (Silver Pin): | $70 |
| | | Pit Badge (Bronze Pin): | $40 |

1993

Emerson Fittipaldi took his Penske/Chevrolet C to victory lane at a speed of 157.2 mph. After his second Indy victory Fittipaldi went on to set single-season records for led laps completed (2,024 of 2,112) and earnings ($2,575,554).

| Program: | $10 | Pit Badge (Silver Pin): | $70 |
| | | Pit Badge (Bronze Pin): | $40 |

Here are two great posters from the 75th Indy 500. The one at top features every winner and his car for all seventy-five races. The one at right details the thirty-three drivers and their cars, as well as their finishing position.

1994

Al Unser scored his second win at Indianapolis in his Penske/Mercedes at a speed of 160.87 mph. Teammates Unser and Fittipaldi dominated the race until Emerson crashed with just sixteen laps to go. For Indy fans, it was the ninth win for the Unser family and the tenth win for one of Roger Penske's cars. Rookie Jacques Villeneuve finished second and drove an outstanding race.

Program:	$10	Pit Badge (Silver Pin):	$65
		Pit Badge (Bronze Pin):	$35

1995

Jacques Villeneuve becomes the first Canadian to capture the race and the youngest winner in four decades. It was Villeneuve's second win in 1995 and it vaulted him to the lead in point standings, where he would finish the season.

Program:	$10	Pit Badge (Silver Pin):	$65
		Pit Badge (Bronze Pin):	$35

NASCAR Winston Cup Series Speedways and Races

* Records are through the 1994 season

Atlanta Motor Speedway
P.O. Box 500
Hampton, GA
404-946-4211

Just south of Atlanta in Georgia's heartland lies Atlanta Motor Speedway. A spectacular facility and a true superspeedway oval, it offers perhaps the best view of any track on the NASCAR Winston Cup Circuit. Whether you're in the grandstand or in the infield, the entire racing surface is within view. The speedway is also complemented by a new state-of-the-art 2.5-mile road course. With Speedway straight-aways measuring one-quarter mile each and turns about one-half mile in length, it is truly a racing fan's delight.

The Atlanta Motor Speedway (Photo courtesy of Atlanta Motor Speedway)

Another view of the Atlanta Motor Speedway (Photo courtesy of Atlanta Motor Speedway)

A pit stop at the Atlanta Motor Speedway (Photo courtesy of Atlanta Motor Speedway)

The Speedway was repaved in August of 1994 as part of an ongoing project to improve the facility for the next decade. Additionally, there are plans to expand seating to 225,000, add another garage area, install over fifty additional luxury suites, and construct a modern frontstretch quad oval to replace the current backstretch. Project 2000 is an aggressive long-range development plan to enhance Atlanta Motor Speedway while taking it into the next decade.

The two Winston Cup events held at the Speedway are the Purolator 500 (Race #4) (formerly the Motorcraft Quality Parts 500, the Motorcraft 500, and the Coca-Cola 500) and the Hooters 500 (Race #31) (formerly the Hardee's 500, the Atlanta Journal 500, and the Dixie 500).

Collector's Note: The Atlanta Motor Speedway Gift Shop is a must for fans and collectors. The shop is packed with a wide selection of track apparel and Winston Cup racing souvenir items. Also remember that your tour ticket is good for $3 off on a purchase of $10 or more. Memorabilia from the Speedway's first race on July 31, 1960, won by Fireball Roberts, is also popular with collectors. Ticket stubs from the inaugural event fall in the $50-$75 range and programs can run $100-$150. Programs from the 1962 Atlanta 500 are somewhat tougher to find in higher grade condition and scarcer than all others except 1960. Richard Petty collectors will have fun grabbing souvenirs from his days at the Speedway. "King Richard" had 66 starts, 6 wins, 4 poles and logged over 17,000 laps at the Speedway.

Richard Petty – Atlanta Motor Speedway Victory Mini-Checklist

Programs:	❑ 1966	❑ 1970	❑ 1971	❑ 1974	❑ 1975	❑ 1977
Tickets:	❑ 1966	❑ 1970	❑ 1971	❑ 1974	❑ 1975	❑ 1977

Track Facts

Distance: 1.522 miles   Banking: 24 degrees

Qualifying Record: Greg Sacks at 185.830 mph on November 11, 1994

Race Record 500 Miles: Dale Earnhardt at 156.849 mph on March 18, 1990

Bristol International Raceway
P.O. Box 3966
Bristol, TN 37625
615-764-1161

Commonly referred to as the "World's Fastest Half-Mile Speedway," Bristol International Speedway offers NASCAR fans some of the most exciting racing as cars fly around its thirty-six-degree banked turns. The slightly over half-mile track is one of the most demanding facilities for both drivers and equipment. Winston Cup racing's oldest night race, the Goody's 500, is held in August at Bristol.

Improvement plans for 1995 included the addition of 3,600 seats and a new permanent lighting system. The lights in particular should be a welcome addition as the track hopes to host its August night race for many years to come.

The two Winston Cup events held at the Raceway are the Food City 500 (Race #6) (formerly the Valleydale Meats 500) and the Goody's 500 (Race #22) (formerly the Busch 500 and the Bud 500).

Collector's Note: Darrell Waltrip collectors will be able to pick up plenty of souvenirs from Bristol, as entering the 1995 season he had won twelve events at the raceway. Waltrip also put together four consecutive wins at the now Food City 500 (1981-1984) and three consecutive victories at the now Goody's 500 (1981-1983). Memorabilia from the 1973 Southeastern 500 is also worth holding on to as Cale Yarborough led all 500 laps. The 1983 Busch 500 was called after 419 laps due to rain, making programs slightly scarcer than others from that period.

Track Facts

Distance: .533 miles   Banking: 36 degrees

Qualifying Record: Chuck Bown at 124.96 mph on April 9, 1994

Race Record 500 Miles: Charlie Glotzbach at 101.074 mph in 1971

Charlotte Motor Speedway
P.O. Box 600
Concord, NC 28026-0600
704-455-3200

The Charlotte Motor Speedway was opened in June of 1960 and became the third superspeedway to join NASCAR's circuit. Located in the Piedmont section of North Carolina, this beautiful facility runs four events under the lights—the only superspeedway capable of such a task.

Boasting over 125,000 seats, 52 condominiums overlooking Turn 1, 63 executive suites, and the unique dining splendor of The Speedway Club, this facility truly sets new standards in motorsports.

The two Winston Cup events held at the Speedway are the Coca-Cola 600 (Race #11) (formerly Coca-Cola World 600) and the Mello-Yello 500 (Race #28) (formerly the National 500, Miller High Life 500, Oakwood Homes 500, and All Pro Auto Parts 500).

Collector's Note: A must stop for both fans and collectors is the Winston Gift Shop, which has one of the largest assortments of Winston Cup racing memorabilia found in this country. The track also has a Souvenir Hotline: 704-455-3202. Price lists from the gift shop are available. On the list you will find T-shirts, jackets, caps, books, die-cast products, and much more. Collectors may find programs from both the 1971 National 500 and the 1968 World 600 slightly harder to find, especially in higher grade conditions. Both these events were shortened to under 400 miles. Good driver memorabilia to collect here includes Bobby Allison, Darrell Waltrip, and Dale Earnhardt.

Track Facts

Distance: 1.5 miles   Banking: 24 degrees
Qualifying Record: Ward Burton at 185.759 mph on October 6, 1994
Race Record 600 Miles: Dale Earnhardt at 145.504 mph on May 30, 1993
Race Record 500 Miles: Ernie Irvan at 154.537 mph on October 10, 1993

Darlington Raceway
P.O. Box 500
Darlington, SC 29532-0500
803-395-8499

On September 4, 1950, the running of the inaugural Southern 500 at Darlington Speedway ushered in the superspeedway era. The track, known as being "Too Tough To Tame," has got the best of many drivers and its mystique has grown into a legend on the NASCAR Winston Cup Series. The 1.366-mile egg-shaped oval is notorious for a tight racing groove and its disproportionately banked east and west turns have ended many a driver's race day prematurely.

Located in the heart of the Deep South, it is littered with tradition and its list of race driver winners reads like a "who's who in racing." Petty, Yarborough, Pearson, Baker, Allison, Lorenzen, Roberts, Weatherly, Elliott, Waltrip, and Earnhardt have all won at this historic facility.

Improvements continue as well at Darlington as "Tyler-Tower," a new ultra-modern grandstand, was dedicated in 1994. More seating and suites are planned for the future.

The track hosts two NASCAR Winston Cup events, the TranSouth Financial 400 (Race #5) (formerly the Rebel 500) and the Mountain Dew Southern 500 (Race #23) (formerly the Southern 500 and the Heinz Southern 500).

One of the elite clubs in motorsports is the Unocal-Darlington Record Club. Membership is awarded to the fastest driver of each make of automobile for the starting field in the Mountain Dew Southern 500.

Collector's Note: Tickets and programs from the Southern 500, especially the early years, are highly prized by collectors. Since the Southern 500 is the anchor event of the "Winston Select Million" program, a $1 million bonus is given to the driver who can win three of Winston Cup racing's "Crown Jewel" events in a single season. Collectors should put away a series of tickets from the only time this has been accomplished. Bill Elliott captured the bonus with three wins in 1985, the program's first year. David Pearson's three consecutive wins from 1972 to 1974 also make a fine ticket or program series to collect, as do any of his souvenirs from this track where he has won ten times. Memorabilia from the 1980 CRC Rebel 500 may be a bit tougher to find than you might expect. The race was shortened to under 260 miles due to conditions.

Track Facts

Distance: 1.366 miles   Banking: 23 degrees - Turn 1 and 2
                                       25 degrees - Turn 3 and 4

Qualifying Record: Geoff Bodine at 166.998 mph on September 2, 1994

Race Record 600 Miles: Dale Earnhardt at 139.958 mph on March 28, 1993

Daytona International Speedway
P.O. Box 2801
Daytona Beach, FL 32120
904-253-7223

"Big Bill" France, founder of NASCAR in 1949, built the Daytona International Speedway. Located on a 450-acre tract, the Speedway features a 2.5-mile tri-oval course and a 3.56-mile road course, both of which use the famous four-story, thirty-one-degree high-banked curves that have brought the site so much notoriety. So vast is the facility that it includes 100,000 grandstand seats and a 44-acre lake in the infield.

The site is home to the most prestigious event in the NASCAR Winston Cup Series, the Daytona 500. Each year this race opens the season, and then at the midway point the Speedway hosts the Pepsi 400.

NASCAR's headquarters, as well as the offices for the International Speedway Corporation and MRN Radio, are located at the facility. A must for all race fans is the World Center of Racing Visitor's Center, which provides a daily comprehensive look at the facility via guided tours, memorabilia, and much more.

The two events the facility hosts are the Daytona 500 (Race #1) and the Pepsi 400 (Race #15) (formerly the Firecracker 400 and the Pepsi Firecracker 400).

Collector's Note: All memorabilia from the Daytona 500, especially old programs and tickets, have seen nice increases in price and increased collector interest. A separate value listing for both programs and tickets from the Daytona 500 is included in Chapter 12 of this book. Daytona 500 programs, especially those races won by Richard Petty, have seen stronger than expected price increases. Petty collectors will find Daytona a haven for memorabilia, as "King Richard" has won ten times at the Speedway. Memorabilia from the 1965 Daytona 500 can be a bit tougher to find than expected, as the race was shortened to 332.5 miles due to rain.

Track Facts

Distance: 2.5 miles   Banking: 31 degrees

Qualifying Record: Bill Elliott at 210.364 mph on February 9, 1987

Race Record 500 Miles: Buddy Baker at 177.602 mph on February 17, 1980

Race Record 400 Miles: Bobby Allison at 173.473 mph on July 4, 1980

Dover Downs International Speedway
P.O. Box 843
Dover, DE 19903
800-441-RACE

"The Monster Mile" is a high-banked one-mile superspeedway that opened in July of 1969. Dover Downs is the first concrete-surfaced superspeedway on the NASCAR Winston Cup circuit. The facility also redesigned entry to the twenty-four-degree banked turns to produce closer racing.

A decade of grandstand expansion raised total spectator capacity to over 100,000. The facility is host to both the first and last NASCAR Winston Cup races of the season in the Northeast. The two events are the Budweiser 500 (Race #12) (formerly the Mason-Dixon 500) and the Splitfire Spark Plug 500 (Race #25) (formerly the Peak Performance 500 and the Peak Antifreeze 500).

Track Facts

Distance: 1.0 miles   Banking: 24 degrees

Qualifying Record: Geoff Bodine at 152.840 mph on September 16, 1994

Race Record 500 Miles: Bill Elliott at 125.945 mph on September 16, 1990

Indianapolis Motor Speedway
P.O. Box 24910
Speedway, IN 46224
317-481-8500

"The Greatest Race Course in the World" opened in 1909, when the 2.5-mile track was used as an automotive testing and competition facility. When the track's crushed stone and tar surface deteriorated, it was replaced with 3.2 million bricks, hence the name "The Brickyard." Since 1991 it has hosted the famed Indianapolis 500, but on August 6, 1994 it began as the new home to the Brickyard 400.

As irony might have it, Indiana native Jeff Gordon won the inaugural race in 1994 and Dale Earnhardt won it in 1995. The capacity crowd in 1994 was the largest ever to witness a NASCAR Winston Cup event, with the following season's race sold out well before it even took place.

The inaugural Brickyard 400 (Race #19) was won at an average speed slightly above 130 mph in just over three hours.

Track Facts

Distance: 2.5 miles   Banking: 9-12 degrees

Qualifying Record: Rick Mast at 172.414 mph on August 4, 1994

Race Record 500 Miles: Jeff Gordon at 131.977 mph on August 6, 1994

Martinsville Speedway
P.O. Box 3311
Martinsville, VA 24115
703-956-3151

One of the original tracks, Martinsville Speedway was built by H. Clay Earles. Originally used as a dirt track, it was opened in 1947 and finally paved in 1955. The slightly over one-half mile track has developed an outstanding reputation and boasts true southern hospitality. The site covers over 200 acres and seats over 56,000. The track, which looks more like a drag strip with turns added, has 800-foot straights and short, tight twelve-degree corners.

The speedway has six corporate suites, a chalet village for tent entertainment, a 115-seat press box, large grandstands, free parking, and a comprehensive medical Infield Care Center.

The site is home to two NASCAR Winston Cup events: the Hanes 500 (Race #8) (formerly Virginia 500, Virginia National Bank 500, Sovran Bank 500, and Pannill Sweatshirts 500) and the Goody's 500 (Race #26) (formerly the Old Dominion 500).

Collector's Note: Another haven for Richard Petty collectors, as he has won fifteen times at Martinsville. Petty's four consecutive victories from 1967 to 1970 in the Old Dominion 500 make a nice series for both ticket and program collectors. Cale Yarborough and Darrell Waltrip also managed to put together three consecutive victories in the same event. The 1961 Grand National 200 only lasted 149 laps or 74.5 miles due to rain, making programs from this event challenging to find. The first formal race at Martinsville was held on September 25, 1949, with the end of the dirt era at the track coming in 1955. Memorabilia from this era is also sought by collectors and not particularly easy to find.

Track Facts

Distance: .526 miles   Banking: 12 degrees

Qualifying Record: Ted Musgrave at 94.185 mph on September 23, 1994

Race Record 263 Miles: Cale Yarborough at 79.185 mph on September 24, 1978

Michigan International Speedway
12626 U.S. 12
Brooklyn, MI 49230
800-354-1010

Situated on 816 acres in the Irish Hills area of southeastern Michigan, the Michigan International Speedway includes a two-mile superspeedway and two 1.9-mile road courses. The multi-purpose racing facility is home to not only NASCAR, but also the PPG Indy Car World Series, and IROC and ARCA events. The track's designers were Charles Moneypenny, who also designed Daytona International Speedway, and the Formula One great, Stirling Moss, who fashioned the MIS road course.

The track, which broke ground in 1967, was purchased by the Penske Corporation in 1973 and immediately modified into one of the country's finest racing facilities.

The speedway hosts two NASCAR Winston Cup events: the Miller Genuine Draft 400 (Race 314) (formerly the Gabriel 400, Miller High Life 400, and the Miller American 400) and the GM Goodwrench Dealer 400 (race #21) (formerly the Champion Spark Plug 400).

Collector's Note: David Pearson, Cale Yarborough, and Bill Elliott collectors will find solace acquiring Michigan International Speedway memorabilia, as each of these drivers has won at least seven times at the track. Bill Elliott's three consecutive victories in both the Champion Spark Plug 400 (1985-1987) and the Miller 400 (1984-1986) make a nice series for both program and ticket collectors. Putting together a complete collection of both programs and tickets from NASCAR events held at Michigan is still possible, with the most challenging memorabilia to find being from the 1969 Yankee 600. This race was shortened to 330 miles due to environmental conditions.

Track Facts

Distance: 2 miles   Banking: 18 degrees

Qualifying Record: Geoff Bodine at 181.082 mph on August 19, 1994

Race Record 400 Miles: Davey Allison at 160.912 mph in June of 1991

New Hampshire International Speedway
P.O. Box 7888
Loudon, NH 03301
603-783-4931

Nestled in the Lake Region of New Hampshire, this facility consists of a one-mile oval and a 1.6-mile road course. As New England's largest spectator sports event with an attendance over 70,000, the New Hampshire International Speedway continues to try to meet the overwhelming demand for the six-state region's only NASCAR Winston Cup race.

The multi-purpose facility, owned and operated by the Bahre family, hosts a variety of racing events including NASCAR, Indy Car, AMA, WKA, and SCCA competition.

Overhead view of the New Hampshire International Speedway (Photo courtesy of the New Hampshire International Speedway)

The Speedway's only NASCAR Winston Cup event is the Slick 50 300 (Race #16) which has only been taking place for three years.

Collector's Note: The Slick 50 300 began in 1993, so collectors will find it relatively easy to acquire older programs and full or partial tickets.

Track Facts

Distance: 1.058 miles   Banking: 12 degrees

Qualifying Record: Ernie Irvan at 127.197 mph on July 9, 1994

Race Record 317.4 Miles: Rusty Wallace at 105.947 mph on July 11, 1993

North Carolina Motor Speedway
P.O. Box 500
Rockingham, NC 28379
910-582-2861

Harold Brasington, who built Darlington Raceway, also built the original North Carolina Motor Speedway. It hosted the inaugural American 500 in 1965, won by Richard Petty, then was redesigned in 1969. Additional changes were added to improve spectator traffic and alter racing styles.

"The Rock" is now one of the most popular superspeedways on the NASCAR circuit and traditionally hosts both the first and last NASCAR Winston Cup events in the Carolinas each year. Just before the AC-Delco 500 in 1994, the track was repaved—just another one of the ongoing improvements to an already great facility.

The Speedway hosts two NASCAR Winston Cup events: the Goodwrench 500 (formerly the Carolina 500) and the AC-Delco 400 (formerly the Nationwide 500).

Collector's Note: Petty collectors will enjoy North Carolina Motor Speedway memorabilia, as Richard has won eleven times at the track with three poles and Kyle has won three times with five poles. Both the general facilities and the infield have souvenir stands for fans and collectors. Memorabilia from the 1965 American 500, followed by the 1967 Carolina 500 and the 1968 American 500, is highly sought by collectors and can present a significant acquisition challenge.

Track Facts

Distance: 1.017 miles   Banking: 22 degrees - Turn 1 and 2
25 degrees - Turn 3 and 4

Qualifying Record: Ricky Rudd at 157.099 mph on October 21, 1994

Race Record 400 Miles: Kyle Petty at 130.748 mph on October 25, 1992

North Wilkesboro Speedway
P.O. Box 337
North Wilkesboro, NC 28659
910-667-6663

Today it is the second-oldest raceway on the Winston Cup circuit. The facility opened its doors in 1947 and gained popularity as a dirt track in the 1940s and 1950s. It was finally paved in 1957, as officials set their sights on long-distance racing.

Nine new enclosed viewing areas, seven large lounges, expansion of the West Grandstand, and the 250-seat Combs Tower are just some of the recent improvements at the facility. With each passing year the Winston Cup's second-oldest raceway is looking more like its newest.

The track hosts two NASCAR Winston Cup events: the First Union 400 (Race #7) (formerly the Staley 400 and the Northwestern Bank 400) and the Tyson Holly Farms 400 (formerly the Wilkes 400 and the Holly Farms 400).

Collector's Note: Richard Petty and Darrell Waltrip collectors will enjoy North Wilkesboro Speedway, as combined these two drivers have twenty-five victories. Richard Petty won both events at the track in 1962—his first time, making a pair of tickets or programs from these events highly collectible. On April 16, 1967, Darel Dieringer led all 400 laps, 250 miles, in his only victory at the track, adding some uniqueness to memorabilia from this event. Memorabilia from the 1963 Gwyn Staley 400, won by Richard Petty, can be elusive, as this race was shortened to 160 miles due to rain.

Track Facts

Distance: .625 miles   Banking: 14 degrees

Qualifying Record: Ernie Irvan at 119.016 mph on April 15, 1994

Race Record 400 Miles: Geoff Bodine at 107.360 mph on October 5, 1992

Phoenix International Raceway
P.O. Box 13088
Phoenix, AZ 85002
602-252-2227

Often considered the world's fastest one-mile oval, Phoenix International Raceway opened its gates in 1964 and now plays host to one of motorsports' most varied schedules. The circle track features the NASCAR Winston Cup Series, the Skoal Bandit Racing Copper World Classic, and the PPG Indy Car World Series. The recent addition of a 1.5-mile road course has added the IMSA Exxon World Sports Car Championship and the AMA National Road Racing Championship for motorcycles.

The "Racing Jewel of the Southwest" continues on its course of improvements, first repaving the facility in 1993, followed by an additional 11,000 grandstands in 1994, with much more planned in upcoming years.

The track hosts one NASCAR Winston Cup event, the Slick 50 500 (Race #30) (formerly the Checkers 500, Autoworks 500, and Pyroil 500).

Collector's Note: Tickets and programs from Davey Allison's back-to-back wins at the Pyroil 500 in 1991 and 1992 make a nice collectibles series and an outstanding tribute to this great driver. With the first NASCAR Winston Cup event dating back only to the 1988 Checker 500, acquiring a complete series of programs and tickets should be a relatively easy task.

Track Facts

Distance: 1.0 miles   Banking: 11 degrees - Turns 1 and 2
                                        9 degrees - Turns 3 and 4

Qualifying Record: Sterling Marlin at 129.833 mph on October 28, 1994

Race Record 400 Miles: Terry Labonte at 107.463 mph on October 30, 1994

Pocono International Raceway
P.O. Box 500
Long Pond, PA 18334
717-646-2300

Located in the heart of the Pocono Mountains resort area, Pocono International Raceway features a unique 2.5-mile tri-oval with three turns, each with a different radius and degree of banking. The track also includes three straights, each a different length, to add to the complexities a driver must face. The intriguing track design often prompts competitors to refer to it as a superspeedway that drives like a road course.

The Raceway hosts two NASCAR Winston Cup events: the UAW-GM Teamwork 500 (Race #13) (formerly the Van Scoy Diamond Mines 500, Miller High Life 500, Miller Genuine Draft 500, and Champion Spark Plug 500) and the Miller Genuine Draft 500 (race #17) (formerly the Purolator 500, Mountain Dew 500, Like Cola 500, Summer 500, and AC Spark Plug 500).

Collector's Note: Darrell Waltrip, Bill Elliott, and Tim Richmond have all won four times at Pocono. Memorabilia from the 1974 Purolator 500, won by Richard Petty, is highly sought by collectors. Back-to-back victories by Bobby Allison, Tim Richmond, and Bill Elliott at Pocono make a series of tickets and programs from these accomplishments very collectible.

Track Facts

Distance: 2.5 miles   Banking: 14 degrees - Turn 1
                                        8 degrees - Turn 2
                                        6 degrees - Turn 3

Qualifying Record: Rusty Wallace at 164.558 mph on June 10, 1994

Race Record 500 Miles: Alan Kulwicki at 144.069 mph on July 14, 1992

Richmond International Raceway
P.O. Box 9257
Richmond, VA 23227
804-345-7223

Located on the Virginia State Fairgrounds in Henrico County outside of Richmond, this multi-use motorsports complex has hosted NASCAR Winston Cup Series races since April of 1953. The Richmond International Raceway is a three-quarter-mile "D" shaped asphalt oval that was redesigned in 1988 primarily to increase its length.

The short-track intimacy is highlighted by grandstand seating for over 70,000, bringing fans close to the action with an unobstructed view. The sixty-foot track width and fourteen-degree banked turns offer plenty of high-speed maneuvering. Originally a horse track, then later a dirt track, the then one-half-mile track was paved in 1968. The track is owned and operated by Paul Sawyer and his family and does a wonderful job catering to the needs of racing fans.

The Raceway hosts two NASCAR Winston Cup Series events: the Pontiac Excitement 400 (Race #3) (formerly the Richmond 400 and the Miller High Life 400) and the Miller Genuine Draft 400 (Race #24) (formerly the Capital City 400, Wrangler san Forrest 400, Wrangler Jeans Indigo 400, and Miller High Life 400).

Collector's Note: Another haven for Petty collectors, as "King Richard" has won thirteen times at Richmond International Speedway. Most sought is memorabilia from the 1961 Richmond 200, which was won by Richard Petty—his first victory at the track. All racing event memorabilia prior to 1960 is also difficult to find, especially from the first season in 1953.

Track Facts

Distance: .750 miles   Banking: 14 degrees

Qualifying Record: Ted Musgrave at 124.052 mph on September 9, 1994

Race Record 400 Miles: Davey Allison at 107.709 mph on March 7, 1993

Sears Point Raceway
Hwys 37 & 121
Sonoma, CA 95476
800-870-RACE

One of only two road courses on the NASCAR Winston Cup Series, Sears Point Raceway is a twelve-turn, 2.52-mile raceway that also hosts Vintage Car Racing, NHRA Drag Racing, IMSA Road Racing, and AMA Motorcycle Racing. Sears Point Raceway opened in 1968 and hosted its first professional race in September of 1969.

During the track's infancy it attracted nearly every great name in motorsports before closing for several years. The track reopened in 1973 and by the mid-1970s was attracting consistently larger crowds to its diverse racing schedule. In addition to its road course, the raceway maintains a world-famous quarter-mile drag strip and has been hosting an NHRA national event every year since 1988. Constant renovations keep the facility state-of-the-art and functional for its race day crowds, which can number well over 90,000.

The track has played host to one NASCAR Winston Cup Series event since 1989, the Save Mart Supermarkets 300 (Race #10) (formerly the Banquet Frozen Foods 300).

Collector's Note: Both Ricky Rudd and Ernie Irvan collectors can enjoy collecting memorabilia from Sears Point Raceway, as both drivers commonly finish in the top two positions. Rudd won the inaugural NASCAR Winston Cup race in 1989 and Irvan has won it twice, in 1992 and 1994. Collectors should find little difficulty in putting together a complete collection of NASCAR Winston Cup programs or ticket stubs from Sears Point.

Track Facts

Distance: 2.52 miles   Turns: 12

Qualifying Record: Dale Earnhardt at 91.838 mph on May 14, 1993

Race Record 187 Miles: Ernie Irvan at 81.412 mph on June 7, 1992

Talladega Superspeedway
P.O. Box 777
Talladega, AL 35160
205-362-9064

The Talladega Superspeedway began construction in 1968 and opened its gates in August of 1969. Conceived as the largest and fastest superspeedway in the world, this 2.66 mile track with four lanes and thirty-three-degree banks invites speeds in excess of 210 mph. The track hosted its first Grand National, now the Winston Cup, on September 14, 1969. Driver Richard Brickhouse won the first Talladega 500, now the DieHard 500, in an event that can seat 70,000 without even using its infield.

The track is so fast that Bill Elliott set a world record for stock car competition at the 1987 Winston 500 by qualifying at 212.809 mph. For race fans it is particularly convenient, as it is adjacent to the International Motorsports Hall of Fame.

The Superspeedway hosts two NASCAR Winston Cup events: the Winston Select 500 (Race #9) (formerly the Alabama 500 and the Winston 500) and the DieHard 500 (Race #18) (formerly the Talladega 500 and the Talladega DieHard 500).

Collector's Note: Dale Earnhardt fans have plenty to collect at Talladega , as "The Intimidator" has won at the superspeedway seven times. Twice Earnhardt has put together back-to-back wins in the now DieHard 500, first in 1983 and 1984, followed by 1990 and 1991. Both of these series' tickets and programs make outstanding collectibles. David Pearson collectors can also opt to collect memorabilia from his three consecutive wins (1972-1974) in the now Winston Select 500. Bill Elliott has also done well at Talladega and holds many qualifying and race speed records.

Track Facts

Distance: 2.66 miles   Banking: 33 degrees

Qualifying Record: Bill Elliott at 212.809 mph on April 30, 1987

Race Record 500 Miles: Bill Elliott at 186.2888 mph on May 5, 1985

Watkins Glen International track in Watkins Glen, New York

Watkins Glen International
Box 500-T
Watkins Glen, NY 14891
607-535-2481

Beautifully situated in wine country at the foot of Seneca Lake, this road course first opened in 1948 as a vision of Cameron Argetsinger. It became a permanent 2.3-mile track in 1956, welcomed the NASCAR Grand National Division in 1957, the International Formula Libre in 1958, and finally the U.S. Grand Prix in 1961. It would host the U.S. Grand Prix for nearly two decades, but by 1981,

"Above the pits" at Watkins Glen

despite a variety of strong events, it was forced to close. It was, however, resurrected in 1983 by a subsidiary of Corning Glass Works, who purchased it and formed a partnership with the International Speedway Corporation.

It was reopened in 1984 and a mere two years later had NASCAR Winston Cup action return. One of only two road courses on the series, it features a unique combination of seven right-hand turns within its eleven corners.

For the last three years crowds in excess of 130,000 have watched Mark Martin win the Bud at the Glen Winston Cup Series. This race is the track's only NASCAR Winston Cup Series race (Race #20) and despite its infancy has seen three different drivers win it at least twice.

The tower at Watkins Glen

Collector's Note: Mark Martin fans have found a new home, Watkins Glen. The road course has seen crowds of over 130,000 watch Martin drive to three consecutive victories. A feat worth commemorating, this series of three programs and tickets is a must for Martin collectors. NASCAR memorabilia from "The Glen" held in 1957, 1964, and 1965 is not easy to find. Most sought of all the memorabilia at Watkins Glen are programs, posters, and tickets from the nineteen U.S. Grand Prix races.

Track Facts

Distance: 2.454 miles   Turns: 11

Qualifying Record: Mark Martin at 119.118 mph on August 6, 1993

Race Record 220.5 Miles: Mark Martin at 98.752 mph on August 14, 1994

1995 Indy Car Driver Profiles

Michael Andretti

Michael Andretti was born October 5, 1962, and is the son of legendary racing champion Mario Andretti. Andretti enters the 1995 season with twenty-nine wins and twenty-seven poles. Mario's retirement and departure from the Newman/Haas Racing Team allowed Michael to return to the top winning driver/team combination of this decade. Andretti finished fourth in the Indy Car standings in 1994, a year that saw him return from Formula One and win his first race back in Australia. His first PPG Cup came in 1991 when he won a record eight Indy Car races and was named Driver of the Year by a panel of journalists. His 234 points in 1991 set a record number under the modern system established in 1983. Andretti picked up three poles and a win at Toronto in 1995 and is now a member of the "30-30" club in auto racing. *Did You Know?* Joining his father at Newman/Haas for 1989, the Andrettis became the first father-son combination in Indy Car racing.

Indy Car Victories: 30
Indy Car Poles: 30

Michael Andretti (Photo courtesy of Kmart Texaco Havoline Racing)

❏ Team Contact: Newman/Haas Racing, 500 Tower Parkway, Lincolnshire, IL 60069

Collector's Note: Andretti began the 1995 season as the leader among active drivers in race wins and pole positions. Andretti collectors will want to seek out memorabilia from his Indy Car debut in 1983 at the Caesar's Palace Grand Prix, his Indianapolis 500 debut in 1984, and his first career Indy Car win at Long Beach in 1986. Also worth picking up are tickets or programs from the 1986 season-opener at Phoenix where racing's first-ever father-son front row was established by the Andrettis. All memorabilia from his championship 1991 season is highly sought, especially from his record eight wins that season.

Side and front views of Michael Andretti's No. 6 (Photo courtesy of Kmart Texaco Havoline Racing)

A Michael Andretti Indy Car wins checklist is provided here for ticket and program collectors:

1986	❏ Long Beach	❏ Milwaukee	❏ Phoenix		
1987	❏ Milwaukee	❏ Michigan 500	❏ Nazareth	❏ Miami
1989	❏ Toronto	❏ Michigan 500		
1990	❏ Detroit	❏ Portland	❏ Meadowlands	❏ Mid-Ohio
	❏ Road America			
1991	❏ Milwaukee	❏ Portland	❏ Cleveland	❏ Toronto
	❏ Vancouver	❏ Mid-Ohio	❏ Road America	❏ Laguna Seca
1992	❏ Portland	❏ Milwaukee	❏ Toronto	❏ Vancouver
	❏ Laguna Seca			
1994	❏ Australia	❏ Toronto		

Ross Bently

Ross Bently was born November 4, 1956, in Vancouver, British Columbia, and since the age of five has had only one ambition—racing. Bently made his PPG Cup debut in his hometown of Vancouver in 1990. Unfortunately Bently has never been able to run a full season due to budget restraints, but it hasn't dampened his spirits. Entering the 1995 season, his best career finish remains eleventh (in Australia, 1992).

Indy Car Victories: 0   Indy Car Poles: 0

Gary Bettenhausen

Gary Bettenhausen was born November 18, 1941, and is the oldest of two sons of Tony Bettenhausen, the 1951 and 1958 Indy Car champion. His father was killed at Indianapolis in 1961, and veteran driver Gary has focused primarily on the 500 during the past few seasons. Bettenhausen has accumulated wins at Phoenix (1968), Michigan (1970), Trenton (1972), and Texas (1973) during his three decades of racing. He qualified for his first Indy 500 in 1968 and finished twenty-fourth. Bettenhausen has been a dominant force in both sprint and dirt car, winning USAC Sprint Championships in 1969 and 1971 and USAC Dirt Championships in 1980 and 1983. *Did You Know?* Gary is the brother of team owner Tony Bettenhausen, Jr.

Indy Car Victories: 4   Indy Car Poles: 2

❏ Team Contact: Menard Racing, 4034 Park 65 Dr., Indianapolis, IN 46254

Raul Boesel and his 1995 Duracell Charger Indy car (Photo courtesy of Rahal Hogan)

Raul Boesel

Raul Boesel was born December 4, 1957, in Curitiba, Brazil. Boesel made his Indy Car debut at Long Beach, CA in 1985. In his first oval track start, an impressive Boesel was the fastest rookie qualifier at the 1985 Indy 500. Boesel finished third at Indy in 1989, behind Fittipaldi and Unser. He finished the 1990 season with eight Top 10 finishes, earning him twelfth place in PPG point standings. Boesel placed second in Detroit in 1992 and in Phoenix, Milwaukee, and Detroit in 1993. He started all sixteen races for Dick Simon Racing in 1994 and finished second at Laguna Seca. *Did You Know?* Boesel was tied with Bobby Rahal for most Top 10 finishes in 1993 with thirteen.

Indy Car Victories: 0   Indy Car Poles: 2

❏ Team Contact: Rahal/Hogan Racing, 4601 Lyman Drive, Hilliard, OH 43026

Scott Brayton

Scott Brayton was born February 20, 1959, and is the son of former Indy Car driver Lee Brayton. Brayton made his PPG Cup debut in 1981 at Phoenix and finished fifteenth. He set a new stock block engine record at Indianapolis (1984) and established a single-lap qualifying record, since broken, in 1985. In 1990 he started every race of the year for the first time in his career and finished the season fifteenth in points. Brayton posted a strong season in 1991 by accumulating nine Top 10 finishes. In 1992 Brayton finished third in Milwaukee for his best career finish to date. Brayton decided to specialize in just the Indianapolis 500 during the 1995 season. His strategy worked, as he captured the 1995 Indy pole position. *Did You Know?* Scott co-drove to a third-place finish during the twenty-four hours of Daytona in 1992 (Porsche 962).

Indy Car Victories: 0   Indy Car Poles: 1

❏ Team Contact: Menard Racing, 4034 Park 65 Dr., Indianapolis, IN 46254

Eddie Cheever

Eddie Cheever was born January 10, 1958, in Phoenix, Arizona, and soon moved to Rome, Italy, where he was raised. The veteran of 132 Grand Prix since his first Formula One race in 1978, his experience has been a valuable asset to many racing teams. Cheever finished sixth overall in the 1993 Formula One rankings. His six point-paying finishes of 1983 included a strong second at the Canadian Grand Prix while driving a Renault Turbo. Cheever's first Indy Car effort was while driving for Arciero at Miami in 1986 and although he qualified eleventh, he crashed on the second lap. Cheever posted a strong 1990 season with third-place finishes at both Detroit and Toronto. His success in 1990 allowed him to capture Rookie of the Year honors. Cheever drove his exciting new Ford-Cosworth to a second-place qualification position at Indy in 1992 and finished second that same year in Phoenix. Cheever was a mid-season addition to the A. J. Foyt Racing Team in 1994, replacing injured Bryan Herta. *Did You Know?* Eddie Cheever finished seventh at Phoenix in 1990 in his first oval race and had nine Top 10 finishes in seventeen starts that season.

Indy Car Victories: 0   Indy Car Poles: 0

❏ Team Contact: A. J. Foyt Enterprises, 6415 Toledo Street, Houston, TX 77008

Christian Danner

Christian Danner was born April 4, 1958, in Munich, Germany. His full-time participation in Formula One racing began in 1986, driving for Osella-Alfa and Arrows BMW. Danner's first Formula One point also came in 1986 with a sixth-place finish at Austria (Arrows). Danner scored two wins in German Touring Car Championship while driving for Alpina Team in 1988. He made his first Indy Car start at Detroit with Antonio Ferrari and Euromotorsport Racing in 1992. Danner's best finish was thirteenth at Nazareth, in seven 1992 starts. He came back in 1993 and with three starts for Euromotorsports, scored his first points with an eleventh place at Elkhart Lake. Driving two races for Project Indy in 1994, he managed two twelfth-place finishes. A partial owner and part-time driver with the Project Indy Team, Danner split his driving talents between PPG Cup competition and European Touring Car racing in 1995. *Did You Know?* Christian Danner won the German Touring Car Championship in 1991.

Indy Car Victories: 0   Indy Car Poles: 0

❏ Team Contact: Project Indy, 434 E. Main St., Brownsburg, IN 46112

Fredrik Ekblom

Fredrik Ekblom was born October 6, 1971, in Kumla, Sweden. He became the youngest driver to enter Swedish Formula Three Series in 1989 and finished third in the championship. In 1991 Ekblom moved to British Formula 3000 Championship, winning three races and finishing second overall. He finished seventh in Indy Lights Championship in 1993, picking up one podium appearance and five Top 5 finishes. Ekblom's first Indy Car race came at Detroit in 1994, driving for McCormack Motorsports. He finished fifteenth. *Did You Know?* In 1989 Fredrik Ekblom received the Ronnie Peterson scholarship for his outstanding performance in his first year of formula racing.

Indy Car Victories: 0   Indy Car Poles: 0

❑ Team Contact: McCormack Racing, 11717 W. Rockville Rd., Indianapolis, IN 46234

Teo Fabi

Teodorico Fabi was born March 9, 1955, in Milan, Italy, and by 1976 he won the European karting title. He made his PPG Cup debut at Atlanta in 1983 and made an enormous impact with his competitive style. He became the first European in twenty years to win the pole at Indy (1993)—in only his second Indy Car start. His 1983 season victories included Pocono, Mid-Ohio, Phoenix, and Laguna Seca. He would finish second in the 1983 standings behind series champion Al Unser by a mere five points. He was awarded the PPG Indy Car World Series 1983 Rookie of the Year, having led 521 laps during the season, more than twice his nearest competitor. In 1984 he started seven races, posted his highest finish at Portland (third), and then made a switch to Formula One. Fabi took the lead driver position for Porsche PPG Cup effort in 1988 and finished fourth in PPG Indy Car World Series rankings in 1989. He competed in sixteen races for Hall Racing in 1994 and scored three fourth-place finishes before announcing plans to move to the newly-formed Forsythe Racing Team, the team he had driven for in the early 1980s. Fabi grabbed the pole at the 1995 Miller Genuine Draft 200. *Did You Know?* Teo Fabi finishes a decade of Indy Car racing with the completion of the 1995 season.

Indy Car Victories: 5   Indy Car Poles: 10

❑ Team Contact: Forsythe Racing Inc., 111 South Willis Ave., Wheeling, IL 60090

Collector's Note: Fabi became the first European to win an Indy pole in twenty years back in 1983, making memorabilia from this race a good acquisition. In fact, the entire 1983 season is a good starting point for Fabi collectors, as he won at Pocono, Mid-Ohio, Laguna Seca, and Phoenix. He also grabbed poles at Milwaukee, Michigan, Riverside, Laguna Seca, and Phoenix that same year.

Gil de Ferran

Gil de Ferran was born November 11, 1967, in Paris, France, and moved to Sao Paolo, Brazil, at the age of nine months. By 1982 he was racing karts in Sao Paolo and a mere three years later would find himself competing aggressively in the Brazilian Formula Ford 1600 Championship. In 1987 he would dominate the circuit by winning seven races en route to winning the Brazilian Formula Ford 1600 Championship. De Ferran captured the British Formula Three Championship in 1992 and scored seven wins. After picking up two wins and placing third in the FIA International Formula 3000 Championship, de Ferran decided to join Halls Racing in 1995 for his rookie PPG Indy Car season. He took the pole at the 1995 Medic Grand Prix of Cleveland and won at the Toyota Grand Prix

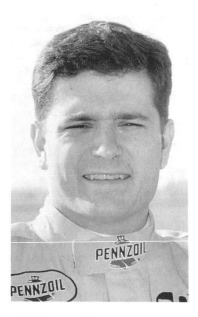

Gil de Ferran (Photo courtesy of Deke Houlgate Enterprises)

Gil de Ferran going through his paces in the Pennzoil Special at Indianapolis Motor Speedway (Photo courtesy of Deke Houlgate Enterprises)

of Monterey. De Ferran also captured the rookie title in 1995. *Did You Know?* Gil de Ferran grabbed one win and finished fourth in the 1993 FIA International Formula 3000 Championship.

Indy Car Victories: 1   Indy Car Poles: 1

❏ Team Contact: Hall Racing, 7700 West Highway 80, Midland, TX 79703-2068

Collector's Note: De Ferran had an outstanding 1995 season and collectors would be smart to put away some memorabilia from his rookie year in PPG Indy Car. Memorabilia from his first pole and win in 1995 are logical starting points for collectors. Watch out in 1996 as de Ferran is going to be a force on the Indy Car circuit!

A front view of Adrian Fernandez' No. 10 car (Photo courtesy of Team Galles)

Adrian Fernandez

Adrian Fernandez was born April 20, 1965, in Mexico City, Mexico, and began racing motorcross at the young age of eight. In 1983 he won the Mexican Marlboro Formula Vee Championship and was named Rookie of the Year in Formula Ford 1600 Championship. Fernandez won the 1991 International Formula Three Championship with four wins and seven pole positions. In 1993, he moved up to Indy Lights and posted a sensational rookie season by setting a record for most rookie wins (four), and for most laps led and most oval wins in a season. Chosen as the 1992 Rookie of the Year, he also finished third in the Indy Lights Championship. In 1993, his rookie Indy Car season, he drove for five races for Galles Racing International and managed to post a top finish of seventh at Detroit. Fernandez started all sixteen races in 1994 for Galles Racing International and grew in comfort level with each race. By mid-season he had scored a top finish of fifth at Road America. *Did You Know?* Adrian Fernandez led his first Indy Car race at Vancouver in 1994 when he paced the field for one lap.

Indy Car Victories: 0   Indy Car Poles: 0

❑ Team Contact: Galles Racing International, P.O. Box 25047, 2725-C Broadbent Pkwy. NE, Albuquerque, NM 87107

1993 was Adrian Fernandez' rookie Indy Car season (Photo courtesy of Team Galles)

Christian Fittipaldi

Christian Fittipaldi was born January 18, 1971, in Sao Paulo, Brazil, and was racing in his first go-kart race by the age of eleven. His first professional race came at the age of seventeen, in Formula Ford 2000. In 1989 Fittipaldi won the Brazilian Formula Three Championship and finished third in the South American Formula Three Championship. In 1990 a near opposite scenario occurred as Fittipaldi won the South American F3 Championship, but finished fourth in the British F3. In one of his most memorable races, he won the F3000 Championship at Nogaro in 1991. He jumped to Formula One World Championship driving in 1993 and collected his first championship point on the way to an overall seventeenth-place showing. Fittipaldi drove all sixteen Formula One events in 1994 and recorded two Top 10 starts and seven Top 10 finishes. Fittipaldi finished second in the 1995 Rookie of the Year standings. An impressive second-place finish at Indy in 1995 gave him that event's Rookie of the Year honors. His overall strong performance in 1995 has led him to sign with Newman/Haas Racing in 1996 to drive the Kmart-Budweiser Lola Ford Cosworth. *Did You Know?* Christian Fittipaldi's father, Wilson, and his uncle, Emerson, have also made their marks in racing history.

Indy Car Victories: 0   Indy Car Poles: 0

❏ Team Contact: Newman/Haas Racing, 500 Tower Parkway, Lincolnshire, IL 60069

Collector's Note: Fittipaldi had an outstanding 1995 season and collectors would be smart to put away some memorabilia from his rookie year in PPG Indy Car. His move to Newman/Haas in 1996 should only enhance his prospects of winning, as well as his collectibility.

Emerson Fittipaldi

Emerson Fittipaldi was born December 12, 1946, in Sao Paulo, Brazil, and by age fifteen was working as a kart mechanic before moving to racing motorbikes and karts. He won his first of two Formula One titles in 1972, becoming the youngest driving champion in that circuit's history. His next Formula One Championship followed two seasons later driving for Team McLaren under Marlboro sponsorship. The following year he would finish runner-up in the Formula One Championship, but not before winning both the U.S. and Brazilian Grand Prix. He returned from a two-year driving retirement in 1984 to make his PPG Cup debut with a fifth at Long Beach. Although he would finish thirteenth in the PPG point standings, Fittipaldi was the runner-up for the Rookie of the Year award. Much more comfortable with the circuit in 1985, he would start all fifteen events and finish sixth in points, scoring an impressive ten Top 10 finishes. The same year he would also win his first event with a very close victory over Al Unser at the Michigan 500. By 1989 Fittipaldi was ready for an assault on the title and he did just that by taking his first PPG Indy Car World Series Championship. On his way he won the first of two Indianapolis 500 victories, taking home more than $1 million and becoming the first foreign driver since Englishman Graham Hill to win the event. Three more solid seasons followed, with Fittipaldi never finishing below fifth in final season standings. In 1993 he made another aggressive assault at the title, taking his second Indy 500, Portland, and Mid-Ohio, but finishing second in the championship. He did however manage to set a single-season record for laps led and earnings that same season. In 1994 he would also finish second in championship, but not before collecting ten Top 10 finishes. His first victory of the 1995 season came at Nazareth. With a career of legendary status, there seems to be no end to this driver's ability. Picked up one win in 1995 at the Bosch Spark Plug Grand Prix. *Did You Know?* Entering 1995, Emerson Fittipaldi has won Indy Car races in ten consecutive seasons.

Indy Car Victories: 22   Indy Car Poles: 17

❏ Team Contact: Marlboro Team Penske, 366 Penske Plaza, P.O. Box 301, Reading, PA 19603

Collector's Note: Fittipaldi has appeared on numerous trading cards, the most popular being the A&S Racing Indy sets from 1985 to 1987. Most of his cards can still be acquired for just a few dollars, making them inexpensive and easy to acquire. Memorabilia from his victories at Indianapolis are a must with Fittipaldi collectors, with some programs and tickets from earlier career victories becoming a bit challenging to find.

Stan Fox

Stan Fox was born July 7, 1952, in Janesville, Wisconsin. Fox started driving midgets in Corona, California in 1971. In 1987, his first successful year of Indy qualifying, he started the race twenty-sixth and finished seventh in an A. J. Foyt car. Fox qualified and started twenty-sixth in the 1988 Indianapolis 500, but had to drop out of the race and finished thirtieth. Fox remained strong on the USAC midget circuit, picking up his ninth career victory at Denver in 1989. In 1991 he began at Indy in the seventeenth position and finished eighth. He qualified for both the 1992 and 1993 Indianapolis 500 but failed to finish either race, in his only Indy Car starts of the season. In 1994, also at Indy, he completed 193 laps to finish thirteenth. He continues to be a top short oval track driver, with his primary Indy Car focus only at "The Brickyard." *Did You Know?* Stan Fox has a career high Indy Car finish of seventh at the Indianapolis 500.

Indy Car Victories: 0   Indy Car Poles: 0

Frank Freon

Frank Freon was born March 16, 1964, in Paris, France. He competed on the French Formula Three circuit before moving to Indy Lights in 1991. He was named Rookie of the Year for that circuit in 1991 and had four podium finishes, ending the season fourth overall in the championship. Freon finished in the runner-up position in both the 1992 and 1993 Indy Lights Championship. His first Indy Car start came at Long Beach where he finished twelfth in 1994. *Did You Know?* Frank Freon won the 1987 Winfield Magny-Cours Racing School award.

Indy Car Victories: 0   Indy Car Poles: 0

Scott Goodyear

Scott Goodyear was born December 20, 1959, in Toronto, Ontario, Canada, and has been racing since the age of nine. He won his third consecutive Canadian Formula Ford title in 1982. Goodyear was a dominant force for many years in the Rothman Porsche Turbo Cup Series, while working his way into Indy Car racing. He grabbed nine Top 10 finishes in sixteen Indy Car races in 1990 and was voted Most Improved Driver by his peers. The season also included his first Indy 500 where he finished tenth. After finishing thirteenth in PPG Cup points in 1990 and 1991, he would impress all by improving to fifth in 1992. Goodyear won the 1992 Marlboro 500, but is best remembered for finishing second, after starting last, in the closest Indianapolis 500 in history—by 0.043 seconds. He scored his first career pole in 1993 at Phoenix, while compiling ten Top 10 season finishes. Goodyear picked up his second career win in 1994 at Michigan. *Did You Know?* Scott Goodyear was twice voted Most Improved Driver by his peers.

Indy Car Victories: 2   Indy Car Poles: 2

Robby Gordon

Robby Gordon was born January 2, 1969, in Cerritos, California, and began motorcross racing by the age of seven. Teamed with his father Bob Gordon, he won four off-road races and the SCORE/HDRA Championship in 1986. In 1990 Gordon won the SCORE/HDRA Class 8 Championship and expressed an interest in moving from dirt to pavement, joining the Jack Roush Racing Team and competing in an IMSA GTO Mercury Cougar. In Atlanta during that same year he captured the pole in his first career ARCA stock car race. His first full season came in 1993, when he finished tenth in the point standings for A. J. Foyt Racing and finished in the Top 10 places ten times. Driving for Derrick Walker Racing in 1994, Gordon competed in all sixteen races and took his first-ever Indy Car pole at Toronto while setting a new track record. He scored five Top 10 finishes en route to fifth place in the PPG Cup standings, with his best a second place at Vancouver. Gordon became the first driver of the 1995 season to earn the maximum twenty-two PPG Cup points—for winning the pole, the race, and leading most laps in Detroit. He had an outstanding 1995, adding two wins and two poles to his statistics. *Did You Know?* Robby Gordon's #5 Valvoline/Cummins Reynard car is in honor of his great-grandfather Huntley Gordon, who wore the same number battling for track positions in 1915.

Indy Car Victories: 2   Indy Car Poles: 4

❏ Team Contact: Walker Racing, 8060 Woodland Road, Indianapolis, IN 46278
Also at 4030 Championship Dr., Indianapolis, IN 46268

Marco Greco

Marco Greco was born December 1, 1963, in Sao Paulo, Brazil. A four-time Brazilian kart champion, he also raced in the 1985 U.S. Motorcycle Grand Prix. A strong competitor on the British Formula 3000 Series, Greco made a move to Indy Lights in 1992 and scored nine Top 10 finishes in ten starts. His first PPG Cup points came at Phoenix in 1993 with an eleventh-place finish. Greco competed in fourteen races during the 1994 season for Arciero Project Indy, with a top finish of eleventh at Michigan. *Did You Know?* A talented driver, Marco Greco is perhaps best known for making the 1994 Indianapolis field on Bubble Day.

Indy Car Victories: 0   Indy Car Poles: 0

❑ Team Contact: Dick Simon Racing, 701 S. Girls School Road, Indianapolis, IN 46231

Mike Groff

Mike Groff was born November 16, 1962, in Van Nuys, California, and entered his first race at the age of ten. In his first full season of Super Vee in 1985, he won the Rookie of the Year title. Groff won the American Racing Series (ARS) Championship in 1989, with four wins, three poles and nine Top 5 finishes. He moved into the Indy Car ranks in 1990, logging twelve starts with his first race taking place in Detroit. Groff started thirteen of seventeen events in 1991 and finished sixteenth in points. The same year he qualified for his first Indianapolis 500 and finished twenty-fourth due to a water leak. In a season marred by engine development, Groff competed in sixteen races for Rahal/Hogan Racing in 1994 and logged a career high finish of sixth at Phoenix. *Did You Know?* Both Mike and Robbie Groff compete in the PPG Indy Car World Series.

Indy Car Victories: 0   Indy Car Poles: 0

❑ Team Contact: Rahal/Hogan Racing, 4601 Lyman Drive, Hilliard, OH 43026

Robbie Groff

Robbie Groff was born January 31, 1966, in San Fernando, California, and he began racing in quarter-midgets before turning seven. He won Super Vee Rookie of the Year in 1987 with six Top 5 finishes. While driving in Super Vees in 1989, Groff won three races, grabbed four poles and captured ten Top 5 finishes en route to a runner-up finish in the championship. He won his first Indy Lights victory in 1990 at Nazareth and finished fifth overall in the championship. Groff finished seventh in the Indy Lights Championship in 1991, fourth in 1992, and fifth in 1993, before starting two Indy Car events for Bettenhausen Motorsports in 1994. *Did You Know?* Robbie Groff finished thirteenth in his first two Indy Car starts.

Indy Car Victories: 0   Indy Car Poles: 0

❑ Team Contact: Bettenhausen Motorsports, 109B Gasoline Alley, Speedway, IN 46222-3964

Roberto Guerrero

Roberto Guerrero was born November 16, 1958, in Medellin, Columbia, and entered Formula Ford Series in England in 1978. He made his PPG Cup debut at Long Beach in 1984 and finished twenty-sixth. During the same year he qualified ninth and finished second to Rick Mears in his first Indianapolis 500. His successful debut season allowed him to finish eleventh in PPG points, while being named Co-Rookie of the Year with Michael Andretti. In 1985 Guerrero started fourteen events and posted a season-high third in his second career Indy 500. Competing in fifteen events during the 1986 season, he earned two second-place finishes and picked up his first career pole in Miami. He finished ninth in PPG points and fourth at Indianapolis the same year. Guerrero's first two career victories were won at Phoenix and Mid-Ohio in 1987. He also grabbed four poles, finished fourth in points, and was runner-up at the Indy 500. In 1992 he set a qualifying record en route to Indy pole, with a four-lap average of 232.428 mph, but crashed on a parade lap. Guerrero started thirteen races in 1993 and accumulated five Top 10 finishes. *Did You Know?* Roberto Guerrero's only Indy Car start in 1994 was the Indianapolis 500, driving for Pagan Racing.

Indy Car Victories: 2   Indy Car Poles: 6

❏ Team Contact: Dick Simon Racing, 701 S. Girls School Road, Indianapolis, IN 46231

Mauricio Gugelmin

Mauricio Gugelmin was born April 20, 1963, in Joinville, Brazil, and began racing at the age of eight. He was the Brazilian Formula Flat Series champion in 1981 before entering British Formula Ford 1600 ranks in 1982 and capturing the national championship. Gugelmin captured the European Formula Ford 2000 title in 1984 and took both the British Formula Three and Macau F3 World Cup titles. His first career Formula One podium finish was third in Brazil during the 1989 season. He entered PPG Indy Car World Series in 1993 and ran in three races. Gugelmin started all sixteen races in 1994, with a career-best finish in Australia by placing sixth. *Did You Know?* Mauricio Gugelmin is a veteran of over seventy Grand Prix events.

Indy Car Victories: 0   Indy Car Poles: 0

❏ Team Contact: Pacwest Racing Group, 150 Gasoline Alley, Indianapolis, IN 46222

Dean Hall

Dean Hall was born November 16, 1957, in Palo Alto, California. He impressed everyone by winning forty-two percent of the races he entered in the first four years of his career. Hall won the Formula Ford National Championship in 1987, scoring seven wins and nine second-place finishes. In 1988 he won five of ten races to capture the Formula Atlantic West Coast Championship. Hall also became the first American to win both the New Zealand Grand Prix and the New Zealand Formula Pacific Championship in 1989. He made his Indy Car debut in 1990 and scored two eleventh-place finishes. Hall also qualified for the Indianapolis 500 and finished seventh that same year. *Did You Know?* Entering the 1995 season, Hall had finished in the Top 5 in eighty percent of the races he had entered.

Indy Car Victories: 0   Indy Car Poles: 0

Bryan Herta

Bryan Herta was born May 23, 1970, in Warren, Michigan, and began racing karts at the age of twelve. In 1989, Herta won the Skip Barber Formula Ford Series, taking fourteen of eighteen events. In 1990 he moved to the Barber Saab Pro Series and won the championship the following year. His first season of competition in the PPG-Firestone Indy Lights Championship Series came in 1992 and he finished a respectable fifth in driver standings. The same year he was awarded the prestigious America's Choice award as one of North America's top young drivers. Winning seven events for Tasman Motorsports Group in 1993, Herta won the PPG-Firestone Indy Lights Championship. His capturing of eight pole positions set a new single-season series record. Herta qualified twenty-second and finished ninth in the 1994 Indianapolis 500. A devastating crash at Toronto cost him the balance of the 1994 season. Herta looked solid in 1995 and was able to pick up a pole at the Slick 50 200. *Did You Know?* Bryan Herta won karting's coveted Sportsman of the Year award in 1986.

Indy Car Victories: 0   Indy Car Poles: 1

❏ Team Contact: Target/Chip Ganassi Racing, 3821 Industrial Blvd., Indianapolis, IN 46254

Stefan Johansson

Stefan Johansson was born September 8, 1956, in Vaxjo, Sweden. With six wins and seven pole positions, Johansson won the 1980 British Formula Three Championship. He quickly moved into the Formula One rankings and established himself as a fierce competitor. Driving for the Ferrari Formula One Team, he scored four podium finishes in 1986 and finished fifth in the World Championship. Johansson drove to a third-place finish at Detroit in his Indy Car debut in 1992. The season found him with five Top 10 finishes and earned him the 1992 Indy Car Rookie of the Year award. He started all sixteen events for Bettenhausen Motorsports in 1994 and scored four Top 5 finishes. Johansson finished sixth at both Long Beach and Michigan in 1995, and recorded his fourth career Indy Car podium visit by placing third at Nazareth. *Did You Know?* When Stefan Johansson led six laps at Australia in 1995, it was the first time ever for both himself and Bettenhausen Motorsports in Indy Car racing.

Indy Car Victories: 0   Indy Car Poles: 0

❑ Team Contact: Bettenhausen Motorsports, 109B Gasoline Alley, Speedway, IN 46222-3964

Parker Johnstone

Parker Johnstone was born March 27, 1961. He established himself on the IMSA circuit and scored his first three wins on the IMSA Camel Lights circuit in 1990. In 1991, Johnstone won eight races and captured his first Camel GT Championship. He went on to win an amazing three consecutive IMSA Camel Lights Championships and even scored poles at all thirteen events in 1992. He had a good 1995 season and was able to pick up his first career pole at the Marlboro 500. *Did You Know?* Parker Johnstone made six starts for Comptech Racing in 1994, with his best finish a thirteenth place at Vancouver.

Indy Car Victories: 0   Indy Car Poles: 1

❑ Team Contact: Comptech Racing, El Dorado Hills, CA

Buddy Lazier

Buddy Lazier was born October 31, 1967, in Loveland Pass, Colorado. The son of 1981 PPG Indy Car Rookie of the Year Bobby Lazier, it was inevitable that Buddy would show an early interest in racing. Like most, he began racing karts and then gradually moved into motorcross, Formula Ford, and then to Formula Vees. He won six of eight AIS events in 1988 to take the championship. Lazier finished thirteenth in his Indy Car debut at Portland in 1990. He drove for a variety of teams in 1991 and finished the season twenty-second in PPG points. In 1992, Lazier started fifteen of sixteen events, scored points in three races, and posted a career-high seventh-place finish at the Marlboro 500. He would start seventeen events during the next two years, with a top finish of thirteenth at Phoenix. *Did You Know?* Buddy Lazier was a national ski racer and Olympic hopeful from 1983 to 1987 in Slalom, Giant Slalom, and Downhill events.

Indy Car Victories: 0   Indy Car Poles: 0

❑ Team Contact: Leader Cards Racers, 8135 W. Crawfordsville Road, Indianapolis, IN 46224

Arie Luyendyk

Arie Luyendyk was born September 21, 1953, in Sommelsdyk, The Netherlands. His father drove in Lotus 7 competitions and Luyendyk began attending races at the age of nine in South Africa. Luyendyk captured the European Super Vee title with nine wins in 1977 and went on to take the U.S. Super Vee title in 1984. That same year he made his Indy Car debut at Elkhart Lake and finished eighth. He scored five Top 10 finishes in 1985, on his way to an eighteenth place in PPG point standings. That same year Luyendyk was also named CART Rookie of the Year and caught the eye of many with his seventh-place finish at his first Indy 500. The next two years would find him finishing seventeenth and seventh in the point standings. By 1990 he had paid his dues and competing in all sixteen events he would finish in ten Top 10 slots. He captured both a front row slot and the victory at the 1990 Indianapolis 500 and finished the season eighth in points. He landed his first Indy pole in 1993 and finished runner-up in a season that would find him eighth in the overall PPG point standings. *Did You Know?* A dominant oval track driver, all three of Arie Luyendyk's Indy Car victories have come on circle tracks.

Indy Car Victories: 3   Indy Car Poles: 1

❑ Team Contact: Team Menard Inc., 4034 Park 65 Dr., Indianapolis, IN 46254

Collector's Note: A very popular driver, Luyendyk is perhaps best known for his 1990 Indianapolis 500 victory. Collectors will want to acquire memorabilia from his 1984 Indy Car debut at his home track at Elkhart Lake's Road America, as well as items from the 1990 Indy 500.

Hiro Matsushita

Hiro Matsushita was born March 14, 1961, in Kobe, Japan. He began racing motorcycles in the late 1970s and into the 1980s. He won the Japanese Motorcross title in 1980 and then turned his interest to auto racing. Matsushita entered his first U.S. race, a Formula Ford event, at Riverside in 1987. He won the 1989 Toyota Atlantic Championship by the largest point margin in series history, winning four out of nine events. He became the first Japanese driver to win the prestigious Lady Wigram Trophy Race in 1989 and to enter the Indy Car ranks in 1990. Matsushita started his first Indianapolis 500 in 1991, beginning twenty-fourth and finishing sixteenth—the first Japanese driver to do so at Indy. Driving for Dick Simon Racing in thirteen starts during the 1994 season, he posted his career-best finish of sixth at Michigan. *Did You Know?* Hiro Matsushita's grandfather is founder of Matsushita Electric Industrial Corporation of Japan.

Indy Car Victories: 0   Indy Car Poles: 0

❑ Team Contact: Arciero-Wells Racing, Anaheim, CA

Andrea Montermini

Andrea Montermini was born May 30, 1964 in Sassuolo, Italy. He finished third overall in the Italian Formula Alfa Romeo Championship in 1987. Montermini then focused his attention to Formula Three racing and managed a third-place finish in the 1989 Italian Formula Three Championship. He entered the Formula 3000 International Championship in 1990 and earned a pole position in his first race at Donnington. He picked up two poles and two third-place finishes in Formula 3000 in 1991. The following year Montermini picked up four poles and four wins to finish as runner-up in the F3000 Championship. In 1993 he started four races with the Euromotorsport Indy Car Team and qualified in the Top 10 twice. With Project Indy, he started two races in 1994, finishing seventh in Toronto and ninth at Laguna Seca. *Did You Know?* Entering the 1995 season Andrea Montermini's best career finish was fourth at Detroit in 1993.

Indy Car Victories: 0   Indy Car Poles: 0

❑ Team Contact: Project Indy, 434 E. Main Street, Brownsburg, IN 46112

Scott Pruett

Scott Pruett was born March 24, 1960, in Sacramento, California, and began driving karts at the age of eight. In 1984 Pruett entered the IMSA GTU ranks and scored his first pro win in GTO Thunderbird at Pocono. With nine poles and seven victories, he won the 1986 IMSA GTO Championship. He added the 1987 SCCA Trans Am Championship to his resume before putting all his savings into his first Indy Car start at long Beach in 1988. Pruett also added a second IMSA GTO point title in 1988, while making his second IROC appearance. He was named to Budweiser Truesports Team in his first full Indy Car season and finished tenth at Indianapolis to earn the Indy Co-Rookie of the Year honors. In a very strong performance, Pruett posted five Top 5 and eleven Top 10 finishes during the 1989 season, with his best a second-place finish at Detroit. Sidelined by an injury in 1990, he returned to test the Jaguar IMSA GTP car later that year. From 1991 to 1993 he finished tenth, eleventh, and twelfth in season point standings. He joined Patrick Racing in 1994 and did extensive testing for Firestone's return to Indy Car racing in 1995. Pruett looked impressive in 1995 and picked up his first career win at the Marlboro 500 in July. *Did You Know?* In 1994, Scott Pruett won the Trans Am Championship and the 24 Hours of Daytona, but did not compete in any Indy Car events.

Indy Car Victories: 1   Indy Car Poles: 0

❑ Team Contact: Patrick Racing, Indianapolis, IN

Bobby Rahal

Bobby Rahal was born January 10, 1953, in Medina, Ohio. He entered 1995, his fourteenth year of competition, with three PPG Cup Championships (1986, 1987, and 1992), and twenty-four Indy Car victories. He became the first champion as owner/driver in 1992. A talented racing mind and competitive driver, he has set numerous marks in racing history. His initial racing experience came from driving his father Michael's Lotus in an SCCA amateur race. Rahal made his first PPG Cup start at Phoenix in 1982 and won his first event that same season in Cleveland. He won the CART Rookie of the Year in 1982 and finished second in PPG Cup points. He had back-to-back Indy Car wins at Phoenix and Laguna Seca in 1984 and finished third in driver standings. Rahal repeated his final standings in 1985 and led all drivers with seven poles. His first PPG Championship in 1986 was secured by winning six events including the Indianapolis 500. In 1987 he became the first driver to win two consecutive championships since Rick

Bobby Rahal and his 1995 Miller Genuine Draft Indy car (Photo courtesy of Rahal Hogan)

Mears (1981-82). Rahal picked up one victory in 1988, but landed nine Top 5 finishes. The year also marked the first time since his rookie season that he did not win a pole. In 1990 he finished second five times in his first ten of sixteen races, including the Indianapolis 500. He rebounded in 1991 by finishing in the Top 5 thirteen times and was runner-up in PPG standings to Michael Andretti. Four wins and eleven Top 5 finishes helped the Driver of the Year capture his third championship in 1992. Rahal finished a respectable fourth in the championship in 1993 and became first Indy Car driver to top the $12 million mark in career earnings. *Did You Know?* Bobby Rahal is an avid golfer with an impressive ten handicap.

Indy Car Victories: 24   Indy Car Poles: 18

❑ Team Contact: Rahal/Hogan Racing, 4601 Lyman Drive, Hilliard, OH 43026

Collector's Note: If you're going to collect Bobby Rahal memorabilia you're going to need a considerable amount of shelf space. Trading card collectors can start by picking up his 1983 A&S Racing Indy card #34, which is still inexpensive and fairly easy to find. Memorabilia from his first Indy Car race at Phoenix in 1982, his first Indy Car victory at Cleveland on July 4, 1982, and his first Indianapolis 500 win on May 31, 1986, are must acquisitions for a Rahal collector.

A Bobby Rahal Indy Car wins checklist is provided here for ticket and program collectors:

1982	❑ Cleveland 500	❑ Michigan 150		
1983	❑ Riverside 500			
1984	❑ Phoenix 150	❑ Laguna Seca 300		
1985	❑ Mid-Ohio 200	❑ Michigan 200	❑ Laguna Seca 300	
1986	❑ Indianapolis 500	❑ Toronto 300	❑ Mid-Ohio 200	❑ Sanair 300
	❑ Michigan 250	❑ Laguna Seca 300		
1987	❑ Portland 200	❑ Laguna Seca 300	❑ Meadowlands 170	
1988	❑ Pocono 500			
1989	❑ Meadowlands 180			
1991	❑ Meadowlands 180			
1992	❑ Phoenix 200	❑ Detroit 200	❑ Nazareth 200	❑ New Hampshire 200

Willy T. Ribbs

Willy T. Ribbs was born January 3, 1956, in San Jose, California. He paid his own way to England in 1977 and rented a Formula Ford to compete and finish third in his first race. Ribbs stepped up to Trans Am Camaros in 1983 and won five of twelve races and SCCA Rookie of the Year. The talented Ribbs would win more races (seventeen) than any other Trans Am driver from 1984 to 1986. He captured IMSA Driver of the Year honors in 1987 by winning four races. Ribbs repeated as IMSA Driver of the Year in 1988 and made his PPG debut at Long Beach in 1990. Driving for Walker Motorsport Team in 1991, Ribbs finished seventeenth in points in nine starts. In 1991, under McDonald's sponsorship, he became the first African-American driver at the Indianapolis 500. He scored five point-paying finishes in 1993 and three in 1994. *Did You Know?* To keep in shape, Willy T. Ribbs boxes with heavyweights such as Ray Mercer.

Indy Car Victories: 0   Indy Car Poles: 0

❑ Team Contact: Walker Racing, 8060 Woodland Road, Indianapolis, IN 46278
Also at 4030 Championship Dr., Indianapolis, IN 46268

Andre Ribeiro

Andre Ribeiro was born January 18, 1966, in Sao Paulo, Brazil, and began racing karts in 1985. He finished second in Sao Paulo Championship and won the two hours of Rio de Janeiro with Christian Fittipaldi in 1988. Ribeiro competed in the Formula Opel European Championship in 1990, before driving a partial season in the British Formula Three Championship in 1991. He claimed two poles and had four podium finishes in the 1993 British Formula Three Championship. Driving in the PPG-Firestone Indy Lights Championship in 1994, he finished the season second, with four wins and four pole positions. Ribeiro looked strong in 1995 and opened a lot of eyes with his impressive performance at the New England 200. Ribeiro took both the pole and win at New England on the one-mile oval. *Did You Know?* Andre Ribeiro was studying to be a lawyer at Sao Paulo University before deciding to enter racing.

Indy Car Victories: 1   Indy Car Poles: 1

❑ Team Contact: Tasman Motorsports Group, Hilliard, OH

Steve Robertson

Steve Robertson was born July 4, 1965, in Hockney, London, England, and was competing in the British Formula Ford Series by 1986. In 1988 he captured the British Formula 2000 Series, winning nine races and grabbing seventeen pole positions. Robertson then focused on the British Formula Three arena, finishing fifth in 1989 and third in 1990. He then moved to the 1993 PPG-Firestone Indy Lights Series and earned Rookie of the Year honors. Not only were his three poles and seven Top 10 finishes impressive, but he also led twenty-eight percent of the laps he raced. The following year Robertson won the PPG-Firestone Indy Lights Championship with four wins, two poles, and seven Top 3 finishes. *Did You Know?* Steve Robertson began his career in Formula Ford and won six races.

Indy Car Victories: 0   Indy Car Poles: 0

Eliseo Salazar

Eliseo Salazar was born November 14, 1954, in Santiago, Chile. He began his career in 1974 as the Chilean Saloon Cars Champion and by 1978 he was the Argentine Formula Ford champion. In 1981 he became the first Chilean to compete in Formula One competition. Salazar won the Sportsman of the Year award from the British magazine *Autosport* in 1990. In 1994 he ran the IMSA World Sports Car season for Momo-Ferrari and won three races, while also placing second three times. *Did You Know?* Eliseo Salazar won the Chilean Champion Rally Hill Climb both in 1984 and in 1985.

Indy Car Victories: 0   Indy Car Poles: 0

❑ Team Contact: Dick Simon Racing, 701 S. Girls School Road, Indianapolis, IN 46231

Mark Smith

Mark Smith was born April 10, 1967, in McMinnville, Oregon, and began racing karts in 1982. Smith quickly moved from Formula Ford Series to Super Vees and was named 1988 Rookie of the Year in New Zealand Tasman Formula Pacific Series. In 1989 he won five races, took four poles, and set six track records on his way to winning the Super Vee Championship. Smith then moved to Indy Lights Series, finishing third and taking Rookie of the Year honors. He won his first Firestone Indy Lights race at Cleveland in 1991 and finished runner-up in the championship. Smith took eight Top 5 starts in twelve Indy Lights events in 1992 and finished seventh overall in the championship. He stepped up to the PPG Cup events in 1993 and entered twelve of sixteen season events. Smith scored a career-best finish of fifth at Michigan in 1994 while starting fourteen races for Derrick Walker Racing. *Did You Know?* Mark Smith became the first "Smith" to compete in any 500-mile event.

Indy Car Victories: 0   Indy Car Poles: 0

❏ Team Contact: Walker Racing, 8060 Woodland Road, Indianapolis, IN 46278
Also at 4030 Championship Dr., Indianapolis, IN 46268

Lyn St. James

Lyn St. James was born March 13, 1947, in Willoughby, Ohio. She won the Kelly American Challenge Series in both 1981 and 1982. St. James was named *Autoweek's* IMSA Camel GT Rookie of the Year in 1984 and became the first woman to win an IMSA GTO race in 1985. She established thirteen national and international speed records for women, including a closed-course record of 204.230 mph, at Talladega. She was voted IMSA's Driver of the Year and Most Improved GT Driver in 1985. St. James drove on the winning GTO Team in 24 Hours of Daytona in 1987, while increasing her records to thirty-one. She was a member of the 1990 GTO Team in both Daytona 24 Hours and Sebring 12 Hours. In 1992, St. James was named the Indianapolis 500 Rookie of the Year, finishing eleventh and becoming only the second woman to start the prestigious race. She entered seven races with Dick Simon Racing in 1993 and finished a season-high thirteenth at Phoenix. St. James broke the women's closed-course speed record for the fourth time in 1994 with a lap of 224.282 at Indy. *Did You Know?* Lyn St. James's best career finish was eleventh at Indianapolis in 1992.

Indy Car Victories: 0   Indy Car Poles: 0

❏ Team Contact: Dick Simon Racing, 701 S. Girls School Rd., Indianapolis, IN 46231

Danny Sullivan

Danny Sullivan was born March 9, 1950, in Louisville, Kentucky, and raced overseas in Formula Three until 1976. He made his PPG Cup racing debut with a strong third at Atlanta in 1982. That same year Sullivan qualified 13th for his first Indianapolis 500, finishing 14th after hitting the turn four wall. He won his first event at Cleveland in 1984, as well as the Pocono 500 and Montreal race. Sullivan's nine Top 10 finishes placed him fourth in the 1984 season standings. In 1985 he joined the Penske Racing Team and won his first Indianapolis 500 despite a near tragic spin in lap 120. Sullivan finished third in PPG points in 1986 and ninth in 1987, before capturing his first PPG Indy Car World Series title in 1988. In a remarkable year, Sullivan won four events, took nine poles and scored 11 Top 5 finishes. He finished seventh in points in 1989, sixth in 1990, seventh in 1992 and twelfth in 1993. Sullivan is one of Indy Car racing's most recognizable personalities and with 17 victories under his belt - through 1994, one of it's all-time finest drivers. *Did You Know?* Danny Sullivan was honored as the 1993 "Auto Racing Legend" at the Eighth Annual Great Sports Legends dinner in October of that year.

Indy Car Victories: 17   Indy Car Poles: 19

❏ Team Contact: Pacwest Racing Group, 150 Gasoline Alley, Indianapolis, IN 46222

Brian Till

Brian Till was born March 26, 1960 in Houston, Texas, and began racing karts in 1983. In 1986 he won the Inaugural Barber Saab race at the Meadowlands and finished second in the championship. Till was the 1990 Toyota Atlantic Eastern champion and Rookie of the Year, grabbing three wins and four seconds in nine races. He moved to the Indy Lights in 1991 and finished fifth overall in his first year. Till started nine Indy Car events in 1992 and scored two points in his debut at Long Beach. He

91

missed six races at the start of the 1993 season, but managed to run in eight of the final ten events and posted a ninth-place finish at Cleveland. Till made his first Indy 500 start in 1994 and despite having only a handful of starts in PPG Cup competition, has driven some very impressive races. *Did You Know?* Until 1992, Brian Till had never finished lower than fifth in points in any series he had entered.

Indy Car Victories: 0   Indy Car Poles: 0

❑ Team Contact: Dale Coyne Racing, 19 Lake Drive, Plainfield, IL 60544

Michael Andretti (left) and Paul Tracy (right) (Photo courtesy of Kmart Texaco Havoline Racing)

Paul Tracy

Paul Tracy was born December 17, 1968, in Toronto, Ontario, Canada. Like many drivers, he began by racing karts and placed sixth in the 1984 World Karting Championships. At the age of sixteen he became the youngest ever Canadian Formula Ford 2000 champion. After two successful years in Formula Ford racing, he entered the American Racing Series (Indy Lights) competition and won the first event he entered at Phoenix. Tracy ended up finishing ninth in points in 1988, eighth in points in 1989, and won his first Indy Lights Championship in 1990. Tracy took nine of fourteen races, set a single-season record for poles (seven), and set four race records and six qualifying records. In 1991 he began his first PPG Cup race at Long Beach for Dale Coyne Racing, but signed on with Penske at mid-year. Tracy started eleven races, filling in for an injured Rick Mears in 1992. He scored six Top 5 qualifying efforts including his first PPG Cup career pole at Elkhart Lake and landed on the podium three times. His first full season came in 1993 and he promptly scored five victories and two poles. Tracy finished third in 1993 points and joined Nigel Mansell as the only driver to win from the pole, accomplishing it twice. In 1994 he started all sixteen races for Penske racing and compiled three victories and four poles. Tracy added two more wins to his total in 1995 by capturing the Indy Car Australia and the Miller Genuine Draft 200. *Did You Know?* Paul Tracy led 757 of 2,112 laps during the 1993 season.

Indy Car Victories: 10   Indy Car Poles: 7

❑ Team Contact: Newman/Haas Racing, 500 Tower Parkway, Lincolnshire, IL 60069

Side and front views of Paul Tracy's No. 3 racing car (Photo courtesy of Kmart Texaco Havoline Racing)

Collector's Note: One of the brightest young stars in the PPG Indy Car World Series, Paul Tracy also has the numbers to back up the claim. In his first two full seasons in 1993 and 1994, he has twice finished third in the final PPG Cup point standings. He has won eight races in the last two years, second only to Unser, Jr.'s nine. Tracy collectors will want to pick up memorabilia from his Indy Car debut in 1991 at Long Beach and from his first pole at Road America in 1992. Tracy makes an excellent driver to collect, as his Indy Car career is only a few years old, making the acquisition of certain memorabilia relatively inexpensive and easy to find. Driving with the prestigious Newman/Haas Racing Team only adds to his popularity.

A Paul Tracy Indy Car wins checklist is provided below for ticket and program collectors:

1993	❑ Long Beach	❑ Cleveland	❑ Toronto	❑ Road America
	❑ Laguna Seca			
1994	❑ Detroit	❑ Nazareth	❑ Laguna Seca	
1995	❑ Australia	❑ Wisconsin		

Al Unser, Jr.

Al Unser, Jr. was born April 19, 1962, in Albuquerque, New Mexico, and began racing karts at the age of nine. Son of legendary driver and PPG Champion Al Unser, it's no surprise that Al Unser, Jr. was destined to become a race car driver. He began racing sprint cars in 1978 and by 1981 he had graduated to Super Vees, where he captured his first championship during his rookie season. The following year Unser added a Can-Am title and made his PPG Cup debut with a fifth-place finish in the California 500. His first full season in Indy Cars found him finishing seventh in 1983, the same year his father won the national championship. In 1984 he won his first PPG Cup event on Father's Day at Portland and finished sixth in point standings. As irony might have it, "Little Al" lost the closest battle in Indy Car history (151-150) to his father in 1985. Al Unser, Jr. became the youngest IROC champion in the history of the series in 1986. He finished third in PPG Cup points in a winless 1987 season, then came back strong in 1988 by winning four races and finishing second in the standings. His first career pole came at Long Beach in 1989 in a race that he would eventually win, but the following year would add "Little Al's" name to the history books. With six wins in sixteen races, Al Unser, Jr. scored his first PPG Indy Car World Series Championship in 1990 and was named "Driver of the Year." In 1992 he won his first Indy 500 by history's closest margin, and scored six podium placements and an Indy Car record twenty-three consecutive point-paying finishes. In 1994 Unser started all sixteen races for Penske Racing, winning his second Indy 500 and PPG Cup. In an extraordinary season, he won eight races, four poles, and clinched the PPG Cup with two races yet remaining on the schedule. Unser added four more victories to his impressive totals in 1995 and should dominate in 1996. *Did You Know?* Al Unser, Jr. was the youngest driver to pass the 200 mph barrier at Indianapolis.

Indy Car Victories: 31   Indy Car Poles: 7

❑ Team Contact: Marlboro Team Penske, 366 Penske Plaza, P.O. Box 301, Reading, PA 19603

Collector's Note: Having driven on both the NASCAR and Indy Car circuits, Al Unser, Jr. has been featured on numerous trading card releases. He appeared first in the 1983 A&S Racing Indy set on card No. 43. A&S then included him in subsequent sets from 1984 to 1987, and even featured him on two cards in 1985. After competing in only one NASCAR event, the Daytona 500, Unser was featured on ten cards in various NASCAR sets in 1993. The card most sought after by collectors is in the 1993 Traks First Run set, a parallel set, card #197. This card commands about three times the value of his regularly issued card in the set. His most valuable Indy Car card is out of the 1993 Hi-Tech Checkered Flag Finishers insert set. This insert #SP1 has an associated value range of $5 to $10. Although he has yet to appear in a Formula One race, he had a card (#162) in the 1992 Grid Formula One card set.

Johnny Unser

Johnny Unser was born October 22, 1958, in Ketchum, Idaho, to the late Jerry Unser, the first Unser to race at the Indianapolis 500. He began racing motorcycles and sprint buggies. In 1986 he scored one pole and one win, with three other Top 3 podium finishes in Formula Russell Mazda Cup Series. Unser took first place at the 1989 Sebring in Huffaker Racing Pontiac GTU, teamed with George Robinson and Bart Kendall. He was awarded the AIS Rookie of the Year in 1990 and finished second in the championship. He returned the following year to AIS and finished fifth in the standings, with his team finishing first. Unser then took to Indy Cars in 1993 and competed in four races. He started only one race for Dale Coyne Racing in 1994 and scored a career-best finish at New Hampshire with a fifteenth-place slot. *Did You Know?* Johnny Unser, the cousin of Al Unser, Jr., worked on his uncle Al's pit crew in the early 1980s.

Indy Car Victories: 0   Indy Car Poles: 0

Jimmy Vasser

Jimmy Vasser was born November 20, 1965, in Canoga Park, California, and started racing quarter midgets at age six. He won three consecutive national midget championships from 1974 to 1978. Vasser scored five victories in eleven starts on the SCCA Formula Ford Series in 1984, gaining him the North American Pro Championship and Rookie of the Year honors. In 1986 he became the SCCA Formula Ford national champion, grabbing seven victories and nine poles. He made two Pro Sports 2000 starts and scored three second-place finishes in the Canadian Formula Ford 2000 Series during 1990. Vasser added the Toyota Atlantic title in 1991, with six wins and eight pole positions. He started eleven Indy Car events in 1992 and posted a seventh-place finish at Long Beach. Vasser placed third at Phoenix, thirteenth at Indy, and finished sixteenth in 1993 PPG Cup standings. Starting all sixteen races with Hayhoe Racing in 1994, Vasser finished fourth at both Australia and Indianapolis in a season that would earn him five point-paying finishes. Vasser put together a strong season in 1995 and picked up his first Indy Car victory at Portland. *Did You Know?* Jimmy Vasser was awarded the SCCA Presidents Cup in 1986.

Indy Car Victories: 0   Indy Car Poles: 0

❏ Team Contact: Target/Chip Ganassi Racing, 3821 Industrial Blvd., Indianapolis, IN 46254

Collector's Note: Jimmy Vasser's strong 1995 season caught the eyes of many collectors. Memorabilia from his first Indy Car victory at Portland, as well as his trading cards, are still inexpensive and easy acquisitions.

Jacques Villeneuve

Jacques Villeneuve was born April 9, 1971, in St-Jean-sur-Richelieu, Canada, to Formula One racer Gilles Villeneuve. He attended both Formula Ford and Formula 2000 racing schools in the mid-1980s. Villeneuve competed in the 1988 Alfa Italian Touring Car Championship before moving to Formula Three in Italy. In 1992 he finished second in points on the Japanese Formula Three Series and made his North American racing debut, finishing third in Trois Riveres Formula Atlantic race. He was named Player's Ltd./Toyota Atlantic Rookie of the Year in 1993 and set five lap and five qualifying records. Villeneuve's first Canadian victory also came in 1993 at the Montreal circuit named after his father. He started sixteen races in his rookie Indy Car season for Forsythe/Green Racing and picked up his first victory at Road America. Villeneuve also finished second at Indianapolis and scored ten point-paying finishes. Both Indy Car and Indy 500 Rookie of the Year, he became the youngest driver to reach the $1 million mark in earnings. Villeneuve dominated the circuit in 1995 by capturing six poles and four wins on his way to the Indy Car Championship. *Did You Know?* Jacques Villeneuve has decided to make a move to the Formula One circuit in 1996.

Indy Car Victories: 1   Indy Car Poles: 0

❏ Team Contact: Team Green, Indianapolis, IN

Collector's Note: The hottest driver to hit Indy Car racing in years, Jacques Villeneuve became the first Canadian to win the Indianapolis 500 and the youngest winner in more than four decades. His first Indy Car win came at Road America in 1994, so memorabilia from this event is a must addition to Villeneuve fans. Memorabilia from his win at the 1995 Indianapolis 500 is also popular with collectors. As far as trading cards, his rookie card (#172) appears in the 1992 Grid set, which was a Formula One release. The 1995 SkyBox Indy set gave the rising star four regular issues and an Heir to Indy insert card.

Dennis Vitolo

Dennis Vitolo was born December 18, 1956, in Massapequa, New York. He began racing Formula Fords in 1981 and won the SCCA Southeast Division Championship in 1982. In 1983 Vitolo drove in both Formula Ford and Sports 2000 races, and made his Super Vee debut at Laguna Seca. He moved to England in 1984 to compete in British Formula Ford 2000 Series and finished in Top 10 in all twenty-five races. Vitolo won the 1985 Camel GT at Pocono in his IMSA debut and entered his own car in the Super Vee Series during 1986. His PPG Cup debut came in Miami in 1988 while driving for Tony Bettenhausen and he finished eleventh after starting twenty-second. Vitolo moved to the GM Lotus Series in 1989 and 1990. In 1991 he entered three PPG Cup events and began a career racing boats, winning a hydroplane event in Maryland. Driving for Dale Coyne in 1992, he started four events and also won his second 2.5-liter hydroplane event. He was the fastest American rookie to qualify at Indy in 1994 and began the race fifteenth. Vitolo had to drop out on Lap 89 after an incident with Nigel Mansell and finished twenty-sixth. *Did You Know?* Entering the 1995 season, Dennis Vitolo's best career finish was eleventh at Miami in 1988.

Indy Car Victories: 0   Indy Car Poles: 0

Jeff Wood

Jeff Wood was born January 20, 1957, in Wichita, Kansas. He grabbed two wins in Formula Ford in 1976 and won the Formula Atlantic Rookie of the Year in 1977. Wood became the youngest winner in Formula Atlantic in 1978 and picked up at least one win in the series for three consecutive years. He joined the Carl Haas' Can-Am Team in 1981 and recorded seven Top 10 finishes. Wood's PPG Cup debut was at Las Vegas driving for Dan Gurney. He qualified thirteenth, but finished twenty-second due to mechanical problems. That same year he finished eighth at Laguna Seca for his best PPG Cup finish to date. He was the Formula Atlantic champion with four wins in 1985, a year in which he would have only one PPG start. Wood entered four races in 1987, five races in 1989, and ten races in 1990. In 1991 he started eight events for a variety of teams, with his best finish thirteenth at Denver. In eighteen races over the next three years, his highest finish was twelfth at Michigan in 1992. *Did You Know?* Jeff Wood's most memorable event was his first professional racing win in 1977 at a Formula Atlantic event in Montreal.

Indy Car Victories: 0   Indy Car Poles: 0

Alessandro Zampedri

Alessandro Zampedri was born October 3, 1969, in Brescia, Italy, and started racing karts at the age of twelve. In 1988 he started his first season in Italian Formula Alfa Boxer Championship and scored five wins and eight poles in the series the following year. In 1990 Zampedri moved into Young Italian Formula Three Series and earned Rookie of the Year honors. He returned to the Italian Formula Three ranks in 1991 and also drove in the South American Formula Three Championship. Zampedri drove in the Formula 3000 Championship the following two years before entering the Indy Car ranks in 1994. He scored a career-best finish of seventh at Portland, while competing in ten races. *Did You Know?* Alessandro Zampedri was named by Italy's *Autosprint Magazine* the Most Promising Young Italian Driver of the Year in 1989.

Indy Car Victories: 0   Indy Car Poles: 0

❑ Team Contact: Payton-Coyne Racing, 19 Lake Drive, Plainfield, IL 60544

1995/1996 NASCAR Winston Cup Series Drivers

John Andretti   **Kmart/Little Caesars (#37)**

John Andretti was born March 12, 1963, and is the son of Aldo Andretti, Mario Andretti's twin brother. After a dynamic 1994 season, Andretti became the initial driver for the Kranefuss-Haas Ford Team. Guided by Indy Car magnate Carl Haas and Ford racing guru Michael Kranefuss, Andretti was also impressed by the addition of crew chief Tim Brewer to the team. Brewer was at the helm during two NASCAR Winston Cup titles—those of Cale Yarborough and Darrell Waltrip. Andretti became the first driver in history to compete in the Indianapolis 500 and the Coca-Cola 600 at Charlotte during the same day in 1994. In addition to two decades of race experience, Andretti's knowledge of all types of racing cars has made him a fierce competitor on the NASCAR circuit. He entered the 1995 season with thirty-three NASCAR Winston Cup races under his belt and strong finishes at both the 1994 Miller Genuine Draft 400 and the 1994 Brickyard 400. He finished eighteenth in the 1995 Winston Cup point standings and is uncertain of his plans yet for 1996. *Did You Know?* John Andretti's godfather is A. J. Foyt.

❑ Team Contact: Chip Williams, Williams Co. of America, 2 Park Crossing Circle, Ormond Beach, FL 32174

First Trading Card: 1991 All World (Indy Set) #4

Collector's Note: As a part of one of racing's most popular families, John Andretti immediately attracted attention from both fans and collectors. As one of NASCAR's top rookies during the 1994 season, he found himself included in many manufacturers' trading card sets. His popularity led him to inserts in both NASCAR and Indy Car sets. Hi-Tech chose him as a Championship Driver insert (#CD3) and Maxx included him in their 1994 Rookie Class insert set. SkyBox also became the first manufacturer to salute his dual performances on Memorial Day 1994 by issuing a commemorative card (#26).

Collect-A-Card randomly inserted one thousand hand-signed cards into its 1992 Andretti Racing foil packs. The one thousand signed cards were equal divided between Mario ($175-$200), Michael ($125-$150), Jeffrey ($100), and John Andretti ($125-$150). The cards are not easy to find. With John Andretti's popularity growing with each passing NASCAR Winston Cup season, beginning a collection of his racing memorabilia today may not be a bad idea.

Johnny Benson   **Pennzoil (#30)**

Johnny Benson was born June 27, 1963, and now makes his home in Grand Rapids, MI. The reigning Busch Grand National titlist graduated to the Pennzoil Pontiac in 1996. He won the 1994 Penrose Rookie Challenge while driving the Staff/America Chevrolet owned by Bill Baumgardner. The team picked up Lipton Tea as a new sponsor in 1995 and raced to the 1995 title. An exciting and young driver, he will be worth watching in 1996. *Did You Know?* Johnny Benson scored his first career win at Dover, DE in September of 1994.

❏ Team Contact: Pennzoil Product Co., Pennzoil Pl., P.O. Box 2967, Houston, TX 77252

Brett Bodine   Lowe's (#11)

Brett Bodine was born January 11, 1959, and is the younger brother of Geoff Bodine. In 1995 he followed in his brother's tracks by driving for legendary car owner Junior Johnson. After spending

five seasons with Kenny Bernstein's Quaker State Fords, Bodine stepped into first-year sponsor Lowe's Stores Ford in 1995. Bodine has posted forty-three Top 10 finishes entering the 1995 season and hopes that reliability improvements will only enhance his performance. During the inaugural running of the Brickyard 400, Bodine finished second after leading late in the race. Bodine posted the highest annual winnings of his career in 1994 and finished nineteenth in Winston Cup standings. *Did You Know?* Brett began racing in 1977 in the comfortable setting of his family-owned Chemung Speedrome in Chemung, New York.

❏ Team Contact: Denise Michaux, Team Lowe's Racing, P.O. Box 484, Winston-Salem, NC 27102

First Trading Card: 1988 Maxx #59

Collector's Note: Bodine ticket and program collectors will want to pick up those from his Winston Cup debut at the World 600 at Charlotte Motor Speedway in 1986, his first Winston Cup win at the North Wilkesboro in the 1990 First Union 400, and his first pole at the 1990 Mello Yello at Charlotte.

Brett Bodine began racing in 1977 (Photo courtesy of Sports Marketing Enterprises)

Geoff Bodine   QVC (#7)

Geoff Bodine was born April 18, 1949, and is the oldest of three racing Bodine brothers. Both car owner and driver in 1994, he finished the season with the highest annual purse of his career. The season was a dichotomy of sorts, as nine engine failures and six accidents put a damper on Bodine's winnings. Geoff started from the pole five times in 1994 and picked up the Busch Pole Award for most poles in a season. His three wins in 1994 helped Bodine finish in the Top 10 ten times during the season. Bringing seventeen career wins into the 1994 season, including a 1986 victory at the Daytona 500, Geoff Bodine is one of the most experienced and respected drivers on the circuit. Bodine purchased Alan Kulwicki's race team from his estate following the racer's death on April 1, 1993. He finished sixteenth in the 1995 Winston Cup point standings. *Did You Know?* Geoff Bodine founded Bo-Dyn Engineering, which developed and built bobsleds for the award-winning USA team.

❏ Team Contact: Cal Lawson, Bodine Racing, 6007 Victory Lane, Harrisburg, NC 28075

First Trading Card: 1986 SportStar no #

Todd Bodine   Factory Stores (#75)

Todd Bodine was born February 27, 1964, and is the youngest of all three Bodine brothers. Todd entered his second full NASCAR Winston Cup season in 1994, behind the wheel of Butch Mock's Factory Stores of America Fords. The new team finished an impressive third in Atlanta and in the Top 10 seven times in 1994. A multi-car accident dampened aspirations at Daytona during the beginning of the 1994 season, as Bodine was in the lead pack. In a tribute to Todd's determination, he failed to finish in only six of the thirty races he ran in 1994. He began the 1995 season with forty-one career Winston Cup starts to his credit. His plans for 1996 are still uncertain at this point. *Did You Know?* Todd Bodine made his NASCAR Winston Cup debut in 1992 at Watkins Glen, NY driving a Diet Pepsi Ford.

❑ Team Contact: Lisa Holleran, Gossage-McFarland Sports Marketing, Smith Tower, Highway 29, Suite 408, Harrisburg, NC 28075

First Trading Card: 1991 Maxx #203, 1991 Traks #34

Jeff Burton   Exide Batteries (#99)

Jeff Burton was born June 29, 1967, and by 1989 was entering the NASCAR Busch Series. Within a year he was among the top drivers and after five seasons he had four victories in 153 Series starts. In 1994 Jeff joined his brother Ward in the NASCAR Winston Cup Series. He won the 1994 Maxx Race Cards Rookie of the Year competition and posted three Top 10 finishes. Burton departed from the Stavola Brothers Raybestos Brakes Fords after the 1995 season and will spend 1996 with Roush Racing. *Did You Know?* Jeff Burton finished fourth in the Winston Select Open in 1994 and earned a berth in the all-star race.

❑ Team Contact: Roush Racing, P.O. Box 1089, Liberty, NC 27298

First Trading Card: 1991 Maxx #201

Ward Burton   MBNA (#22)

Ward Burton was born October 25, 1961, and he and his brother Jeff became another outstanding brother combination in NASCAR Winston Cup racing. Ward helped bring the A. G. Dillard Hardee's racing team to Winston Cup from the Busch Series in 1994. After a rocky start in 1994, the team regrouped and finished a strong second in the Miller 500, just a second behind winner Geoff Bodine. The team also won the pole for the 1994 Mello Yello 500 at Charlotte. Burton stayed with the Hardee's race team until August of 1995, when he was replaced by Greg Sacks. Burton came on strong in 1995 and picked up his first Winston Cup victory at Rockingham in the AC-Delco 400. *Did You Know?* In 1993 Ward finished sixth in season point standings on the Busch Series circuit and won three races.

❏ Team Contact: Bob Boyles, A. G. Dillard Motorsports, 1000 River Road, Charlottesville, VA 22901

First Trading Card: 1991 Maxx #123

Collector's Note: Burton collectors had much to cheer about in 1995, as Ward picked up his first NASCAR Winston Cup victory at the AC-Delco 400 in Rockingham. Memorabilia from this race is a must for all Burton collectors.

Ward Burton (Photo courtesy of The Source Int., Inc.)

Derrike Cope   Straight Arrow (#12)

Derrike Cope was born November 3, 1958. He began the 1994 season with Cale Yarborough's racing team, but was dismissed midway through the season. His departure from behind the wheel would only be a short one, as after running three races for the T. W. Taylor Team, Cope found himself driving Bobby Allison Team's Fords at Watkins Glen in August. Allison had been searching for a sponsor throughout the season and finally signed Straight Arrow Products simultaneously with Cope's arrival. Now with competitive financing, Cope drove a brand new Ford at Charlotte, qualified seventh, and finished ninth. The end of the 1994 season found a confident Derrike Cope qualifying fourth at Rockingham and finishing seventh at Atlanta. Anticipation was high as the Straight Arrow Ford racing team entered the 1995 season and the team seemed to improve with each race. Cope finished a season high second at the 1995 Dura-Lube 500 in Phoenix. Cope finished fifteenth in the 1995 Winston Cup point standings. *Did You Know?* In twenty-nine NASCAR Winston Cup races during the 1990 season, Derrike Cope finished six times in the Top 10.

❏ Team Contact: Carolyn Carrier, Bobby Allison Motorsports, 5254 Pit Road South, Harrisburg, NC 28075

First Trading Card: 1988 Maxx #92

Ricky Craven   Kodiak (#41)

Ricky Craven was born May 24, 1966, in Newburgh, ME. After capturing the 1992 NASCAR Busch Series Rookie of the Year award, Craven compiled two strong second-place finishes in Busch Series Championship point standings during the 1993 and 1994 seasons. In 1995, his first year of driving for Larry Hedrick Motorsports and his first season on the Winston

Derrike Cope (Photo courtesy of Bobby Allison Motorsports Team, Inc.)

Cup Circuit, Craven was quick to establish himself as a contender. He qualified third and finished tenth in the 1995 Coca-Cola 600 at Charlotte in May and finished tenth in the Budweiser at the Glen in August. Craven battled Robert Pressley all season in the Maxx Race Cards Rookie of the Year point standings, with both highly-talented drivers finishing strong in 1995. The 1995 Rookie of the Year finished twenty-fourth in Winston Cup point standings. *Did You Know?* Ricky Craven won the 1991 Busch Grand National North Series Championship, with ten victories and six poles.

❑ Team Contact: Bob Hice, Muhleman Marketing, 6000 Monroe Road, Suite 300, Charlotte, NC 28212

First Trading Card: 1991 Winner's Choice #98

Collector's Note: Ricky Craven is no stranger to race fans, particularly those who witnessed him win the 1991 Busch Grand National North Series Championship. That same year Winner's Choice issued a thirty-card set saluting the young driver. The company also issued a regional set saluting the drivers of the Northeast, which included Craven. Both of these trading card sets are highly sought by Craven collectors.

By 1992, Craven's first regular issue trading cards began appearing in Winston Cup sets, as it became common to include the top Busch drivers. His autographed insert card in the Winner's Choice Busch set is also popular with his fans.

Craven collectors had a field day when their driver joined the Winston Cup circuit in 1995. Any and all items relating to his inaugural year are certainly worth collecting, as are career milestone items such as tickets and programs. Some 1995 free promotional items included a Kodiak racing schedule, "One Hungry Bear" bumper sticker, and a (9" x 7") handout.

Dale Earnhardt   GM Goodwrench (#3)

In search of his eighth NASCAR Winston Cup title, Dale Earnhardt entered the 1995 season as one of the greatest drivers in the history of the sport. His record-tying seven Winston Cup titles leaves him in the company of only the king—Richard Petty. The magic formula of Richard Childress and Earnhardt, accompanied by the dedication and consistency of the GM Goodwrench Racing Team, have set new standards for the sport. Dale Earnhardt was born April 29, 1951, in Kannapolis, NC. In addition to his record-tying championships, Earnhardt entered the 1995 season with sixty-three career Winston Cup wins in 480 starts—sixth on the all-time list. The two-time American Driver of the Year (1987, 1994) has set all-time career marks for earnings both in American motorsports ($24 M) and in Winston Cup ($22 M). He was Rookie of the Year in 1979 and holds numerous track records. Earnhardt finished an impressive second in the 1995 Winston Cup point standings, a mere thirty-four points from Jeff Gordon. *Did You Know?* Dale Earnhardt's first Winston Cup victory was at the Southeastern 500 at Bristol on April 19, 1979, and his first pole followed shortly after at Riverside in the NAPA 400 on June 8 of the same year.

"The Man in Black" Dale Earnhardt

❑ Team Contact: J. R. Rhodes, Championship Sports Group, Inc., 5015B West, WT Harris Boulevard, Charlotte, NC 28269

First Trading Card: 1986 SportStar no#

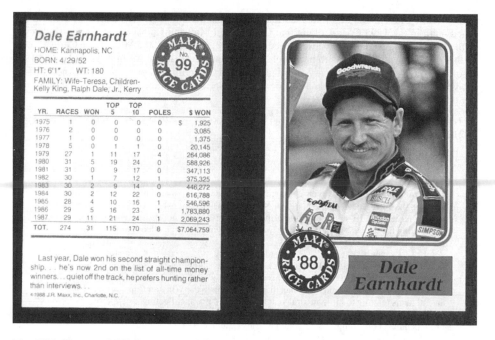

Dale Earnhardt

HOME: Kannapolis, NC
BORN: 4/29/52
HT: 6'1"   WT: 180
FAMILY: Wife-Teresa, Children-
Kelly King, Ralph Dale, Jr., Kerry

YR.	RACES	WON	TOP 5	TOP 10	POLES	$ WON
1975	1	0	0	0	0	$ 1,925
1976	2	0	0	0	0	3,085
1977	1	0	0	0	0	1,375
1978	5	0	1	1	0	20,145
1979	27	1	11	17	4	264,086
1980	31	5	19	24	0	588,926
1981	31	0	9	17	0	347,113
1982	30	1	7	12	1	375,325
1983	30	2	9	14	0	446,272
1984	30	2	12	22	0	616,788
1985	28	4	10	16	1	546,596
1986	29	5	16	23	1	1,783,880
1987	29	11	21	24	1	2,069,243
TOT.	274	31	115	170	8	$7,064,759

Last year, Dale won his second straight championship. . . he's now 2nd on the list of all-time money
winners. . . quiet off the track, he prefers hunting rather
than interviews. . .
© 1988 J.R. Maxx, Inc., Charlotte, N.C.

Dale Earnhardt

The 1988 Maxx card #99 was excluded from the original set when Earnhardt refused to grant the company rights to issue the card. The cards that were already produced had to be pulled or were kept by the company.

Collector's Note: An entire book can be written about the collectibles surrounding Dale Earnhardt's fabulous career. The demand for his collectibles parallels his racing ability. Just when you think it can't get any better, it does. Earnhardt is to racing, what Michael Jordon's been to basketball—a huge drawing card. The Score Board Incorporated's pursuit and capture of Earnhardt for a broad two-year marketing deal is just one of many examples of Dale's strong appeal to racing fans. Among the products authorized under the agreement are autographed products, used race equipment, trading cards, ceramic sculptures and plates, ceramic and pewter figurines, computer and video game software products, coins and medallions, artwork, and much more. Most industry experts believe Earnhardt memorabilia outsells the next tier of drivers by three to six times. If you have ever been at a NASCAR race you won't find this statement hard to believe, as Sports Images, which operates seven Earnhardt souvenir trailers, takes five trailers to most races. Although Earnhardt resists exclusive agreements, he approaches each license with guarded optimism, which also benefits Earnhardt collectors.

Both Racing Collectibles by Action and Racing Champions have had die cast agreements with the Intimidator. Action's deal covered over twenty different collectibles including cars, car banks, haulers, and even show trailers most at 1:24, 1:64, and 1:94 scale. Quantities range from slightly over 2,500 to issues as high as 16,000. Needless to say, Earnhardt's Wrangler-sponsored Monte Carlos that he drove in the mid-1980s became immediate hits in the collectibles market. Sales of select #3 Goodwrench Chevrolets, especially low-number limited editions, have remained strong and should continue.

Perhaps the most common question asked by Earnhardt trading card collectors is, where did the 1988 Maxx card #99 of Dale Earnhardt come from? The Maxx card #99 was slated for inclusion in the original 1988 Maxx set. The card was excluded when Earnhardt refused to grant the company rights to issue the card. The cards that were already produced had to be pulled or kept by the company. They then became the source for inserts in 1994 Maxx Medallion boxes. The difference between the insert and the original is sequential numbering and a permanent gold foil label on the latter. Only a handful of uncut sheets, consisting of twenty-four assorted cards, and a few dozen singles are known to exist, making them treasured with Earnhardt collectors. Earnhardt insert singles in demand include 1995 Action Packed Race For Eight, an eight-card set, 1995 Press Pass VIP Emerald #9, and the 1995 Press Pass Cup Chase #9.

In June of 1995, a beautiful 1:43-scale pewter replica of the 1995 Monte Carlo driven by Earnhardt was created by Action Collectables and distributed through The Racing Collectables Club of America. Limited to 1,500 pieces, at a price of $99.95, this reproduction sold out as fast as you could read the sponsor stickers depicted on the replica.

Collectors of unique Earnhardt memorabilia might want to look to Frost Cutlery of Chattanooga, Tennessee, which produced a unique line of "'The Intimidator' Rolls a 7" commemorative knives ranging in price from $21.99 to $439.99 (prices may vary).

Earnhardt's "Intimidator" nickname can also be applied to his dealings off the track, as the driver exercises strong control over his collectibles production. For Earnhardt collectors this is an excellent testament to the driver's dedication to his fans and his vigilance for quality.

Included here for all Earnhardt ticket and program collectors are a few key dates:

❏ First Start   Charlotte Motor Speedway in the World 600, May 25, 1975
❏ First Race Win   Bristol International Raceway in the Southern 500, April 19, 1979
❏ First Pole   Riverside Raceway in NAPA 400, June 8, 1979
❏ First Speedway Win   Atlanta 500 on March 16, 1980
Winston Cup Champion: ❏ 1980 ❏ 1986 ❏ 1987 ❏ 1990 ❏ 1991 ❏ 1993
                       ❏ 1994

Bill Elliott

McDonald's (#94)

The sport's Most Popular Driver, as voted by the fans for the ninth time, in 1994 was Bill Elliott. The award, presented by the National Motorsports Press Association first in 1956, reflects the most received by any driver during its history. Bill Elliott was born October 8, 1955, and won his first Winston Cup Championship in 1988, one of only two Ford champions since 1969. He has finished in the Top 10 in Winston Cup points an impressive eleven out of twelve years (through 1994). In 1985 Elliott became the first driver to win the Daytona 500, Winston 500, and Southern 500, three of the four "Crown Jewel" events on the Winston Cup circuit. He captured two Daytona 500s (1985 and 1987), winning both from the pole. Elliott rejoined his brothers in 1995 to share the responsibility of team ownership along with Charles Hardy. The McDonald's Team Ford Thunderbird also added the sponsorship of Reese's and Coca-Cola during the 1995 season. He finished eighth in Winston Cup point standings in 1995. *Did You Know?* Bill Elliott's first career win was at Riverside on November 20, 1983, and his first pole came on April 12, 1981, at Darlington.

❏ Team Contact: Keith Parsons, Camp & Associates, P.O. Box 3378, One Buffalo Avenue, Lock Mill Plaza, Suite 2207, Concord, NC 28025

First Trading Card: 1986 SportStar no #

"Awesome Bill from Dawsonville" (Georgia) (Photo courtesy of Elliott-Hardy Promotions)

Collector's Note: Similar to Dale Earnhardt, you could probably write a book solely about Bill Elliott memorabilia. This extremely popular driver has had his likeness adorn just about everything imaginable during the last two decades. Elliott collectors should be sure to add both tickets and programs from Elliott's first start on February 23, 1976, at Rockingham, his first pole April 12, 1981, at Darlington, and his first win on November 20, 1983 at Riverside International Raceway. Elliott is still the only driver to win three of four "Crown Jewel" events. It happened in 1985 and series of tickets or programs from these events make a great Elliott display.

Perhaps the most frequently asked question by Elliott card collectors is, "What's the difference between the 1991 and 1992 Maxx Bill Elliott autographed cards?" There are two versions of both the 1991 Maxx Bill Elliott autograph and the 1992 Maxx Bill Elliott autograph. Maxx produced a special retail only factory set in 1991 and 1992 that came with a Bill Elliott autograph card and certificate of authenticity. These sets were sold only through JC Penney stores. Then in 1994, as a redemption, the 1991 and 1992 Elliott autographed cards were included in the Maxx Medallion packs. These cards include a Maxx seal instead of the certificate of authenticity. Fewer than 150 of each of these cards were inserted into the packs, making them considerably more valuable than those found in retail sets.

Be sure to contact or visit the Bill Elliott Museum and Souvenir Centre, P.O. Box 435, Dawsonville, GA 30534 or call for a catalog at 706-265-2718. Remember to sign up for his fan club and receive a 10% discount.

Jeff Gordon   Du Pont (#24)

Jeff Gordon was born August 4, 1971, in Vallejo, CA. His rise to prominence as a NASCAR driver has been swift, picking up fourteen Top 10 finishes in 1994 and his first Winston Cup

Championship in 1995. After winning an impressive two NASCAR Winston Cup Series races in 1994, including the Inaugural Brickyard 400 at Indianapolis Motor Speedway, everyone became aware of his potential and knew that 1995 could be Jeff Gordon's year. Without disappointment Gordon captured an astounding seven Winston Cup Series wins in 1995. Consistency, reliability, and performance have become the hallmark for the Hendrick Motorsports Team. Sporting three impressive racing teams during the 1995 season—Jeff Gordon, Terry Labonte, and Ken Schrader—Rick Hendrick is finding a second home in victory lane. *Did You Know?* Jeff Gordon has won more than six hundred events in open-wheel and NASCAR competition.

❑ Team Contact: Ron Miller, Performance PR

Jeff Gordon has won more than 600 events in open-wheel and NASCAR competition

Plus, 529 N. College Street, Charlotte, NC 28202

First Trading Card: 1987 World of Outlaws #52

Collector's Note: Jeff Gordon collectibles are almost as hot as the sport itself. While novice collectors may focus only on the Du Pont collectibles, more serious collectors find themselves seeking out Gordon's Baby Ruth or Carolina Ford Dealers memorabilia. A favorite of die cast collectors is the 1:64 two-car pack of Mark Martin-Jeff Gordon cars by Pro Sports Marketing. Since both drivers drove the car on the Busch Grand National circuit, the car also includes a Mark Martin paint job. Of Gordon's Du Pont cars, the 1:18 bank produced by Ertl for White Rose Collectibles has received considerable attention. It was reported that damaged product shipments forced a recall by the manufacturer, and as such less than 5,000 appear to remain in the market. The 1994 Kellogg's Jeff Gordon three-car mail-in offer was a big hit with Gordon collectors, who finally had a chance to pick up a replica of his 1988 Sprint car.

Of the paper-based collectibles receiving attention is a postcard used to publicize Gordon's Busch Series Team. The postcard features Gordon standing behind the blue Carolina Ford Dealers car and a profile insert of the driver. The top of the postcard reads "JEFF GORDON AND CAROLINA FORD DEALERS THUNDERBIRD." Sources claim that only 5,000 of the postcards were produced, making them highly sought by collectors.

Trading card collectors have migrated toward the 1987 and 1988 World of Outlaws Gordon cards, with the 1987 #52 card exhibiting some nice price increases. Collectors will also find many exclusive sets featuring Gordon including the 1992 Traks Baby Ruth set (four cards), the 1993 Maxx Jeff Gordon set (twenty cards), and the 1993 Limited Editions Race Cards Gordon set (fifteen cards). The 1992 Traks autograph insert card (A7) has also been in demand as the first of many insert cards to salute the young driver's career. Other inserts in demand include 1995 Press Pass VIP Emerald #11, 1995 Crown Jewels Dual Jewels Ruby #DJ1, 1995 Traks Series Stars #8, 1995 Press Pass Cup Chase #10, 1995 Press Pass Optima XL Gorden four-card insert set (Card #4 is the toughest 1:276), 1995 Action Packed Silver Speed #61, and the 1995 Select Dream Machine #8.

Memorabilia surrounding Gordon's win at the Inaugural Brickyard 400 continues to capture collectors' interest. Autographed Brickyard 400 programs have been widely marketed through many outlets including various cable shopping networks. Don't forget about tickets and programs from all of Gordon's career milestones, as many have already shown significant collector demand. Often overlooked are "Press Kits" and "Media Guides" produced earlier in Gordon's career, although it may be awhile before these types of items are accepted as collectibles.

Steve Grissom

Cartoon Network (#29)

Steve Grissom was born June 26, 1963, and had his first solid run of NASCAR Winston Cup Series racing in 1995. He finished second to Jeff Burton in the 1994 Maxx Race Cards Rookie of the Year competition and had three Top 10 finishes. Grissom, the 1993 NASCAR Busch Grand National Series Champion, put together a solid performance in 1995 that included a sixth-place finish at the Goodwrench 500, a fifth-place finish at the First Union 500, and a seventh-place showing at the Daytona 500. One of Winston Cup's exciting new drivers, Grissom and the entire Diamond Ridge Racing Team are emerging as serious contenders on the NASCAR circuit. Grissom will make a move to the new Hanna-Barbera car in 1996. *Did You Know?* Steve Grissom, through 1993, has compiled eight wins and thirty-four Top 5 finishes on the Busch Grand National circuit.

❏ Team Contact: Peggy Schrock, 2220 Highway 49, Harrisburg, NC 28075

First Trading Card: 1989 Maxx #204

Steve Grissom and the entire Diamond Ridge Racing Team are emerging as serious contenders on the NASCAR circuit (Photo courtesy of Diamond Ridge Motorsports)

Collector's Note: Steve Grissom was first pictured in the 1989 Maxx trading card set (#204). But not until he became the 1993 Busch Grand National champion did his cardboard likenesses really start growing. With the championship came numerous card company offers. His popularity has also earned him several inserts in manufacturers' card sets, including Traks, Finish Line, Press Pass, and Wheels.

Popular with Grissom die cast car collectors are the 1994 1:24 Racing Champions, Racing Champions 1:24 banks, and the 1994 1:64 Racing Champions. Although Grissom transporters are few, the 1993 1:64 Winross ($50) is a must. As this exciting driver's Winston Cup career begins to take shape, it's an excellent time to begin a Steve Grissom memorabilia collection. Watch for exciting new die cast releases of his Cartoon Network car in 1996.

The year for collecting Steve Grissom memorabilia should be 1996, as collector interest in his new "Wacky Racing" Hanna-Barbera car started at the end of the 1995 season. Collectors should anticipate a strong demand for products associated with the team in 1996.

Bobby Hamilton   STP (#43)

Bobby Hamilton was born May 29, 1957, and was named NASCAR Rookie of the Year in 1991. With 106 career NASCAR Winston Cup starts under his belt, he entered the 1995 season as the fifth driver in just three seasons to drive Richard Petty's famed STP Pontiacs. Petty, who had been searching sometime for just the right winning combination, wasn't disappointed in 1995 as Hamilton pushed the Pontiacs to some premier positions including a strong second-place finish at Dover. It has become increasingly apparent that Petty has found the magic formula with Bobby Hamilton and his crew. Next year should find the "43" car back in victory lane for the first time since 1983. Hamilton won the miles completed award in 1995 and finished fourteenth in the Winston Cup point standings. *Did You Know?* Bobby Hamilton logged thirty races in 1994 for the Kendall Oil Pontiacs of the Felix Sabates Team, with a best place finish of ninth at the Bristol Food City 500.

❑ Team Contact: Chuck Spicer, STP Racing, 8603 NC Highway, Suite B, Clemmons, NC 27012
First Trading Card: 1990 Maxx #151

Collector's Note: Hamilton collectors should make space on their shelves for new memorabilia, as the STP Pontiacs will sport three new paint jobs in 1996.

Bobby Hillin   Jasper Motorsports (#77)

Bobby Hillin was born June 5, 1964, in Midland, Texas. As a high school student he made his Winston Cup debut in the 1982 and by the age of 22 years, 1 month, and 22 days, he had become the youngest driver ever to win a superspeedway race. Hillin's first win came at the 1986 Talladega 500, in his 78th start. He made his debut in the Jasper Engines/US Air Ford at Dover Downs in June of 1995. Hillin finished twelfth for the team in a terrific effort at Pocono Raceway in July, and the increased confidence level in 1995 will know doubt carry over to 1996. *Did You Know?* Bobby Hillin was the youngest driver in NASCAR history to qualify in excess of 200 mph.

❑ Team Contact: Diane Sawyer, U*S Motorsports, One Knob Hill Road, Mooresville, NC 28115
First Trading Card: 1988 Maxx #52

Collector's Note: For Hillin collectors, memorabilia from his first win at the 1986 Talladega 500 is a must.

Ernie Irvan   Texaco Havoline (#28)

Ernie Irvan was born January 13, 1959, in Salinas, California. Twenty races into the 1994 season, Irvan had already logged fifteen Top 10 finishes while battling with Dale Earnhardt for the lead in the NASCAR Winston Cup point race. While practicing at Michigan International Speedway in August, he had a serious accident ending his bid for a 1994 championship. Vowing to return to his seat in the Texaco Havoline Fords, Irvan has been the embodiment of courage, will, and determination. He set an example for racing and for all his fans by returning to the NASCAR circuit in the 1995 Tyson Holly Farms 400 at Monroeville and finishing an impressive sixth place. Up until the accident, Irvan had compiled an astonishing seventy-seven Top 10 career NASCAR Winston Cup finishes. The 1994 season saw him in the winner's circle three times, first at the Pontiac Excitement 400, followed by the Purolator 500 and finally the Save Mart Supermarkets 300. An extremely popular driver, Irvan has won over the hearts of all racing fans with promises to return to contention in the NASCAR Winston Cup Series. He ran a great race at Phoenix in the 1995 Dura-Lube 500 and was leading before losing a cylinder and having to drop out. Irvan put on a nice display of driving skills at the NAPA 500 in Atlanta at the end of the season, showing everyone that he will be back strong in 1996. *Did You Know?* Ernie Irvan was the recipient of three major awards in 1994, the Maxwell House Spirit Award, the Mike Rich Memorial Award, and the True Value Hard Charger Award.

❑ Team Contact: Brian Vandercock, 8701 Mallard Creek Road, Charlotte, NC 28262
First Trading Card: 1988 Maxx #95

Collector's Note: Adversity is certainly nothing to salute, but courage is, and this is why so many collectibles have been produced acknowledging this driver's return to NASCAR. An extremely popular individual to begin with, Irvan's fame has only been enhanced by his great spirit and faith. Action Packed should be acknowledged first for producing 5,000 gold-plated pins, which sold for $25 each, with all proceeds sent directly to the Irvan family. Hi-Tech also produced a nice "Thank You" trading card, 60,000 of which were signed and mailed to fans who sent Irvan letters. At the time of the driver's injury, he had been working with Hi-Tech and Case Knife on a line of collectibles that would combine both manufacturers' products. Following the injury, three different versions of the Case Knife cards were produced, all with "We Miss You ... Ernie" adorning the front left side of the card. Other types of memorabilia also paid tribute to the driver's courage. A beautiful limited edition lithograph printed on museum quality, acid-free paper (20" x 26") was also produced by Jeanne Barnes Studio of Concord, NC. The print, titled "Behind Every Cloud ...," features Irvan perched over his #28 car against a cloud backdrop with a ray of light cascading out from the top right-hand corner. The print was limited to an edition of 750, with 150 signed by Irvan.

Dale Jarrett   Ford Quality Care (#88)

Dale Jarrett was born November 26, 1956, in Newton, North Carolina, to the racing parents of Ned and Martha Jarrett. While Ernie Irvan continued to recover from the injuries he suffered last August, Jarret took over driving the Texaco Havoline Ford for 1995. Jarrett was able to agree to terms with Joe Gibbs in order to join Robert Yates Racing. Jarret had competed strongly for Gibbs in 1993, while finishing fourth in the standings. He entered the 1995 season with fifty Top 10 career finishes, including three wins. In 1995 he proved his competitiveness with many strong races and finished thirteenth in the Winston Cup point standings. *Did You Know?* Dale Jarret was a natural athlete in high school and by the age of seventeen he was a scratch golfer.

❑ Team Contact: Brian Vandercock, 8701 Mallard Creek Road, Charlotte, NC 28262

First Trading Card: 1988 Maxx #61

Collector's Note: Dale Jarrett collectors will want to pick up both programs and tickets from his first Winston Cup start at Martinsville on April 29, 1984, and from his first victory at Michigan in the Champion Spark Plug 400 on August 18, 1991.

Bobby Labonte   Interstate Batteries (#18)

Bobby Labonte was born May 8, 1964, in Corpus Christi, Texas. In 1995 Labonte joined the #18 Interstate Batteries Chevrolet Monte Carlo Team owned by Joe Gibbs, replacing Dale Jarrett. Labonte won the 1994 NASCAR Busch Grand National Championship as a first-year car owner, while also competing as a regular on the Winston Cup Circuit. His first season of Winston Cup racing found him nineteenth in points and runner-up in the 1993 Rookie of the Year standings. Bobby Labonte, like his older brother Terry, is a fierce and determined competitor and is destined for stardom on NASCAR Winston Cup racing circuit. Bobby's wife Donna gave birth to the couple's first child in 1994, just a month after his private plane crashed on the way home from a race. Thankfully no one was injured in the plane crash. Labonte finished strong in 1995, while compiling three wins and finishing tenth in the Winston Cup point standings. *Did You Know?* Bobby Labonte began racing quarter midgets in 1969 at age five and won his first national quarter midget race at age six.

❑ Team Contact: Larry M. Camp, Camp & Associates, P.O. Box 3378, Concord, NC 28025

First Trading Card: 1991 Maxx #53

Collector's Note: Popular among Bobby Labonte trading card collectors is the 1991 Maxx #53 and the 1991 Maxx Update #53, which included a statistical correction. Both of these cards can still be picked up at very reasonable prices, often under $1.00. In 1991 Labonte's sponsors Slim Jim and Penrose commissioned a twenty-nine-card set commemorating the new Busch champion. It has become increasingly hard to find and is a must for any Labonte collector. Other popular trading cards include: 1993 Traks #176 (Silver Series), the 1993 Action Packed #62 (alone), and #156 (Young Guns). Labonte has also been featured

on many popular insert cards, particularly those produced by Action Packed. His 1995 Finish Line Printer's Proof issue is also a favorite among Labonte collectors. These cards were random inserts in hobby packs, with the Labonte card commanding an average of $15.

Labonte transporters, especially the 1993 1:87 Racing Champions Premier ($20) and both the 1:64 Action Racing Collectibles (Maxwell House and Penrose, $75), are also popular with collectors. For the Labonte die cast car collectors, most of the Maxwell House issues are a must before delving into the Interstate Batteries releases. That Labonte only has a few seasons under his belt makes it a good time to begin collecting his material.

Bobby Labonte finished strong in 1995, while compiling three wins and finishing tenth in the Winston Cup point standings (Photo courtesy of Camp & Associates, Inc.)

Terry Labonte   Kellogg's (#5)

Terry Labonte was born November 16, 1956, in Corpus Christi, Texas. A fierce, consistent, and competitive driver, he takes 248 career finishes into 1995. Labonte, after three years with Billy Hagan, took his Kellogg's sponsorship to Rick Hendrick's racing team. The three-car team of Labonte, Schrader, and Gordon could be the most dominant force in NASCAR racing during this decade. Labonte started strong in 1994 and won at North Wilkesboro in his seventh race for the team. He dominated at Richmond and Phoenix, picking up his second and third wins of the 1994 season. Labonte's strong finish in 1994 followed him into 1995, picking up a win at the Goody's 500. During the 1995 MBNA 500 he marked his 500th consecutive start at NASCAR's major level. The record is 513 in a row held by Richard Petty. A strong finisher, Labonte is like a good wine, getting better with age. He finished sixth in the 1995 Winston Cup point standings. *Did You Know?* Terry Labonte brought a career record of 159,700 laps into the 1995 season, completing 88% of his laps, as well as 77.3% of his races—fifth among all active drivers with 145 or more starts (five full seasons) in DNF (did not finish) percentage in the Winston Cup Series.

Terry Labonte is like a good wine, getting better with age

❏ Team Contact: Bill Armour, Wilson Marketing, Bldg. 200, Galleries Parkway, Ste. 1750, Atlanta, GA 30339

First Trading Card: 1986 SportStar no#

Collector's Note: Labonte collectors will want to pick up memorabilia associated with his first Winston Cup start in the Southern 500 at Darlington in 1978, his first win on September 1, 1980 also at the Southern 500 in Darlington, and his first pole in the spring race at Atlanta on March 15, 1981. Entering the 1995 season he had thirteen Winston Cup Series wins, making a collection of tickets or programs from all his victories certainly attainable. The most difficult challenge will be getting your hands on memorabilia from his first win at the Southern 500.

Perhaps the most enjoyable element of being a Terry Labonte collector is acquiring all the Kellogg's products that he has been featured on. From Kellogg's Pop Tarts to Kellogg's Corn Flakes, Labonte fans can not only enjoy the product, but add an often inexpensive and unique item to their collection. A checklist of these products is provided in the Miscellaneous chapter.

Naturally, Labonte collectors will also want to focus on collecting all memorabilia associated with his 1984 Winston Cup Championship. Labonte trading card collectors can start with his first issue, the 1986 SportStar release that has no number. Some of his most valuable cards are from the 1994 Action Packed 24K Gold insert set (#32G and 184G) and the 1995 High Gear (#TLS1).

Die cast collectors will find both the 1:24 Action No. 5 Kellogg's bank and the 1991 Winross 1:64 transporter challenging acquisitions. The die cast bank ran into production problems that eventually limited its release to just over 1,000 (originally 2,500 plus). The Winross 1:64 transporter with the Sunoco logo is popular with Labonte collectors who often have to pay over $100 for the piece.

Randy LaJoie

Randy LaJoie was born August 28, 1961, in Norwalk, Connecticut. He began racing in 1980 at Danbury Race arena. The following year LaJoie won fourteen of twenty-two modified sportsman events. In 1983 he won the Busch Grand National North Series Rookie of the Year, winning two races and finishing fourth overall in point standings. LaJoie won the Busch North Series in 1985, then set his sights on Winston Cup racing. Entering the 1995 season with thirteen Winston Cup events under his belt, LaJoie looks forward to his first full season. *Did You Know?* Randy LaJoie led the 1994 Busch point standings after nine races, but a rash of problems resulted in a late-season fade.

❏ Team Contact: Teddi Smith, The Source, P.O. Box 1788, Kernersville, NC 27285

First Trading Card: 1992 Maxx #19

Sterling Marlin   Kodak Film (#4)

Sterling Marlin was born June 30, 1957, in Columbia, Tennessee. He drove in his first Winston Cup race in a car owned and prepared by his father, the legendary Clifton "Coo-Coo" Marlin. In 1983, the former three time Nashville Speedway Champion captured the Winston Cup Rookie of the Year title. While driving for Billy Hagen from 1987 to 1990, Marlin claimed an astounding sixteen Top 5 and twenty-eight Top 10 finishes. A quick stint with Junior Johnson picked up seven poles and ten Top 5 finishes. After a year with Stavola Brothers racing, 1994 found Marlin driving for Morgan-McClure, picking up his first career win at the Daytona 500 and posting five Top 5 finishes. Marlin finished an impressive third in the 1995 Winston Cup point standings. *Did You Know?* In addition to water sports, Sterling Marlin enjoys Civil War history.

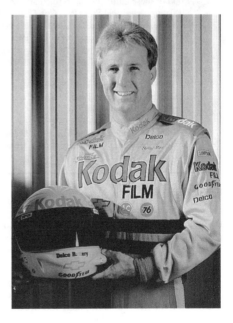

❏ Team Contact: Steve Crisp, Delco Battery, 375 Windrose Lane, Concord, NC 28025

First Trading Card: 1988 Maxx #80

Collector's Note: Although Sterling Marlin has appeared on over 200 cards, most within the last two years, it wasn't until his first Winston Cup victory at the Daytona 500 that collectors really stopped and took an interest in his memorabilia. Since that time he has appeared in almost every set produced, often multiple times and on inserts. The

Sterling Marlin (Photo courtesy of Kodak Film Racing)

1988 Maxx #80 card, his first card, is a must for all Marlin collectors. Also popular with Marlin trading card collectors are his 1993 Wheels Rookie Thunder #24 and his 1994 Maxx Rookies of the Year #5 insert set. His inclusion in the 1995 Press Pass Cup Chase redemption game, and his repeat at Daytona, allowed collectors to redeem the special card for a unique holoprism card.

Marlin collectors will also delight at the selection of die cast cars and transporters available, many of which carry earlier sponsors such as Piedmont, Maxwell House, and Raybestos. The 1989-90 Matchbox White Rose 1:87 Super Star Series transporter is very popular with Marlin die cast collectors. There were two versions of the transport, one with Marlin's name on the cab ($300) and one without ($225).

Mark Martin   Valvoline (#6)

Mark Martin was born January 9, 1959, in Batesville, Arkansas. Although he makes his home in Batesville, Arkansas, many think that with his third consecutive win at Watkins Glen in 1995, he may take up residence in New York State. Martin is a consistent finisher, an outstanding competitor, and a very popular driver on the NASCAR Winston Cup circuit. Mark and Roush Racing began their eighth year together in 1995 and what a magic combination it has been. This incredible team has put together 124 Top 10 finishes and fourteen wins entering the 1995 season. Martin finished second in the final 1994 NASCAR Winston Cup standings. Martin picked up three wins in 1995 including Watkins Glen and Monroeville. He finished fourth place in the 1995 Winston Cup point standings. *Did You Know?* Perhaps the most formidable challenger on the Winston Cup circuit, Mark Martin had a 1994 season average race finish of 11.6. He is a driver who consistently finishes near the top!

❑ Team Contact: Diana Hollingsworth, Roush Racing, P.O. Box 1089, Liberty, NC 27298

First Trading Card: 1988 Maxx #48

Collector's Note: Mark Martin racing memorabilia is bountiful and it's no surprise when you consider his talent and popularity in Winston Cup racing. He has appeared on hundreds of trading cards and been commemorated in numerous die cast issues. With multiple cards in a wide variety of sets, collectors have many options. Popular Martin cards include the 1998 Maxx #48, a five-card subset in the 1994 Action Packed Series III, and the 1994 Finish Line Gold Autograph Set (#81 with signature). Also highly sought is his 1994 High Gear #MMS1 Autograph insert. With only 1,000 of these cards produced, the card has shown some significant value, hovering around the $100 range. His 1994 Press Pass Cup Chase card received some attention as a part of an interactive fan game. Because Martin finished second in the final point standings, the card could be redeemed by collectors for an uncut sheet of five Press Pass Prospects.

Because Martin frequents the Busch Grand National circuit under a different sponsor, he is also able to generate a great deal of attention from die cast manufacturers. Martin's 1994 Racing Champions Maxx combo set, a 1:64 Racing Champions car accompanied by a Maxx chromium card, was met with fine reviews from collectors. Martin's transporters have also shown considerable collector interest. His 1990 1:87 scale Matchbox White Rose transporter carrying the Folgers company logo is a must for any Martin collector. Other popular haulers include the 1993 1:64 scale Winross and the 1994 1:24 scale Raceway Replicas.

Martin's boundless appeal has even led to milk caps produced by Reese's as a promotional program. With so many items to choose from, the question most Mark Martin collectors ask is, "Where do I begin?"

Rick Mast   Skoal Racing (#1)

Rick Mast was born March 4, 1957, and now makes his home in Rockbridge Baths, Virginia. He began racing on dirt tracks at the age of sixteen in 1973. Mast started NASCAR racing in 1977 and logged his first full year on the Busch Grand National circuit in 1985. He captured his first pole on November 13, 1992, at the Hooters 500 and had the distinct honor of pole sitter for the inaugural 1994 Brickyard 400 at the Indianapolis Motor Speedway, posting a speed of 172.414 mph. Mast took ten Top 10 finishes during the 1994 season in a year that exhibited his greatest consistency thus far in Winston Cup racing. *Did You Know?* Coming off his finest NASCAR Winston Cup season thus far in his career in 1994, he competed and finished in all thirty-one track events.

❑ Team Contact: Jay Wells, United States Tobacco Motorsports, P.O. Box 1117, Mooresville, NC 28115

First Trading Card: 1989 Maxx #66

Jeremy Mayfield   RCA (#98)

Jeremy Mayfield was born May 27, 1969, and hails from Owensboro, Kentucky. Like Owensboro drivers who have gone before him, the Waltrips and the Greens, Mayfield hopes to leave his mark on the NASCAR Winston Cup circuit. Chosen by Cale Yarborough to guide the Fingerhut Fords, Mayfield came into the 1995 season with twenty-one career races under his belt. While on the ARCA Series in 1993, he ran nineteen races and captured eight Top 5 finishes along with Rookie of the Year. A short driving stint with Sadler Racing in 1994 found him impressing everyone with an eleventh-place start at the First Union 400. Accompanied by the knowledge of Cale Yarborough, this young and skillful driver is soon to make his mark on the NASCAR Winston Cup circuit. *Did You Know?* Jeremy Mayfield's first start with Cale Yarborough's Fingerhut Team came at Pocono.

❑ Team Contact: Richard Sceery, Jr., RAM Sports Marketing, Providence Civic Center, 1 LaSalle Square, Providence, RI 02903

First Trading Card: 1994 Traks II #107

Teddy Musgrave   The Family Channel (#16)

Teddy Musgrave was born December 18, 1955, in Evanston, Illinois. He was the 1987 ASA Rookie of the Year, and finished fifth in the ASA Championship. Musgrave finished third in '88 and fourth in '89 while driving on the ASA circuit. He stepped into his first NASCAR Winston Cup race in 1990. Musgrave was runner-up for the 1991 Winston Cup Rookie of the Year and competed in twenty-nine races during the season. Finishing eighteenth in the 1992 Winston Cup standings, Musgrave impressed all onlookers with seven Top 10 finishes. He took three poles in '94 and finished thirteenth overall in season standings. Unfailing and determined, Musgrave challenges for a Top 10 position in every race and parallels Roush Racing teammate Mark Martin in competitive spirit. Musgrave took the pole at the 1995 Tyson Holly Farms 400 in an all Roush Racing front line. He also finished second at both the Hanes 500 and the UAW Teamwork 500 in 1995. Musgrave took seventh place in the 1995 Winston Cup point standings. *Did You Know?* Teddy Musgrave had an impressive twenty Top 10 finishes to his credit entering the 1995 season.

❑ Team Contact: Stephanie Smith, Roush Racing, P.O. Box 1089, Liberty, NC 27298

First Trading Card: 1991 Pro Set #103, 1991 Traks #55

Joe Nemechek   **Burger King (#87)**

Joe Nemechek was born September 26, 1963, and now makes his home in Lakeland, Florida. Nemechek, the 1992 NASCAR Busch Series champion, turned his head to Winston Cup racing in 1993 and ran in five races. In his rookie season of 1994, he raced for Meineke Mufflers and Larry Hedrick's team and finished third in the Maxx Race Cards Rookie of the Year standings. Nemechek won the pole for the 1994 Winston Select Open and qualified second for the Coca-Cola 600. The Miller Genuine Draft 500 would be the climax of the season as Nemechek finished third, the team's best season finish and a personal best. He finished twenty-seventh in the final NASCAR Winston Cup standings and announced late in 1994 that he would leave Hedrick Motorsports and form his own team for 1995. An impressive Burger King #87 car rolled out onto the track at Daytona in 1995, primed for a serious year of NASCAR Winston Cup racing. *Did You Know?* Joe Nemechek started in twenty-third position for the 1994 The Bud At The Glen and managed to persevere for an eighth-place finish.

❏ Team Contact: Kristen Helsel, NEMCO Motorsports, P.O. Box 177, Mooresville, NC 28115
First Trading Card: 1991 Maxx #139, 1991 Traks #87

Kyle Petty   **Coors Light (#42)**

Kyle Petty was born June 20, 1960, to arguably the greatest name in U.S. motorsports history, Richard Petty. As history might have it, Kyle Petty strapped himself into an ARCA (Automobile

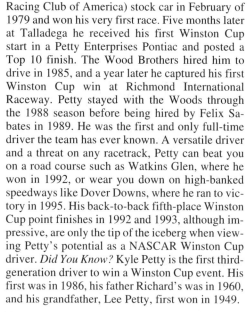

Racing Club of America) stock car in February of 1979 and won his very first race. Five months later at Talladega he received his first Winston Cup start in a Petty Enterprises Pontiac and posted a Top 10 finish. The Wood Brothers hired him to drive in 1985, and a year later he captured his first Winston Cup win at Richmond International Raceway. Petty stayed with the Woods through the 1988 season before being hired by Felix Sabates in 1989. He was the first and only full-time driver the team has ever known. A versatile driver and a threat on any racetrack, Petty can beat you on a road course such as Watkins Glen, where he won in 1992, or wear you down on high-banked speedways like Dover Downs, where he ran to victory in 1995. His back-to-back fifth-place Winston Cup point finishes in 1992 and 1993, although impressive, are only the tip of the iceberg when viewing Petty's potential as a NASCAR Winston Cup driver. *Did You Know?* Kyle Petty is the first third-generation driver to win a Winston Cup event. His first was in 1986, his father Richard's was in 1960, and his grandfather, Lee Petty, first won in 1949.

Kyle Petty is the first third-generation driver to win a Winston Cup event (Photo courtesy of SABCO Racing)

❏ Team Contact: Jon Sands, SABCO Racing, 5901 Orr Road, Charlotte, NC 28213
First Trading Card: 1989 Maxx #42 & #220

Collector's Note: Kyle Petty's distinctive personality and rock star looks have only complemented his popularity. He is commonly photographed with a variety of personalities, occasionally even in obscure settings. Petty was the subject for one of the most unique racing collectibles ever produced. Action Packed produced a 1994 (#92D) portrait insert that had an actual diamond chip on the card where Petty wears his earring. Although collectors had slim odds of pulling one of these cards from a pack (1 in 1,650), 1,000 of the cards were produced. The card typically ranges in price from $200 to $350.

Of the over 300 cards Petty has appeared on, his first card, the 1989 Maxx (#42) has remained very popular with collectors. The card features Kyle in his driving uniform with his long hair blowing from a racing breeze. Kyle also appears with his father Richard on card #220, the last card in this set. This card has also shown consistent demand over time.

Team set collectors have two options, the 1991 Traks Mello Yello Set ($10-$12) and the 1992 Wheels Kyle Petty Set ($7-$9). The Wheels set is the lesser of the two in value and comes in two versions, regular and gold. No significant price variation has been noted with either variation of the Wheels set.

Serious Petty collectors will want to pick the driver's "No Fear Racing" video game for Super NES and a copy of the soundtrack that is available on compact disk.

Petty's move to the Coors Light sponsorship in 1995 prompted a run on some of his vintage die cast and other Mello Yello memorabilia. The Coors Light sponsorship has also led to a plethora of new products and marketing tools, from Petty full-size cardboard stand-ups to restaurant table tents. Petty collectors will no doubt have their hands full trying to keep up with this aggressive sponsor's marketing of their new driver.

It will be interesting to see if any of the die cast manufacturers release a version of Petty's 1995 Halloween car with his daughter's pumpkin painted on the hood.

Robert Pressley
Skoal Bandit (#33)

Robert Pressley was born April 8, 1959, and was inspired to become a racing car driver by watching his father Bob race stock cars. His first race was at Hickory Speedway in October of 1982. From 1985 to 1988, Pressley estimates that he won 150 races on the short tracks of Carolina. He gained considerable attention racing on the Busch Grand National circuit in 1993 and won three races including a beauty at Darlington. Then when Harry Gant retired, car owner Leo Jackson gave the seat to Pressley. He spent most of the 1995 season battling Ricky Craven for the Rookie of the Year honors and managed some very respectable runs on many of the circuit's toughest tracks. *Did You Know?* Robert Pressley spent so much of his time at race tracks while he was growing up that at one point he vowed never to become a driver.

❑ Team Contact: Brian Buchauer, U.S. Tobacco Motorsports, P.O. Box 1117, Mooresville, NC 28115

First Trading Card: 1991 Bull Ring #59, 1991 Maxx #147, 1991 Traks #59

Collector's Note: Pressley collectors were thrilled when they found out that their favorite driver would join the NASCAR Winston Cup circuit in 1995. No stranger to racing collectibles, Pressley appeared on two Maxx trading cards (#147) and one Traks card in 1991. Since then, he's appeared in numerous other sets with most featuring him as a Busch driver.

In 1992, Traks decided to issue an exclusive twelve-card set on the Alliance Racing Team, which Pressley was driving for at the time. The set is a must for any Pressley collector and generally available for around $10.

Pressley trading card collectors will also find autographed inserts available in the 1992 Winner's Choice Busch, 1994 Finish Line Gold Autograph, 1994 Traks Autograph insert, and 1994 Maxx Medallion Autograph insert.

Any and all items relating to his inaugural year are certainly worth collecting, as are career milestone items such as tickets and programs.

Ricky Rudd
Tide (#10)

Ricky Rudd was born September 12, 1956, and ran in his first Winston Cup race in 1975, starting twenty-sixth and finishing eleventh at Rockingham, NC. By 1977 Rudd had been named the NASCAR Rookie of the Year. He joined DiGard Racing in 1981 and picked up three poles including the first of his career on April 24 at Martinsville. In 1982 Rudd teamed up with Richard Childress, grabbed two poles, and had thirteen Top 10 finishes. His first Winston Cup victory was the Budweiser 400 at Riverside, California, in June of 1983. During the thirty races he ran in 1983, Rudd would add fourteen Top 10 finishes, seven Top 5 finishes, and two wins to his career record. Rudd joined Hendrick Motorsports in 1990 and in 1991 finished second in the Winston Cup Points Championship, the highest in his career to date. Consistency, reliability, and performance were easy labels to add to the 1991 season, as Rudd finished 11,427.2 miles out of a possible 11,677. In 1994 he began his first season as owner and driver of his own racing team, Rudd

Performance Motorsports. The team, sponsored by Tide Detergent, surpassed all expectations by claiming fifteen Top 10 finishes and a win at New Hampshire. In what many believed impossible, Ricky Rudd finished the 1994 season fifth in the final NASCAR Winston Cup standings. His win in Phoenix in 1995 marked his thirteenth straight year with a victory. Rudd finished ninth in the 1995 Winston Cup point standings. *Did You Know?* Ricky Rudd started his 500th career NASCAR Winston Cup race in the Hooters 500 at the Atlanta Motor Speedway on November 13, 1994.

❑ Team Contact: Kirby Boone, P.O. Box 1857, Davidson, NC 28036

First Trading Card: 1989 Maxx #26

Collector's Note: Although it certainly won't be easy to acquire, a must for all Ricky Rudd collectors is memorabilia that relates to his streak of thirteen straight years with at least one win on the NASCAR Winston Cup circuit. Can you imagine having a set of full or partial tickets representing each of his wins during the thirteen seasons? It certainly would make an outstanding display!

Prized Rudd memorabilia include items from his first start at Rockingham in 1975, his first pole at Martinsville on April 24, 1981, and his first win at Riverside in the Budweiser 400.

Greg Sacks

Greg Sacks was born November 3, 1952. He began his quest for the Winston Cup ranks by becoming one of the finest Modified drivers in the Northeast. In 1994 Sacks began his second full season on the Winston Cup circuit and finished thirty-first in the final standings. Driving US Air-sponsored Fords for US Motorsports in the team's first year of existence, he qualified in the Top 9 eight times. He opened the 1994 season with a sixth-place finish in the Daytona 500 and closed it with an impressive pole position in Atlanta. He entered the 1995 season with 210 career NASCAR Winston Cup races to his credit. *Did You Know?* Greg Sacks made his Winston Cup debut at the 1983 Pepsi 400.

❑ Team Contact: Michael Rompf, Gossage-McFarland Sports Marketing, Inc., Smith Tower, Highway 29, Suite 408, Harrisburg, NC 28075

First Trading Card: 1988 Maxx #65

Collector's Note: The Daytona International Speedway is a good place to begin your Greg Sacks memorabilia collection, as this where he started his Winston Cup career in the 1983 Firecracker 400 and grabbed his first win in the same event two years later. Of course every Greg Sacks fan has their own copy of "Days of Thunder," as he stunt doubled behind the wheel for motion picture star Tom Cruise.

Elton Sawyer   Hooters (#27)

Elton Sawyer was born November 5, 1959, in Norfolk, Virginia. He began his racing career in 1977 while attending high school and his first Busch Grand National win came during the 1994 Carolina Pride/Budweiser 250 at Myrtle Beach Speedway. His first NASCAR Winston Cup start came in 1995 in the Hanes 500 at Martinsville, Virginia. Sawyer drove his #27 Hooters Ford Thunderbird to a very respectable twentieth finish, while starting ninth. In 1995 he also competed full-time in his twelfth season on the NASCAR Busch Grand National circuit. Working in conjunction with owner Junior Johnson, Elton Sawyer continued to impress many in 1995, with a seventeenth-place finish at the Daytona 500 and a fourteenth-place finish at the DieHard 500. *Did You Know?* Elton Sawyer married a fellow Busch Grand National competitor, Patty Moise.

❑ Team Contact: Jill Horton, Hooters Racing Inc., 125-D Commerce Drive, Fayetteville, GA 30214

First Trading Card: 1989 Maxx #175

Ken Schrader

Budweiser (#25)

Ken Schrader was born May 29, 1955. In 1985, his first full season of NASCAR Winston Cup racing, he claimed three Top 10 finishes and picked up Rookie of the Year honors. Schrader's first

$1M year came in 1989, grabbing fourteen Top 10 finishes, ten Top 5 finishes, and his second career win. He entered the 1995 season coming off his highest finish in the point standings of his career, taking fourth. Schrader claimed an amazing eighteen Top 10 finishes and nine Top 5 finishes in 1994. In 1995, Schrader found himself behind the wheel of a red Hendrick Motorsport Chevrolet Monte Carlo emblazoned with an all too familiar Budweiser logo. It was a dream come true to work with the brewery from his hometown (Fenton, MO is a suburb of St. Louis) and the combination is exciting for all race fans. An outstanding competitor and dedicated driver, Schrader commemorates the 1995 season with his 300th career NASCAR Winston Cup race. Schrader finished seventeenth in the 1995 Winston Cup point standings. *Did You Know?* Ken Schrader had a banner year in 1991, grabbing eighteen Top 10 finishes, ten Top 5 finishes, and two wins.

❏ Team Contact: Joy Pinto, Muhleman Marketing, 6000 Monroe Road, Suite 300, Charlotte, NC 28212

Ken Schrader

First Trading Card: 1988 Maxx #74

Morgan Shepherd   **Remington Arms (#75)**

Morgan Shepherd was born October 12, 1941. He became a mainstay in the NASCAR Sportsman Class (now Busch Series) compiling many victories during the division "Golden Age," the mid- and late '70s. Just prior to moving to NASCAR he won the 1980 NASCAR Sportsman National Championship. In 1981, his first full NASCAR Winston Cup season, he claimed ten Top 10 finishes and his first career win. Shepherd entered 1995 coming off his best earnings year and perhaps even his most consistent NASCAR Winston Cup season. He compiled sixteen Top 10 finishes and nine Top 5 finishes, while taking home more than $1M in race purses, the first time in his career. Behind the wheel of Wood Brothers Thunderbirds for the fourth year in 1995, Shepherd hoped to become the oldest driver in the history of NASCAR Winston Cup to win an event, a spot now held by Harry Gant (age 52). When it happens it will surprise nobody, as Shepherd is one of the most respected drivers on the circuit. Shepherd finished a strong eleventh in 1995 and announced a move to a new sponsor in 1996—Remington Arms. *Did You Know?* Entering the 1995 season, Morgan Shepherd has won more than $5.7 million in 383 NASCAR Winston Cup starts.

❏ Team Contact: Doug Cox, McLean Marketing, Inc., 12033 East Independence, Suite A, Matthews, NC 28105

First Trading Card: 1988 Maxx #25

Lake Speed   **Spam (#9)**

Lake Speed was born January 17, 1948, in Jackson, Mississippi. Before his Winston Cup career he won the World Karting Championship in LeMans, France, in 1978. In 1980, Speed's first year in NASCAR Winston Cup, he had five Top 10 finishes in nineteen races and finished second for Rookie of the Year. Speed won his first Winston Cup race at Darlington in 1988. Coming off a strong 1994, a season that saw Speed accumulate nine Top 10 finishes and four Top 5 finishes, the future is looking very bright for this competitive driver. His chances were only improved in 1995 as he teamed with Harry Melling. With one Winston Cup Series Championship, thirty-four Winston Cup victories, and forty poles to his credit, Melling is no stranger to assembling and operating a winning team. Behind the wheel of the #9 Spam Ford Thunderbird, Lake Speed looks like he's going to be a force to contend with for a long time. Speed finished twenty-third in Winston Cup point standings in 1995. *Did You Know?* Lake Speed finished eleventh in the 1994 Winston Cup Points Championship and competed in his 300th career Winston Cup event in 1995.

❏ Team Contact: Melling Racing Enterprises, Concord, NC

First Trading Card: 1988 Maxx #46

Collector's Note: An excellent eight-page Spam Racing #9 Gift Catalog is available by calling this toll-free number: 1-800-LUV-SPAM. Various shirts, hats, and jackets are available in this must catalog for all Lake Speed fans. Memorabilia from his first win at Darlington in the 1988 Tran-South 500 is also sought by Speed collectors.

Jimmy Spencer   **Camel Cigarettes (#23)**

Jimmy Spencer was born February 15, 1957. In his first year as a NASCAR Winston Cup driver in 1989, he ran in seventeen races and picked up three Top 10 finishes. Driving for Junior Johnson in the McDonald's Ford during the 1994 season, he took four Top 10 finishes and won both the Pepsi 400 and the DieHard 400. In a dramatic victory, Spencer gradually moved through the pack to win his first career victory in the Pepsi 400. He repeated the task a few weeks later and emerged from the pack during the final laps to win again at Talladega. Spencer also picked up his first career NASCAR Winston Cup pole at the second North Wilkesboro race, the Tyson Holly Farms 400. Unfortunately, Spencer broke a shoulder blade twice during the season and was hindered for most of 1994. In 1995 he rejoins car owner Travis Carter to drive the Smokin' Joe's Ford. Spencer had driven previously for Carter during the 1991 season. *Did You Know?* In addition to his two victories in 1994, Jimmy Spencer also finished tenth in the Purolator 500 and fourth in the Winston Select 500.

❏ Team Contact: Rob Goodman, Sports Marketing Ent., P.O. Box 484, Winston-Salem, NC 27102

First Trading Card: 1989 Maxx #208

Hut Stricklin   **Circuit City (#8)**

Hut Stricklin was born June 24, 1961. He was NASCAR Goody's Dash Series Champion in 1986, winning nine of seventeen races and ten poles. Stricklin drove for Rod Osterlund's team in his first full season in NASCAR Winston Cup in 1989, and finished second in the Rookie of the Year standings. His strongest season thus far came in 1991 while he was driving for Bobby Allison's team. He picked up seven Top 10 finishes, along with three Top 5 finishes, and claimed sixteenth in the 1991 point standings. Coming off a lackluster season in 1994, Stricklin assumed driving duties in 1995 for King Racing Team on a race-to-race basis beginning with the Hanes 500 at Martinsville. The Quaker State Team went on the auction blocks following the 1995 season. *Did You Know?* Hut Stricklin recorded a career best second-place finish in the 1991 Miller Genuine Draft 400.

❑ Team Contact: Kirk Weeks, King Sports, Inc., 11611 N. Meridian, Suite 701, Carmel, IN 46032

First Trading Card: 1988 Maxx #28

Hut Stricklin (Photo courtesy of King Sports, Inc.)

Dick Trickle   **Purina (#63)**

Dick Trickle was born October 27, 1941, in Wisconsin Rapids, Wisconsin. He established himself on Midwest short tracks by winning more than 1,200 feature races since he began driving competitively in 1956. In 1989, the Stavola Brothers asked Trickle to replace Mike Alexander as their Winston Cup driver. It was the break he had been waiting for and he seized the opportunity by finishing in the Top 10 in nine races and taking three third-place finishes. At the age of forty-eight, Dick Trickle became the NASCAR Winston Cup Rookie of the Year. In 1990 he captured his first pole position at Dover's Budweiser 500 and had four Top 10 finishes during the season. With 167 career NASCAR Winston Cup races under his belt through the 1994 season, Dick Trickle combined efforts with veteran car owner Bud Moore in 1995. Driving Moore's Quality Care Fords, he finished eleventh at the Daytona 500, ninth at the Winston Select Open, and tenth at Pocono. Trickle finished twenty-fifth in Winston Cup point standings in 1995. *Did You Know?* Dick Trickle's first NASCAR Winston Cup start was at the 1970 Daytona 500.

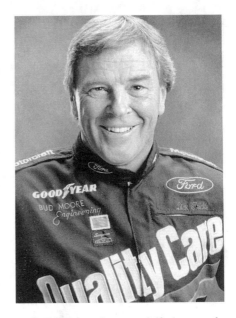

Dick Trickle, at the age of 48, became the NASCAR Winston Cup Rookie of the Year (Photo courtesy of Ford Quality Care Racing)

Using his own car, he finished twenty-sixth after starting thirty-sixth.

❑ Team Contact: Marti Rompf, Campbell & Co., 3363 Greenfield Road, Dearborn, MI 48120
   First Trading Card: 1990 Maxx #150

Kenny Wallace   Square D / TIC Financial Systems (#81)

Kenny Wallace was born August 23, 1963. He established himself as driver in the Midwest ASA ranks and captured the 1986 ASA Rookie of the Year. Driving in the NASCAR Busch Series, Wallace would earn the rookie title in 1989 and finish runner-up for the title in 1991. Driving for Felix Sabates in cars sponsored by Dirt Devil vacuum cleaners, he finished his first full season of Winston Cup racing with three Top 10 finishes. During the final third of the 1994 season, Wallace accepted an opportunity to drive for Robert Yates in the Texaco Havoline Thunderbirds. He would replace the injured Ernie Irvan. Wallace finished fourth at the Goody's 500 and grabbed tenth place at the Tyson Holly Farms 400. In 1995, Wallace and car owner Fil Martocci decided to move up from the NASCAR Busch Series to compete at the Winston Cup level. *Did You Know?* Kenny Wallace finished third in the 1993 Rookie of the Year honors.

❑ Team Contact: Filmar Racing, 2602 Westwood Drive, Nashville, TN 37204
   First Trading Card: 1989 Maxx #178

Collector's Note: Kenny Wallace's success on the Busch Grand National circuit, his terrific personality, and his family bloodline have all contributed to his interest with both fans and collectors. With racing experts predicting nothing but a brilliant future for this young driver, collectors are being increasingly drawn to Wallace memorabilia. He has already appeared on numerous trading card issues including Busch subsets, prospect and rising star subsets, and insert series. Wallace trading card collectors should make his first card from the 1989 Maxx set #178 an acquisition priority. Wallace insert cards are also in demand, including the 1994 Press Pass Cup Chase card #CC27, his 1994 Finish Line Gold Autograph #37, and the 1993 Action Packed Young Guns subset, which also touts a 24K Gold insert equivalent.

Mike Wallace   Heilig-Myers (#90)

Mike Wallace was born March 10, 1959. He gained notoriety by participating in over 300 short-track events throughout the Midwest during the '70s. In 1990 he took the Mid-America Region Championship in the NASCAR Winston Racing Series by winning an astounding twenty-one of twenty-nine events. The following four years Wallace would participate in both the NASCAR Busch Series and ARCA races. When Bobby Hillin left Junie Donlavey's Heilig-Meyers Team in early 1994, Wallace was chosen to drive the teal Thunderbirds. Wallace finished twelfth in the Pepsi 400 at Daytona and came from the back of the pack to finish fifth at the Hooters 500, closing out the 1994 season. The team's strong finish in 1994 made them a force to be reckoned with in 1995. *Did You Know?* Mike Wallace brought thirty-one career NASCAR starts into the 1995 season, twenty-two in a Heilig-Myers Ford.

❑ Team Contact: Keystone Marketing, 101 S. Stratford Rd., Suite 501, Winston-Salem, NC 27104

First Trading Card: 1991 Traks #18

Mike Wallace (Photo courtesy of Keystone Marketing Co., Inc.)

Rusty Wallace and his Ford Thunderbird (Photo courtesy of Miller Genuine Draft Racing Team)

Rusty Wallace   Miller Genuine Draft (#2)

Rusty Wallace was born August 14, 1956, in Fenton, Missouri. In over two decades of racing he has ascended from short-track racing upstart to Winston Cup stardom. His determination, knowledge, and skill can no doubt be traced to his father Russ who was a consistent race winner on the short tracks of the Midwest. The oldest of three racing brothers, he reached the first pinnacle of his career when he won the 1989 NASCAR Winston Cup Championship. His numerous other career accomplishments include: USAC (1979) and Winston Cup Rookie of the Year (1984) honors, an American Speed Association Championship (1983), an IROC title, and thirty-nine Winston Cup race wins through the 1994 season. Entering the 1995 season he was fourteenth in Winston Cup competition's all-time career win standings and has a career 172 Top 10 finishes. As one of the sport's greatest drivers, Rusty Wallace continues to add to his many racing records with each passing season. Finished fifth in Winston Cup point standings in 1995 and previewed a new paint scheme for 1996 at the NAPA 500. *Did You Know?* Rusty Wallace's first NASCAR Winston Cup race was at the Atlanta 500 on March 16, 1980. Driving in his #16 Penske Chevrolet he would finish second in the race (runner-up to Dale Earnhardt).

❑ Team Contact: Tom Roberts, Tom Roberts Public Relations, P.O. Box 890, Guntersville, AL 35976

First Trading Card: 1988 Maxx #14

Collector's Note: Not only could you write a book about the sensational career Rusty Wallace has had in racing, but you could also write one about the memorabilia commemorating it. With the exception of die cast collectibles, his image has adorned a variety of objects. Wallace die cast collectors have had to respect Miller's decision to exclude corporate logos from appearing on products available to youngsters. The predictable result has been inexpensive replicas of little accuracy and minor appeal, however a viable alternative has been to target market expensive Wallace collectibles only to adults. Product attempts in this direction have met with less approval resistance. This has not always been the case, as some older products were less scrutinized. A predictable result of this policy is: unlicensed issues that may carry Miller logos entering the collector market—buyer beware.

The benefit of Miller's wonderful association with Wallace is some nice and often unique direct marketing pieces with the driver's likeness. Wallace full-size stand-ups, autographed hoods, banners, clocks, and restaurant table tents are just a few items that end up finding their way into collectors' hands. The company has also produced its own set of cards as a product promotion in packs of Miller Genuine Draft. The promotion, which was target marketed only at adults, was held primarily in the Southeast.

Wallace trading card collectors have many issues to choose from, however many favor the 1988 and 1989 Maxx cards, as well as valuable insert cards. Popular Wallace insert cards include the 1992 Traks Autograph #A2, the Press Pass Cup Chase #CC28, the 1994 Wheels High Gear Dominators #D2, and his Press Pass VIP Exchange 24K #EC7.

Included here for all Wallace ticket and program collectors are a few key dates:

❏ First Race   1980 Atlanta 500 (This race was also his first Top 10 and Top 5 finish)
❏ First Lap Led   April 14, 1984, Lap 49 in the TranSouth 500 at Darlington
❏ First Race Win   April 6, 1986, Valleydale 500 at Bristol
❏ First Pole   June 26, 1987, Miller 400 at Michigan International

Darrell Waltrip   Western Auto (#17)

Darrell Waltrip was born February 5, 1947. A former three-time champion, Waltrip completed two decades of racing in 1995. He entered the '95 season with an incredible 84 career wins and 374 Top 10 finishes. One of NASCAR's all-time great drivers, Waltrip is determined to reach the 100 win milestone and win a fourth NASCAR Winston Cup Championship before retirement. As a car owner and driver, he is confident that his Western Auto Chevrolets have enough good races left in them to reach his final goals. In 1994, Waltrip captured thirteen Top 10 finishes and took ninth place in the final NASCAR Winston Cup standings. A brilliant and extremely talented driver, Darrell Waltrip has left an indelible mark on the sport. Finished nineteenth in Winston Cup point standings in 1995 and finished the season strong by taking the pole at the NAPA 500. *Did You Know?* In 1981, Darrell Waltrip won twelve races and finished in the Top 5 an amazing twenty-one times.

❏ Team Contact: Keith Waltz, Cotter Communication, 6525 Hudspeth Road, Harrisburg, NC 28075

First Trading Card: 1986 SportsStar no#

Collector's Note: Many hobbyists agree that even though Darrell Waltrip is the most successful driver of his era, he has yet to gain the full respect of collectibles manufacturers. Certainly his accomplishments are deserving of a dedicated card set, yet to date nothing has been produced. The lack of product can certainly be due to timing, as Waltrip enjoyed much of his success before the boom in racing collectibles. With any luck the manufacturers will correct their short-sightedness and produce a set dedicated to this outstanding three-time Winston Cup champion. Waltrip trading card collectors rank his 1988 Maxx #10, his first card, as the most collectible. It wasn't included in the set's first press run, but debuted in the so-called "Charlotte" cards of a later printing. This card replaced the rare Talladega Streaks card from the Myrtle Beach, SC, print run.

Michael Waltrip   Citgo (#21)

Michael Waltrip was born April 30, 1963, in Owensboro, Kentucky. He is a seven-time winner on the Busch Grand National circuit and a two-time Busch pole winner. In 1988 he posted his best career Winston Cup finish, second at Pocono in the Miller 500. His most lucrative win entering the 1995 season was an eighth-place finish at the Brickyard 400 in 1994. After spending half the season in the Top 10, Waltrip finished a career best twelfth in Winston Cup point standings. He finished the 1994 season with ten Top 10 finishes in one of his finest years on the Winston Cup circuit. Showing consistent improvement, the Pennzoil-sponsored Pontiacs of Bahari' Racing have found a winning combination with Waltrip, and nothing but potential for the future. Waltrip finished twelfth in Winston Cup point standings in 1995 and will make a move to Woods Brothers in 1996. *Did You Know?* Michael Waltrip brings 268 career starts into the 1995 season with forty-eight Top 10 finishes.

❑ Team Contact: Drew Brown, Cohn & Wolfe, 225 Peachtree Street N.E., Suite 2300, Atlanta, GA 30303

First Trading Card: 1988 Maxx #98

Michael Waltrip (Photo courtesy of Cohn & Wolfe)

NHRA Winston Drag Racing Speedways and Races

* Data is through the 1994 season

Chief Internationals

Pomona Raceway
NHRA Communications Department
P.O. Box 5555
Glendora, CA 91740
818-914-1491

The season opener and one of the "Big Four" NHRA national events. This race, which takes place in early February, draws more than 100,000 spectators to watch 500 drivers compete at Pomona Raceway. In 1994, Kenny Bernstein set a course record in Top Fuel at 314.46 mph, while John Force did the same in the Funny Car class by hitting 303.95 mph.

Motorcraft Nationals

Firebird International Raceway
Box 5023, 20000 Maricopa Rd.
Chandler, AZ 85226
602-268-0200

Event number two on the nineteen-race NHRA Winston Drag Racing Series is held in late February and typically draws over 50,000 people. In 1994, Cory McClenathan won the Top Fuel title with the McDonald's Dragster at a speed of 304.87 mph, while Al Hofmann set the Firebird International Raceway Funny Car speed mark of 301.10 mph.

Slick 50 Nationals

Houston Raceway Park
2525 FM 565 South
Baytown, Texas 77520
713-383-2666

This event held in early March can draw nearly 90,000 spectators. In 1994, Scott Kalitta set the NHRA elapsed-time national record for Top Fuel with a run of 4.726 seconds, while Don "The Snake" Prudhomme won his first title of the season. Also in 1994, Al Hofmann captured the Funny Car class at a speed of 287.44 mph.

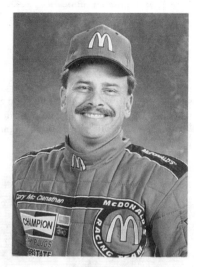

Cory McClenathan
Top Fuel Driver

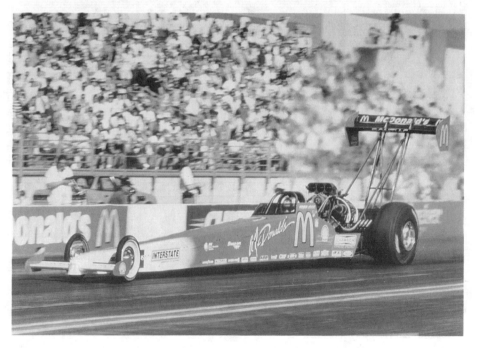

McDonald's Top Fuel Dragster. Driver: Cory McClenathan.

(Photo courtesy of Joe Gibbs Racing)

Mac Tools Gatornationals

Gainesville Raceway
11211 North County Rd. 225
Gainesville, FL 32609
904-377-0046

Celebrating its twenty-fifth anniversary in 1994, this very popular event can draw over 110,000 spectators. In 1994, Connie Kalitta and Scott Kalitta met in the first father-and-son Top Fuel final round in NHRA history. Connie prevailed at a speed of 290.79 mph. John Force captured the 1994 Funny Car class with a speed of 263 mph.

Scott Kalitta
1994 NHRA/Winston Top Fuel Champion

The American International Airways/Sequent Top Fuel Dragster of Scott Kalitta

The American International Airways Top Fuel Dragster of Connie Kalitta

Connie Kalitta

(Photo courtesy of American International Motorsports)

Winston Select Invitational

Rockingham Dragway
US Highway 1 North
Rockingham, NC 28379
910-582-3400

This event held in early April can draw over 50,000 people. In 1994, Don Prudhomme took the Top Fuel class at 288 mph, while Chuck Etchells swept Funny Car at a speed of 276.15 mph. Also in 1994, Al Hoffman ran the first 300 mph speed at the freshly paved dragway with a 300.80 mph run.

Fram Nationals

Atlanta Dragway
500 E. Ridgeway Road
Commerce, GA 30529
706-335-2301

This very popular event draws over 90,000 spectators in late April. In 1994 the Top Fuel class saw two experienced warriors battle it out as Connie Kalitta triumphed over Eddie Hill. It marked the oldest Top Fuel round ever as Kalitta, age fifty-six, earned his second straight victory of the year over Hill, who is fifty-eight. In the Funny Car class it was once again John Force picking up his third title out of only five events held so far that season.

Mid-South Nationals

Memphis International Motorsports Park
5500 Taylor-Forge Dr.
Millington, TN 38053
901-358-7223

This event held in mid-May typically draws over 60,000 spectators. Earning his second career Top Fuel victory, Tommy Johnson set new performance records with an exciting run of 305.08 mph and an elapsed time of 4.773 seconds. Gordie Bonin in his '94 Mustang captured his first Funny Car title of the season at 288.55 mph.

Gordie Bonin, Funny Car Driver (Photo courtesy of Smokin' Joe's Racing)

Mopar Parts Nationals

Old Bridge Township Raceway Park
230 Pension Rd.
Englishtown, NJ 07726
908-446-6331

Celebrating the silver anniversary of the Mopar Parts Nationals in 1994, this event held in late May can draw over 100,000 spectators. With an elapsed time of 4.690 seconds, Michael Brotherton became the quickest Top Fuel driver in NHRA history. Also in 1994, Pat Austin captured Top Fuel honors and Mark Oswald took the Funny Car title.

Virginia Nationals

Virginia Motorsports Park
P.O. Box 600
Dinwiddie, VA 23841
804-862-3174

This state-of-the-art facility opened in Spring 1994. It played host to a divisional event in 1994 and its success led to the Virginia Nationals being added to the 1995 NHRA Winston Drag Racing Series. It's the first time nineteen events have been on the schedule since 1990.

Oldsmobile Spring Nationals

National Trail Raceway
NHRA Communications Department
P.O. Box 5555
Glendora, CA 91740

Three decades of the Oldsmobile Spring Nationals were celebrated in 1994. Most will remember the event for Scott Kalitta's motor-exploding slide across the finish line during his Top Fuel victory. For Kalitta it would be the first of a four-race winning streak. He also scored two performance records during the event with an elapsed time of 4.847 seconds and a speed of 299.30 mph. Gordie Bonin took the Funny Car class for the second consecutive year.

Western Auto Nationals

Heartland Park Topeka
1805 SW 71st St.
Topeka, KS 66619
913-862-4781

The 1995 Western Auto Nationals featured qualifying and final eliminations primarily during the late afternoon and evening hours thanks to a new state-of-the-art lighting system at Heartland Park. This marks the first time since 1984 that this format has been done. In 1994, Scott Kalitta took the Top Fuel event at 299.40 mph, while John Force won the Funny Car class at 292.11 mph.

Mopar Parts Mile-High Nationals

Bandimere Speedway
3051 South Rooney Road
Morrison, CO 80465
303-697-6001

This mid-July event attracts over 80,000 spectators to Bandimere Speedway. For the participants it begins a tough stretch of three events in three weeks. In 1994, while en route to victory, Scott Kalitta set both ends of the Top Fuel track record at 4.890 seconds and 290.51 mph. John Force picked up his first victory in this event with a track record Funny Car elapsed time of 5.232 seconds.

Autolite Nationals

Sears Point Raceway
Highway 37 and 121
Sonoma, CA 95476
707-938-8430

The picturesque Sears Point Raceway attracts over 75,000 spectators for this late July event. The 1994 Autolite Nationals featured three drivers who had won at the Mopar Parts Mile-High Nationals, then repeated their performance here: Scott Kalitta (Top Fuel), John Force (Funny Car), and Darrell Alderman (Pro Stock). Alderman used the forum to set the NHRA speed national record for Pro Stock at 197.80 mph, the fastest Pro Stock speed in NHRA national event history. Scott Kalitta, with his fourth straight win, set an NHRA record for consecutive victories in Top Fuel.

Northwest Nationals

Seattle International Raceway
31001 144th Ave. S.E.
Kent, WA 98042
206-631-1550

The grueling three West-ended events in three weeks ends here at the Northwest Nationals. In 1994 the spectators were not disappointed as Scott Kalitta made the raceway's first 300 mph run with a stunning 302.72 mph. Joe Amato ended Kalitta's streak with a fine 295.08 mph performance in Top Fuel. John Force landed his fourth consecutive Funny Car title here at 291.82 mph.

Joe Amato, Top Fuel Driver (Photo courtesy of Joe Amato Racing)

Champion Auto Store Nationals

Brainerd International Raceway
4343 Highway 371
North Brainerd, MN 56401
218-829-9836

All four professional racing categories shined at the 1994 Champion Auto Stores National at Brainerd International Raceway. The Budweiser King Dragster driven by Kenny Bernstein set both ends of the Top Fuel track record at 4.774 seconds and 304.77 mph. Don Prudhomme won his second Top Fuel title of the season over Scott Kalitta. The ever impressive Kalitta made his sixth straight final round appearance. John Force continued his Funny Car dominance by picking up his fifth consecutive win, tying him for the record in that category.

U.S. Nationals

Indianapolis Raceway Park
P.O. Box 34300
Indianapolis, IN 46234
317-291-4090

This early September event draws over 150,000 spectators to a city famous for its motorsports. A rain-delayed start to the 1994 event caused eliminations to begin at 3 p.m. on Labor Day. The rain didn't dampen anyone's spirits, but caused the event to go under the lights for the first time. Connie Kalitta edged Eddie Hill to capture the Top Fuel title, while Cruz Pedregon stopped K. C. Spurlock in the Funny Car final.

Keystone Nationals

Maple Grove Raceway
R.D. 3
Box 3420
Mohnton, PA 19540
610-856-7812

Cruz Pedregon, Funny Car Driver (Photo courtesy of Joe Gibbs Racing/Pedregon Motorsports)

The 1994 Keystone Nationals provided a list of winners that was beginning to look far too familiar. Eventual Winston champions Scott Kalitta, John Force, and Darrell Alderman won their respective titles in Top Fuel, Funny Car, and Pro Stock. Kalitta knocked out a speed of 304.87 mph, while Force also cracked the 300 mark at 302.11 mph. It was by far the fastest Keystone National in history and a magic one with drivers in both categories cracking the formidable 300 mph barrier.

Sears Craftsman Nationals

Heartland Park Topeka
1805 SW 71st St.
Topeka, KS 66619
913-862-4781

The 1994 Sears Craftsman Nationals at Heartland Park Topeka was dominated by the golden arches as the McDonald's Racing Team doubled up in Top Fuel and Funny Car. Both Cory McClenathan and Cruz Pedregon scored impressive victories. John Force turned some heads as he set the NHRA elapsed-time national record for Funny Car at 4.939 seconds and also clinched the $150,000 Winston Championship.

127

Chief Nationals

Texas Motorplex
P.O. Box 1439
Ennis, TX 75120
214-875-2641

Rain got the best of the 1994 Chief Auto Parts Nationals, as the mid-October event was delayed one week for the first time. A little rain didn't affect Scott Kalitta as he advanced to the semifinal round to clinch his first NHRA Winston Top Fuel Championship. Don Prudhomme, who never backs down, won his third Top Fuel title of the season at 290.51 mph. Cruz Pedregon notched back-to-back circuit victories, as did Scott Geoffrion in Pro Stock.

Winston Select Finals

Pomona Raceway
NHRA Communications Department
P.O. Box 5555
Glendora, CA 91740
818-914-4761

To say that the 1994 NHRA Winston Drag Racing Series ended in a spectacular fashion might be an understatement. In an event that draws over 100,000 spectators, Shelly Anderson set the NHRA elapsed-time national record for Top Fuel at 4.718 seconds on her way to winning the $50,000 Budweiser Classic title. Kenny Bernstein knocked down speed records like they were bowling pins as he earned his first Top Fuel victory of the season. Bernstein recorded the two fastest speeds in NHRA national event history, 311.85 mph and an NHRA speed national record of 314.46 mph in the final round. John Force, whose season dominance was so very impressive, didn't let anyone down as he picked up his tenth victory and ran the all-time fastest Funny Car speed of 303.95 mph for the NHRA speed national record. Darrell Alderman also clinched his third NHRA Winston Pro Stock Championship.

Defunct Races

Defunct Event	Dates	Venue
NHRA Cajun Nationals	1977-1990	State Capitol Dragway, Erwinville, LA
Le Grandnational	1971-1992	Sanair Int. Drag Strip, St. Pie, Quebec
Supernationals	1970-1973	Ontario Motor Speedway, Ontario, CA
Golden Gate Nationals	1981-1983	Baylands Raceway, Fremont, CA
Fall Nationals	1975-1980	Seattle Raceway, Kent, WA

Die Cast Racing Collectibles

Die cast collectors are often die-hard racing fans. Like any area of the hobby, there are those who collect purely for fun and others who collect only for investment. For those who collect only the merchandise of their favorite driver, die cast can offer an interesting option. From airplanes to panel trucks, die cast has a fascinating product offering for the racing enthusiast.

It's not unusual for die cast collectors to purchase more than one of each product. One for fun and one for investment. One to open, examine, or display and the other to preserve in its original state without altering the packaging. The latter is the preferred method for the investor. Die cast original packaging is often as important to the value of the collectible as the replica itself, so if you are collecting die cast merchandise for investment, preserving the item in its original state is of paramount importance.

Production is always a concern to die cast collectors, especially when value is the objective. Many collectors prefer limited number or serialized offerings over mass marketed replicas. If you collect memorabilia from only the top ten racing teams, then collecting limited edition quality products is probably an excellent strategy. With so many products on the market today, accurate production numbers can be a key to value.

In recent years, accuracy in duplication has become a critical factor to the serious collector. From proper color shades to proper decals, all characteristics of a replica are examined for accuracy.

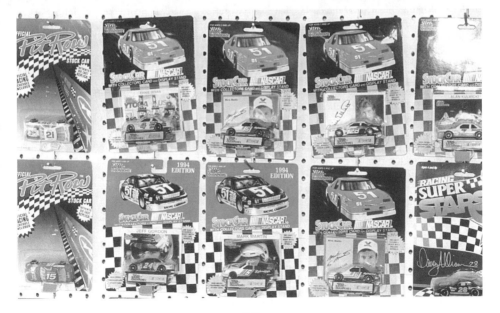

Many collectors prefer limited number or serialized offerings over mass marketed replicas

Size

Die cast collectibles come in many different shapes and sizes, making it a bit confusing for beginning collectors. Once the scales and ratios are understood however, the world of die cast can become a fascinating element of the hobby. If you can remember studying fractions, such as 1/2 or 1/3, during your math lessons in school, then die cast scales will be easy to understand. A fraction consists of a numerator (the top number) and a denominator (the bottom number). So in die cast the bigger the bottom number gets, the smaller the car. Just as a half is bigger than a quarter, so is a 1:18 die cast car bigger than a 1:24 or 1:43 scale version.

The intriguing element of die cast is that scales or ratios actually apply to the real thing. For example, if you were to take a 1:24 die cast car of Dale Earnhardt's (#3) Goodwrench Chevrolet Monte Carlo and make it 24 times larger, it would be exactly the same size.

Typically, die cast manufacturers use scale sizes of 1:8, 1:24, 1:43, 1:64, and 1:87. Other scales such as 1:16, 1:25, 1:55, and 1:96 can be used, but they are less common.

For years toy manufacturers have produced automotive replicas to a 1:64 scale size. Recognizing this, the most common size for racing replicas is 1:64. Many model manufacturers popularized the 1:24 scale and today it is a common size for most die cast banks. But in the dynamic world of die cast, what is uncommon today, may be typical tomorrow.

Ertl, a popular manufacturer of die cast, has long opted for 1:18 scale primarily because of the company's success in producing farming equipment replicas in this size. But scale can also be an important factor to manufacturers of larger sized vehicles such as transporters. The vehicles that carry your favorite NASCAR drivers' cars from track to track can be equally impressive in die cast. But being that they are much larger, the smaller scales such as 1:87 are very popular. With accuracy in both scale and detail being a paramount concern to all die cast collectors, size is a key concern to all manufacturers.

Die Cast Size Comparison

1:64	Approximately 3 inches
1:43	Approximately 4-1/25 inches
1:24	Approximately 7-3/4 inches
1:18	Approximately 10-3/4 inches

Production

Die cast production varies from manufacturer to manufacturer, with most companies following both competitor and consumer trends. Some companies may produce 10,000 to 15,000 NASCAR transporters, and between 15,000 and 20,000 cars, depending upon scale and driver popularity. Promotional products and limited editions typically have lower production runs of 2,500 to 5,000. Manufacturers can differ dramatically depending upon the type of product release or anticipated popularity. For example, Racing Champions produced 1:64 scale 1993 Premier Edition Transporters that ranged in production from 1,500 (Sterling Marlin/Raybestos) to 15,000 (Jeff Gordon/Du Pont).

Most collectors agree that for blister packaged cars in the $2-$3 range, production isn't an issue, but when manufacturers move from mass marketed pieces to 1:24 scale cars, banks, and premier items, production is critical and levels of about 3,000 to 4,000 should be maintained. The problem is obvious—the market for die cast of the top ten drivers just can't be met. Three thousand Lake Speed banks may be plenty, but it will not be enough for an Earnhardt or Gordon.

Not all companies release production information, although it has become increasingly popular and often advantageous to do so in recent years. Manufacturers realize that an increased knowledge level in their collector base has almost necessitated the procedure. Most die cast collectors want to preserve the value of their purchases, and understanding an item's production is the first step toward completing that task.

Die cast collectors are first to bring to the attention of manufacturers that too many products with too much production turns the collectible business into a toy business.

The intriguing element of die cast is that scales or ratios actually apply to the real thing. For example, if you were to take a 1:18 scale die cast car of Dale Earnhardt's (#3) Goodwrench Chevrolet Monte Carlo (as shown above) and make it eighteen times larger, it would be exactly the same size as the real car.

Products

Not all die cast manufacturers keep or release a product checklist to the public, even though doing so can only enhance a collector's willingness to buy additional items from a quality manufacturer's product line. White Rose Collectibles of York, Pennsylvania, is one example of a company that circulates checklists of their products. Fortunately for collectors, companies that don't produce or circulate checklists are often monitored by many hobby periodicals, thereby bringing the information into collectors' hands.

It is not unusual for die cast manufacturers to produce several versions of a product. For example, Action Racing Collectables produced three versions of the Dale Earnhardt Winston Select Silver 1:64 car. The Platinum Series version, which comes with a SkyBox trading card, had a production of about 70,000. This product was distributed through the manufacturer's distributors, Chevy dealerships, Earnhardt's racetrack trailers, and Action's track trailer. A second version came in a blister pack with black windows added. This version had a production of 20,000 and the same distribution as its predecessor. The final "hood open" version was for the Racing Collectors Club of America (RCCA), a "Club Item" release. This version had a production of 20,000 and was distributed to club members or through Action's track trailer. At the time of this writing, Action had produced six Earnhardt silver cars: three 1:64s, a 1:43 pewter, a 1:24 bank, and a 1:24 car. A 1:18 version was also planned for later release in 1995.

Variations

A die cast collectible, like any manufactured product, is subject to a certain amount of variation, whether intended or not by the manufacturer. Typically this variation occurs with the replica (wheels, tires, body style), its detailing (decals, paint, accessories) or the cards, stands, or packaging.

Replica – Wheels and Tire Variations

It is not uncommon for manufacturers to vary wheel, design, color, or material. Die cast collectors must monitor these changes in order to correctly identify and price a particular issue. For example, there are three known variations of wheels on the Racing Champions, Inc. cars: a solid center style (1989-90), spokes version (1992-95), and a cut-out or mag version (1992-95). Additionally, there were several color variations, with silver wheels believed to be the scarcest.

There were also several different styles of tires on Racing Champions, Inc. cars: rubber removable tires (1989/90), plastic non-removable tires (1990-92) with "Racing Champions" printed in white letters on one side only, and plastic non-removable tires (1992-95) with "Goodyear Eagles" printed in white or yellow letters on one side only.

Replica – Body Style Variations

Die cast replicas can also vary in body styles, particularly as it applies to front and back end pieces. If certain body styles are found that do not reflect the correct style of the driver, they are most often considered mistakes. Quantities manufactured with large enough production runs to be considered collectible are referred to as variations. Design changes made by car manufacturers are the underlying reason for the existence of these body style variations. Certainly a surplus of old die cast parts and lack of new updated parts can lead to the decision to produce a variation of a new model with some old pieces. Although it doesn't make collectors happy, it is an alternative to stopping a manufacturer's production.

Some variations to body styles worth noting, particularly as they apply to Racing Champions, Inc. cars, are the following:

* Pontiac	Current Mold (1992/95): small front grille openings, no metal straps down the rear window and has roof rails.
	Previous Style (1990/91): large front grille openings, two metal straps down the rear window (painted same color as the car), and a smooth roof. * Some 1991 models did not have the rear window straps – only GM body cars.
	Previous Style (1989/90): small front grille openings, two metal straps down the rear window (painted same color as the car), and a smooth roof.

Variations in die cast accessories and packaging are common. Above are examples of die cast packages, some containing cards and display stands.

* Ford	Current Mold (1993/95): two front grille openings, with detail lower roof line.
	Previous Style (1992): no roof rails, same as below.
	Previous Style (1992): roof rails, no rear window straps.
	Previous Style (1991/92): smooth detailess front grille, smooth roof, rear window straps and headlight circles.
	Previous Style (1989/91): detailed front grille area, smooth roof and rear window straps.
* Oldsmobile	Current Model (1992/94): detailed front grille area with two air inlets, roof rails, no rear window straps.
	Previous Style (1989/91): flat front grille area, two raised areas on the outside of the lower front bumper, smooth roof, and rear window straps.
* Lumina	Current Model (1992-94): improved front grille detailing, roof rails, no rear window straps.
	Previous Style (1989/91): defined front grille with smooth lower bumper, smooth roof, rear window straps.
* Buick	Current Model (1992/94): defined front grille, two small grille areas on the outside of the lower bumper, roof rails, no rear window straps.
	Previous Style (1989/91): defined complex front grille, smaller lower bumper that includes dots between raised areas, smooth roof, rear window straps.

Detailing – Paint and Decal Variations

Detailing variations are common in die cast products, with the most significant changes noted in the enclosed checklist of selected die cast products. Whereas the paint variations would be far too numerous to mention here, collectors should acquaint themselves with various manufacturers' releases to better understand what significant changes to expect with certain products.

Decal variations can occur and are especially prevalent in earlier die cast releases. For example, Racing Champions Inc. in 1991 had the STP and Mac Tools decals show up behind the front tire on cars in the Dale Earnhardt back packaging. Some had shown up on 1990 series one cars, but they were scarce. Inconsistency in decal application should be noted and understood by die cast collectors.

Cards, Stands, and Packaging Variations

Variations in die cast accessories and packaging are common characteristics of the hobby. Elements inserted into a die cast product such as a card or a stand are also subject to variations. Various style stands, cards with no names on the front, or changes to the front or back of certain types of packaging can be either mistakes or purposeful marketing changes. Since most serious die cast hobbyists prefer to leave their acquisitions in the original packaging, all accessory variations are noted. The difficulty these variations present is determining what, if any, additional value should be added to the product as a result. Most dealers add one to three dollars on the price of a difficult die cast product accessory or package variation.

Sponsorship

The dynamic world of racing, with its seasonal changes in drivers and sponsors, keeps the die cast collector busy. Just take a look at NASCAR's makeover in 1995. McDonald's put their golden arches on the hood of veteran Bill Elliott. Bobby Labonte decided to take up residence in Joe Gibbs' Interstate Batteries car. Kyle Petty changed his choice of beverage from Mello Yello to Coors Light, and Maxwell House decided to perk elsewhere.

For the collector these changes often mean intensifying their collecting, seeking out harder to find pieces under the old sponsor, while gearing up for new products. Die cast collectors of drivers with alcohol or tobacco products often find sponsorship changes frustrating because of the difficulties involved

Although Rusty Wallace hasn't changed sponsors in over five years, die cast cars with the Miller logo didn't appear until last year. Above is a photo of Rusty's Ford Thunderbird with the Miller logo. (Photo courtesy of Miller Genuine Draft Racing Team)

with such licensing and the restrictions that apply. Although Rusty Wallace hasn't changed sponsors in over five years, die cast cars with the Miller logo didn't appear until last year. Fans want to see cars reproduced exactly the way they are, and a Wallace car without the Miller logo was no substitute.

With collectors being more driver-oriented rather than sponsor-oriented, often the changes spark new interest with collectors. Many collectors applauded the Elliott shift to McDonald's as a way to add a little color contrast to their collection. For a driver as popular as Elliott, the change led to a plethora of new collectibles, from combination appearances on merchandise with Ronald McDonald to the debut of the "Thunderbat." In conjunction with McDonald's and Warner Brothers Studio, Elliott's familiar red car was transformed into a black McDonald's/Batman Forever design in one of the most unique promotions in the history of the sport. The "Thunderbat" flew at Charlotte, Pocono, and Michigan as part of the summer release of the movie.

Earnhardt collectors went crazy over Action's line of Dale Earnhardt silver Monte Carlos. Earnhardt drove the car for The Winston Select at Charlotte Motor Speedway. The approach of associating die cast releases with legitimate racing events excited both fans and dealers. Additionally, that this type of item didn't enter mass retail outlets also seemed to add to its legitimacy.

An interesting element to add to the sponsorship shifting is when you see your favorite driver decide to move his decals to another model car or decide to add additional paint schemes during the season. The 1996 STP NASCAR Winston Cup Pontiacs are one example of a team planning to introduce three different paint schemes during the season. No doubt certain die cast manufacturers will replicate the paint changes in their 1996 product line. All of this adds an additional twist to the already very exciting element of collecting auto racing memorabilia.

The Future of Die Cast May Be the Past

While Super Trucks will certainly be popular with die cast collectors in 1996, Action Performance Companies decided to revisit the past and issue die cast cars of the last 25 Winston Cup champions. Collectors of certain drivers such as Dale Earnhardt can now add versions of every car driven by the seven-time champion to their collection. The popularity of the nostalgic issues will no doubt add considerable interest to the hobby.

Haulers, dirt cars, golf cart banks, and other forms of die cast, some of which may be produced in multiple versions, will add to collector interest. Vintage team sets such as those offered by Peachstate Classics should also score big with collectors. Cars of Ralph Moody, Parnelli Jones, and Curtis Turner can now find themselves alongside Kyle Petty's No. 42 Coors Light Pontiac on collectors' shelves. Even a two-sided 1:64 hauler with Dale Earnhardt on one side and Richard Petty on the other can be expected from Action this year. Racing Champions, who added dragsters and Indy Cars to its product line last year, should find increased collector interest in these forms during the coming year. Special edition replicas, such as the car Mark Martin drove at the 1995 Brickyard, will also continue this year, as special commemorative paint jobs seem to be a trend. Additionally, expect the popularity of 1:18 cars to continue in 1996 as bigger seems to be better.

Selected Price Guide
(not intended to be comprehensive)

Action Racing Collectables

1:16 Pit Wagon Banks
(Formerly known as RCI)
* Varied production from 2,500 to 7,500

❑ 2	R. Wallace, Ford Motor Co.	$	45
❑ 3	D. Earnhardt, Goodwrench	$	65
❑ 3	D. Earnhardt, Goodwrench / 7 Time	$	65
❑ 11	B. Elliott, Budweiser	$	45
❑ 16	T. Musgrave, Family Channel	$	35
❑ 18	D. Jarrett, Interstate Batteries	$	35
❑ 24	J. Gordon, Du Pont	$	70
❑ 28	D. Allison, Havoline	$	50
❑ 28	D. Allison, Havoline Mac Tools	$	40
❑ 28	E. Irvan, Havoline	$	45
❑ 28	E. Irvan, Mac Tools	$	40
❑ 30	M. Waltrip, Pennzoil	$	30
❑ 41	J. Nemechek, Meineke	$	30
❑ 42	K. Petty, Mello Yello	$	35
❑ 51	N. Bonnett, Country Time	$	40

Action Racing Collectables

1:24
(Formerly known as RCI)

❑ 1	R. Mast, Skoal	$	55
❑ 2	R. Craven, Du Pont	$	35
❑ 2	R. Wallace, Ford Motor, B	$	90
❑ 2	R. Wallace, MGD	$	45
❑ 2	R. Wallace, MGD, B	$	50
❑ 3	D. Earnhardt, Goodwrench, LUM B	$	60
❑ 3	D. Earnhardt, Goodwrench, 95MC B	$	50
❑ 3	D. Earnhardt, Goodwrench Silver B	$	80
❑ 3	D. Earnhardt, Wrangler 84MC B	$	80
❑ 3	D. Earnhardt, Wrangler 85MC B	$	80
❑ 3	D. Earnhardt, Wrangler 87MC B	$	80
❑ 5	T. Labonte, Kellogg's B	$	100
❑ 11	B. Elliott, Budweiser	$	50
❑ 11	B. Elliott, Budweiser B	$	55
❑ 11	D. Waltrip, Budweiser	$	50
❑ 11	D. Waltrip, Budweiser 85MC B	$	55
❑ 11	D. Waltrip, Budweiser 87MC B	$	55
❑ 12	N. Bonnett, Budweiser 85MC B	$	55
❑ 12	N. Bonnett, Budweiser 87MC B	$	45
❑ 15	L. Speed, Quality Care	$	35
❑ 16	T. Musgrave, Family Channel B	$	100
❑ 21	D. Pearson, Chattanooga Chew B	$	50
❑ 25	K. Schrader, Budweiser B	$	55

❑ 28	E. Irvan, Havoline B Employee	$	125
❑ 28	E. Irvan, Havoline B Retail	$	35
❑ 41	J. Nemechek, Meineke	$	35
❑ 42	K. Petty, Mello Yello	$	35
❑ 51	N. Bonnett, Country Time B	$	55
❑ 94	B. Elliott, Thunderbat B	$	50
❑ 98	D. Cope, Fingerhut	$	35

Action Racing Collectables

1:64
(Formerly known as RCI)
ACR - AC Racing '93 Series
DR - Delco Remy
PLS - Platinum Series
VT - Valvoline Team

❑ 2	R. Craven, Du Pont PLS	$	8
❑ 2	R. Wallace, Ford Motor PLS	$	9
❑ 2	R. Wallace, MGD	$	12
❑ 2	R. Wallace, Pontiac Exc. ACR	$	10
❑ 2	R. Wallace, Pontiac Exc. DR	$	10
❑ 3	D. Earnhardt, Goodwrench ACR	$	14
❑ 3	D. Earnhardt, Goodwrench 94LUM PLS	$	12
❑ 3	D. Earnhardt, Goodwrench 88MC PLS	$	12
❑ 3	D. Earnhardt, Goodwrench 95MC PLS	$	14
❑ 3	D. Earnhardt, Good Silver	$	25
❑ 3	D. Earnhardt, Good Silver PLS	$	20
❑ 3	D. Earnhardt, Wrangler 84MC PLS	$	15
❑ 4	E. Irvan, Kodak ACR	$	9
❑ 4	E. Irvan, Kodak DR	$	8
❑ 5	T. Labonte, Kellogg's PLS	$	8
❑ 6	T. Houston, Roses	$	8
❑ 6	M. Martin, Valvoline VT	$	8
❑ 8	D. Earnhardt, 85Cam. ASA PLS	$	10
❑ 11	B. Elliott, Budweiser PLS	$	14
❑ 11	D. Waltrip, Budweiser PLS	$	14
❑ 12	N. Bonnett, Budweiser PLS	$	14
❑ 15	L. Speed, Quality Care PLS	$	8
❑ 16	W. Dallenbach, Roush VT	$	8
❑ 16	T. Musgrave, Family Channel PLS	$	8
❑ 17	D. Waltrip, Western Auto ACR	$	9
❑ 17	D. Waltrip, Western Auto DR	$	8
❑ 24	J. Gordon, Du Pont ACR	$	16
❑ 24	J. Gordon, Du Pont 94LUM PLS	$	14
❑ 24	J. Gordon, Du Pont 95MC PLS	$	16
❑ 24	J. Gordon, Du Pont VT	$	16
❑ 25	K. Schrader, GMAC ACR	$	9
❑ 25	K. Schrader, GMAC VT	$	8

❑ 25	K. Schrader, Budweiser PLS	$	12
❑ 26	S. Swindell, Bull Hannah P	$	8
❑ 27	T. Richmond, Old Milwaukee	$	12
❑ 28	E. Irvan, Havoline	$	12
❑ 28	D. Jarrett, Texaco PLS	$	12
❑ 35	S. Robinson, Polaroid	$	12
❑ 40	K. Wallace, Dirt Devil ACR	$	9
❑ 41	J. Nemechek, Meineke PLS	$	8
❑ 41	P. Parsons, ACR	$	9
❑ 42	K. Petty, Mello Yello ACR	$	9
❑ 42	K. Petty, Mello Yello PLS	$	8
❑ 46	A. Unser, Jr., Valvoline VT	$	10
❑ 51	N. Bonnett, Country Time PLS	$	14
❑ 93	NDA, Lumina Prototype	$	8
❑ 93	NDA, Pontiac Prototype	$	8
❑ 93	NDA, TB Prototype	$	8
❑ 94	B. Elliott, McDonald's PLS	$	10
❑ 94	B. Elliott, Thunderbat PLS	$	12
❑ 94	C. Elliott, RCI	$	12
❑ 98	D. Cope, Fingerhut PLS	$	8

Action / RCCA

1:24

❑ 2	R. Wallace, Ford Motor Co.	$	80
❑ 2	R. Wallace, MGD	$	60
❑ 3	D. Earnhardt, Goodwrench 94LUM	$	55
❑ 3	D. Earnhardt, Goodwrench 95MC	$	40
❑ 3	D. Earnhardt, Goodwrench Silver	$	85
❑ 18	D. Jarrett, Interstate Batteries	$	40
❑ 25	K. Schrader, Budweiser	$	45
❑ 51	N. Bonnett, Country Time	$	45

Action / RCCA

1:64

CO - Club Only
HO - Hood Open Series
REV - Revell

❑ 1	J. Gordon, Baby Ruth REV	$	17
❑ 2	R. Wallace, Pontiac Excite REV	$	8
❑ 2	R. Wallace, MGD CO	$	18
❑ 2	R. Wallace, MGD HO	$	15
❑ 3	D. Earnhardt, Goodwrench CO	$	32
❑ 3	D. Earnhardt, Goodwrench 94LUM HO	$	20
❑ 3	D. Earnhardt, Goodwrench 95MC HO	$	18
❑ 3	D. Earnhardt, Goodwrench Silver HO	$	22
❑ 3	D. Earnhardt, Wrangler 85MC NB	$	22
❑ 3	D. Earnhardt, Wrangler 87MC FB	$	22
❑ 3	D. Earnhardt Jr., Mom-n-Pop's	$	17
❑ 5	T. Labonte, Kellogg's HO	$	12
❑ 5	R. Rudd, Tide REV P	$	10
❑ 6	M. Martin, Folgers P	$	25
❑ 6	M. Martin, Stroh's Light, 2 cars	$	25
❑ 6	M. Martin, Valvoline HO	$	15
❑ 6	M. Martin, Valvoline REV	$	8
❑ 8	K. Earnhardt, Mom-n-Pop's	$	16
❑ 9	B. Elliott, Melling CO	$	12
❑ 10	D. Cope, Purolator REV	$	10
❑ 11	B. Elliott, Budweiser HO	$	15
❑ 11	D. Waltrip, Budweiser 84MC NB	$	20
❑ 12	N. Bonnett, Budweiser 84MC NB	$	20
❑ 12	H. Stricklin, Raybestos REV	$	8

❑ 15	L. Speed, Quality Care HO	$	15
❑ 15	NDA, Motorcraft REV	$	8
❑ 16	T. Musgrave, Family Channel HO	$	15
❑ 17	D. Waltrip, Western Auto REV CO	$	20
❑ 17	D. Waltrip, Western Auto 94LUM HO	$	12
❑ 18	D. Jarrett, Interstate Batteries HO	$	12
❑ 18	D. Jarrett, Interstate Batteries REV	$	8
❑ 21	D. Pearson, Chattanooga Chew	$	15
❑ 21	D. Pearson, Pearson Racing	$	7
❑ 21	M. Shepherd, Cheer, Morema	$	10
❑ 21	M. Shepherd, Citgo REV	$	8
❑ 22	S. Marlin, Maxwell House REV	$	8
❑ 24	J. Gordon, Du Pont 94LUM HO	$	25
❑ 24	J. Gordon, Du Pont 95MC HO	$	21
❑ 25	R. Craven, 91 BGN Champ P	$	15
❑ 25	K. Schrader, Budweiser HO	$	15
❑ 25	B. Venturini, Rain X REV	$	8
❑ 26	B. Bodine, Quaker State REV	$	8
❑ 27	T. Richmond, Old Milwaukee	$	15
❑ 28	D. Allison, Havoline CO	$	25
❑ 28	D. Allison, Mac Tools P	$	25
❑ 28	D. Allison, Texaco HO Black/Gold	$	16
❑ 28	D. Allison, Texaco HO Black/Orange	$	16
❑ 28	D. Jarrett, Texaco HO	$	15
❑ 30	M. Waltrip, Pennzoil HO	$	12
❑ 30	M. Waltrip, Pennzoil REV	$	8
❑ 36	K. Wallace, Cox Lumber REV	$	8
❑ 36	K. Wallace, Dirt Devil REV	$	8
❑ 38	K. Earnhardt, Mom-n-Pop's	$	16
❑ 42	K. Petty, Mello Yello HO	$	12
❑ 42	K. Petty, Mello Yello REV	$	8
❑ 43	R. Petty, STP REV	$	8
❑ 44	L. Caudill, Army REV	$	8
❑ 51	N. Bonnett, Country Time HO	$	20
❑ 63	C. Bown, Nescafe HO	$	12
❑ 66	J. Hensley, TropArtic REV	$	8
❑ 68	B. Hamilton, Country Time REV	$	8
❑ 87	J. Nemechek, Texas Pete REV	$	8
❑ 89	J. Sauter, Evinrude REV	$	8
❑ 90	B. Hillin, Heilig-Meyers P	$	12
❑ 92	NDA, Circle Track Show P	$	12
❑ 93	M. Wallace, NS REV	$	8
❑ 94	B. Elliott, McDonald's HO	$	15
❑ 94	C. Elliott, NS HO	$	14
❑ 98	D. Cope, Fingerhut HO	$	12
❑ 99	R. Craven, Du Pont REV	$	8

Action / RCCA

1:64

1991 Oldsmobile Series

❑ 20	R. Moroso, Swi. Sweet, 2 cars	$	30
❑ 22	E. Berrier, Greased Lightning	$	8
❑ 22	R. Moroso, Moroso Racing	$	6
❑ 22	R. Moroso, Prestone	$	6
❑ 33	H. Gant, Skoal with mug	$	25
❑ 44	B. Labonte, Penrose	$	8
❑ 44	S. Marlin, Piedmont	$	17
❑ 73	P. Barkdoll, XR-1	$	8
❑ 88	B. Baker, Red Baron	$	13
❑ 91	C. Allison, Mac Tools	$	20
❑ 93	NDA, Christmas Car	$	15

Action / RCCA

1:64
1983-86 T-Bird Series

☐ 7	K. Petty, 7-Eleven	$	12
☐ 9	B. Elliott, Melling	$	20
☐ 15	D. Earnhardt, Wrangler	$	35
☐ 15	R. Rudd, Motorcraft	$	8
☐ 21	B. Baker, Valvoline, V on deck lid	$	8
☐ 21	B. Baker, Valvoline on deck lid	$	20
☐ 21	D. Pearson, Black Bumper	$	20
☐ 21	D. Pearson, Brown Bumper	$	8
☐ 22	B. Allison, Gold Wheels	$	15
☐ 22	B. Allison, Silver Wheels	$	23
☐ 28	D. Allison, Havoline	$	20
☐ 28	C. Yarborough, Hardee's	$	8
☐ 35	A. Kulwicki, Quincy's	$	56
☐ 35	D. May, Hanover Printing	$	8
☐ 57	J. Ridley, Nationwise	$	8
☐ 64	R. Combs, Sunny King, Small Roof No.	$	10
☐ 64	R. Combs, Sunny King, Big Roof No.	$	8
☐ 67	B. Arrington, Arrington Racing	$	8
☐ 70	J. D. McDuffie, Lockhart	$	10
☐ 71	D. Marcis, Shoney's	$	8
☐ 90	J. Donlavey, Chameleon	$	8
☐ 90	K. Schrader, Red Baron	$	16
☐ 90	K. Schrader, Sunny King	$	8
☐ NNO	NDA, Primer, Lumina, Pontiac, HO	$	10

Ertl

1:18

☐ 3	D. Earnhardt, Goodwrench	$	60
☐ 4	E. Irvan, Kodak	$	45
☐ 6	M. Martin, Valvoline	$	45
☐ 7	G. Bodine, Exide GMP	$	65
☐ 7	A. Kulwicki, Army BF	$	90
☐ 7	A. Kulwicki, Hooters BF	$	90
☐ 7	A. Kulwicki, Zerex BF	$	90
☐ 10	D. Cope, Purolator	$	90
☐ 11	B. Elliott, Budweiser	$	45
☐ 12	J. Spencer, Meineke WRC B	$	125
☐ 14	J. Andretti, Kanawha	$	60
☐ 15	G. Bodine, Motorcraft	$	80
☐ 16	C. Chaffin, 31W Insulation	$	55
☐ 17	D. Waltrip, Western Auto	$	45
☐ 18	D. Jarrett, Interstate Batteries	$	40
☐ 20	B. Hamilton, Fina Lube B	$	75
☐ 21	B. Bowsher, Quality Farm	$	70
☐ 21	M. Shepherd, Cheerwine	$	70
☐ 23	J. Spencer, Smokin' Joe's	$	75
☐ 24	J. Gordon, Du Pont WRC B	$	500
☐ 24	J. Gordon, Du Pont, WRC B No Serial #	$	149
☐ 26	S. Kinser, Quaker State HO	$	60
☐ 28	D. Allison, Havoline	$	75
☐ 30	M. Waltrip, Pennzoil	$	30
☐ 33	B. Loney, Winnebago	$	60
☐ 42	A. Hillenburg, Budget Gourmet P B	$	75
☐ 42	K. Petty, Mello Yello	$	35
☐ 43	R. Petty, STP	$	50
☐ 44	D. Green, Slim Jim	$	60
☐ 59	A. Belmont, Dr. Die Cast	$	60
☐ 59	C. Chaffin, Dr. Die Cast	$	45

☐ 59	R. Pressley, Alliance	$	350
☐ 59	D. Setzer, Alliance 5000	$	75
☐ 59	D. Setzer, Alliance, 2 car set	$	225
☐ 60	M. Martin, Winn Dixie GMP	$	65
☐ 84	B. Senneker, Lane Auto	$	70
☐ 87	J. Nemechek, Dent. WRC B	$	175
☐ 98	J. Mayfield, Fingerhut	$	60

Funstuf Pit Row

1:43

☐ Cars (6/11/12/18/21)		$	5
☐ Cars (22/33/49/75/98)		$	5
☐ 1	J. Gordon, Baby Ruth	$	10
☐ 16	W. Dallenbach, Jr., Roush	$	6
☐ 41	G. Sacks, Kellogg's	$	6
☐ 66	J. Hensley, TropArtic	$	5
☐ 66	C. Little, TropArtic	$	5
☐ 83	J. McClure, Collector's World	$	6

Funstuf Pit Row

1:64
*WD - Winston decal on fender

☐ Cars (2/4/5/7/8/22/33)		$	3
☐ Cars (55/71/82/98)		$	3
☐ 1	J. Gordon, Baby Ruth	$	5
☐ 11	B. Elliott, Amoco Deck Lid	$	3
☐ 11	B. Elliott, Amoco Hood	$	3
☐ 11	NDA, Baby Ruth	$	3
☐ 12	K. Schultz, Piggly Wiggly	$	5
☐ 15	M. Shepherd, Motorcraft	$	3
☐ 15	M. Shepherd, Motorcraft WD	$	7
☐ 15	NDA, Motorcraft	$	3
☐ 18	D. Jarrett, Interstate Batteries	$	3
☐ 18	NDA, Interstate Batteries	$	3
☐ 20	M. Wallace, Orkin	$	5
☐ 21	D. Jarrett, Citgo	$	3
☐ 21	D. Jarrett, Citgo WD	$	7
☐ 21	M. Shepherd, Citgo	$	3
☐ 23	E. Bierschwale, AutoFinders	$	5
☐ 27	W. Burton, Gaultney	$	5
☐ 41	G. Sacks, Kellogg's	$	5
☐ 43	R. Petty, STP	$	3
☐ 43	R. Petty, STP WD	$	7
☐ 49	S. Smith, Ameritron Battery	$	7
☐ 66	J. Hensley, TropArtic	$	3
☐ 66	C. Little, TropArtic	$	3
☐ 66	L. Speed, TropArtic	$	3
☐ 75	NDA, Dinner Bell	$	3
☐ 75	J. Ruttman, Dinner Bell	$	3
☐ 83	J. McClure, Collector's World	$	5
☐ 94	T. Labonte, Sunoco	$	3
☐ 94	T. Labonte, Sunoco Busch	$	5

Matchbox White Rose

1:64
1990-1992
Super Stars Series 1
BX = Boxed
BL = Blister Pack

☐ 1	J. Gordon, Baby Ruth Red BX92	$	15

❏ 1	J. Gordon, Baby Ruth Orange BX92	$	20
❏ 2	R. Wallace, Penske BL92	$	5
❏ 3	D. Earnhardt, GM BX90	$	43
❏ 3	D. Earnhardt, GM Parts BX91	$	33
❏ 3	D. Earnhardt, Goodwrench BL92	$	15
❏ 3	D. Earnhardt, Mom-n-Pop's PBG92	$	12
❏ 4	E. Irvan, Kodak BL92	$	6
❏ 7	H. Gant, Mac Tools BX92	$	10
❏ 7	J. Hensley, WRC BX92	$	10
❏ 7	A. Kulwicki, Hooters BL92	$	25
❏ 7	A. Kulwicki, Hooters National Fresh BL92	$	16
❏ 8	J. Burton, TIC Financial BX92	$	4
❏ 8	D. Trickle, Snickers BL92	$	4
❏ 9	NDA, Melling BL92	$	4
❏ 10	D. Cope, Purolator BL92	$	4
❏ 10	E. Irvan, Mac Tools BX91	$	27
❏ 11	B. Elliott, Amoco BL92	$	4
❏ 12	H. Stricklin, Raybestos BL92	$	4
❏ 15	NDA, Motorcraft BL92	$	4
❏ 15	M. Shepherd, Motorcraft BL92	$	6
❏ 18	D. Jarrett, Interstate Batteries BL92	$	4
❏ 22	S. Marlin, Maxwell House BL92	$	4
❏ 26	B. Bodine, Quaker State BL92	$	4
❏ 28	D. Allison, Havoline BL92	$	20
❏ 28	D. Allison, Havoline MT BL92	$	20
❏ 29	NDA, MB Racing, WRC BX92	$	5
❏ 29	P. Parsons, Parsons BX92	$	32
❏ 30	M. Waltrip, Pennzoil BL92	$	4
❏ 41	J. Smith, White House AJ BL92	$	6
❏ 42	K. Petty, Mello Yello BL92	$	4
❏ 43	R. Petty, STP BL92	$	4
❏ 44	B. Labonte, Penrose BX92	$	8
❏ 44	B. Labonte, Slim Jim BX92	$	8
❏ 48	J. Hylton, Valtrol BL92	$	4
❏ 49	E. Feree, Fergaed Racing BX92	$	4
❏ 55	T. Musgrave, Jasper BL92	$	4
❏ 66	C. Little, Phillips 66 BL92 Red	$	5
❏ 66	NDA, Phillips 66 BL92 Black	$	4
❏ 68	B. Hamilton, Country Time BL92	$	4
❏ 87	J. Nemechek, Texas Pete BX92	$	4
❏ 89	J. Sauter, Evinrude BL92	$	4
❏ 92	NDA, White Rose Coll. BL92	$	45
❏ 92	H. Stricklin, Stanley Tools BX92	$	4

Matchbox White Rose

1:64

1993 Super Stars Series 1

BX = Boxed

BL = Blister Pack

❏ Cars (9/12/14/21/22/25/29/31)		$	4
❏ Cars (40/41/48/71/83/87/94)		$	4
❏ 1	R. Combs, Luxaire BL	$	18
❏ 1	R. Combs, Goody's BX	$	16
❏ 6	M. Martin, Valvoline	$	5
❏ 7	J. Hensley, Bobsled BX	$	9
❏ 7	J. Hensley, Bojangles BL	$	9
❏ 7	J. Hensley, Cellular One BX	$	9
❏ 7	J. Hensley, Family Channel BX	$	9
❏ 7	J. Hensley, Hanes BX	$	9
❏ 7	J. Hensley, Matchbox BX	$	9
❏ 8	J. Burton, TIC Financial BX	$	4

❏ 8	J. Burton, Baby Ruth BX	$	4
❏ 8	S. Marlin, Raybestos BL	$	4
❏ 08	B. Dotter, Dewalt BX	$	4
❏ 24	J. Gordon, Du Pont BL	$	10
❏ 28	D. Allison, Havoline BL	$	18
❏ 32	J. Horton, Active Racing BL	$	4
❏ 32	D. Jarrett, Pic-N-Pay BX	$	4
❏ 69	J. Sparker, WFE Chall. BL	$	12
❏ 93	Generic, White Rose Coll. BL	$	40
❏ 93	Generic, American Zoom PBG	$	10
❏ 98	D. Cope, Bojangles BL	$	4
❏ 98	J. Spencer, Moly Black Gold BL	$	4
❏ 98	R. Craven, Du Pont BX	$	4

Matchbox White Rose

1:64

1994 Super Stars Series 2

BX = Boxed

BL = Blister Pack

FCS - Future Cup Stars '94

SSA - Super Star Awards

❏ Cars (5/6/8/12/15/16)		$	4
❏ Cars (17/19/26/30/32/34)		$	4
❏ Cars (40/41/52/75/92/98)		$	4
❏ 0	J. Burton, TIC Financial FCS BX	$	9
❏ 2	R. Craven, Du Pont BX	$	4
❏ 2	R. Wallace, Ford Motor Co. BX	$	5
❏ 3	D. Earnhardt, Gold LUM SSA BX	$	32
❏ 4	S. Marlin, Kodak BX	$	4
❏ 4	S. Marlin, Kodak Fun Saver BX	$	4
❏ 7	G. Bodine, Exide BX	$	8
❏ 7	H. Gant, Manheim BX	$	4
❏ 23	H. Stricklin, Smokin' Joe's BX	$	20
❏ 24	J. Gordon, Du Pont BX	$	10
❏ 29	P. Parsons, Baltimore CFL BL	$	20
❏ 29	P. Parsons, MB, WRC BX	$	4
❏ 33	H. Gant, Gold LUM SSA BX	$	22
❏ 37	L. Allen, Nat. Fresh FCS BX	$	8
❏ 43	R. Combs, Black Flag BX	$	8
❏ 43	R. Combs, French's Black Flag BL	$	25
❏ 43	R. Combs, French's BX	$	8
❏ 46	S. Robinson, Polaroid BL	$	12
❏ 55	J. Hensley, Petron Plus BL	$	15
❏ 60	M. Martin, Winn Dixie BX	$	8
❏ 66	M. Wallace, Duron Paint FCS BX	$	8
❏ 87	J. Nemechek, Cintas FCS BX	$	8
❏ 94	Generic, MB, WRC BL	$	25
❏ 94	Generic, Series 2, Preview BX	$	8

Matchbox White Rose

1:64

1995 Super Stars Series 2

❏ 2	R. Craven, Du Pont	$	5
❏ 8	J. Burton, Raybestos Gold	$	20
❏ 11	B. Bodine, Lowe's	$	5
❏ 12	D. Cope, Straight Arrow	$	5
❏ 26	S. Kinser, Quaker State	$	5
❏ 72	T. Leslie, Detroit Gasket	$	5
❏ 74	J. Benson Jr., Lipton Tea	$	5
❏ 90	M. Wallace, Heilig-Meyers	$	5
❏ 94	B. Elliott, McDonald's	$	5

❑ 94	B. Elliott, Thunderbat	$	15
❑ 95	J. Tanner, Caterpillar	$	5

Raceway Replicas

1:24

❑ 6	M. Martin, Valvoline 94	$	130
❑ 11	B. Elliott, Budweiser 92	$	130
❑ 27	H. Stricklin, McDonald's 93	$	130
❑ 28	D. Allison, Havoline 93	$	130

Racing Champions

1:24
1991-92
(In black boxes)

❑ 1	J. Gordon, Baby Ruth	$	320
❑ 1	R. Mast, Majik Market	$	40
❑ 2	R. Wallace, AC-Delco	$	40
❑ 2	R. Wallace, Pontiac Excitement	$	40
❑ 3	D. Earnhardt, Goodwrench, Fen. Stick.	$	24
❑ 3	D. Earnhardt, Goodwrench, Tampo Dec.	$	32
❑ 4	E. Irvan, Kodak	$	20
❑ 5	R. Rudd, Tide	$	20
❑ 6	M. Martin, Valvoline	$	20
❑ 7	H. Gant, Morema	$	50
❑ 7	Generic, Easy Off	$	50
❑ 7	Generic, French's	$	60
❑ 7	Generic, Gulf Lite	$	60
❑ 7	J. Hensley, Bojangles	$	50
❑ 7	T. Kendall, Family Channel	$	50
❑ 7	A. Kulwicki, Hooters	$	75
❑ 9	B. Elliott, Melling	$	22
❑ 10	D. Cope, Purolator	$	20
❑ 11	B. Elliott, Amoco	$	22
❑ 15	G. Bodine, Motorcraft	$	20
❑ 15	M. Shepherd, Motorcraft	$	20
❑ 16	W. Dallenbach, Jr., Roush	$	50
❑ 17	D. Waltrip, Western Auto, Fen. Stick.	$	20
❑ 17	D. Waltrip, Western Auto, Tampo	$	22
❑ 18	D. Jarrett, Interstate Batteries	$	20
❑ 18	G. Trammell, Melling	$	20
❑ 21	D. Jarrett, Citgo	$	20
❑ 21	M. Shepherd, Citgo	$	20
❑ 22	S. Marlin, Maxwell House	$	20
❑ 25	K. Schrader, NS Large K	$	30
❑ 25	K. Schrader, NS (No Sponsor)	$	20
❑ 25	B. Venturini, Rain X	$	150
❑ 28	D. Allison, Havoline	$	30
❑ 30	M. Waltrip, Pennzoil	$	20
❑ 33	H. Gant, NS Olds	$	30
❑ 33	H. Gant, NS Chevy	$	30
❑ 36	K. Wallace, Cox Lumber	$	275
❑ 36	K. Wallace, Dirt Devil	$	275
❑ 42	B. Hillin, Mello Yello	$	40
❑ 42	K. Petty, Mello Yello	$	20
❑ 43	R. Petty, STP Blue Wheels	$	22
❑ 49	S. Smith, Ameritron Battery	$	125
❑ 51	Generic, Racing Champions	$	175
❑ 59	A. Belmont, FDP Brakes	$	100
❑ 60	M. Martin, Winn Dixie, Red No.	$	100
❑ 60	M. Martin, Winn Dixie, White No.	$	60
❑ 63	C. Bown, Nescafe	$	150

❑ 66	J. Hensley, TropArtic	$	22
❑ 66	C. Little, TropArtic	$	22
❑ 66	Generic, TropArtic, Red Car	$	20
❑ 66	C. Yarborough, TropArtic	$	20
❑ 68	B. Hamilton, Country Time	$	22
❑ 70	J. D. McDuffie, Son's Auto	$	20
❑ 71	D. Marcis, Big Apple Market	$	20
❑ 75	B. Miller, Food Country	$	150
❑ 83	L. Speed, Purex	$	125
❑ 87	J. Nemechek, Texas Pete	$	150
❑ 94	T. Labonte, Sunoco	$	20
❑ 94	T. Labonte, Sun. Arrow at tire	$	22

Racing Champions

1:24
1993
(In red boxes)

❑ 2	D. Allison, True Value, IROC	$	45
❑ 2	R. Wallace, Pontiac Excitement	$	25
❑ 3	D. Earnhardt, Goodwrench Goodyear White	$	25
❑ 3	D. Earnhardt, Goodwrench Goodyear Yellow	$	25
❑ 3	D. Earnhardt, Goodwrench Mom-n-Pop's	$	25
❑ 4	E. Irvan, Kodak Gold Film	$	20
❑ 4	E. Irvan, Kodak Gold Film Plus	$	20
❑ 5	R. Rudd, Tide Exxon	$	20
❑ 5	R. Rudd, Tide Valvoline	$	20
❑ 6	M. Martin, Valvoline	$	22
❑ 7	A. Kulwicki, Hooters	$	60
❑ 8	S. Marlin, Raybestos	$	20
❑ 8	S. Marlin, Raybestos Doug. Battery	$	22
❑ 10	B. Elliott, True Value, IROC	$	22
❑ 11	B. Elliott, Amoco	$	20
❑ 12	J. Spencer, Meineke	$	20
❑ 14	T. Labonte, Kellogg's	$	20
❑ 15	G. Bodine, Motorcraft	$	20
❑ 17	D. Waltrip, Western Auto	$	20
❑ 18	D. Jarrett, Interstate Batteries	$	20
❑ 21	M. Shepherd, Citgo, Red Pillar Post	$	20
❑ 21	M. Shepherd, Citgo, Tri-Color Pillar Post	$	20
❑ 22	B. Labonte, Maxwell House	$	20
❑ 24	J. Gordon, Du Pont	$	30
❑ 25	K. Schrader, NS	$	40
❑ 26	B. Bodine, Quaker State	$	20
❑ 27	H. Stricklin, McDonald's	$	20
❑ 28	D. Allison, Havoline, Black/Gold	$	30
❑ 28	D. Allison, Havoline, Black/White	$	35
❑ 30	M. Waltrip, Pennzoil	$	40
❑ 42	K. Petty, Mello Yello	$	20
❑ 44	R. Wilson, STP	$	22
❑ 49	S. Smith, Ameritron Battery	$	55
❑ 59	A. Belmont, FDP Brakes	$	75
❑ 60	M. Martin, Winn Dixie	$	22
❑ 75	NDA, Auto Value	$	25
❑ 75	NDA, Factory Stores	$	20
❑ 87	J. Nemechek, Dentyne	$	20
❑ 98	D. Cope, Bojangles	$	20

Racing Champions

1:24
1994

(In red or black boxes)

❏ 0	D. McCabe, Fisher Snow Plows	$	20
❏ 1	R. Mast, Precision Products	$	18
❏ 2	R. Craven, Du Pont	$	18
❏ 2	R. Wallace, Black Ford Oval	$	20
❏ 2	R. Wallace, Blue Ford Oval	$	20
❏ 3	D. Earnhardt, Goodwrench	$	25
❏ 4	S. Marlin, Kodak	$	18
❏ 5	T. Labonte, Kellogg's	$	18
❏ 6	M. Martin, Valvoline Reese's	$	18
❏ 7	G. Bodine, Exide	$	18
❏ 7	H. Gant, Manheim	$	25
❏ 7	A. Kulwicki, Zerex	$	35
❏ 8	J. Burton, Raybestos Goodyear	$	18
❏ 8	J. Burton, Raybestos Hoosier	$	18
❏ 8	K. Wallace, TIC Financial	$	22
❏ 12	C. Allison, Sports Image	$	30
❏ 14	J. Andretti, Kanawha	$	25
❏ 14	T. Labonte, MW Windows	$	18
❏ 15	L. Speed, Quality Care	$	18
❏ 16	C. Chaffin, Dr. Die Cast	$	26
❏ 16	T. Musgrave, Family Channel	$	18
❏ 17	D. Waltrip, Western Auto	$	18
❏ 18	D. Jarrett, Interstate Batteries	$	18
❏ 19	L. Allen, Hooters	$	18
❏ 20	B. Hillin, Fina	$	22
❏ 20	R. LaJoie, Fina	$	22
❏ 21	M. Shepherd, Citgo	$	18
❏ 22	B. Labonte, Maxwell House	$	19
❏ 23	C. Little, Bayer	$	18
❏ 23	H. Stricklin, Smokin' Joe's	$	35
❏ 24	J. Gordon, Brickyard Purple Box	$	45
❏ 24	J. Gordon, Coca-Cola Win	$	50
❏ 24	J. Gordon, Du Pont	$	25
❏ 24	J. Gordon, Du Pont Snickers	$	25
❏ 25	K. Schrader, GMAC	$	35
❏ 26	B. Bodine, Quaker State	$	18
❏ 27	J. Spencer, McDonald's	$	18
❏ 28	E. Irvan, Havoline	$	18
❏ 30	M. Waltrip, Pennzoil	$	18
❏ 31	S. Grissom, Channellock	$	22
❏ 31	T. Peck, Channellock	$	18
❏ 33	H. Gant, NS(No Sponsor)	$	18
❏ 33	H. Gant, Leo Jackson Motor.	$	18
❏ 33	H. Gant, Manheim Auctions	$	30
❏ 33	B. Labonte, Dentyne	$	18
❏ 34	M. McLaughlin, Fiddle Faddle	$	18
❏ 35	S. Robinson, Polaroid Captiva	$	22
❏ 38	E. Sawyer, Ford Credit	$	18
❏ 40	B. Hamilton, Kendall	$	18
❏ 42	K. Petty, Mello Yello	$	18
❏ 44	D. Green, Slim Jim	$	22
❏ 44	B. Hillin, Buss Fuses	$	18
❏ 46	S. Robinson, Polaroid	$	22
❏ 52	K. Schrader, AC-Delco	$	18
❏ 54	R. Pressley, Manheim	$	25
❏ 59	A. Belmont, Metal Arrester	$	25
❏ 59	D. Setzer, Alliance	$	30
❏ 60	M. Martin, Winn Dixie	$	26
❏ 63	J. Bown, Lysol	$	18
❏ 70	J. D. McDuffie, Son's Auto	$	22
❏ 75	T. Bodine, Factory Stores	$	18

❏ 79	D. Rezendes, Lipton Tea	$	22
❏ 83	S. Blakeley, Ramses	$	30
❏ 92	L. Pearson, Stanley Tools	$	18
❏ 94	Generic, Auto Value	$	25
❏ 94	Generic, Brickyard 400, Purple Box	$	22
❏ 97	J. Bessy, Johnson	$	18
❏ 98	D. Cope, Fingerhut	$	18

Racing Champions

1:24
1995 Previews
(In red boxes)

❏ 2	R. Wallace, Ford Motor	$	18
❏ 6	M. Martin, Valvoline	$	18
❏ 7	G. Bodine, Exide Goodyear	$	18
❏ 7	G. Bodine, Exide Hoosier	$	18
❏ 10	R. Rudd, Tide	$	18
❏ 57	J. Keller, Budget Gourmet	$	18
❏ 63	C. Markham, Lysol	$	18
❏ 94	B. Elliott, McDonald's	$	18
❏ 98	J. Mayfield, Fingerhut	$	18

Racing Champions

1:24
1995
(in red boxes)

❏ 2	R. Wallace, Ford Motorsports	$	20
❏ 4	S. Marlin, Kodak	$	18
❏ 4	J. Purvis, Kodak Fun Saver	$	18
❏ 5	T. Labonte, Kellogg's	$	18
❏ 6	T. Houston, Red Devil	$	18
❏ 6	M. Martin, Valvoline	$	18
❏ 7	G. Bodine, Exide	$	18
❏ 8	J. Burton, Raybestos	$	18
❏ 10	R. Rudd, Tide	$	18
❏ 12	D. Cope, Mane and Tail	$	18
❏ 16	T. Musgrave, Family Channel	$	18
❏ 17	D. Waltrip, Western Auto	$	18
❏ 18	B. Labonte, Interstate Batteries	$	18
❏ 24	J. Gordon, Du Pont	$	23
❏ 26	S. Kinser, Quaker State	$	24
❏ 27	L. Allen, Hooters	$	18
❏ 28	D. Jarrett, Havoline	$	18
❏ 40	P. Moise, Dial Purex	$	20
❏ 41	R. Craven, Larry Hedrick	$	18
❏ 60	M. Martin, Winn Dixie	$	20
❏ 90	M. Wallace, Heilig-Meyers	$	18
❏ 94	B. Elliott, McDonald's	$	18
❏ 94	B. Elliott, Thunderbat	$	26

Racing Champions

Super Trucks 1:24
1995

❏ 1	P. J. Jones, Sears DieHard	$	20
❏ 2	D. Ashley, Ultra Wheels	$	20
❏ 06	M. Bliss, Ultra Wheels	$	20
❏ 06	B. Gilliland, Ultra Wheels	$	20
❏ 7	G. Bodine, Exide	$	20
❏ 08	M. Bliss, Ultra Wheels	$	20
❏ 12	R. MacCachren, Venable	$	20

❏ 21	T. Butler, Ortho Green Nose	$	20
❏ 21	T. Butler, Ortho Yellow Nose	$	20
❏ 23	T. J. Clark, ASE Blue	$	20
❏ 23	T. J. Clark, ASE White	$	20
❏ 38	S. Swindell, Channellock	$	20

Racing Champions

1:24

1992-94 Banks

❏ 0	D. McCabe, Fisher Snow Plows	$	30
❏ 1	R. Mast, Precision Products	$	22
❏ 2	W. Burton, Hardee's	$	32
❏ 2	R. Craven, Du Pont	$	22
❏ 2	R. Wallace, Ford Motorsports	$	40
❏ 2	R. Wallace, Pontiac Excitement	$	175
❏ 3	D. Earnhardt, Goodwrench, No. BX	$	40
❏ 3	D. Earnhardt, Goodwrench, no No. BX	$	35
❏ 3	D. Earnhardt, Goodwrench, BGN	$	35
❏ 3	D. Earnhardt, Goodwrench Snap On	$	35
❏ 3	D. Earnhardt, Mom-n-Pop's	$	40
❏ 4	E. Irvan, Kodak	$	32
❏ 4	S. Marlin, Kodak	$	22
❏ 4	S. Marlin, Kodak Fun Saver	$	25
❏ 5	T. Labonte, Kellogg's	$	25
❏ 5	R. Rudd, Tide	$	25
❏ 6	M. Martin, Valvoline	$	30
❏ 6	M. Martin, Valvoline Reese's	$	25
❏ 7	G. Bodine, Exide	$	25
❏ 7	H. Gant, Black Flag	$	45
❏ 7	H. Gant, Easy Off	$	45
❏ 7	H. Gant, French's	$	45
❏ 7	H. Gant, Gulf Lite	$	45
❏ 7	H. Gant, Manheim	$	45
❏ 7	H. Gant, Morema	$	45
❏ 7	H. Gant, Woolite	$	45
❏ 7	J. Hensley, Bojangles	$	25
❏ 7	T. Kendall, Family Channel	$	30
❏ 7	A. Kulwicki, Army	$	50
❏ 7	A. Kulwicki, Hooters	$	180
❏ 7	A. Kulwicki, Zerex	$	80
❏ 8	S. Marlin, Raybestos	$	22
❏ 8	K. Wallace, TIC Financial	$	32
❏ 10	J. Spencer, Kleenex	$	60
❏ 11	B. Elliott, Amoco	$	37
❏ 11	B. Elliott, Budweiser	$	45
❏ 11	B. Elliott, Budweiser Hardy Boys	$	48
❏ 12	C. Allison, Sports Image	$	45
❏ 12	J. Spencer, Meineke	$	65
❏ 14	J. Andretti, Kanawha	$	30
❏ 14	T. Labonte, MW Windows	$	25
❏ 15	G. Bodine, Motorcraft	$	22
❏ 15	L. Speed, Quality Care	$	22
❏ 16	C. Chaffin, Dr. Die Cast	$	25
❏ 16	T. Musgrave, Family Channel	$	25
❏ 17	D. Waltrip, Tide Orange	$	40
❏ 17	D. Waltrip, Tide Primer	$	30
❏ 17	D. Waltrip, Western Auto	$	100
❏ 18	D. Jarrett, Interstate Batteries	$	22
❏ 20	R. LaJoie, Fina	$	32
❏ 20	J. Ruttman, Fina	$	45
❏ 20	J. Ruttman, Fina 520	$	45

❏ 21	M. Shepherd, Cheerwine	$	32
❏ 21	M. Shepherd, Citgo	$	22
❏ 22	B. Labonte, Maxwell House	$	22
❏ 23	C. Little, Bayer	$	22
❏ 24	J. Gordon, Du Pont	$	50
❏ 24	J. Gordon, Du Pont Brickyard	$	70
❏ 24	J. Gordon, Du Pont Coke 600	$	150
❏ 24	J. Gordon, Du Pont Snickers	$	32
❏ 25	H. Sadler, VA. Lovers	$	30
❏ 26	B. Bodine, Quaker State	$	22
❏ 27	H. Stricklin, McDonald's	$	30
❏ 28	D. Allison, Havoline	$	80
❏ 28	D. Allison, Havoline Black/Gold	$	90
❏ 28	D. Allison, Havoline Black/White	$	50
❏ 28	D. Allison, Mac Tools	$	80
❏ 28	E. Irvan, Havoline	$	40
❏ 28	E. Irvan, Mac Tools	$	40
❏ 30	M. Waltrip, Pennzoil	$	22
❏ 31	S. Grissom, Channellock	$	22
❏ 31	T. Peck, Channellock	$	22
❏ 33	H. Gant, Farewell Tour	$	32
❏ 33	H. Gant, Leo Jackson	$	25
❏ 33	H. Gant, Manheim Auctions	$	75
❏ 33	H. Gant, Manheim Auctions, AUTO	$	125
❏ 33	B. Labonte, Dentyne	$	25
❏ 34	M. McLaughlin, Fiddle Faddle	$	22
❏ 35	S. Robinson, Polaroid Captiva	$	30
❏ 38	E. Sawyer, Ford Credit	$	25
❏ 41	E. Irvan, Mac Tools	$	40
❏ 42	K. Petty, Mello Yello	$	30
❏ 43	R. Combs, French's	$	25
❏ 43	W. Dallenbach, STP	$	25
❏ 43	R. Petty, STP	$	50
❏ 44	D. Green, Slim Jim	$	32
❏ 44	B. Hillin, Buss Fuses	$	25
❏ 44	R. Wilson, STP	$	25
❏ 46	S. Robinson, Polaroid	$	30
❏ 51	Generic, Racing Champions	$	135
❏ 52	K. Schrader, AC-Delco	$	25
❏ 52	K. Schrader, Morema	$	35
❏ 54	R. Pressley, Manheim Auctions	$	35
❏ 55	T. Musgrave, US Air	$	50
❏ 59	A. Belmont, Metal Arrester	$	32
❏ 59	R. Pressley, Alliance	$	70
❏ 59	D. Setzer, Alliance	$	40
❏ 60	M. Martin, Winn Dixie 5000	$	55
❏ 60	M. Martin, Winn Dixie 10000	$	32
❏ 63	J. Bown, Lysol	$	22
❏ 70	J. D. McDuffie, Son's Auto	$	30
❏ 71	D. Marcis, Earnhardt Chevy	$	45
❏ 75	T. Bodine, Factory Stores	$	22
❏ 77	G. Sacks, US Air	$	30
❏ 83	S. Blakeley, Ramses	$	35
❏ 87	J. Nemechek, Dentyne	$	25
❏ 92	L. Pearson, Stanley Tools	$	22
❏ 94	Generic, Brickyard 400	$	32
❏ 97	J. Bessey, Auto Palace	$	30
❏ 97	J. Bessey, Johnson AC-Delco	$	30
❏ 98	D. Cope, Bojangles, Black	$	32
❏ 98	D. Cope, Bojangles, Yellow	$	32
❏ 98	J. Ridley, Ford Motorsports	$	40

Racing Champions

1:24
1995 Banks

❏ 2	R. Wallace, Ford Motorsports	$	25
❏ 6	M. Martin, Valvoline	$	25
❏ 7	G. Bodine, Exide	$	25
❏ 8	J. Burton, Raybestos	$	25
❏ 27	L. Allen, Hooters	$	25
❏ 59	D. Setzer, Alliance	$	32
❏ 94	B. Elliott, McDonald's	$	32
❏ 94	B. Elliott, Thunderbat	$	40

Action Racing Collectables

1:16 Pit Wagon Banks
(Formerly known as RCI)
* Varied production from 2,500 to 7,500

❏ 2	R. Wallace, Ford Motor Co.	$	45
❏ 3	D. Earnhardt, Goodwrench	$	65
❏ 3	D. Earnhardt, Goodwrench / 7 Time	$	65
❏ 11	B. Elliott, Budweiser	$	45
❏ 16	T. Musgrave, Family Channel	$	35
❏ 18	D. Jarrett, Interstate Batteries	$	35
❏ 24	J. Gordon, Du Pont	$	70
❏ 28	D. Allison, Havoline	$	50
❏ 28	D. Allison, Havoline Mac Tools	$	40
❏ 28	E. Irvan, Havoline	$	45
❏ 28	E. Irvan, Mac Tools	$	40
❏ 30	M. Waltrip, Pennzoil	$	30
❏ 41	J. Nemechek, Meineke	$	30
❏ 42	K. Petty, Mello Yello	$	35
❏ 51	N. Bonnett, Country Time	$	40

Action Racing Collectables

1:24
(Formerly known as RCI)

❏ 1	R. Mast, Skoal	$	55
❏ 2	R. Craven, Du Pont	$	35
❏ 2	R. Wallace, Ford Motor B	$	90
❏ 2	R. Wallace, MGD	$	45
❏ 2	R. Wallace, MGD B	$	50
❏ 3	D. Earnhardt, Goodwrench LUM B	$	60
❏ 3	D. Earnhardt, Goodwrench 95MC B	$	50
❏ 3	D. Earnhardt, Goodwrench Silver B	$	80
❏ 3	D. Earnhardt, Wrangler 84MC B	$	80
❏ 3	D. Earnhardt, Wrangler 85MC B	$	80
❏ 3	D. Earnhardt, Wrangler 87MC B	$	80
❏ 5	T. Labonte, Kellogg's B	$	100
❏ 11	B. Elliott, Budweiser	$	50
❏ 11	B. Elliott, Budweiser B	$	55
❏ 11	D. Waltrip, Budweiser	$	50
❏ 11	D. Waltrip, Budweiser 85MC B	$	55
❏ 11	D. Waltrip, Budweiser 87MC B	$	55
❏ 12	N. Bonnett, Budweiser 85MC B	$	55
❏ 12	N. Bonnett, Budweiser 87MC B	$	45
❏ 15	L. Speed, Quality Care	$	35
❏ 16	T. Musgrave, Family Channel B	$	100
❏ 21	D. Pearson, Chattanooga Chew B	$	50
❏ 25	K. Schrader, Budweiser B	$	55
❏ 28	E. Irvan, Havoline B Employee	$	125
❏ 28	E. Irvan, Havoline B Retail	$	35

❏ 41	J. Nemechek, Meineke	$	35
❏ 42	K. Petty, Mello Yello	$	35
❏ 51	N. Bonnett, Country Time B	$	55
❏ 94	B. Elliott, Thunderbat B	$	50
❏ 98	D. Cope, Fingerhut	$	35

Action Racing Collectables

1:64
(Formerly known as RCI)
ACR - AC Racing '93 Series
DR - Delco Remy
PLS - Platinum Series
VT - Valvoline Team

❏ 2	R. Craven, Du Pont PLS	$	8
❏ 2	R. Wallace, Ford Motor PLS	$	9
❏ 2	R. Wallace, MGD	$	12
❏ 2	R. Wallace, Pontiac Exc. ACR	$	10
❏ 2	R. Wallace, Pontiac Exc. DR	$	10
❏ 3	D. Earnhardt, Goodwrench ACR	$	14
❏ 3	D. Earnhardt, Goodwrench 94LUM PLS	$	12
❏ 3	D. Earnhardt, Goodwrench 88MC PLS	$	12
❏ 3	D. Earnhardt, Goodwrench 95MC PLS	$	14
❏ 3	D. Earnhardt, Good Silver	$	25
❏ 3	D. Earnhardt, Good Silver PLS	$	20
❏ 3	D. Earnhardt, Wrangler 84MC PLS	$	15
❏ 4	E. Irvan, Kodak ACR	$	9
❏ 4	E. Irvan, Kodak DR	$	8
❏ 5	T. Labonte, Kellogg's PLS	$	8
❏ 6	T. Houston, Roses	$	8
❏ 6	M. Martin, Valvoline VT	$	8
❏ 8	D. Earnhardt, 85Cam. ASA PLS	$	10
❏ 11	B. Elliott, Budweiser PLS	$	14
❏ 11	D. Waltrip, Budweiser PLS	$	14
❏ 12	N. Bonnett, Budweiser PLS	$	14
❏ 15	L. Speed, Quality Care PLS	$	8
❏ 16	W. Dallenbach, Roush VT	$	8
❏ 16	T. Musgrave, Family Channel PLS	$	8
❏ 17	D. Waltrip, Western Auto ACR	$	9
❏ 17	D. Waltrip, Western Auto DR	$	8
❏ 24	J. Gordon, Du Pont ACR	$	16
❏ 24	J. Gordon, Du Pont 94LUM PLS	$	14
❏ 24	J. Gordon, Du Pont 95MC PLS	$	16
❏ 24	J. Gordon, Du Pont VT	$	16
❏ 25	K. Schrader, GMAC ACR	$	9
❏ 25	K. Schrader, GMAC VT	$	8
❏ 25	K. Schrader, Budweiser PLS	$	12
❏ 26	S. Swindell, Bull Hannah P	$	8
❏ 27	T. Richmond, Old Milwaukee	$	12
❏ 28	E. Irvan, Havoline	$	12
❏ 28	D. Jarrett, Texaco PLS	$	12
❏ 35	S. Robinson, Polaroid	$	12
❏ 40	K. Wallace, Dirt Devil ACR	$	9
❏ 41	J. Nemechek, Meineke PLS	$	8
❏ 41	P. Parsons, ACR	$	9
❏ 42	K. Petty, Mello Yello ACR	$	9
❏ 42	K. Petty, Mello Yello PLS	$	8
❏ 46	A. Unser, Jr., Valvoline VT	$	10
❏ 51	N. Bonnett, Country Time PLS	$	14
❏ 93	NDA, Lumina Prototype	$	8
❏ 93	NDA, Pontiac Prototype	$	8
❏ 93	NDA, TB Prototype	$	8

❑ 94	B. Elliott, McDonald's PLS	$	10
❑ 94	B. Elliott, Thunderbat PLS	$	12
❑ 94	C. Elliott, RCI	$	12
❑ 98	D. Cope, Fingerhut PLS	$	8

Action / RCCA

1:24

❑ 2	R. Wallace, Ford Motor Co.	$	80
❑ 2	R. Wallace, MGD	$	60
❑ 3	D. Earnhardt, Goodwrench 94LUM	$	55
❑ 3	D. Earnhardt, Goodwrench 95MC	$	40
❑ 3	D. Earnhardt, Goodwrench Silver	$	85
❑ 18	D. Jarrett, Interstate Batteries	$	40
❑ 25	K. Schrader, Budweiser	$	45
❑ 51	N. Bonnett, Country Time	$	45

Action / RCCA

1:64

CO - Club Only

HO - Hood Open Series

REV - Revell

❑ 1	J. Gordon, Baby Ruth REV	$	17
❑ 2	R. Wallace, Pontiac Excite REV	$	8
❑ 2	R. Wallace, MGD CO	$	18
❑ 2	R. Wallace, MGD HO	$	15
❑ 3	D. Earnhardt, Goodwrench CO	$	32
❑ 3	D. Earnhardt, Goodwrench 94LUM HO	$	20
❑ 3	D. Earnhardt, Goodwrench 95MC HO	$	18
❑ 3	D. Earnhardt, Goodwrench Silver HO	$	22
❑ 3	D. Earnhardt, Wrangler 85MC NB	$	22
❑ 3	D. Earnhardt, Wrangler 87MC FB	$	22
❑ 3	D. Earnhardt Jr., Mom-n-Pop's	$	17
❑ 5	T. Labonte, Kellogg's HO	$	12
❑ 5	R. Rudd, Tide REV P	$	10
❑ 6	M. Martin, Folgers P	$	25
❑ 6	M. Martin, Stroh's Light, 2 cars	$	25
❑ 6	M. Martin, Valvoline HO	$	15
❑ 6	M. Martin, Valvoline REV	$	8
❑ 8	K. Earnhardt, Mom-n-Pop's	$	16
❑ 9	B. Elliott, Melling CO	$	12
❑ 10	D. Cope, Purolator REV	$	10
❑ 11	B. Elliott, Budweiser HO	$	15
❑ 11	D. Waltrip, Budweiser 84MC NB	$	20
❑ 12	N. Bonnett, Budweiser 84MC NB	$	20
❑ 12	H. Stricklin, Raybestos REV	$	8
❑ 15	L. Speed, Quality Care HO	$	15
❑ 15	NDA, Motorcraft REV	$	8
❑ 16	T. Musgrave, Family Channel HO	$	15
❑ 17	D. Waltrip, Western Auto REV CO	$	20
❑ 17	D. Waltrip, Western Auto 94LUM HO	$	12
❑ 18	D. Jarrett, Interstate Batteries HO	$	12
❑ 18	D. Jarrett, Interstate Batteries REV	$	8
❑ 21	D. Pearson, Chattanooga Chew	$	15
❑ 21	D. Pearson, Pearson Racing	$	7
❑ 21	M. Shepherd, Cheer, Morema	$	10
❑ 21	M. Shepherd, Citgo REV	$	8
❑ 22	S. Marlin, Maxwell House REV	$	8
❑ 24	J. Gordon, Du Pont 94LUM HO	$	25
❑ 24	J. Gordon, Du Pont 95MC HO	$	21
❑ 25	R. Craven, 91 BGN Champ P	$	15
❑ 25	K. Schrader, Budweiser HO	$	15

❑ 25	B. Venturini, Rain X REV	$	8
❑ 26	B. Bodine, Quaker State REV	$	8
❑ 27	T. Richmond, Old Milwaukee	$	15
❑ 28	D. Allison, Havoline CO	$	25
❑ 28	D. Allison, Mac Tools P	$	25
❑ 28	D. Allison, Texaco HO Black/Gold	$	16
❑ 28	D. Allison, Texaco HO Black/Orange	$	16
❑ 28	D. Jarrett, Texaco HO	$	15
❑ 30	M. Waltrip, Pennzoil HO	$	12
❑ 30	M. Waltrip, Pennzoil REV	$	8
❑ 36	K. Wallace, Cox Lumber REV	$	8
❑ 36	K. Wallace, Dirt Devil REV	$	8
❑ 38	K. Earnhardt, Mom-n-Pop's	$	16
❑ 42	K. Petty, Mello Yello HO	$	12
❑ 42	K. Petty, Mello Yello REV	$	8
❑ 43	R. Petty, STP REV	$	8
❑ 44	L. Caudill, Army REV	$	8
❑ 51	N. Bonnett, Country Time HO	$	20
❑ 63	C. Bown, Nescafe HO	$	12
❑ 66	J. Hensley, TropArtic REV	$	8
❑ 68	B. Hamilton, Country Time REV	$	8
❑ 87	J. Nemechek, Texas Pete REV	$	8
❑ 89	J. Sauter, Evinrude REV	$	8
❑ 90	B. Hillin, Heilig-Meyers P	$	12
❑ 92	NDA, Circle Track Show P	$	12
❑ 93	M. Wallace, NS REV	$	8
❑ 94	B. Elliott, McDonald's HO	$	15
❑ 94	C. Elliott, NS HO	$	14
❑ 98	D. Cope, Fingerhut HO	$	12
❑ 99	R. Craven, Du Pont REV	$	8

Action / RCCA

1:64

1991 Oldsmobile Series

❑ 20	R. Moroso, Swi. Sweet, 2 cars	$	30
❑ 22	E. Berrier, Greased Lightning	$	8
❑ 22	R. Moroso, Moroso Racing	$	6
❑ 22	R. Moroso, Prestone	$	6
❑ 33	H. Gant, Skoal with mug	$	25
❑ 44	B. Labonte, Penrose	$	8
❑ 44	S. Marlin, Piedmont	$	17
❑ 73	P. Barkdoll, XR-1	$	8
❑ 88	B. Baker, Red Baron	$	13
❑ 91	C. Allison, Mac Tools	$	20
❑ 93	NDA, Christmas Car	$	15

Action / RCCA

1:64

1983-86 T-Bird Series

❑ 7	K. Petty, 7-Eleven	$	12
❑ 9	B. Elliott, Melling	$	20
❑ 15	D. Earnhardt, Wrangler	$	35
❑ 15	R. Rudd, Motorcraft	$	8
❑ 21	B. Baker, Valvoline, V on deck lid	$	8
❑ 21	B. Baker, Valvoline on deck lid	$	20
❑ 21	D. Pearson, Black Bumper	$	20
❑ 21	D. Pearson, Brown Bumper	$	8
❑ 22	B. Allison, Gold Wheels	$	15
❑ 22	B. Allison, Silver Wheels	$	23
❑ 28	D. Allison, Havoline	$	20
❑ 28	C. Yarborough, Hardee's	$	8

❏ 35	A. Kulwicki, Quincy's	$	56
❏ 35	D. May, Hanover Printing	$	8
❏ 57	J. Ridley, Nationwise	$	8
❏ 64	R. Combs, Sunny King, Small Roof No.	$	10
❏ 64	R. Combs, Sunny King, Big Roof No.	$	8
❏ 67	B. Arrington, Arrington Racing	$	8
❏ 70	J. D. McDuffie, Lockhart	$	10
❏ 71	D. Marcis, Shoney's	$	8
❏ 90	J. Donlavey, Chameleon	$	8
❏ 90	K. Schrader, Red Baron	$	16
❏ 90	K. Schrader, Sunny King	$	8
❏ NNO	NDA, Primer, Lumina, Pontiac, HO	$	10

Ertl

1:18

❏ 3	D. Earnhardt, Goodwrench	$	60
❏ 4	E. Irvan, Kodak	$	45
❏ 6	M. Martin, Valvoline	$	45
❏ 7	G. Bodine, Exide GMP	$	65
❏ 7	A. Kulwicki, Army BF	$	90
❏ 7	A. Kulwicki, Hooters BF	$	90
❏ 7	A. Kulwicki, Zerex BF	$	90
❏ 10	D. Cope, Purolator	$	90
❏ 11	B. Elliott, Budweiser	$	45
❏ 12	J. Spencer, Meineke WRC B	$	125
❏ 14	J. Andretti, Kanawha	$	60
❏ 15	G. Bodine, Motorcraft	$	80
❏ 16	C. Chaffin, 31W Insulation	$	55
❏ 17	D. Waltrip, Western Auto	$	45
❏ 18	D. Jarrett, Interstate Batteries	$	40
❏ 20	B. Hamilton, Fina Lube B	$	75
❏ 21	B. Bowsher, Quality Farm	$	70
❏ 21	M. Shepherd, Cheerwine	$	70
❏ 23	J. Spencer, Smokin' Joe's	$	75
❏ 24	J. Gordon, Du Pont WRC B	$	500
❏ 24	J. Gordon, Du Pont WRC B No Serial #	$	140
❏ 26	S. Kinser, Quaker State HO	$	60
❏ 28	D. Allison, Havoline	$	75
❏ 30	M. Waltrip, Pennzoil	$	30
❏ 33	B. Loney, Winnebago	$	60
❏ 42	A. Hillenburg, Budget Gourmet P B	$	75
❏ 42	K. Petty, Mello Yello	$	35
❏ 43	R. Petty, STP	$	50
❏ 44	D. Green, Slim Jim	$	60
❏ 59	A. Belmont, Dr. Die Cast	$	60
❏ 59	C. Chaffin, Dr. Die Cast	$	45
❏ 59	R. Pressley, Alliance	$	350
❏ 59	D. Setzer, Alliance 5000	$	75
❏ 59	D. Setzer, Alliance, 2 car set	$	225
❏ 60	M. Martin, Winn Dixie GMP	$	65
❏ 84	B. Senneker, Lane Auto.	$	70
❏ 87	J. Nemechek, Dent. WRC B	$	175
❏ 98	J. Mayfield, Fingerhut	$	60

Funstuf Pit Row

1:43

❏ Cars (6/11/12/18/21)		$	5
❏ Cars (22/33/49/75/98)		$	5
❏ 1	J. Gordon, Baby Ruth	$	10
❏ 16	W. Dallenbach, Jr., Roush	$	6
❏ 41	G. Sacks, Kellogg's	$	6

❏ 66	J. Hensley, TropArtic	$	5
❏ 66	C. Little, TropArtic	$	5
❏ 83	J. McClure, Collector's World	$	6

Funstuf Pit Row

1:64

WD - Winston decal on fender

❏ Cars (2/4/5/7/8/22/33)		$	3
❏ Cars (55/71/82/98)		$	3
❏ 1	J. Gordon, Baby Ruth	$	5
❏ 11	B. Elliott, Amoco Deck Lid	$	3
❏ 11	B. Elliott, Amoco Hood	$	3
❏ 11	NDA, Baby Ruth	$	3
❏ 12	K. Schultz, Piggly Wiggly	$	5
❏ 15	M. Shepherd, Motorcraft	$	3
❏ 15	M. Shepherd, Motorcraft WD	$	7
❏ 15	NDA, Motorcraft	$	3
❏ 18	D. Jarrett, Interstate Batteries	$	3
❏ 18	NDA, Interstate Batteries	$	3
❏ 20	M. Wallace, Orkin	$	5
❏ 21	D. Jarrett, Citgo	$	3
❏ 21	D. Jarrett, Citgo WD	$	7
❏ 21	M. Shepherd, Citgo	$	3
❏ 23	E. Bierschwale, AutoFinders	$	5
❏ 27	W. Burton, Gaultney	$	5
❏ 41	G. Sacks, Kellogg's	$	5
❏ 43	R. Petty, STP	$	3
❏ 43	R. Petty, STP WD	$	7
❏ 49	S. Smith, Ameritron Battery	$	7
❏ 66	J. Hensley, TropArtic	$	3
❏ 66	C. Little, TropArtic	$	3
❏ 66	L. Speed, TropArtic	$	3
❏ 75	NDA, Dinner Bell	$	3
❏ 75	J. Ruttman, Dinner Bell	$	3
❏ 83	J. McClure, Collector's World	$	5
❏ 94	T. Labonte, Sunoco	$	3
❏ 94	T. Labonte, Sunoco Busch	$	5

Matchbox White Rose

1:64

1990-1992

Super Stars Series 1

BX = Boxed

BL = Blister Pack

❏ 1	J. Gordon, Baby Ruth Red BX92	$	15
❏ 1	J. Gordon, Baby Ruth Orange BX92	$	20
❏ 2	R. Wallace, Penske BL92	$	5
❏ 3	D. Earnhardt, GM BX90	$	43
❏ 3	D. Earnhardt, GM Parts BX91	$	33
❏ 3	D. Earnhardt, Goodwrench BL92	$	15
❏ 3	D. Earnhardt, Mom-n-Pop's PBG92	$	12
❏ 4	E. Irvan, Kodak BL92	$	6
❏ 7	H. Gant, Mac Tools BX92	$	10
❏ 7	J. Hensley, WRC BX92	$	10
❏ 7	A. Kulwicki, Hooters BL92	$	25
❏ 7	A. Kulwicki, Hooters National Fresh BL92	$	16
❏ 8	J. Burton, TIC Financial BX92	$	4
❏ 8	D. Trickle, Snickers BL92	$	4
❏ 9	NDA, Melling BL92	$	4
❏ 10	D. Cope, Purolator BL92	$	4

145

❏ 10	E. Irvan, Mac Tools BX91	$	27
❏ 11	B. Elliott, Amoco BL92	$	4
❏ 12	H. Stricklin, Raybestos BL92	$	4
❏ 15	NDA, Motorcraft BL92	$	4
❏ 15	M. Shepherd, Motorcraft BL92	$	6
❏ 18	D. Jarrett, Interstate Batteries BL92	$	4
❏ 22	S. Marlin, Maxwell House BL92	$	4
❏ 26	B. Bodine, Quaker State BL92	$	4
❏ 28	D. Allison, Havoline BL92	$	20
❏ 28	D. Allison, Havoline MT BL92	$	20
❏ 29	NDA, MB Racing, WRC BX92	$	5
❏ 29	P. Parsons, Parsons BX92	$	32
❏ 30	M. Waltrip, Pennzoil BL92	$	4
❏ 41	J. Smith, White House AJ BL92	$	6
❏ 42	K. Petty, Mello Yello BL92	$	4
❏ 43	R. Petty, STP BL92	$	4
❏ 44	B. Labonte, Penrose BX92	$	8
❏ 44	B. Labonte, Slim Jim BX92	$	8
❏ 48	J. Hylton, Valtrol BL92	$	4
❏ 49	E. Feree, Fergaed Racing BX92	$	4
❏ 55	T. Musgrave, Jasper BL92	$	4
❏ 66	C. Little, Phillips 66 BL92 Red	$	5
❏ 66	NDA, Phillips 66 BL92 Black	$	4
❏ 68	B. Hamilton, Country Time BL92	$	4
❏ 87	J. Nemechek, Texas Pete BX92	$	4
❏ 89	J. Sauter, Evinrude BL92	$	4
❏ 92	NDA, White Rose Coll. BL92	$	45
❏ 92	H. Stricklin, Stanley Tools BX92	$	4

Matchbox White Rose

1:64
1993 Super Stars Series 1
BX = Boxed
BL = Blister Pack

❏ Cars (9/12/14/21/22/25/29/31)		$	4
❏ Cars (40/41/48/71/83/87/94)		$	4
❏ 1	R. Combs, Luxaire BL	$	18
❏ 1	R. Combs, Goody's BX	$	16
❏ 6	M. Martin, Valvoline	$	5
❏ 7	J. Hensley, Bobsled BX	$	9
❏ 7	J. Hensley, Bojangles BL	$	9
❏ 7	J. Hensley, Cellular One BX	$	9
❏ 7	J. Hensley, Family Channel BX	$	9
❏ 7	J. Hensley, Hanes BX	$	9
❏ 7	J. Hensley, Matchbox BX	$	9
❏ 8	J. Burton, TIC Financial BX	$	4
❏ 8	J. Burton, Baby Ruth BX	$	4
❏ 8	S. Marlin, Raybestos BL	$	4
❏ 08	B. Dotter, Dewalt BX	$	4
❏ 24	J. Gordon, Du Pont BL	$	10
❏ 28	D. Allison, Havoline BL	$	18
❏ 32	J. Horton, Active Racing BL	$	4
❏ 32	D. Jarrett, Pic-N-Pay BX	$	4
❏ 69	J. Sparker, WFE Chall. BL	$	12
❏ 93	Generic, White Rose Coll. BL	$	40
❏ 93	Generic, American Zoom PBG	$	10
❏ 98	D. Cope, Bojangles BL	$	4
❏ 98	J. Spencer, Moly Black Gold BL	$	4
❏ 98	R. Craven, Du Pont BX	$	4

Matchbox White Rose

1:64
1994 Super Stars Series 2
BX = Boxed
BL = Blister Pack
FCS - Future Cup Stars '94
SSA - Super Star Awards

❏ Cars (5/6/8/12/15/16)		$	4
❏ Cars (17/19/26/30/32/34)		$	4
❏ Cars (40/41/52/75/92/98)		$	4
❏ 0	J. Burton, TIC Financial FCS BX	$	9
❏ 2	R. Craven, Du Pont BX	$	4
❏ 2	R. Wallace, Ford Motor Co. BX	$	5
❏ 3	D. Earnhardt, Gold LUM SSA BX	$	32
❏ 4	S. Marlin, Kodak BX	$	4
❏ 4	S. Marlin, Kodak Fun Saver BX	$	4
❏ 7	G. Bodine, Exide BX	$	8
❏ 7	H. Gant, Manheim BX	$	4
❏ 23	H. Stricklin, Smokin' Joe's BX	$	20
❏ 24	J. Gordon, Du Pont BX	$	10
❏ 29	P. Parsons, Baltimore CFL BL	$	20
❏ 29	P. Parsons, MB, WRC BX	$	4
❏ 33	H. Gant, Gold LUM SSA BX	$	22
❏ 37	L. Allen, Nat. Fresh FCS BX	$	8
❏ 43	R. Combs, Black Flag BX	$	8
❏ 43	R. Combs, French's Black Flag BL	$	25
❏ 43	R. Combs, French's BX	$	8
❏ 46	S. Robinson, Polaroid BL	$	12
❏ 55	J. Hensley, Petron Plus BL	$	15
❏ 60	M. Martin, Winn Dixie BX	$	8
❏ 66	M. Wallace, Duron Paint FCS BX	$	8
❏ 87	J. Nemechek, Cintas FCS BX	$	8
❏ 94	Generic, MB, WRC BL	$	25
❏ 94	Generic, Series 2, Preview BX	$	8

Matchbox White Rose

1:64
1995 Super Stars Series 2

❏ 2	R. Craven, Du Pont	$	5
❏ 8	J. Burton, Raybestos Gold	$	20
❏ 11	B. Bodine, Lowe's	$	5
❏ 12	D. Cope, Straight Arrow	$	5
❏ 26	S. Kinser, Quaker State	$	5
❏ 72	T. Leslie, Detroit Gasket	$	5
❏ 74	J. Benson Jr., Lipton Tea	$	5
❏ 90	M. Wallace, Heilig-Meyers	$	5
❏ 94	B. Elliott, McDonald's	$	5
❏ 94	B. Elliott, Thunderbat	$	15
❏ 95	J. Tanner, Caterpillar	$	5

Raceway Replicas

1:24

❏ 6	M. Martin, Valvoline 94	$	130
❏ 11	B. Elliott, Budweiser 92	$	130
❏ 27	H. Stricklin, McDonald's 93	$	130
❏ 28	D. Allison, Havoline 93	$	130

Racing Champions

1:24
1991-92

(In black boxes)

❑ 1	J. Gordon, Baby Ruth	$	320
❑ 1	R. Mast, Majik Market	$	40
❑ 2	R. Wallace, AC-Delco	$	40
❑ 2	R. Wallace, Pontiac Excitement	$	40
❑ 3	D. Earnhardt, Goodwrench, Fen. Stick.	$	24
❑ 3	D. Earnhardt, Goodwrench, Tampo Dec.	$	32
❑ 4	E. Irvan, Kodak	$	20
❑ 5	R. Rudd, Tide	$	20
❑ 6	M. Martin, Valvoline	$	20
❑ 7	H. Gant, Morema	$	50
❑ 7	Generic, Easy Off	$	50
❑ 7	Generic, French's	$	60
❑ 7	Generic, Gulf Lite	$	60
❑ 7	J. Hensley, Bojangles	$	50
❑ 7	T. Kendall, Family Channel	$	50
❑ 7	A. Kulwicki, Hooters	$	75
❑ 9	B. Elliott, Melling	$	22
❑ 10	D. Cope, Purolator	$	20
❑ 11	B. Elliott, Amoco	$	22
❑ 15	G. Bodine, Motorcraft	$	20
❑ 15	M. Shepherd, Motorcraft	$	20
❑ 16	W. Dallenbach, Jr., Roush	$	50
❑ 17	D. Waltrip, Western Auto, Fen. Stick.	$	20
❑ 17	D. Waltrip, Western Auto, Tampo	$	22
❑ 18	D. Jarrett, Interstate Batteries	$	20
❑ 18	G. Trammell, Melling	$	20
❑ 21	D. Jarrett, Citgo	$	20
❑ 21	M. Shepherd, Citgo	$	20
❑ 22	S. Marlin, Maxwell House	$	20
❑ 25	K. Schrader, NS Large K	$	30
❑ 25	K. Schrader, NS (No Sponsor)	$	20
❑ 25	B. Venturini, Rain X	$	150
❑ 28	D. Allison, Havoline	$	30
❑ 30	M. Waltrip, Pennzoil	$	20
❑ 33	H. Gant, NS Olds	$	30
❑ 33	H. Gant, NS Chevy	$	30
❑ 36	K. Wallace, Cox Lumber	$	275
❑ 36	K. Wallace, Dirt Devil	$	275
❑ 42	B. Hillin, Mello Yello	$	40
❑ 42	K. Petty, Mello Yello	$	20
❑ 43	R. Petty, STP Blue Wheels	$	22
❑ 49	S. Smith, Ameritron Battery	$	125
❑ 51	Generic, Racing Champions	$	175
❑ 59	A. Belmont, FDP Brakes	$	100
❑ 60	M. Martin, Winn Dixie, Red No.	$	100
❑ 60	M. Martin, Winn Dixie, White No.	$	60
❑ 63	C. Bown, Nescafe	$	150
❑ 66	J. Hensley, TropArtic	$	22
❑ 66	C. Little, TropArtic	$	22
❑ 66	Generic, TropArtic, Red Car	$	20
❑ 66	C. Yarborough, TropArtic	$	20
❑ 68	B. Hamilton, Country Time	$	22
❑ 70	J. D. McDuffie, Son's Auto	$	20
❑ 71	D. Marcis, Big Apple Market	$	20
❑ 75	B. Miller, Food Country	$	150
❑ 83	L. Speed, Purex	$	125
❑ 87	J. Nemechek, Texas Pete	$	150
❑ 94	T. Labonte, Sunoco	$	20
❑ 94	T. Labonte, Sun. Arrow at tire	$	22

Racing Champions

1:24
1993
(In red boxes)

❑ 2	D. Allison, True Value, IROC	$	45
❑ 2	R. Wallace, Pontiac Excitement	$	25
❑ 3	D. Earnhardt, Goodwrench Goodyear White	$	25
❑ 3	D. Earnhardt, Goodwrench Goodyear Yellow	$	25
❑ 3	D. Earnhardt, Goodwrench Mom-n-Pop's	$	25
❑ 4	E. Irvan, Kodak Gold Film	$	20
❑ 4	E. Irvan, Kodak Gold Film Plus	$	20
❑ 5	R. Rudd, Tide Exxon	$	20
❑ 5	R. Rudd, Tide Valvoline	$	20
❑ 6	M. Martin, Valvoline	$	22
❑ 7	A. Kulwicki, Hooters	$	60
❑ 8	S. Marlin, Raybestos	$	20
❑ 8	S. Marlin, Raybestos Doug. Battery	$	22
❑ 10	B. Elliott, True Value, IROC	$	22
❑ 11	B. Elliott, Amoco	$	20
❑ 12	J. Spencer, Meineke	$	20
❑ 14	T. Labonte, Kellogg's	$	20
❑ 15	G. Bodine, Motorcraft	$	20
❑ 17	D. Waltrip, Western Auto	$	20
❑ 18	D. Jarrett, Interstate Batteries	$	20
❑ 21	M. Shepherd, Citgo, Red Pillar Post	$	20
❑ 21	M. Shepherd, Citgo, Tri-Color Pillar Post	$	20
❑ 22	B. Labonte, Maxwell House	$	20
❑ 24	J. Gordon, Du Pont	$	30
❑ 25	K. Schrader, NS	$	40
❑ 26	B. Bodine, Quaker State	$	20
❑ 27	H. Stricklin, McDonald's	$	20
❑ 28	D. Allison, Havoline, Black/Gold	$	30
❑ 28	D. Allison, Havoline, Black/White	$	35
❑ 30	M. Waltrip, Pennzoil	$	40
❑ 42	K. Petty, Mello Yello	$	20
❑ 44	R. Wilson, STP	$	22
❑ 49	S. Smith, Ameritron Battery	$	55
❑ 59	A. Belmont, FDP Brakes	$	75
❑ 60	M. Martin, Winn Dixie	$	22
❑ 75	NDA, Auto Value	$	25
❑ 75	NDA, Factory Stores	$	20
❑ 87	J. Nemechek, Dentyne	$	20
❑ 98	D. Cope, Bojangles	$	20

Racing Champions

1:24
1994
(In red or black boxes)

❑ 0	D. McCabe, Fisher Snow Plows	$	20
❑ 1	R. Mast, Precision Products	$	18
❑ 2	R. Craven, Du Pont	$	18
❑ 2	R. Wallace, Black Ford Oval	$	20
❑ 2	R. Wallace, Blue Ford Oval	$	20
❑ 3	D. Earnhardt, Goodwrench	$	25
❑ 4	S. Marlin, Kodak	$	18
❑ 5	T. Labonte, Kellogg's	$	18
❑ 6	M. Martin, Valvoline Reese's	$	18
❑ 7	G. Bodine, Exide	$	18
❑ 7	H. Gant, Manheim	$	25
❑ 7	A. Kulwicki, Zerex	$	35

147

❑ 8	J. Burton, Raybestos Goodyear	$	18
❑ 8	J. Burton, Raybestos Hoosier	$	18
❑ 8	K. Wallace, TIC Financial	$	22
❑ 12	C. Allison, Sports Image	$	30
❑ 14	J. Andretti, Kanawha	$	25
❑ 14	T. Labonte, MW Windows	$	18
❑ 15	L. Speed, Quality Care	$	18
❑ 16	C. Chaffin, Dr. Die Cast	$	26
❑ 16	T. Musgrave, Family Channel	$	18
❑ 17	D. Waltrip, Western Auto	$	18
❑ 18	D. Jarrett, Interstate Batteries	$	18
❑ 19	L. Allen, Hooters	$	18
❑ 20	B. Hillin, Fina	$	22
❑ 20	R. LaJoie, Fina	$	22
❑ 21	M. Shepherd, Citgo	$	18
❑ 22	B. Labonte, Maxwell House	$	19
❑ 23	C. Little, Bayer	$	18
❑ 23	H. Stricklin, Smokin' Joe's	$	35
❑ 24	J. Gordon, Brickyard Purple Box	$	45
❑ 24	J. Gordon, Coca-Cola Win	$	50
❑ 24	J. Gordon, Du Pont	$	25
❑ 24	J. Gordon, Du Pont Snickers	$	25
❑ 25	K. Schrader, GMAC	$	35
❑ 26	B. Bodine, Quaker State	$	18
❑ 27	J. Spencer, McDonald's	$	18
❑ 28	E. Irvan, Havoline	$	18
❑ 30	M. Waltrip, Pennzoil	$	18
❑ 31	S. Grissom, Channellock	$	22
❑ 31	T. Peck, Channellock	$	18
❑ 33	H. Gant, NS(No Sponsor)	$	18
❑ 33	H. Gant, Leo Jackson Motor.	$	18
❑ 33	H. Gant, Manheim Auctions	$	30
❑ 33	B. Labonte, Dentyne	$	18
❑ 34	M. McLaughlin, Fiddle Faddle	$	18
❑ 35	S. Robinson, Polaroid Captiva	$	22
❑ 38	E. Sawyer, Ford Credit	$	18
❑ 40	B. Hamilton, Kendall	$	18
❑ 42	K. Petty, Mello Yello	$	18
❑ 44	D. Green, Slim Jim	$	22
❑ 44	B. Hillin, Buss Fuses	$	18
❑ 46	S. Robinson, Polaroid	$	22
❑ 52	K. Schrader, AC-Delco	$	18
❑ 54	R. Pressley, Manheim	$	25
❑ 59	A. Belmont, Metal Arrester	$	25
❑ 59	D. Setzer, Alliance	$	30
❑ 60	M. Martin, Winn Dixie	$	26
❑ 63	J. Bown, Lysol	$	18
❑ 70	J. D. McDuffie, Son's Auto	$	22
❑ 75	T. Bodine, Factory Stores	$	18
❑ 79	D. Rezendes, Lipton Tea	$	22
❑ 83	S. Blakeley, Ramses	$	30
❑ 92	L. Pearson, Stanley Tools	$	18
❑ 94	Generic, Auto Value	$	25
❑ 94	Generic, Brickyard 400, Purple Box	$	22
❑ 97	J. Bessy, Johnson	$	18
❑ 98	D. Cope, Fingerhut	$	18

Racing Champions

1:24
1995 Previews
(In red boxes)

❑ 2	R. Wallace, Ford Motor	$	18

❑ 6	M. Martin, Valvoline	$	18
❑ 7	G. Bodine, Exide Goodyear	$	18
❑ 7	G. Bodine, Exide Hoosier	$	18
❑ 10	R. Rudd, Tide	$	18
❑ 57	J. Keller, Budget Gourmet	$	18
❑ 63	C. Markham, Lysol	$	18
❑ 94	B. Elliott, McDonald's	$	18
❑ 98	J. Mayfield, Fingerhut	$	18

Racing Champions

1:24
1995
(In red boxes)

❑ 2	R. Wallace, Ford Motorsports	$	20
❑ 4	S. Marlin, Kodak	$	18
❑ 4	J. Purvis, Kodak Fun Saver	$	18
❑ 5	T. Labonte, Kellogg's	$	18
❑ 6	T. Houston, Red Devil	$	18
❑ 6	M. Martin, Valvoline	$	18
❑ 7	G. Bodine, Exide	$	18
❑ 8	J. Burton, Raybestos	$	18
❑ 10	R. Rudd, Tide	$	18
❑ 12	D. Cope, Mane and Tail	$	18
❑ 16	T. Musgrave, Family Channel	$	18
❑ 17	D. Waltrip, Western Auto	$	18
❑ 18	B. Labonte, Interstate Batteries	$	18
❑ 24	J. Gordon, Du Pont	$	23
❑ 26	S. Kinser, Quaker State	$	24
❑ 27	L. Allen, Hooters	$	18
❑ 28	D. Jarrett, Havoline	$	18
❑ 40	P. Moise, Dial Purex	$	20
❑ 41	R. Craven, Larry Hedrick	$	18
❑ 60	M. Martin, Winn Dixie	$	20
❑ 90	M. Wallace, Heilig-Meyers	$	18
❑ 94	B. Elliott, McDonald's	$	18
❑ 94	B. Elliott, Thunderbat	$	26

Racing Champions

Super Trucks 1:24
1995

❑ 1	P. J. Jones, Sears DieHard	$	20
❑ 2	D. Ashley, Ultra Wheels	$	20
❑ 06	M. Bliss, Ultra Wheels	$	20
❑ 06	B. Gilliland, Ultra Wheels	$	20
❑ 7	G. Bodine, Exide	$	20
❑ 08	M. Bliss, Ultra Wheels	$	20
❑ 12	R. MacCachren, Venable	$	20
❑ 21	T. Butler, Ortho Green Nose	$	20
❑ 21	T. Butler, Ortho Yellow Nose	$	20
❑ 23	T. J. Clark, ASE Blue	$	20
❑ 23	T. J. Clark, ASE White	$	20
❑ 38	S. Swindell, Channellock	$	20

Racing Champions

1:24
1992-94 Banks

❑ 0	D. McCabe, Fisher Snow Plows	$	30
❑ 1	R. Mast, Precision Products	$	22
❑ 2	W. Burton, Hardee's	$	32
❑ 2	R. Craven, Du Pont	$	22

❏ 2	R. Wallace, Ford Motorsports	$ 40
❏ 2	R. Wallace, Pontiac Excitement	$ 175
❏ 3	D. Earnhardt, Goodwrench, No. BX	$ 40
❏ 3	D. Earnhardt, Goodwrench, no No. BX	$ 35
❏ 3	D. Earnhardt, Goodwrench, BGN	$ 35
❏ 3	D. Earnhardt, Goodwrench Snap On	$ 35
❏ 3	D. Earnhardt, Mom-n-Pop's	$ 40
❏ 4	E. Irvan, Kodak	$ 32
❏ 4	S. Marlin, Kodak	$ 22
❏ 4	S. Marlin, Kodak Fun Saver	$ 25
❏ 5	T. Labonte, Kellogg's	$ 25
❏ 5	R. Rudd, Tide	$ 25
❏ 6	M. Martin, Valvoline	$ 30
❏ 6	M. Martin, Valvoline Reese's	$ 25
❏ 7	G. Bodine, Exide	$ 25
❏ 7	H. Gant, Black Flag	$ 45
❏ 7	H. Gant, Easy Off	$ 45
❏ 7	H. Gant, French's	$ 45
❏ 7	H. Gant, Gulf Lite	$ 45
❏ 7	H. Gant, Manheim	$ 45
❏ 7	H. Gant, Morema	$ 45
❏ 7	H. Gant, Woolite	$ 45
❏ 7	J. Hensley, Bojangles	$ 25
❏ 7	T. Kendall, Family Channel	$ 30
❏ 7	A. Kulwicki, Army	$ 50
❏ 7	A. Kulwicki, Hooters	$ 180
❏ 7	A. Kulwicki, Zerex	$ 80
❏ 8	S. Marlin, Raybestos	$ 22
❏ 8	K. Wallace, TIC Financial	$ 32
❏ 10	J. Spencer, Kleenex	$ 60
❏ 11	B. Elliott, Amoco	$ 37
❏ 11	B. Elliott, Budweiser	$ 45
❏ 11	B. Elliott, Budweiser Hardy Boys	$ 48
❏ 12	C. Allison, Sports Image	$ 45
❏ 12	J. Spencer, Meineke	$ 65
❏ 14	J. Andretti, Kanawha	$ 30
❏ 14	T. Labonte, MW Windows	$ 25
❏ 15	G. Bodine, Motorcraft	$ 22
❏ 15	L. Speed, Quality Care	$ 22
❏ 16	C. Chaffin, Dr. Die Cast	$ 25
❏ 16	T. Musgrave, Family Channel	$ 25
❏ 17	D. Waltrip, Tide Orange	$ 40
❏ 17	D. Waltrip, Tide Primer	$ 30
❏ 17	D. Waltrip, Western Auto	$ 100
❏ 18	D. Jarrett, Interstate Batteries	$ 22
❏ 20	R. LaJoie, Fina	$ 32
❏ 20	J. Ruttman, Fina	$ 45
❏ 20	J. Ruttman, Fina 520	$ 45
❏ 21	M. Shepherd, Cheerwine	$ 32
❏ 21	M. Shepherd, Citgo	$ 22
❏ 22	B. Labonte, Maxwell House	$ 22
❏ 23	C. Little, Bayer	$ 22
❏ 24	J. Gordon, Du Pont	$ 50
❏ 24	J. Gordon, Du Pont Brickyard	$ 70
❏ 24	J. Gordon, Du Pont Coke 600	$ 150
❏ 24	J. Gordon, Du Pont Snickers	$ 32
❏ 25	H. Sadler, VA. Lovers	$ 30
❏ 26	B. Bodine, Quaker State	$ 22
❏ 27	H. Stricklin, McDonald's	$ 30
❏ 28	D. Allison, Havoline	$ 80
❏ 28	D. Allison, Havoline Black/Gold	$ 90
❏ 28	D. Allison, Havoline Black/White	$ 50
❏ 28	D. Allison, Mac Tools	$ 80
❏ 28	E. Irvan, Havoline	$ 40
❏ 28	E. Irvan, Mac Tools	$ 40
❏ 30	M. Waltrip, Pennzoil	$ 22
❏ 31	S. Grissom, Channellock	$ 22
❏ 31	T. Peck, Channellock	$ 22
❏ 33	H. Gant, Farewell Tour	$ 32
❏ 33	H. Gant, Leo Jackson	$ 25
❏ 33	H. Gant, Manheim Auctions	$ 75
❏ 33	H. Gant, Manheim Auctions, AUTO	$ 125
❏ 33	B. Labonte, Dentyne	$ 25
❏ 34	M. McLaughlin, Fiddle Faddle	$ 22
❏ 35	S. Robinson, Polaroid Captiva	$ 30
❏ 38	E. Sawyer, Ford Credit	$ 25
❏ 41	E. Irvan, Mac Tools	$ 40
❏ 42	K. Petty, Mello Yello	$ 30
❏ 43	R. Combs, French's	$ 25
❏ 43	W. Dallenbach, STP	$ 25
❏ 43	R. Petty, STP	$ 50
❏ 44	D. Green, Slim Jim	$ 32
❏ 44	B. Hillin, Buss Fuses	$ 25
❏ 44	R. Wilson, STP	$ 25
❏ 46	S. Robinson, Polaroid	$ 30
❏ 51	Generic, Racing Champions	$ 135
❏ 52	K. Schrader, AC-Delco	$ 25
❏ 52	K. Schrader, Morema	$ 35
❏ 54	R. Pressley, Manheim Auctions	$ 35
❏ 55	T. Musgrave, US Air	$ 50
❏ 59	A. Belmont, Metal Arrester	$ 32
❏ 59	R. Pressley, Alliance	$ 70
❏ 59	D. Setzer, Alliance	$ 40
❏ 60	M. Martin, Winn Dixie 5000	$ 55
❏ 60	M. Martin, Winn Dixie 10000	$ 32
❏ 63	J. Bown, Lysol	$ 22
❏ 70	J. D. McDuffie, Son's Auto	$ 30
❏ 71	D. Marcis, Earnhardt Chevy	$ 45
❏ 75	T. Bodine, Factory Stores	$ 22
❏ 77	G. Sacks, US Air	$ 30
❏ 83	S. Blakeley, Ramses	$ 35
❏ 87	J. Nemechek, Dentyne	$ 25
❏ 92	L. Pearson, Stanley Tools	$ 22
❏ 94	Generic, Brickyard 400	$ 32
❏ 97	J. Bessey, Auto Palace	$ 30
❏ 97	J. Bessey, Johnson AC-Delco	$ 30
❏ 98	D. Cope, Bojangles, Black	$ 32
❏ 98	D. Cope, Bojangles, Yellow	$ 32
❏ 98	J. Ridley, Ford Motorsports	$ 40

Racing Champions

1:24
1995 Banks

❏ 2	R. Wallace, Ford Motorsports	$ 25
❏ 6	M. Martin, Valvoline	$ 25
❏ 7	G. Bodine, Exide	$ 25
❏ 8	J. Burton, Raybestos	$ 25
❏ 27	L. Allen, Hooters	$ 25
❏ 59	D. Setzer, Alliance	$ 32
❏ 94	B. Elliott, McDonald's	$ 32
❏ 94	B. Elliott, Thunderbat	$ 40

Racing Champions

1:43
1991

❏ Cars (4/9/11/15/18/21/22/25)		$	6
❏ Cars (36/42/43/66/70/72/89)		$	6
❏ 2	R. Wallace, Pontiac Excitement	$	8
❏ 6	M. Martin, Valvoline	$	8

Racing Champions

1:43
1992

❏ Cars (1/5/11/18/30/66/72)		$	6
❏ 3	D. Earnhardt, Goodwrench	$	12
❏ 7	A. Kulwicki, Hooters	$	32
❏ 17	D. Waltrip, Western Auto	$	6
❏ 17	D. Waltrip, Western Auto P	$	6
❏ 28	D. Allison, Havoline	$	20

Racing Champions

1:43
1993

❏ Cars (4/5/11/14/15/17/21)		$	6
❏ Cars (26/27/33/42/44)		$	6
❏ 2	R. Wallace, Pontiac Excitement	$	8
❏ 3	D. Earnhardt, Goodwrench	$	12
❏ 6	M. Martin, Valvoline	$	8
❏ 7	A. Kulwicki, Hooters BX	$	20
❏ 8	S. Marlin, Raybestos	$	20
❏ 24	J. Gordon, Du Pont	$	15
❏ 25	B. Venturini, Rain X	$	12
❏ 28	D. Allison, Havoline	$	12
❏ 51	Generic, Chevy Primer	$	12
❏ 51	Generic, Ford Primer	$	12
❏ 51	Generic, Pontiac Primer	$	12
❏ 59	A. Belmont, FDP Brakes	$	12
❏ 60	M. Martin, Winn Dixie	$	10

Racing Champions Premier

1:43
1993
(In black boxes)

❏ 2	W. Burton, Hardee's	$	18
❏ 3	D. Earnhardt, Goodwrench	$	33
❏ 5	R. Rudd, Tide	$	14
❏ 6	M. Martin, Valvoline	$	14
❏ 7	A. Kulwicki, Hooters	$	58
❏ 8	S. Marlin, Raybestos	$	14
❏ 11	B. Elliott, Amoco	$	14
❏ 11	B. Elliott, Budweiser	$	25
❏ 17	D. Waltrip, Western Auto	$	14
❏ 24	J. Gordon, Du Pont	$	35
❏ 27	H. Stricklin, McDonald's	$	14
❏ 28	D. Allison, Havoline	$	30
❏ 28	D. Allison, Havoline, Black/White	$	30
❏ 28	E. Irvan, Havoline	$	22
❏ 33	H. Gant, Skoal	$	14
❏ 42	K. Petty, Mello Yello	$	14
❏ 59	R. Pressley, Alliance	$	25
❏ 60	M. Martin, Winn Dixie	$	25
❏ 97	J. Bessey, AC-Delco	$	16
❏ 98	D. Cope, Bojangles RCCA	$	40

Racing Champions

1:43
1994

❏ Cars (1/4/5/10/19/26/42)		$	5
❏ 24	J. Gordon, Du Pont	$	15
❏ 24	J. Gordon, Du Pont Coke Win	$	30
❏ 33	H. Gant, Farewell Tour	$	16
❏ 33	H. Gant, Leo Jackson	$	5
❏ 60	M. Martin, Winn Dixie	$	10

Racing Champions Premier

1:43
1994
(In black boxes)

❏ 1	R. Mast, Precision Products	$	15
❏ 2	R. Wallace, Ford Motorsports	$	16
❏ 3	D. Earnhardt, Goodwrench	$	20
❏ 4	S. Marlin, Kodak	$	15
❏ 5	T. Labonte, Kellogg's	$	15
❏ 6	M. Martin, Valvoline	$	18
❏ 7	H. Gant, Manheim	$	25
❏ 7	J. Hensley, Bojangles	$	20
❏ 7	T. Kendall, Family Channel	$	20
❏ 7	A. Kulwicki, Army	$	25
❏ 7	A. Kulwicki, Zerex	$	25
❏ 12	C. Allison, Sports Image	$	20
❏ 15	L. Speed, Quality Care	$	15
❏ 16	T. Musgrave, Family Channel	$	15
❏ 21	M. Shepherd, Cheerwine	$	20
❏ 22	B. Labonte, Maxwell House	$	15
❏ 24	J. Gordon, Du Pont Snickers	$	20
❏ 25	K. Schrader, GMAC	$	15
❏ 26	B. Bodine, Quaker State	$	15
❏ 28	E. Irvan, Havoline	$	20
❏ 28	E. Irvan, Mac Tools	$	25
❏ 30	M. Waltrip, Pennzoil	$	15
❏ 33	H. Gant, Farewell Tour	$	16
❏ 33	H. Gant, Leo Jackson	$	15
❏ 59	D. Setzer, Alliance	$	20
❏ 60	M. Martin, Winn Dixie	$	20
❏ 77	G. Sacks, US Air	$	18

Racing Champions

1:64
1989 Flat Bottom

❏ 3	D. Earnhardt, Goodwrench	$	135
❏ 9	B. Elliott, Motorcraft, Melling	$	90
❏ 16	L. Pearson, No Sponsor	$	45
❏ 28	D. Allison, Havoline	$	100
❏ 30	M. Waltrip, Country Time	$	50
❏ 94	S. Marlin, Sunoco	$	50

Racing Champions

1:64
1990
(add $5-$10 for rubber wheels)
* Additional variations to list below

❏ 1	T. Labonte, Olds	$	40
❏ 3	D. Earnhardt, Goodwrench on trunk	$	140
❏ 3	D. Earnhardt, GM Performance Parts	$	40

#	Description		Price
❑ 9	B. Elliott, Orange/Blue Stripe, No Melling	$	120
❑ 9	B. Elliott, Orange/Blue Stripe with Melling	$	35
❑ 9	B. Elliott, Red/Blue Stripe with Melling	$	45
❑ 10	D. Cope, Chevy Lumina	$	75
❑ 14	A. J. Foyt, Buick	$	70
❑ 14	A. J. Foyt, Chevy Lumina	$	70
❑ 14	A. J. Foyt, Old Pontiac	$	50
❑ 14	A. J. Foyt, Olds	$	35
❑ 14	A. J. Foyt, Pontiac	$	35
❑ 15	M. Shepherd, Red White	$	25
❑ 15	M. Shepherd, Red Cream	$	30
❑ 16	L. Pearson, Buick, White Bumper	$	125
❑ 16	L. Pearson, Buick, Brown Bumper, Script	$	35
❑ 16	L. Pearson, Buick, Brown Bumper, Print	$	20
❑ 16	L. Pearson, Lumina, Brown Bumper	$	90
❑ 16	L. Pearson, Old Pontiac, Brown Bumper	$	90
❑ 16	L. Pearson, Olds, Brown Bumper	$	90
❑ 16	L. Pearson, Pontiac, Brown Bumper	$	20
❑ 20	R. Moroso, Red Stripe	$	40*
❑ 21	N. Bonnett, Citgo	$	30
❑ 21	N. Bonnett, No Citgo	$	40
❑ 26	K. Bernstein, Buick	$	20
❑ 26	K. Bernstein, Chevy Lumina	$	50
❑ 26	K. Bernstein, Old Pontiac	$	50
❑ 26	K. Bernstein, Olds	$	40
❑ 27	R. Wallace, Old Pontiac, MGD	$	90
❑ 27	R. Wallace, Olds	$	100
❑ 27	R. Wallace, Pontiac, MGD	$	60
❑ 27	R. Wallace, Pontiac, Miller	$	60
❑ 27	R. Wallace, Pontiac, Silver Decals	$	80
❑ 28	D. Allison, Black/White	$	90
❑ 28	D. Allison, Black/no name	$	50
❑ 30	M. Waltrip, Country Time	$	60*
❑ 30	M. Waltrip, Maxwell House	$	25*
❑ 33	H. Gant, Pontiac	$	30
❑ 42	K. Petty, Buick, Blue/White	$	125
❑ 42	K. Petty, Lumina, Blue/White	$	125
❑ 42	K. Petty, Old Pontiac, Blue/White	$	125
❑ 42	K. Petty, Olds, Blue/White	$	125
❑ 42	K. Petty, Sabco on Deck Lid	$	30
❑ 42	K. Petty, Without Sabco, Blue/Pink	$	30
❑ 43	R. Petty, Pontiac	$	40
❑ 91	C. Friedman, Winston Cup Scene	$	25
❑ 94	S. Marlin, Buick	$	90
❑ 94	S. Marlin, Chevy Lumina	$	75
❑ 94	S. Marlin, Old Pontiac	$	90
❑ 94	S. Marlin, Olds	$	20

Racing Champions

1:64
1991
EB - Earnhardt on the back of the blister pack
NP - NASCAR properties on stand
PB - Petty on the back of the blister pack

#	Description		Price
❑ 1	T. Labonte, Olds, EB	$	15
❑ 1	T. Labonte, Olds, NP	$	35
❑ 1	T. Labonte, Olds, PB	$	15
❑ 1	R. Mast, Buick, PB	$	6
❑ 1	R. Mast, Olds, PB	$	5
❑ 2	R. Wallace, Pontiac, EB	$	15
❑ 2	R. Wallace, Pontiac, PB	$	10
❑ 3	D. Earnhardt, Chevy Lumina, EB	$	45
❑ 3	D. Earnhardt, Chevy Lumina, NP	$	75
❑ 3	D. Earnhardt, Chevy Lumina, PB	$	30
❑ 4	E. Irvan, Kodak, PB	$	5
❑ 5	J. Fogelman, Chevy Lumina, PB	$	5
❑ 9	B. Elliott, Ford, PB	$	5
❑ 9	B. Elliott, Ford, EB 1/2 Blue	$	25
❑ 9	B. Elliott, Ford, EB 3/4 Blue	$	15
❑ 9	B. Elliott, Old Ford, Orange/White, EB	$	20
❑ 9	B. Elliott, Old Ford, Orange/White, NP	$	35
❑ 10	D. Cope, 2 Checkered Rows, EB	$	6
❑ 10	D. Cope, 3 Checkered Rows, EB	$	20
❑ 10	D. Cope, 2 Checkered Rows, PB	$	5
❑ 10	D. Cope, 3 Checkered Rows, PB	$	15
❑ 11	G. Bodine, Ford, EB	$	5
❑ 11	G. Bodine, Ford, PB	$	5
❑ 12	B. Allison, Buick, PB	$	5
❑ 12	H. Stricklin, Buick, PB	$	5
❑ 12	H. Stricklin, Chevy Lumina, PB	$	6
❑ 14	A. J. Foyt, Buick, PB	$	20
❑ 14	A. J. Foyt, Olds, EB	$	20
❑ 14	A. J. Foyt, Olds, NP	$	35
❑ 14	A. J. Foyt, Olds, PB	$	10
❑ 15	M. Shepherd, Ford, Red, EB	$	10
❑ 15	M. Shepherd, Ford, Red/White, EB	$	15
❑ 15	M. Shepherd, Ford, PB	$	5
❑ 15	M. Shepherd, Old Ford, EB	$	10
❑ 15	M. Shepherd, Old Ford, NP	$	30
❑ 16	L. Pearson, Buick, EB	$	6
❑ 16	L. Pearson, Buick, NP	$	30
❑ 16	L. Pearson, Buick, PB	$	6
❑ 16	L. Pearson, Chevy Lumina, PB	$	25
❑ 18	G. Trammell, Ford Melling, PB	$	5
❑ 20	R. Moroso, Olds, EB	$	20
❑ 20	R. Moroso, Olds, STP Decal, NP	$	50
❑ 21	N. Bonnett, Old Ford, EB	$	25
❑ 21	N. Bonnett, Old Ford, NP	$	50
❑ 21	D. Jarrett, Ford, EB	$	6
❑ 21	D. Jarrett, Ford, PB	$	5
❑ 22	S. Marlin, Ford, Black Wheels, PB	$	5
❑ 22	S. Marlin, Ford, Silver Wheels, PB	$	20
❑ 25	K. Schrader, Chevy Lumina, PB	$	5
❑ 26	K. Bernstein, Buick, EB	$	6
❑ 26	K. Bernstein, Buick, Quaker State, NP	$	20
❑ 26	K. Bernstein, Buick, PB	$	5
❑ 26	K. Bernstein, Olds, PB	$	10
❑ 26	B. Bodine, Buick, Quaker State, PB	$	5
❑ 26	B. Bodine, Chevy Lumina, PB	$	5
❑ 27	R. Wallace, Pontiac, MGD, EB	$	55
❑ 27	R. Wallace, Pontiac, MGD, NP	$	100
❑ 27	R. Wallace, Pontiac, no MGD, EB	$	30
❑ 27	R. Wallace, Pontiac, Miller, EB	$	45
❑ 28	D. Allison, Ford, EB	$	40
❑ 28	D. Allison, Ford, PB	$	35
❑ 28	D. Allison, Old Ford, EB	$	40
❑ 28	D. Allison, Old Ford, NP	$	90
❑ 28	D. Allison, Old Ford, PB	$	30
❑ 30	M. Waltrip, Pontiac, Country Time, EB	$	25
❑ 30	M. Waltrip, Pontiac, Pen. with STP, EB	$	12

❑ 30	M. Waltrip, Pontiac, Pen. no STP, EB	$	12
❑ 30	M. Waltrip, Pontiac, NP	$	40
❑ 30	M. Waltrip, Pontiac, PB	$	5
❑ 33	H. Gant, Buick, PB	$	20
❑ 33	H. Gant, Olds, EB	$	15
❑ 33	H. Gant, Olds, PB	$	12
❑ 33	H. Gant, Pontiac, EB	$	15
❑ 33	H. Gant, Pontiac, NP	$	50
❑ 34	T. Bodine, Chevy Lumina, Welco	$	5
❑ 36	K. Wallace, Pontiac, Cox Lumber	$	5
❑ 42	K. Petty, Pontiac, Peak, EB	$	15
❑ 42	K. Petty, Pontiac, Peak, NP	$	35
❑ 42	K. Petty, Pontiac, Peak, PB	$	20
❑ 42	K. Petty, Pontiac, Mello Yello, PB	$	5
❑ 43	R. Petty, Pontiac, EB	$	15
❑ 43	R. Petty, Pontiac, NP	$	50
❑ 43	R. Petty, Pontiac, PB	$	5
❑ 52	J. Means, Pontiac, PB	$	5
❑ 59	R. Pressley, Alliance	$	5
❑ 66	C. Yarborough, Pontiac, PB	$	5
❑ 68	B. Hamilton, Olds, PB	$	5
❑ 68	B. Hamilton, Buick, PB	$	20
❑ 70	J. D. McDuffie, Son's Auto	$	5
❑ 71	D. Marcis, Chevy Lumina, PB	$	5
❑ 72	K. Bouchard, Pontiac, ADAP, PB	$	20
❑ 72	T. Leslie, Olds, Detroit Gaskets, PB	$	5
❑ 89	J. Sauter, Pontiac, PB	$	5
❑ 89	J. Sauter, Pontiac, Day Glow, PB	$	10
❑ 94	T. Labonte, Buick, PB	$	10
❑ 94	T. Labonte, Olds, PB	$	5
❑ 94	S. Marlin, Olds, EB	$	10
❑ 94	S. Marlin, Olds, NP	$	25
❑ 96	T. Peck, Chevy Lumina, PB	$	35
❑ 96	T. Peck, Olds, PB	$	5

Racing Champions

1:64
1992
(Back of blister pack has either Petty or a copyright list)

❑ 1	J. Gordon, Baby Ruth	$	18
❑ 1	R. Mast, Majik Market	$	3
❑ 2	R. Wallace, Pontiac Excitement	$	5
❑ 3	D. Earnhardt, Goodwrench	$	8
❑ 4	E. Irvan, Kodak	$	4
❑ 5	J. Fogleman, InnKeeper	$	3
❑ 5	R. Rudd, Tide	$	3
❑ 6	M. Martin, Valvoline	$	5
❑ 7	H. Gant, Mac Tools	$	15
❑ 7	A. Kulwicki	$	20
❑ 08	B. Dotter, Team R	$	3
❑ 9	J. Bessey, AC-Delco	$	5
❑ 9	B. Elliott, Melling	$	4
❑ 9	C. Little, Melling Performance	$	5
❑ 10	D. Cope, Purolator Adam's Mark	$	5
❑ 10	D. Cope, Purolator, Blue Name	$	5
❑ 10	D. Cope, Purolator, White Name	$	15
❑ 10	S. Marlin, Maxwell House	$	8
❑ 11	G. Bodine, NS	$	5
❑ 11	B. Elliott, Amoco	$	4
❑ 12	B. Allison, NS	$	5
❑ 12	H. Stricklin, Raybestos	$	4

❑ 14	A. J. Foyt, NS	$	13
❑ 15	G. Bodine, Motorcraft	$	3
❑ 16	W. Dallenbach Jr., Roush	$	13
❑ 17	D. Waltrip, Western Auto	$	3
❑ 18	D. Jarrett, Interstate Batteries	$	3
❑ 18	G. Trammell, Melling	$	3
❑ 19	C. Little, Tyson	$	3
❑ 20	M. Wallace, First Aide	$	8
❑ 21	D. Jarrett, Citgo	$	3
❑ 21	M. Shepherd, Citgo	$	3
❑ 22	S. Marlin, Maxwell House	$	3
❑ 25	K. Schrader, Hendrick	$	5
❑ 25	B. Venturini, Amoco Rain X	$	5
❑ 26	B. Bodine, Quaker State	$	5
❑ 28	D. Allison, Havoline	$	15
❑ 28	B. Hillin, Havoline	$	6
❑ 30	M. Waltrip, Pennzoil	$	3
❑ 31	B. Hillin, Team Ireland	$	5
❑ 33	H. Gant, NS	$	5
❑ 34	T. Bodine, Welco Quick Stop	$	5
❑ 36	K. Wallace, Cox Lumber	$	5
❑ 36	K. Wallace, Dirt Devil	$	6
❑ 42	B. Hillin, Mello Yello	$	8
❑ 42	K. Petty, Mello Yello	$	3
❑ 43	R. Petty, STP, Black Wheels	$	3
❑ 43	R. Petty, STP, Blue Wheels	$	3
❑ 44	B. Caudill, Army	$	5
❑ 49	S. Smith, Ameritron	$	10
❑ 55	T. Musgrave, Jasper	$	10
❑ 56	J. Glanville, Atlanta Falcons	$	6
❑ 59	A. Belmont, FDP Brakes	$	6
❑ 60	M. Martin, Winn Dixie	$	6
❑ 63	C. Bown, Nescafe	$	5
❑ 66	J. Hensley, TropArtic	$	3
❑ 66	C. Little, TropArtic	$	3
❑ 66	C. Yarborough, TropArtic, Ford	$	5
❑ 66	C. Yarborough, Trop Artic, Pontiac	$	3
❑ 68	B. Hamilton, Country Time	$	3
❑ 70	J. D. McDuffie, Son's Auto	$	3
❑ 71	D. Marcis, Big Apple Market	$	3
❑ 72	K. Bouchard, ADAP	$	8
❑ 72	T. Leslie, Detroit Gasket	$	3
❑ 75	B. Miller, Food Country	$	5
❑ 83	L. Speed, Purex	$	6
❑ 87	J. Nemechek, Texas Pete	$	5
❑ 89	J. Sauter, Evinrude	$	3
❑ 94	T. Labonte, Sunoco, Blue Bumper	$	5
❑ 94	T. Labonte, Sunoco, Yellow Bumper	$	6
❑ 96	T. Peck, Thomas Bros.	$	3

Racing Champions Premier

1:64
1992
(In black boxes)

❑ 3	D. Earnhardt, Goodwrench	$	30
❑ 11	B. Elliott, Amoco	$	13
❑ 17	D. Waltrip, Western Auto	$	12
❑ 28	D. Allison, Havoline	$	27
❑ 43	R. Petty, STP	$	25

152

Racing Champions

1:64
1993
Blister Pack

❑ 0	D. McCabe, Fisher Snow Plows	$	5
❑ 2	R. Wallace, Pontiac Excitement	$	5
❑ 3	D. Earnhardt, Goodwrench	$	6
❑ 3	D. Earnhardt, Goodwrench, Mom-n-Pop's	$	6
❑ 4	E. Irvan, Kodak	$	5
❑ 5	R. Rudd, Tide	$	4
❑ 6	M. Martin, Valvoline	$	5
❑ 7	A. Kulwicki, Hooters	$	13
❑ 8	S. Marlin, Raybestos	$	4
❑ 11	B. Elliott, Amoco	$	5
❑ 12	J. Spencer, Meineke	$	4
❑ 14	T. Labonte, Kellogg's	$	4
❑ 15	G. Bodine, Motorcraft	$	4
❑ 17	D. Waltrip, Western Auto	$	4
❑ 18	D. Jarrett, Interstate Batteries	$	4
❑ 21	M. Shepherd, Citgo	$	4
❑ 22	B. Labonte, Maxwell House	$	4
❑ 24	J. Gordon, Du Pont	$	6
❑ 25	K. Schrader, Kodiak	$	10
❑ 25	B. Venturini, Rain X	$	6
❑ 26	B. Bodine, Quaker State	$	4
❑ 27	H. Stricklin, McDonald's	$	4
❑ 28	D. Allison, Havoline	$	8
❑ 28	D. Allison, Havoline, Black/White	$	11
❑ 28	E. Irvan, Havoline	$	10
❑ 33	H. Gant, NS, Lumina	$	4
❑ 22	H. Gant, NS, Olds	$	4
❑ 42	K. Petty, Mello Yello	$	4
❑ 44	R. Wilson, STP	$	4
❑ 59	A. Belmont, FDP Brakes	$	8
❑ 59	R. Pressley, Alliance	$	8
❑ 60	M. Martin, Winn Dixie	$	5
❑ 71	D. Marcis, STG	$	4
❑ 75	B. Mock, Factory Stores	$	4
❑ 87	J. Nemechek, Dentyne	$	4
❑ 98	D. Cope, Bojangles	$	4

Racing Champions Premier

1:64
1993
(In black boxes)

❑ 1	R. Combs, Jebco Clocks	$	10
❑ 2	W. Burton, Hardee's	$	12
❑ 02	F. Kimmel, Harley-Davidson	$	15
❑ 2	R. Wallace, Pontiac Excitement	$	7
❑ 3	D. Earnhardt, Goodwrench	$	20
❑ 3	D. Earnhardt, DEI package	$	15
❑ 4	E. Irvan, Kodak	$	6
❑ 4	J. Purvis, Kodak	$	15
❑ 5	R. Rudd, Tide	$	6
❑ 6	M. Martin, Valvoline	$	7
❑ 6	M. Martin, Valvoline, 4 in Row P	$	14
❑ 6	M. Stefnik, Valvoline Auto Palace	$	15
❑ 7	J. Hensley, A. Kulwicki Racing	$	30
❑ 7	A. Kulwicki, Hooters	$	40
❑ 7	A. Kulwicki, Zerex	$	30

❑ 8	S. Marlin, Raybestos	$	6
❑ 11	B. Elliott, Budweiser P	$	20
❑ 12	J. Spencer, Meineke	$	6
❑ 14	T. Labonte, Kellogg's	$	6
❑ 15	G. Bodine, Motorcraft	$	6
❑ 18	D. Jarrett, Interstate Batteries	$	6
❑ 21	M. Shepherd, Citgo	$	6
❑ 24	J. Gordon, Du Pont	$	18
❑ 26	B. Bodine, Quaker State	$	6
❑ 27	H. Stricklin, McDonald's	$	6
❑ 27	H. Stricklin, Mr. Pibb	$	6
❑ 28	D. Allison, Havoline, Black	$	20
❑ 28	D. Allison, Havoline, CF Black/Gold	$	20
❑ 28	D. Allison, Havoline, CF Black/Orange	$	20
❑ 28	D. Allison, Havoline, CF Black/White	$	20
❑ 28	E. Irvan, Havoline	$	20
❑ 31	N. Bonnett, Mom-n-Pop's	$	50
❑ 33	H. Gant, NS	$	8
❑ 41	E. Irvan, Mac Tools	$	15
❑ 42	K. Petty, Mello Yello	$	6
❑ 44	J. Hensley, STP	$	12
❑ 59	R. Pressley, Alliance	$	20
❑ 59	D. Setzer, Alliance	$	15
❑ 60	M. Martin, Winn Dixie	$	20
❑ 87	J. Nemechek, Dentyne	$	6
❑ 97	J. Bessey, Auto Palace	$	12
❑ 98	D. Cope, Bojangles, Black	$	12
❑ 98	D. Cope, Bojangles, Yellow	$	12

Racing Champions

1:64
1993 PVC Box

❑ 3	D. Earnhardt, Back in Black	$	17
❑ 3	D. Earnhardt, Darlington Win	$	17
❑ 3	D. Earnhardt, Busch Clash Win	$	17
❑ 3	D. Earnhardt, Twin 125 Win	$	17
❑ 4	E. Irvan, Kodak, Talladega Win	$	10
❑ 7	H. Gant, Morema	$	10
❑ 7	J. Hensley, Hanes	$	15
❑ 7	J. Hensley, Purolator	$	15
❑ 8	S. Marlin, Raybestos	$	15
❑ 12	D. Bonnett, Plasti-Kote	$	10
❑ 18	D. Jarrett, Interstate Batteries	$	10
❑ 24	J. Gordon, Du Pont	$	30
❑ 24	J. Gordon, Du Pont Fan Club	$	30
❑ 24	J. Gordon, Du Pont Daytona	$	30
❑ 24	J. Gordon, Du Pont Twin 125	$	30
❑ 27	H. Stricklin, McDonald's, All-American	$	10
❑ 27	H. Stricklin, McDonald's Daytona	$	20
❑ 27	H. Stricklin, McDonald's 250	$	50
❑ 27	H. Stricklin, McDonald's, Taylors	$	10
❑ 28	A. Kulwicki, Hardee's	$	40
❑ 28	D. Allison, Havoline	$	20
❑ 28	E. Irvan, Havoline	$	20
❑ 28	E. Irvan, Havoline Charlotte	$	20
❑ 40	K. Wallace, Dirt Devil	$	25
❑ 42	K. Petty, Mello Yello	$	20
❑ 44	D. Green, Slim Jim	$	20
❑ 44	R. Wilson, STP	$	20
❑ 46	A. Unser, Jr., Valvoline	$	25

❏ 51	Generic, Pontiac, Racing Champions	$	40
❏ 51	Generic, Lumina, Racing Champions	$	40
❏ 51	Generic, Thunderbird, Racing Champions	$	40
❏ 51	Generic, Racing Champions, Mascot	$	40
❏ 52	K. Schrader, Morema	$	12
❏ 56	E. Irvan, Earnhardt Chevrolet	$	25
❏ 59	R. Pressley, Alliance	$	20
❏ 59	R. Pressley, Alliance, Sept. 93	$	35
❏ 59	R. Pressley, Alliance, 1994 PRE	$	20
❏ 60	M. Martin, Winn Dixie	$	15
❏ 68	B. Hamilton, Country Time	$	75
❏ 89	J. McClure, Bero Motors	$	12
❏ 93	Generic, Budweiser 500	$	15
❏ 93	Generic, Food City 500	$	15
❏ 93	Generic, Slick 50 300	$	15
❏ 93	Generic, Racing Champions Club Car	$	15

Racing Champions

1:64
1994
Blister Pack

❏ 00	J. Rumley, Big Dog Coal	$	6
❏ 1	R. Mast, Precision Products	$	4
❏ 2	R. Craven, Du Pont	$	4
❏ 2	R. Wallace, Ford Motorsports	$	5
❏ 2	R. Wallace, Ford Motorsports, No Blue	$	8
❏ 4	S. Marlin, Kodak	$	4
❏ 5	T. Labonte, Kellogg's	$	4
❏ 6	M. Martin, Valvoline	$	4
❏ 7	G. Bodine, Exide	$	4
❏ 7	H. Gant, Manheim	$	8
❏ 8	J. Burton, Raybestos	$	4
❏ 8	K. Wallace, TIC	$	4
❏ 10	R. Rudd, Tide	$	4
❏ 12	C. Allison, Sports Image	$	10
❏ 14	J. Andretti, Kanawha	$	6
❏ 15	L. Speed, Quality Care	$	4
❏ 16	T. Musgrave, Family Channel	$	4
❏ 17	D. Waltrip, Western Auto	$	4
❏ 18	D. Jarrett, Interstate Batteries	$	4
❏ 19	L. Allen, Hooters	$	4
❏ 20	R. LaJoie, Fina	$	4
❏ 21	M. Shepherd, Citgo	$	4
❏ 22	B. Labonte, Maxwell House	$	4
❏ 23	H. Stricklin, Smokin' Joe's, PVC BX	$	12
❏ 24	J. Gordon, Du Pont	$	8
❏ 24	J. Gordon, Du Pont Brickyard	$	18
❏ 25	H. Sadler, VA Lovers	$	4
❏ 25	K. Schrader, GMAC	$	4
❏ 26	B. Bodine, Quaker State	$	4
❏ 27	J. Spencer, McDonald's	$	4
❏ 28	E. Irvan, Havoline	$	5
❏ 30	M. Waltrip, Pennzoil	$	4
❏ 31	T. Peck, Channellock	$	6
❏ 33	H. Gant, Manheim	$	4
❏ 38	E. Sawyer, Ford Credit	$	4
❏ 40	B. Hamilton, Kendall	$	4
❏ 42	K. Petty, Mello Yello	$	4
❏ 44	B. Hillin, Buss Fuses	$	4
❏ 46	S. Robinson, Polaroid	$	4
❏ 52	K. Schrader, AC-Delco	$	4

❏ 54	R. Pressley, Manheim	$	6
❏ 60	M. Martin, Winn Dixie	$	5
❏ 63	J. Bown, Lysol	$	4
❏ 75	T. Bodine, Factory Stores	$	4
❏ 83	S. Blakely, Ramses	$	6
❏ 92	L. Pearson, Stanley Tools	$	4
❏ 94	Generic, Brickyard 400	$	4
❏ 97	J. Bessey, Johnson	$	4
❏ 98	D. Cope, Fingerhut	$	6

Racing Champions

1:64
1994 Hobby
(In yellow boxes)

❏ Cars (1/5/7/8/14/15/16/17)		$	4
❏ Cars (18/19/22/23/25/26)		$	4
❏ Cars (27/30/31/34/38/40)		$	4
❏ Cars (42/46/63/75/92/98)		$	4
❏ 2	R. Craven, Du Pont	$	4
❏ 2	R. Wallace, Ford Motorsports	$	5
❏ 4	S. Marlin, Kodak	$	4
❏ 4	S. Marlin, Kodak Fun Saver	$	4
❏ 6	M. Martin, Valvoline	$	5
❏ 24	J. Gordon, Du Pont	$	8
❏ 33	H. Gant, No Sponsor	$	8
❏ 94	Generic, Brickyard 400	$	6

Racing Champions Premier

1:64
1994
(In black boxes)

❏ 0	D. McCabe, Fisher Snow Plows	$	10
❏ 1	D. Allison, Lancaster	$	20
❏ 2	R. Craven, Du Pont	$	6
❏ 2	R. Wallace, MGD	$	8
❏ 2	R. Wallace, Mac Tools	$	20
❏ 3	D. Earnhardt, Goodwrench	$	18
❏ 4	S. Marlin, Kodak	$	6
❏ 4	S. Marlin, Kodak Fun Saver	$	8
❏ 5	T. Labonte, Kellogg's	$	6
❏ 6	M. Martin, Valvoline	$	6
❏ 6	M. Martin, Valvoline, 4 in Row	$	15
❏ 7	G. Bodine, Exide	$	8
❏ 7	H. Gant, Manheim	$	15
❏ 7	A. Kulwicki, Army	$	25
❏ 8	J. Burton, Raybestos	$	6
❏ 8	K. Wallace, TIC Financial	$	12
❏ 12	C. Allison, Sports Image	$	15
❏ 15	L. Speed, Quality Care	$	6
❏ 16	C. Chaffin, 31W Insulation	$	12
❏ 16	T. Musgrave, Family Channel	$	6
❏ 18	D. Jarrett, Interstate Batteries	$	6
❏ 19	L. Allen, Hooters	$	6
❏ 21	J. Benson, Jr., Berger	$	14
❏ 24	J. Gordon, Du Pont	$	18
❏ 24	J. Gordon, Du Pont, 1993 ROY	$	20
❏ 25	H. Sadler, VA Lovers	$	12
❏ 25	K. Schrader, Kodiak	$	8
❏ 26	B. Bodine, Quaker State	$	6
❏ 27	J. Spencer, McDonald's	$	6
❏ 28	E. Irvan, Mac Tools, Yellow BX	$	18

❑ 31	S. Grissom, Channellock	$	12
❑ 33	B. Labonte, Dentyne	$	6
❑ 34	M. McLaughlin, Fiddle Faddle	$	6
❑ 35	S. Robinson, Polaroid Captiva	$	15
❑ 40	B. Hamilton, Kendall	$	6
❑ 43	R. Combs, French's	$	15
❑ 43	W. Dallenbach, Jr., STP	$	15
❑ 54	R. Pressley, Alliance	$	12
❑ 59	A. Belmont, Metal Arrester	$	12
❑ 59	D. Setzer, Alliance, 2000	$	25
❑ 59	D. Setzer, Alliance	$	15
❑ 60	M. Martin, Winn Dixie	$	15
❑ 70	J. D. McDuffie, Son's Auto	$	20
❑ 71	D. Marcis, Earnhardt Chevy	$	15
❑ 75	T. Bodine, Factory Stores	$	6
❑ 77	G. Sacks, US Air Jasper	$	15
❑ 85	J. Sauter, Rheem AC	$	10
❑ 89	J. McClure, FSU Seminoles	$	10

Racing Champions Premier

1:64
1994 Brickyard 400
(In purple boxes)

❑ 3	D. Earnhardt, Goodwrench	$	35
❑ 6	M. Martin, Valvoline	$	10
❑ 18	D. Jarrett, Interstate Batteries	$	7
❑ 21	M. Shepherd, Citgo	$	7
❑ 24	J. Gordon, Du Pont	$	75
❑ 26	B. Bodine, Quaker State	$	7
❑ 27	J. Spencer, McDonald's	$	7
❑ 30	M. Waltrip, Pennzoil	$	7
❑ 42	K. Petty, Mello Yello	$	7

Racing Champions

1:64
1994 To The Maxx
Series One

❑ 2	R. Wallace, Ford Motorsports	$	8
❑ 4	S. Marlin, Kodak	$	7
❑ 5	T. Labonte, Kellogg's	$	7
❑ 6	M. Martin, Valvoline	$	7
❑ 16	T. Musgrave, Family Channel	$	7
❑ 24	J. Gordon, Du Pont	$	12
❑ 28	E. Irvan, Havoline	$	7
❑ 42	K. Petty, Mello Yello	$	7

Racing Champions

1:64
1995 Previews

❑ 1	R. Mast, Precision Products	$	4
❑ 2	R. Craven, Du Pont	$	4
❑ 2	R. Wallace, Ford Motorsports	$	7
❑ 4	S. Marlin, Kodak	$	4
❑ 6	M. Martin, Valvoline	$	4
❑ 7	G. Bodine, Exide	$	4
❑ 10	R. Rudd, Tide	$	4
❑ 14	T. Labonte, MW Windows	$	4
❑ 16	T. Musgrave, Family Channel	$	4
❑ 21	M. Shepherd, Citgo	$	4
❑ 23	C. Little, Bayer	$	4

❑ 24	J. Gordon, Du Pont	$	9
❑ 25	K. Shelmerdine, Big Johnson	$	6
❑ 26	S. Kinser, Quaker State	$	4
❑ 28	D. Jarrett, Havoline	$	4
❑ 30	M. Waltrip, Pennzoil	$	4
❑ 38	E. Sawyer, Ford Credit	$	4
❑ 40	B. Hamilton, Kendall	$	4
❑ 40	P. Moise, Dial Purex	$	4
❑ 52	K. Schrader, AC-Delco	$	4
❑ 57	J. Keller, Budget Gourmet	$	4
❑ 63	C. Markham, Lysol	$	4
❑ 75	T. Bodine, Factory Stores	$	4
❑ 92	L. Pearson, Stanley Tools	$	4
❑ 94	B. Elliott, McDonald's	$	4
❑ 98	J. Mayfield, Fingerhut	$	4

Racing Champions

1:64
1995

❑ 1	R. Mast, Precision Products	$	4
❑ 2	R. Craven, Du Pont	$	4
❑ 2	R. Wallace, Ford Motorsports	$	7
❑ 4	S. Marlin, Kodak	$	4
❑ 4	J. Purvis, Kodak Fun Saver	$	5
❑ 5	T. Labonte, Kellogg's	$	4
❑ 6	T. Houston, Red Devil	$	5
❑ 6	M. Martin, Valvoline	$	5
❑ 7	G. Bodine, Exide	$	4
❑ 8	J. Burton, Raybestos	$	4
❑ 08	B. Dotter, Hyde Tools	$	4
❑ 10	R. Rudd, Tide	$	4
❑ 12	D. Cope, Straight Arrow	$	5
❑ 14	T. Labonte, MW Windows	$	5
❑ 15	D. Trickle, Ford Quality	$	4
❑ 17	D. Waltrip, Western Auto	$	4
❑ 18	B. Labonte, Interstate Batteries	$	4
❑ 22	R. LaJoie, MBNA	$	5
❑ 24	J. Gordon, Du Pont	$	9
❑ 24	J. Gordon, Du Pont Coke	$	9
❑ 25	K. Schrader, Hendrick	$	5
❑ 25	K. Shelmerdine, Big Johnson	$	4
❑ 26	S. Kinser, Quaker State	$	5
❑ 27	L. Allen, Hooters	$	4
❑ 28	D. Jarrett, Havoline	$	4
❑ 34	M. McLaughlin, French's	$	4
❑ 40	P. Moise, Dial Purex	$	5
❑ 41	R. Craven, Hedrick	$	4
❑ 47	J. Fuller, Sunoco	$	4
❑ 51	J. Bown, Luck's	$	5
❑ 52	K. Schrader, AC-Delco	$	4
❑ 57	J. Keller, Budget Gourmet	$	5
❑ 60	M. Martin, Winn Dixie	$	7
❑ 92	L. Pearson, Stanley Tools	$	4
❑ 94	B. Elliott, McDonald's	$	4
❑ 94	B. Elliott, Thunderbat	$	7

Racing Champions Premier

1:64
1995

❑ 2	R. Wallace, Ford Motorsports	$	7
❑ 4	S. Marlin, Kodak	$	6

❏ 18	B. Labonte, Interstate Batteries	$	6
❏ 24	J. Gordon, Du Pont	$	10
❏ 26	S. Kinser, Quaker State	$	6
❏ 40	P. Moise, Dial Purex	$	6
❏ 59	D. Setzer, Alliance	$	6
❏ 94	B. Elliott, McDonald's	$	20

Racing Champions

1:64
1995 To The Maxx
Series Two

❏ 7	G. Bodine, Exide	$	7
❏ 12	D. Cope, Mane and Tail	$	7
❏ 17	D. Waltrip, Western Auto	$	7
❏ 21	M. Shepherd, Citgo	$	7
❏ 23	C. Little, Bayer	$	7
❏ 26	S. Kinser, Quaker State	$	7
❏ 52	K. Schrader, AC-Delco	$	7
❏ 94	B. Elliott, McDonald's	$	7

Racing Champions

Super Trucks 1:64
1995

❏ 1	P. J. Jones, Sears DieHard	$	6
❏ 2	D. Ashley, Ultra Wheels	$	5
❏ 3	M. Skinner, Goodwrench	$	6
❏ 6	R. Carelli, Total Petroleum	$	5
❏ 06	M. Bliss, Ultra Wheels	$	5
❏ 7	G. Bodine, Exide	$	5
❏ 8	C. Huartson, AC-Delco	$	5
❏ 12	R. MacCachren, Venable	$	5
❏ 21	T. Butler, Ortho Green Nose	$	5
❏ 21	T. Butler, Ortho Yellow Nose	$	5
❏ 23	T. J. Clark, ASE Blue	$	5
❏ 23	T. J. Clark, ASE White	$	5
❏ 24	Generic, Du Pont, Gordon Card	$	8
❏ 38	S. Swind, Chann White Goodyear	$	6
❏ 38	S. Swind, Chann Yellow Goodyear	$	6

Revell

1:24

❏ 1	J. Gordon, Baby Ruth, RCI	$	70
❏ 3	D. Earnhardt, Goodwrench, Kellogg's P	$	35
❏ 3	D. Earnhardt, Goodwrench, Black/White SI	$	30
❏ 3	D. Earnhardt, Goodwrench, Silver Wheels	$	20
❏ 3	D. Earnhardt, Goodwrench, 94 SI	$	30
❏ 3	D. Earnhardt, Goodwrench, 6-Time	$	30
❏ 4	R. Wilson, Kodak, GMP	$	25
❏ 6	M. Martin, Valvoline	$	18
❏ 7	H. Gant, Mac Tools, RCI	$	40
❏ 7	H. Gant, Morema	$	40
❏ 8	D. Trickle, Snickers	$	18
❏ 8 1/2	Generic, Racing For Kids	$	18
❏ 10	D. Cope, Purolator	$	18
❏ 15	G. Bodine, Ford Motorsports	$	35
❏ 17	D. Waltrip, Western Auto	$	16
❏ 18	D. Jarrett, Interstate Batteries	$	18
❏ 21	M. Shepherd, Cheerwine	$	25
❏ 21	M. Shepherd, Citgo	$	18
❏ 22	S. Marlin, Maxwell House	$	18

❏ 26	B. Bodine, Quaker State	$	18
❏ 28	D. Allison, Havoline	$	30
❏ 28	D. Allison, Mac Tools	$	50
❏ 28	E. Irvan, Mac Tools	$	40
❏ 30	M. Waltrip, Pennzoil	$	18
❏ 32	D. Jarrett, Mac Tools	$	35
❏ 33	H. Gant, NS, Farewell Tour	$	30
❏ 42	K. Petty, Mello Yello	$	16
❏ 52	K. Schrader, NS, Morema	$	30
❏ 57	Generic, Heinz 57	$	18
❏ 59	R. Pressley, Alliance, RCI	$	55
❏ 60	M. Martin, Winn Dixie, GMP	$	30
❏ 66	D. Trickle, Phillips 66, TropArtic	$	40
❏ 66	Generic, Phillips 66, TropArtic	$	18
❏ 68	B. Hamilton, Country Time	$	18
❏ 75	J. Ruttman, Dinner Bell	$	18
❏ 83	L. Speed, Purex, GMP	$	25
❏ 90	B. Hillin, Heilig-Meyers	$	25
❏ 94	T. Labonte, Sunoco	$	18

Revell

1:24
1994 Hobby
(In yellow and black boxes)

❏ 4	S. Marlin, Kodak	$	20
❏ 5	T. Labonte, Kellogg's	$	20
❏ 7	G. Bodine, Exide	$	20
❏ 15	L. Speed, Quality Care	$	20
❏ 24	J. Gordon, Du Pont	$	30
❏ 31	W. Burton, Hardee's	$	30
❏ 41	J. Nemechek, Meineke	$	30
❏ 43	W. Dallenbach, Jr., STP	$	20

Action

1:24
Dually Truck
B= Bank

❏ 2	R. Wallace, MGD B	$	60
❏ 3	D. Earnhardt, Goodwrench B	$	85
❏ 5	T. Labonte, Kellogg's B	$	70
❏ 11	B. Elliott, Bud B	$	80
❏ 16	T. Musgrave, Family Channel B	$	45
❏ 18	D. Jarrett, Interstate Batteries B	$	45
❏ 21	M. Shepherd, Cheerwine B	$	40
❏ 22	B. Labonte, Maxwell House B	$	50
❏ 24	J. Gordon, Du Pont B	$	110
❏ 24	J. Gordon, Du Pont Coke B	$	110
❏ 28	D. Allison, Havoline	$	160
❏ 51	N. Bonnett, Country Time B	$	50
❏ 59	D. Setzer, Alliance	$	45
❏ 98	D. Cope, Fingerhut B	$	45

Action

1:64
Dually Truck

❏ 3	D. Earnhardt, Goodwrench	$	25
❏ 18	D. Jarrett, Interstate Batteries	$	15
❏ 24	J. Gordon, Du Pont	$	60
❏ 30	M. Waltrip, Pennzoil	$	15

Action / RCCA Transporters

1:64
BGN = Busch Grand National
GMP = Georgia Marketing and Promotions

❏	D. Allison, Havoline, RCCA	$	125
❏	D. Allison, Mac Tools	$	80
❏	D. Allison, Texaco	$	80
❏	N. Bonnett, Country Time, RCCA	$	90
❏	D. Earnhardt, RCCA CO with cars	$	155
❏	D. Earnhardt, Goodwrench, DEI BGN	$	110
❏	D. Earnhardt, Goodwrench, RCR	$	110
❏	D. Earnhardt, Goodwrench, Dually/Show	$	110
❏	D. Earnhardt, Wrangler	$	110
❏	D. Earnhardt, Kids, Mom-n-Pop's	$	75
❏	B. Elliott, Melling, RCCA	$	90
❏	B. Elliott, Budweiser	$	90
❏	H. Gant, Mac Tools, Morema	$	80
❏	H. Gant, Morema	$	80
❏	J. Gordon, Baby Ruth, PS (Peachstate)	$	100
❏	J. Gordon, Du Pont, GMP	$	140
❏	J. Gordon, Du Pont Dually/Show	$	75
❏	E. Irvan, Kodak, PS	$	75
❏	E. Irvan, Delco Remy, PLS	$	75
❏	D. Jarrett, Interstate Batteries, Dually/Show	$	60
❏	B. Labonte, Maxwell House, PS	$	75
❏	B. Labonte, Penrose	$	75
❏	T. Labonte, Kellogg's, PS	$	75
❏	S. Marlin, Raybestos, PS	$	75
❏	M. Martin, Winn Dixie, PS	$	90
❏	M. Martin, Valvoline	$	90
❏	R. Moroso, Swisher, RCCA	$	75
❏	T. Musgrave, Family Channel, PS	$	75
❏	NDA, TropArtic	$	50
❏	J. Nemechek, Dentyne, PS	$	75
❏	J. Nemechek, Meineke, PLS	$	60
❏	D. Pearson, Chattanooga Chew	$	75
❏	L. Pearson, Stanley Tools, PS	$	75
❏	K. Petty, Mello Yello, PS	$	75
❏	R. Petty, STP, RCCA	$	75
❏	R. Pressley, Alliance	$	75
❏	R. Pressley, Alliance, Fan Club	$	90
❏	D. Rezendes, KPR Racing	$	60
❏	T. Richmond, Old Milwaukee	$	80
❏	S. Robinson, Polaroid	$	75
❏	M. Shepherd, Cheerwine	$	75
❏	M. Shepherd, Citgo, Dually/Show	$	60
❏	K. Wallace, Dirt Devil, PS	$	75
❏	R. Wallace, Delco Remy, PLS	$	75
❏	D. Waltrip, Western Auto, RCCA	$	75
❏	D. Waltrip, Delco Remy, PLS	$	75

Ertl White Rose

Transporters 1:64
Past and Present

❏	D. Allison, Havoline	$	125
❏	G. Bodine, Exide	$	60
❏	N. Bonnett, Warner Hodgdon	$	90
❏	D. Cope, Bojangles	$	45
❏	D. Earnhardt, Wrangler	$	175
❏	D. Earnhardt, Goodwrench	$	160
❏	J. Gordon, Du Pont	$	120

❏	D. Jarrett, Interstate Batteries	$	45
❏	J. Johnson, Mountain Dew	$	50
❏	A. Kulwicki, Zerex	$	70
❏	A. Kulwicki, Hooters	$	150
❏	T. Labonte, Kellogg's	$	50
❏	S. Marlin, Piedmont	$	45
❏	T. Musgrave, Family Channel	$	45
❏	P. Parson, Manheim	$	45
❏	K. Petty, 7-Eleven	$	50
❏	K. Petty, R. Petty, STP Combo	$	125
❏	M. Shepherd, Citgo	$	45
❏	L. Speed, Quality Care	$	45
❏	J. Spencer, Meineke	$	45
❏	K. Wallace, Dirt Devil	$	45
❏	D. Waltrip, Western Auto	$	45
❏	C. Yarborough, Hardee's	$	50

Ertl White Rose

Transporters 1:64
BGN / Promos
BGN = Busch Grand National

❏	J. Burton, Baby Ruth, BGN	$	50
❏	R. Craven, Du Pont, P(Promo)	$	50
❏	B. Elliott, Bud, Wood Case P	$	125
❏	H. Gant, Manheim, BGN	$	50
❏	J. Gordon, Baby Ruth, BGN	$	90
❏	A. Kulwicki, 92 WC Champ P	$	175
❏	J. Nemechek, Dentyne, BGN	$	45
❏	J. Nemechek, 93 BGN Champ P	$	75
❏	P. Parson, White Rose, BGN	$	45
❏	R. Petty, Petty Anniversary, P	$	185
❏	K. Schrader, AC-Delco, BGN	$	45
❏	J. Smith, White House AJ, BGN	$	45
❏	J. Sprague, Staff America, BGN	$	45
❏	H. Stricklin, Smokin' Joe's, Plexi P	$	60
❏	K. Wallace, Dirt Devil, BGN	$	45

Matchbox White Rose

Transporters 1:80 1994
Super Star Series

❏	Trans (2/4/5/15/16/17/19/29/32)	$	10
❏	Trans (40/43/46/52/75/94/98)	$	10
❏ 3	D. Earnhardt, Goodwrench	$	25
❏ 7	G. Bodine, Exide	$	10
❏ 7	H. Gant, Manheim Auctions	$	10
❏ 24	J. Gordon, Du Pont	$	30
❏ 41	J. Smith, White House AJ	$	10
❏ 41	J. Smith, White House AJ, Gold BX	$	18

Matchbox White Rose

Transporters 1:80 1995
Super Stars Series

❏ 2	R. Craven, Du Pont	$	12
❏ 3	D. Earnhardt, Snap On	$	25
❏ 12	D. Cope, Straight Arrow	$	12
❏ 26	S. Kinser, Quaker State	$	12
❏ 72	T. Leslie, Detroit Gasket	$	12
❏ 74	J. Benson Jr., Lipton Tea	$	12
❏ 90	M. Wallace, Heilig-Meyers	$	12
❏ 94	B. Elliott, McDonald's	$	12

❑ 95	J. Tanner, Caterpillar	$	12
❑ 99	P. Parsons, Luxaire	$	12

Matchbox White Rose

Transporters 1:87 1989-90
Super Stars Series

❑ 3	D. Earnhardt, Goodwrench 89	$	320
❑ 3	D. Earnhardt, Goodwrench 90	$	135
❑ 6	M. Martin, Folgers 90	$	125
❑ 9	B. Elliott, Melling 90	$	100
❑ 20	R. Moroso, Crown 90	$	80
❑ 21	N. Bonnett, Citgo 89	$	160
❑ 28	C. Yarborough, Hardee's 89	$	150
❑ 43	R. Petty, STP 89	$	350
❑ 43	R. Petty, STP 90	$	125
❑ 66	D. Trickle, TropArtic 90	$	50
❑ 94	S. Marlin, Sunoco 90 (name on cab)	$	300
❑ 94	S. Marlin, Sunoco 90 (no name)	$	225

Matchbox White Rose

Transporters 1:87 1991
Super Stars Series

❑ Trans (22/25/66/68)		$	16
❑ 3	D. Earnhardt, Goodwrench	$	45
❑ 4	E. Irvan, Kodak	$	18
❑ 6	M. Martin, Folgers Mack Cab	$	30
❑ 6	M. Martin, Folgers Ford Cab	$	20
❑ 9	B. Elliott, Melling Mack Cab	$	40
❑ 9	B. Elliott, Melling Ford Cab	$	20
❑ 10	D. Cope, Purolator Pink	$	20
❑ 10	D. Cope, Purolator Red	$	40
❑ 10	E. Irvan, Mac Tools	$	30
❑ 17	D. Waltrip, Western Auto	$	20
❑ 28	D. Allison, Texaco Kenworth	$	75
❑ 42	K. Petty, Mello Yello	$	18
❑ 43	R. Petty, STP 20th Anniversary	$	25
❑ 59	R. Pressley, Alliance	$	25

Matchbox White Rose

Transporters 1:87 1992
Super Stars Series

❑ Trans (8/12/15/18/26)		$	10
❑ Trans (30/31/49/89/92)		$	10
❑ 1	J. Gordon, Baby Ruth	$	25
❑ 2	R. Wallace, Penske	$	16
❑ 3	D. Earnhardt, Goodwrench	$	25
❑ 7	H. Gant, Mac Tools	$	25
❑ 7	A. Kulwicki, Hooters	$	50
❑ 9	B. Elliott, Melling	$	12
❑ 28	D. Allison, Texaco Ford Cab	$	30
❑ 43	R. Petty, STP	$	12
❑ 44	B. Labonte, Slim Jim	$	12
❑ 55	T. Musgrave, Jasper Engines	$	12
❑ 72	K. Bouchard, ADAP	$	16

Matchbox White Rose

Transporters 1:87 1993
Super Star Series

❑ Trans (6/12/14/21/22/25)		$	10
❑ Trans (29/32/34/41/48)		$	10

❑ Trans (75/83/87/94/99)		$	10
❑ 8	J. Burton, TIC Financial	$	10
❑ 8	J. Burton, Baby Ruth	$	10
❑ 8	S. Marlin, Raybestos	$	10
❑ 08	B. Dotter, Dewalt	$	10
❑ 28	D. Allison, Mac Tools	$	25
❑ 36	K. Wallace, Dirt Devil	$	18
❑ 59	R. Pressley, Alliance	$	25
❑ 98	D. Cope, Bojangles	$	10
❑ 98	J. Spencer, Moly Black/Gold	$	10

Racing Champions

Transporters 1:64
1991

❑ 2	R. Wallace, Penske Racing	$	30
❑ 9	B. Elliott, Melling Red	$	100
❑ 11	G. Bodine	$	20
❑ 28	D. Allison, Havoline	$	50

Racing Champions

Transporters 1:64
1992

❑ Trans (14/15/18/21/30)		$	12
❑ Trans (42/66/71/72)		$	12
❑ 1	J. Gordon, Baby Ruth	$	55
❑ 1	R. Mast, Majik Market	$	20
❑ 2	R. Wallace, Penske	$	20
❑ 3	D. Earnhardt, Goodwrench	$	30
❑ 4	E. Irvan, Kodak	$	16
❑ 5	J. Fogelman, InnKeeper	$	15
❑ 5	R. Rudd, Tide	$	15
❑ 6	M. Martin, Valvoline	$	16
❑ 7	A. Kulwicki, Hooters	$	50
❑ 9	B. Elliott, Melling Blue	$	25
❑ 9	C. Little, Melling	$	25
❑ 9	J. Bessey, Auto Palace	$	15
❑ 10	D. Cope, Purolator	$	15
❑ 11	B. Elliott, Amoco	$	16
❑ 12	B. Allison, Allison Motorsports	$	15
❑ 12	H. Stricklin, Raybestos	$	12
❑ 16	W. Dallenbach Jr., Roush	$	20
❑ 17	D. Waltrip, Western Auto	$	12
❑ 17	D. Waltrip, Western Auto P	$	15
❑ 20	J. Ruttman, Fina	$	25
❑ 21	M. Shepherd, Citgo	$	15
❑ 22	S. Marlin, Maxwell House	$	12
❑ 25	K. Schrader	$	15
❑ 25	B. Venturini, Rain X	$	50
❑ 26	B. Bodine, Quaker State	$	12
❑ 28	D. Allison, Havoline	$	25
❑ 33	H. Gant, Food Lion	$	20
❑ 36	K. Wallace, Dirt Devil	$	25
❑ 43	R. Petty, Fan Appreciation Tour	$	20
❑ 43	R. Petty, STP	$	15
❑ 49	S. Smith, Ameritron Battery	$	30
❑ 59	A. Belmont, FDP Brakes	$	30
❑ 59	R. Pressley, Alliance	$	50
❑ 60	M. Martin, Winn Dixie	$	30
❑ 68	B. Hamilton, Country Time	$	12
❑ 70	J. D. McDuffie, Son's Auto	$	30
❑ 90	W. Dallenbach, Ford Motorsports	$	30
❑ 97	T. Labonte, Sunoco	$	20

Racing Champions

Transporters 1:64
1993

❏ Trans (8/12/15/18/21/22)		$	12
❏ Trans (26/30/42/75/87/98)		$	12
❏ 1	R. Mast, Majik Market	$	18
❏ 2	R. Wallace, Penske	$	16
❏ 3	D. Earnhardt, Goodwrench	$	22
❏ 3	D. Earnhardt, Goodwrench P	$	22
❏ 4	E. Irvan, Kodak	$	16
❏ 5	R. Rudd, Tide	$	15
❏ 6	M. Martin, Valvoline	$	16
❏ 7	A. Kulwicki, Hooters	$	50
❏ 11	B. Elliott, Amoco	$	16
❏ 14	T. Labonte, Kellogg's	$	16
❏ 17	D. Waltrip, Western Auto	$	12
❏ 17	D. Waltrip, Western Auto P	$	15
❏ 24	J. Gordon, Du Pont	$	30
❏ 26	B. Bodine, Quaker State	$	12
❏ 27	H. Stricklin, McDonald's	$	12
❏ 27	H. Stricklin, McDonald's P	$	16
❏ 28	D. Allison, Havoline	$	25
❏ 33	H. Gant, Food Lion	$	15
❏ 44	R. Wilson, STP	$	15
❏ 59	A. Belmont, FDP Brakes	$	25
❏ 60	M. Martin, Winn Dixie	$	20

Racing Champions Premier

Transporters 1:64
1993

❏ 2	R. Wallace, Ford Motorsports	$	35
❏ 3	D. Earnhardt, Goodwrench	$	65
❏ 5	R. Rudd, Tide	$	35
❏ 7	A. Kulwicki, Hooters	$	75
❏ 8	S. Marlin, Raybestos	$	30
❏ 11	B. Elliott, Budweiser	$	35
❏ 24	J. Gordon, Du Pont	$	60
❏ 26	B. Bodine, Quaker State	$	30
❏ 27	H. Stricklin, McDonald's	$	30
❏ 28	D. Allison, Havoline	$	60
❏ 28	E. Irvan, Mac Tools	$	45
❏ 33	H. Gant, Chevrolet	$	35
❏ 42	K. Petty, Mello Yello	$	35
❏ 51	Generic, Primer Ford Cab	$	30
❏ 51	Generic, Primer Kenworth	$	25
❏ 94	Generic, Brickyard 400	$	50

Racing Champions

Transporters 1:64
1994
YBH - Yellow Box Hobby Only

❏ 1	R. Mast, Majik Market	$	12
❏ 1	R. Mast, Precision Products	$	12
❏ 2	R. Craven, Du Pont	$	12
❏ 2	R. Wallace, Penske	$	15
❏ 2	R. Wallace, Penske YBH	$	20
❏ 3	D. Earnhardt, Goodwrench P	$	20
❏ 4	S. Marlin, Kodak	$	12
❏ 4	S. Marlin, Kodak, YBH	$	15
❏ 5	T. Labonte, Kellogg's	$	15
❏ 5	T. Labonte, Kellogg's YBH	$	20
❏ 6	M. Martin, Valvoline	$	15
❏ 7	G. Bodine, Exide Batteries	$	12
❏ 7	H. Gant, Manheim Auctions	$	20
❏ 8	J. Burton, Raybestos	$	12
❏ 10	R. Rudd, Tide	$	12
❏ 11	B. Elliott, Amoco	$	12
❏ 15	L. Speed, Quality Care	$	12
❏ 16	T. Musgrave, Family Channel	$	12
❏ 17	D. Waltrip, Western Auto	$	12
❏ 18	D. Jarrett, Interstate Batteries	$	12
❏ 18	D. Jarrett, Interstate Batteries YBH	$	20
❏ 19	L. Allen, Hooters	$	12
❏ 22	B. Labonte, Maxwell House	$	12
❏ 24	J. Gordon, Du Pont	$	23
❏ 26	B. Bodine, Quaker State	$	12
❏ 27	J. Spencer, McDonald's	$	12
❏ 28	E. Irvan, Havoline	$	15
❏ 30	M. Waltrip, Pennzoil	$	12
❏ 30	M. Waltrip, Pennzoil YBH	$	15
❏ 33	H. Gant, Leo Jackson	$	15
❏ 33	H. Gant, Leo Jackson YBH	$	16
❏ 40	B. Hamilton, Kendall	$	12
❏ 41	J. Nemechek, Meineke	$	12
❏ 42	K. Petty, Mello Yello	$	12
❏ 42	K. Petty, Mello Yello YBH	$	15
❏ 52	K. Schrader, AC-Delco	$	12
❏ 60	M. Martin, Winn Dixie	$	14
❏ 75	T. Bodine, Factory Stores	$	12
❏ 87	J. Nemechek, Dentyne	$	12
❏ 98	D. Cope, Fingerhut	$	12

Racing Champions Premier

Transporters 1:64
1994

❏ 3	D. Earnhardt, Goodwrench	$	45
❏ 4	S. Marlin, Kodak	$	30
❏ 33	H. Gant, Farewell Tour	$	35

Racing Champions

Transporters 1:64
1995 Previews

❏ 2	R. Wallace, Penske	$	14
❏ 7	G. Bodine, Exide	$	14
❏ 10	R. Rudd, Tide	$	14
❏ 14	T. Labonte, MW Windows	$	14
❏ 16	T. Musgrave, Family Channel	$	14
❏ 24	J. Gordon, Du Pont	$	17
❏ 38	E. Sawyer, Red Carpet	$	14
❏ 40	B. Hamilton, Kendall	$	14
❏ 57	J. Keller, Budget Gourmet	$	14

Racing Champions

Transporters 1:64
1995

❏ 2	R. Wallace, Penske	$	14
❏ 5	T. Labonte, Kellogg's	$	14
❏ 6	M. Martin, Valvoline	$	15
❏ 7	G. Bodine, Exide	$	14
❏ 10	R. Rudd, Tide	$	14

❑ 24	J. Gordon, Du Pont	$	20
❑ 26	S. Kinser, Quaker State	$	14
❑ 27	L. Allen, Hooters	$	14
❑ 28	D. Jarrett/E. Irvan, Texaco	$	14
❑ 40	P. Moise, Dial	$	14
❑ 60	M. Martin, Winn Dixie	$	16
❑ 94	B. Elliott, McDonald's	$	15
❑ 94	B. Elliott, Thunderbat	$	20

Racing Champions Premier

Transporters 1:64
1995

❑ 2	R. Wallace, Penske B	$	40
❑ 26	S. Kinser, Quaker State B	$	40
❑ 27	L. Allen, Hooters	$	20
❑ 40	B. Hamilton, Kendall	$	20
❑ 94	B. Elliott, McDonald's	$	20

Racing Champions

Transporters 1:87
1993-94
YBH - Yellow Box Hobby Only

❑ Trans (9/11/12/14/15/17/21)		$	6
❑ Trans (22/25/27/43/44/87/98)		$	6
❑ 1	R. Mast, Precision Products, YBH	$	10
❑ 2	R. Wallace, Penske, YBH	$	12
❑ 2	R. Wallace, Penske	$	8
❑ 3	D. Earnhardt, Goodwrench	$	15
❑ 4	E. Irvan, Kodak	$	6
❑ 4	S. Marlin, Kodak, YBH	$	10
❑ 5	T. Labonte, Kellogg's, YBH	$	10
❑ 5	R. Rudd, Tide	$	6
❑ 6	M. Martin, Valvoline	$	6
❑ 6	M. Martin, Valvoline, YBH	$	10
❑ 7	H. Gant, Manheim Auctions	$	10
❑ 7	H. Gant, Morema	$	8
❑ 7	A. Kulwicki, Hooters	$	20
❑ 8	J. Burton, Raybestos, YBH	$	10
❑ 8	S. Marlin, Raybestos	$	6
❑ 18	D. Jarrett, Interstate Batteries	$	6
❑ 18	D. Jarrett, Interstate Batteries, YBH	$	10
❑ 24	J. Gordon, Du Pont	$	15
❑ 24	J. Gordon, Du Pont, YBH	$	25
❑ 26	B. Bodine, Quaker State	$	6
❑ 26	B. Bodine, Quaker State, YBH	$	10
❑ 28	D. Allison, Havoline	$	12
❑ 28	D. Allison, Havoline Black/White	$	14
❑ 30	M. Waltrip, Pennzoil	$	6
❑ 30	M. Waltrip, Pennzoil, YBH	$	10
❑ 33	H. Gant, Food Lion	$	8
❑ 33	H. Gant, Morema	$	12
❑ 33	H. Gant, Leo Jackson, YBH	$	10
❑ 35	B. Venturini, Amoco	$	20
❑ 42	K. Petty, Mello Yello	$	6
❑ 42	K. Petty, Mello Yello, YBH	$	10
❑ 52	K. Schrader, AC-Delco	$	6
❑ 52	K. Schrader, Morema	$	10

❑ 66	C. Yarborough, TropArtic	$	12
❑ 75	T. Bodine, Factory Stores, YBH	$	10

Racing Champions Premier

Transporters 1:87
1993

Trans (4/5/6/8/12/14/15/18)		$	20
Trans (21/22/27/33/42/87)		$	20
❑ 2	W. Burton, Hardee's	$	20
❑ 2	R. Wallace, Penske	$	30
❑ 3	D. Earnhardt, Goodwrench	$	35
❑ 3	D. Earnhardt, Goodwrench DEI	$	35
❑ 7	A. Kulwicki, Hooters	$	75
❑ 11	B. Elliott, Bud	$	35
❑ 11	B. Elliott, Amoco	$	20
❑ 24	J. Gordon, Du Pont	$	30
❑ 28	D. Allison, Havoline, Black	$	35
❑ 28	D. Allison, Havoline, Black/White	$	35
❑ 28	E. Irvan, Havoline	$	25
❑ 44	D. Green, Slim Jim	$	20
❑ 44	R. Wilson, STP	$	20
❑ 51	Generic, Primer, Kenworth	$	20
❑ 51	Generic, Primer, Ford	$	20
❑ 59	R. Pressley, Alliance	$	35
❑ 60	M. Martin, Winn Dixie	$	40

Racing Champions Premier

Transporters 1:87
1994

❑ Trans (2/5/8/15/16)		$	20
❑ Trans (19/32/40/98)		$	20
❑ 3	D. Earnhardt, Goodwrench	$	27
❑ 4	S. Marlin, Kodak	$	20
❑ 4	S. Marlin, Kodak Fun Saver	$	20
❑ 7	G. Bodine, Exide	$	25
❑ 7	H. Gant, Manheim Auctions	$	25
❑ 17	D. Waltrip, Western Auto	$	25
❑ 21	M. Shepherd, Cheerwine	$	25
❑ 28	E. Irvan, Havoline	$	25
❑ 28	E. Irvan, Mac Tools	$	25
❑ 52	K. Schrader, AC-Delco	$	25
❑ 60	M. Martin, Winn Dixie	$	25
❑ 94	NDA, Brickyard 400	$	35

Racing Champions

Transporters 1:87
1995

❑ 2	R. Wallace, Penske	$	6
❑ 5	T. Labonte, Kellogg's	$	6
❑ 6	M. Martin, Valvoline	$	6
❑ 7	G. Bodine, Exide	$	6
❑ 10	R. Rudd, Tide	$	6
❑ 24	J. Gordon, Du Pont	$	10
❑ 26	S. Kinser, Quaker State	$	6
❑ 27	L. Allen, Hooters	$	6
❑ 28	D. Jarrett/E. Irvan, Texaco	$	6
❑ 40	P. Moise, Dial Purex	$	6

Winross Transporters

1:64
1987-1990

❏	B. Elliott, Coors 90	$	225
❏	B. Gerhart, ARCA 88	$	300
❏	S. Marlin, Sunoco 90	$	100
❏	S. Smith, Hamilton Trucking 88	$	150
❏	R. Wilson, Kodak, Ford 87	$	325
❏	R. Wilson, Kodak, Mack 87	$	450

Winross Transporters

1:64
1991

❏	K. Bouchard, ADAP	$	75
❏	B. Elliott, Coors Light	$	125
❏	B. Elliott, Fan Club	$	90
❏	B. Elliott, Museum Blue	$	90
❏	T. Ellis, Polaroid	$	175
❏	T. Labonte, Sunoco	$	125
❏	R. Petty, STP	$	150
❏	K. Schrader, Kodak	$	90

Winross Transporters

1:64
1992

❏	J. Donlavey, Truxmore	$	90
❏	B. Elliott, Fan Club	$	90
❏	B. Elliott, Museum Red	$	90
❏	D. Earnhardt, Goodwrench WRC	$	160
❏	D. Earnhardt, Goodwrench Wood BX	$	320
❏	T. Ellis, Polaroid	$	90
❏	B. Hamilton, Country Time	$	60
❏	T. Labonte, Sunoco	$	75
❏	T. Lund	$	75
❏	J. McClure, Superior Performance	$	90

❏	J. D. McDuffie, Son's Auto	$	75
❏	P. Parsons	$	90
❏	K. Petty, Mello Yello	$	90
❏	R. Petty, STP, Fan Appreciation Tour	$	90
❏	R. Pressley, Alliance	$	150
❏	F. Roberts	$	75
❏	D. Waltrip, Western Auto	$	90
❏	D. Waltrip, Western Auto Red	$	125

Winross Transporters

1:64
1993

❏	J. Bessey, AC-Delco	$	50
❏	B. Elliott, Fan Club	$	75
❏	D. Ford, NASCAR Flags	$	75
❏	J. Gordon, Du Pont	$	100
❏	S. Grissom, Channellock	$	50
❏	D. Jarrett, Interstate Batteries	$	60
❏	A. Kulwicki, Hooters	$	150
❏	S. Marlin, Maxwell House	$	60
❏	M. Martin, Valvoline	$	75
❏	R. Pressley, Alliance	$	90
❏	M. Stefanik, Auto Palace	$	50
❏	Generic/McClure Racing, Kodak	$	125

Winross Transporters

1:64
1994

❏	D. Allison, Havoline ERR	$	125
❏	D. Allison, Havoline COR	$	100
❏	B. Elliott, Budweiser	$	75
❏	H. Gant, Farewell Tour	$	90
❏	T. Labonte, Kellogg's	$	75
❏	M. Waltrip, Pennzoil	$	60

Plastic Model Kits

When one thinks of the term "model car" it's easy to envision a father at the kitchen table helping his son build a plastic model kit of one of his favorite cars. Few baby boomers of the 1950s, especially males, went through their adolescence without building a plastic model race car. Like baseball cards, these items became a fond reminder of our childhood and perhaps the hours we spent together with our fathers. As adults we never forgot about those times, and our urge for model building continued. That's why it is no surprise to learn that the market of adult model car builders has grown significantly during the past two decades. Outstanding publications such as *Scale Auto Enthusiast* have dedicated themselves to serving this growing base of collectors. How many plastic model kits builders and collectors are out there? Consider this: since 1979 over four million copies of *Scale Auto Enthusiast* have been printed.

The National Model and Hobby Show held in late October is one of the platforms used by plastic model manufacturers to announce their new product offerings for the upcoming year. As expected, in 1996 the NASCAR Super Truck model offerings should be "red hot" with collectors. AMT/Ertl will be offering both Ford and Chevy versions, with other manufacturers expected to follow their lead.

The Chevrolet Monte Carlo was hot back in 1995 and more popular than ever with collectors. The winningest car in Winston Cup history was first available to collectors in the early 1970s (1970-72) in race car kits made by AMT and MPC. Two subsequent generations of the car followed during the decade, but were never offered by the major kit manufacturers or simply not raced in Winston Cup competition. The 1980s saw it represented by Monogram until it was replaced by the Lumina in 1989. In 1995 it captured the interest of auto racing collectors with plastic kit introductions by Monogram of the #3 GM/Goodwrench car and the #4 Kodak Film car.

Like the collector, plastic kit manufacturers have also evolved, with considerably more attention paid to detailing each model. Correct proportions and crisp, clean molding is now expected by collectors. Any modifications made by NASCAR should be reflected in all updated kits. Cost restrictions or oversights by plastic kit manufacturers often necessitate collectors delving into old kits looking for parts to interchange. For example, in the Monogram kits previously mentioned, two front wheel hubs need to be exchanged with parts from other previously manufactured kits that contained rear hubs in order to have the correct configuration.

The craving by collectors for exact model kit representation is exemplified most by the aftermarket for decals. Although plastic kit manufacturers have made considerable strides in trying to improve in every area, it is difficult to keep up with changes in sponsorship. Companies such as UpScale Graphics produce updated decals for collectors to substitute for outdated versions that may be included in some manufacturers kits. Instruction sheets are included with these decals and in UpScale's offerings five different angles are given of the subject's car. Although these sheets also give color information, they don't give exact decal information for each race, so in some instances a collector will have to know which sticker was used on which car during certain races.

Since molds are expensive, it's not surprising to see manufacturers' kit offerings identical except for the color of the plastic. This is an important point to understand especially if you need to inter-

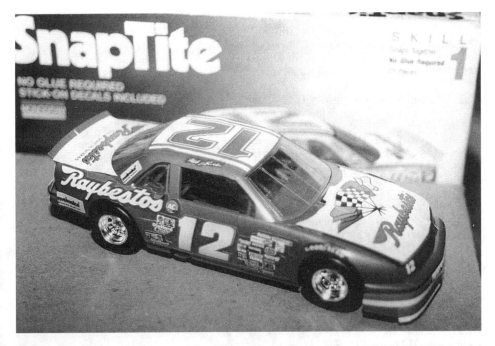

Monogram's SnapTite plastic model line offers collectors three different skill levels. Skill Level 1 snaps together and requires no glue.

change a piece for some unexpected reason. Many manufacturers such as Monogram Models, Inc. will replace missing parts as long as you include the kit number, part number, description and your return address.

If you are a beginning collector, it is also important to note that some manufacturers like Monogram have different skill levels. This company's SnapTite line offers collectors three different skill levels, from no glue required to a challenging line for the experienced builder.

For the die-hard auto racing fan there is no better niche of the hobby than plastic model kit building and collecting. It will constantly test your knowledge of the sport from modifications to engines to changes in sponsorship. It will also force you to become completely knowledgeable of not only auto racing history but also that of plastic kit manufacturers' product offerings. It also gives each builder an opportunity to showcase his patience, knowledge, and skills with each new kit—an element unlike any other niche of the hobby.

A final note: As you read through the values of the kits provided in this chapter, you may see why it's worthwhile to buy more than one kit. The prices reflected here are for mint condition kits still in original packaging.

Selected Model Kit Price Listings

All prices are mint condition kits still in original packaging

AMT 1:25 Kits

T229	1976 Dodge Dart #43 (R. Petty)	$	145
T373	1973 Chevy Malibu #12 (B. Allison)	$	135
T380	1974 Diegard Chevelle #88 (D. Allison)	$	110
T391	1972 Jo Han Rebox #90	$	65
T395	1974 Chevelle #28 (G. Johncock)	$	110
T421	1973 Coca-Cola Chevy #12 (B. Allison)	$	145
T429	1974 King's Row Chevy #72 (Parsons)	$	125

T430	1975 Penske Matador #16 (B. Allison)	$	110
T430	1975 Coca-Cola/Penske (B. Allison)	$	110
T443	1975 Chevy Malibu #54 (L. Pond)	$	100
T565	1976 Penske/Van/Trlr #16 (B. Allison)	$	220
T569	1976 Dodge/Ford Truck Set #43 (Petty)	$	240
1895	1975 Chevy Malibu	$	30
3030	1973 Matador Sportsman #12 (Allison)	$	75
3688	1972-1976 Chevelle/Malibu (Generic Kit)	$	70
6019	Trailer #9 "Coors" (Elliott - 1:24)	$	50
6162	1992 T-Bird #15 "Motorcraft" (Bodine)	$	20
6457	1991 T-Bird #22 "Maxwell House" (Marlin)	$	20
6727	1991 Chevy #4 "Kodiak" (Irvan)	$	20
6728	1990 Pontiac #43 "STP" (Petty)	$	20
6730	1991 T-Bird #15 "Motorcraft" (Shepherd)	$	20
6731	1990 Olds Cutlass #4 "Kodiak" (Wilson)	$	22
6732	1990 Pontiac #30 "Country Time" (Waltrip)	$	22
6733	1990 T-Bird #21 "Citgo" (Bonnett/Jarrett)	$	55
6738	1990 Olds #94 "Sunoco" (Marlin)	$	22
6739	1990 T-Bird #7 "Zerex" (Kulwicki)	$	60
6740	1991 T-Bird #9 "Coors Light" (Elliott)	$	25
6802	Trailer #4 "Kodak" (Irvan - 1:24)	$	45
6807	1993 T-Bird #7 "Hooters" (Kulwicki)	$	30
6819	1991 Olds #68 "Country Time" (Hamilton)	$	20
6852	1993 Lumina #24 "Du Pont" (Gordon)	$	15
6892	1993 Pontiac 344 "STP" (Wilson)	$	13
6894	1993 T-Bird #26 "Quaker State" (Bodine)	$	13
6961	1990 Pontiac #27 "MGD" (Wallace)	$	35
6962	1990 T-Bird #9 "Coors" (Elliott)	$	30
8042	1983 T-Bird #21 "Valvoline" (Baker)	$	75
8043	1983 Chevy #11 "Pepsi" (D. Waltrip)	$	85
8044	1984 Pontiac GP #43 "STP" (R. Petty)	$	45
8045	1983 Chevy #28 "Hardee's" (Yarborough)	$	75
8046	1984 T-Bird 315 "Wrangler" (Earnhardt)	$	70
8047	1983 Pontiac #7 "7-Eleven" (K. Petty)	$	85
8106	1991 Pontiac #42 "Mello Yello" (K. Petty)	$	17
8115	1971 Plymouth Roadrunner #43 (Petty)	$	14	*re-issue
8116	1975 Matador #16 "Coca-Cola/AMC" (Allison)	$	13
8752	1991 Chevy #18 "Interstate Batteries" (Jarrett)	$	12
8754	1992 T-Bird #66 "Phillips 66" (Little)	$	16
8756	1992 T-Bird #6 "Valvoline" (Martin)	$	22
8910	Gift set – three piece		
	(Kodak #4, STP #43, Maxwell House #2)	$	60

AMT 1:32 Snap Kits

8707	1992 Lumina #4 "Kodak" (Irvan)	$	14
8708	1992 T-Bird #22 "Maxwell House" (Marlin)	$	14
8709	1992 Pontiac #43 "STP" (R. Petty)	$	14
8712	1993 Pontiac #44 "STP" (Wilson)	$	9
8721	1993 T-Bird #21 "Citgo" (Shepherd)	$	9
8722	1992 Lumina #10 "Purolator" (Cope)	$	14
8723	1993 T-Bird #26 "Quaker State" (Bodine)	$	9
8727	1992 Pontiac #42 "Mello Yello" (K. Petty)	$	14
8728	1992 Chevy #18 "Interstate Batteries" (Jarrett)	$	14
8729	1992 T-Bird #6 "Valvoline" (Martin)	$	15
8730	1992 T-Bird 315 "Motorcraft" (Bodine)	$	14
8799	1992 T-Bird 366 "Phillips" (Little)	$	14

AMT 1:16 Kits

6717	1985 T-Bird #28 "Hardee's" (Yarborough)	$	105
6718	1985 T-Bird #7 "7-Eleven" (K. Petty)	$	105
6741	1985 Grand Prix #43 "STP" (R. Petty)	$	110
6746	1985 Pontiac #75 "Nationwise" (Speed)	$	85

Monogram 1:24 Kits

DA124	1993 T-Bird #28 "Mac Tools" (D. Allison)	$	65	
EI124	1994 T-Bird #28 "Mac Tools" (Irvan)	$	35	
HG124	1993 Lumina #7 "Mac Tools" (Gant)	$	35	
646	1994 T-Bird #21 "Cheerwine" (Shepherd)	$	35	
664	1981-83 Buick Regal (Generic Kit)	$	22	
898	1993 Lumina #7 "Mac Tools" (Gant)	$	85	
2204	1983 Buick Regal #11 "Mountain Dew" (Waltrip)	$	80	
2205	1982 Buick Regal #1 "UNO" (Baker)	$	105	
2206	1983 T-Bird #15 "Wrangler" (Earnhardt)	$	85	
2207	1983 T-Bird #9 "Melling" (Elliott)	$	75	
2244	1985 T-Bird #9 SH "Coors" (Elliott)	$	80	
2244	1984 T-Bird #9 LH "Coors" (Elliott)	$	80	
2244	1984 T-Bird #9 SH "Coors" Winston (Elliott)	$	105	
2244	1985 T-Bird #9 "Melling Speedway" (Elliott)	$	80	
2245	1984 Budweiser #11 or #12 (Waltrip/Bonnett)	$	95	
2298	1984 Buick GN #22 "Miller" (B. Allison)	$	80	
2298	1984 Buick #22 "Miller" Speedway (B. Allison)	$	80	
2299	1984 Chevy #44 "Piedmont" (T. Labonte)	$	100	
2428	1991 Pontiac #42 "Mello Yello" (K. Petty)	$	13	
2430	1991 T-Bird #28 "Havoline" (D. Allison)	$	13	
2431	1991 Buick #12 "Raybestos" (Stricklin)	$	16	
2432	1991 Olds #75 "Dinner Bell" (Ruttman)	$	25	
2440	1993 Lumina #5 "Tide" (Rudd)	$	25	
2441	1993 Lumina #24 "Du Pont" (Gordon)	$	14	
2442	1993 T-Bird #27 "McDonald's" (Stricklin)	$	12	
2447	1995 Monte Carlo GM Goodwrench (Earnhardt)	$	13	
2448	1995 Monte Carlo Kodak (Marlin)	$	11.50	
2449	1994 T-Bird #10 "Tide" (Rudd)	$	12	
2450	1994 T-Bird #7 "Exide" (Bodine)	$	12	
2451	1994 T-Bird #15 "Quality Care" (Speed)	$	12	
2465	1995 T-Bird #16 "Family Channel" (Musgrave)	$	12	
2466	1995 T-Bird Stock Car	$	11	
2469	1995 McDonald's Thunderbat, (Elliott)	$	13	
2476	1995 Monte Carlo #24 "Du Pont" (Gordon)	$	8	
2706	1985 Lumina #3 "Skoal" (Gant)	$	90	
2707	1984 Buick #47 "Valvoline" (Bouchard)	$	105	
2722	1985 Pontiac #43 "STP/CURB" (Petty)	$	95	
2723	1986 T-Bird #15 "Motorcraft" (Rudd)	$	60	
2734	1987 Chevy #25 "Folgers" (Richmond)	$	65	
2754	1987 Olds #29 "Hardee's" (Yarborough)	$	60	
2755	1987 Chevy #17 "Tide" (Waltrip)	$	75	
2779	1987 Olds #83 "Kmart" (Speed)	$	40	
2786	1989 Buick 326 "Quaker State" (Rudd)	$	30	
2787	1989 Pontiac #75 "Valvoline" (Bonnett)	$	80	
2900	1988 M/C #3 "Goodwrench" (Earnhardt)	$	45	
2900	1991 M/C #3 "Goodwrench" (Earnhardt)	$	13	*re-issue
2906	1989 Pontiac #42 "Peak" (K. Petty)	$	35	
2908	1989 T-Bird #7 "Zerex" (Kulwicki)	$	60	
2914	1990 Pontiac #57 "Heinz" (Stricklin/Spencer)	$	30	

2915	1989 Buick #8, #84, #12 "Miller"	$	70
2916	1989 T-Bird #28 "Havoline" (D. Allison)	$	80
2917	1990 Lumina #46 "City Chevy" "Days of Thunder"	$	40
2920	1990 Lumina #18 "Hardee's" "Days of Thunder"	$	30
2921	1990 Lumina #51 "Mello Yello" "Days of Thunder"	$	45
2927	1990-1992 Lumina #3 Goodwrench (Earnhardt)	$	30
2928	1990-1992 T-Bird #6 "Folgers" (Martin)	$	30
2930	1990 Pontiac #66 "TropArtic" (Trickle)	$	35
2932	1990 Pontiac #30 "K. Aid/Country Time"(Waltrip)	$	35
2939	1991 Pontiac #30 "Pennzoil" (Waltrip)	$	30
2940	1990-1991 Buick #8 "Snickers" (Wilson and Hillin)	$	30
2941	1991 Lumina #10 "Purolator" (Cope)	$	30
2942	1991 T-Bird #22 "Maxwell House" (Marlin)	$	30
2949	1991 Lumina #17 "Western Auto" (Waltrip)	$	12
2959	1992 T-Bird #36 "Valvoline" (Martin)	$	12
2960	1992 Pontiac #32 "Pontiac Excitement" (Wallace)	$	12
2961	1992 T-Bird #21 "Citgo" (Shepherd)	$	12
2973	1994 Pontiac #40 "Dirt Devil" (Wallace)	$	12
2974	1994 Lumina #5 "Kellogg's" (T. Labonte)	$	12
6182	1983-1986 T-Bird (Generic Kit)	$	60
6298	Combo Set #3 "Wrangler" (Earnhardt)	$	25
6367	Combo Set #4 "Kodak Film" (Irvan/Wilson)	$	25
6368	Combo Set "Rookie of the Year" (Kulwicki/Schrader)	$	25
6389	Combo Set #42/#43 "Racing Pettys"	$	25
6391	Combo Set #11 Waltrip "Pepsi and Mt. Dew"	$	25
9460	1994 T-Bird #60 "Winn Dixie" (Martin)	$	40

Monogram's plastic model of Jeff Gordon's Du Pont Automotive Finishes Monte Carlo. The Skill Level 3 kit contains ninety-five pieces.

Monogram 1:32 Snap Kits

1086	1992 T-Bird #28 "Havoline" (D. Allison)	$	10
1087	1992 T-Bird #6 "Valvoline" (Martin)	$	10
1088	1992 Lumina #3 "Goodwrench" (Earnhardt)	$	20
1089	1992 Chevy 312 "Raybestos" (Stricklin)	$	10
1090	Race Set #3 "Goodwrench" (Earnhardt)	$	45
1091	Race Set #28 "Havoline" (D. Allison)	$	30
1094	1993 T-Bird #68 "Country Time" (Hamilton)	$	10
1095	1993 T-Bird #26 "Quaker State" (Bodine)	$	20
1700	1994 T-Bird #2 "Penske Racing" (Wallace)	$	12
1701	1994 McDonald's Thunderbat (Elliott)	$	10

MPC 1:25 Kits

681	1976 Malibu #1 "Hawaiian Tropic"	$	95
731	1971 "K&K Insurance" (Issac)	$	240
	1972 Ford Torino #15 (Issac)	$	220
738	1983 S Stocker Monte Carlo #37	$	55
845	1982 S Stocker Buick #58	$	55
846	1982 S Stocker Grand Prix #20	$	55
1701	1971 Daytona Charger #43 (Petty)	$	180
1702	1971 NASCAR Charger #11 (Baker)	$	180
1703	1971 NASCAR Chevelle #56 (Hurtubise)	$	90
1704	1971 NASCAR Mercury #21 (D. Allison)	$	150
1705	1971 NASCAR Charger #22 (Brooks)	$	180
1706	1971 NASCAR GTO #3 (Pearson)	$	140
1707	1972 Monte Carlo #11 (Coo Coo Martin)	$	160
1708	1973 NASCAR Charger #43 (Petty)	$	150
1709	1973 Chevy #22 Jr. Johnson (Yarborough)	$	125
1710	1973 Ford Torino #25 (Issac)	$	155
1711	1973 NASCAR Charger #71 (Baker)	$	140
1712	1977 Chevelle #39 "Pepsi" (Hurtubise)	$	80
1713	1978 NASCAR Charger #43 (Petty)	$	140
6365	1985 Chevy #2 "Chattanooga Chew" (Pearson)	$	95
6366	1985 Chevy #55 "Copenhagen" (Parsons)	$	100
6367	1985 Pontiac #2 "Alugard" (Wallace)	$	100
6368	1985 Chevy #66 "Skoal Bandit" (Parsons)	$	95

MPC 1:16 Kits

3053	1973 Charger #43 (Petty)	$	260
3055	1973 Charger #71 (Baker)	$	240

Jo Han 1:25 Kits

GC964	1964 Plymouth #43 (Petty)	$	30
GC1470	1970 Superbird #43, #40 (Petty/Hamilton)	$	30
GC1970	1970 Superbird/Plymouth #43 (Petty)	$	30
GC2200	1969 Oval Track #22	$	40
GC3372	1970 Oval Track #27	$	40

Auto Racing Cards

Over the last few years the increased popularity of both NASCAR and Indy Car trading cards has prompted collector interest in vintage trading cards sets, as well as cards of other forms of racing. The interest has led collectors to seek out not only vintage sets produced here the United States, but also sets produced in Europe. Europe itself has a long and fascinating history of motor racing, especially Formula One.

European Auto Racing Cards

Some analysts have divided card collecting in Europe into two distinct geographic areas: United Kingdom/England and the continent of Europe. The reason for this is that certain forms of cards, such as cigarette cards and commercial card sets, were far more prevalent in England than on the continent of Europe.

From about 1870 to 1939, virtually every conceivable subject was transformed into cigarette cards. When sports card collectors think of cigarette or "tobacco" cards, their minds often jump to the famous T-206 Honus Wagner cigarette card. The American Tobacco Company popularized baseball players on tobacco cards, but they would not be the only subject. Animals, famous people, aircraft and of course automobiles, racing cars, and racing personalities also were depicted on these small cards.

Although the first cigarette card was indeed American, the British actually out-produced the number of issues created in the United States. British tobacco manufacturers found themselves employing full staffs just to keep up with the demand for artwork. Often many of the British cigarette issues ended up being a series of twenty-five or fifty cards.

The beginning of World War II essentially brought an end to cigarette card production. An attempt was made by Carreras Cigarettes to revive the cards during the mid-seventies, but it was unsuccessful. The Imperial Tobacco Company has distributed a few sets with "Tom Thumb" cigars in England. One such release was a thirty-card set called "History of Motor Racing." This set presented a nice overview of the history of Grand Prix racing from 1986 to the present day. The beautiful set featured the artwork of renowned artist Graham Turner and included two variations. The more common set included the copyright "Imperial Group Plc." on the back, while the rarer set has "Imperial Tobacco Ltd." The first set can run collectors about $40-$60, while the latter can sell for $125-$150 depending upon the market.

Although many sets were dedicated to racing or automobile subjects, there were also sets that included famous sportsmen and included athletes from boxing, soccer, track & field and even motor racing.

Non-tobacco cards have been issued for years in conjunction with numerous products. The Topps Company of Brooklyn, New York, for example, issued sets during the 1960s and 1970s under the trade name of "A. & B. C. Gum" (American and British Chewing Gum). These sets include "Grand Prix" (1958, 27 cards) and "Car Stamps" (1971, 120 stamps) to name a few. Although the sets are a bit smaller in size, the content is often identical.

Selected Pre-1940 Cigarette Card Sets

Manufacturer	Title	Date	Comments
Ardath	Speed, Land, Sea and Air	1935	50 card set, 10 on racing – includes Campbell's "Blue Bird"
	Sports Champions	1935	50 card set, 5 on racing

168

B.A.T.	Motor Cycles	1927	50 card set, reprinted
Churchman	Kings of Speed	1939	50 card set, 22 cards on racing
Cope	Sports & Pastimes	1925	25 card set, 1 on racing
Lambert & Butler	Motors	1908	25 card set, reprinted
	Motor Cars 1st and 2nd Series	1922/23	50 card set, reprinted
	Motorcycles	1923	50 card set, reprinted
	Motor Cars	1934	25 card set, reprinted
Ogden's	Famous Dirt Track Riders	1929	50 card set, motorcyclists
	Motor Race 1931	1931	50 card set, rare, includes auto and motorcycle racing
Pattreioux	Dirt Track Riders	1929	50 card set, motorcyclists
Player	Motor Cars, A series	1936	50 card set, reprinted
Wills	Motor Cycles	1926	50 card set
	Speed	1930	50 card set, 10 cards on racing cars and cycles
	Speed	1931	50 card set, 13 cards on racing cars and cycles

Sets that were produced and marketed solely as complete card sets without a product attachment are often referred to as commercial card sets. Although some of these sets were created in the 1930s, most were created after 1950. These sets carried on the tradition of reproducing artwork rather than photographs, as the latter are less appealing for framing, which is popular with European collectors.

Selected Pre-1970 Commercial Card Sets

Year	No. of Cards	Manufacturer/Title	Comments
1933	12	Amalgamated Press – Sports Queriosities	
1937	48	D. C. Thomson – Speed	Four racing cards
1952	56	Bake-a-Cake, Ltd. – Motor Cars	
1954	50	Kane Products Ltd. – Modern Racing Cars	Black & white set
1955	50	Miranda – 100 Years of Motoring	
	12	News Chronicle – Story of Stirling Moss	Black & white set
	18	Castrol – Famous Riders	
1956	24	Castrol – Racing Cars	
1957	24	British Automatic Co. – Racing and Sports Cars	Your weight printed on back of card
1959	48	Merrysweets, Ltd. – World Racing Cars	
1960	25	Mitcham Foods – Motor Racing	Black & white set
1961	12	Brook Motors – Veteran Cars	Postcard size
1962	25	B. T. Ltd. – Modern Motor Cars	
1963	30	Avon Rubber Co. – Leading Riders of 1963	Motorcyclists
	50	Sweetule Products – Motorcycles Old & New	Scarce
1965	25	Amaran Tea – Veteran Racing Cars	1900-30 cars
	25	Autobrite – Vintage Cars	
	50	Plant, Ltd. – Racing Cars of the World	Rare
1966	40	J. Lyons & Co. – Famous Cars	
	24	Mobil Oil – Vintage Cars	
	35	Petpro, Ltd. – Grand Prix of Racing Cars	
	36	Prescott – Speed Kings	
	66	D. C. Thomson – Motor Cars of 1966	
	50	Brook Bond – History of the Motor Car	

Panini, the most popular name in stickers worldwide, produced a number of motor racing and automobile sets. These include "Grand Prix" (48), "Formula One Grand Prix" (144), "Moto Sport" (324), "Super Auto" (200), and "Super Moto" (200). None of these sets are dated but most were issued in the mid-1980s.

Many European playing card manufacturers also produce other types of card sets. Popular among these sets are "trump" games or "quartettes." These games are designed for play by four people and are typically produced in 32-card sets. The game, which is similar to the American "Go Fish," involves matching a statistic from your card with the same category of statistic from your opponents' cards. The popularity of the game has attracted fierce competition among manufacturers, who constantly try to outdo each other. The flood of constant releases makes it difficult to account for many of the sets issued, as well as their production.

Calendar card sets are also issued in Europe. Typically eight- to twelve-card sets, these feature a subject on the front, such as racing, and a calendar with a business name on the back. The cards, which are typically given away like business cards or flyers, often have low production runs (under 5,000).

169

Additionally, telephone cards, which have also become popular in America, are typically issued in Europe. These cards come in a variety of designs and denominations, with auto racing a very popular subject. All of these cards have expiration dates for using the calling time and pin numbers that are revealed when scratched. The format of the phone cards has led to a dilemma with collectors, which is whether or not to use the value associated with it. In Europe most collectors use the phone time on high denomination phone cards and leave the lower value cards unscratched and unused. American collectors however, have been trained to keep cards in mint condition in order for them to maintain their value.

How to determine an accurate value for phone cards is another issue that is perplexing to collectors. For example, the Jeff Gordon 1995 Press Pass Premium Phone Card was issued at a denomination of $1,995. With only eighteen of these cards in existence, all of them signed, how can you determine an accurate value? Typically the face value is used as a starting point, as there is that much phone time associated with the card. But what happens after the phone time expires? Does scarcity alone become the key in determining the card's value? Is an unused Jeff Gordon card going to be worth more than a used one after the expiration date? These are all issues still to be played out in the relatively new American phone card market. What has appeared as trend in the hobby is not to use the lower denomination phone cards.

American Auto Racing Cards

A popular starting point with collectors of American vintage racing cards is either the "Automobile Drivers" set (circa 1911, twenty-five cards) produced by American Tobacco under its Mecca/Hassan brand, or the "Automobile" Series (circa 1911, fifty cards), produced by the same company under its Turkey Red brand. Cards from either of these sets are difficult to find in higher grade conditions and if you are lucky enough to run across just one it will probably run in the $10 to $25 price range. Often racers ended up as part of a general sporting series, such as the "Series of Champions" (T-227) produced in 1912 by the American Tobacco Company for its Honest Long Cut brand. This set included Ralph Mulford, one of the great American racers of the early twentieth century. In 1911, one of his finest years in racing, Mulford was flagged first but placed second in a controversial inaugural Indianapolis 500 and won the prestigious Vanderbilt Cup at Savannah. The Mulford card, also difficult to find in higher grade conditions, can run a collector $60 in very good condition.

Collectors who find some of the cigarette card sets either too challenging or out of their price range may want to begin collecting with one of the many promotional sets offered during the 1950s, such as "Sports Cars" from Mother's Cookies or "Indy Speedway Winners" by Stark & Wetzell. Both these sets are under fifty cards and although they are often found in better condition than cigarette cards, they can still be a challenge to find. A Stark & Wetzell card can be had for under $30 in mint condition, while a similar Mother's Cookies card can be purchased for under $20.

Selected Pre-1980 Auto Racing Sets

Year	Name of Set	Company	Cards	Price/Condition = NR MT + Single card from set
1950*	Sports Cars	Hood Ice Cream	42	Price Range: $18-$23 NR MT+
1953	Antique Autos	Bowman	48	PR: $6-$10 NR MT +
1953	Sports Cars	Mother's Cookies	42	PR: $10-$17 NR MT +
1953	Antique Autos	Signal Oil	63	PR: $10-$13 NR MT +
1953-55	World on Wheels	Topps	180	
	#1-160			PR: $2-$4
	#161-170			PR: $22-$35
	#171-180, red backs			PR: $25-$60
	#171-180, blue backs			PR: $25-$60
1955	Sports Cars	Parkhurst	42	PR: $15-$20, French and English text
1955	Old Time Cars	Parkhurst/Zip	42	PR: $15-$20, French and English text
1955	Indy Speedway Winners	Stark & Wetzell **	37***	PR: $22-$27, blank backs
1950*	Antique Autos	Premiere/Oak	63	PR: $5-$7
1950*	Sports Cars	Skinner's Raisin Bran	10	PR: $17-$23
1950*	Sports Cars	Tip Top Bread	28	PR: $25-$40
1960	Hawes Wax Indy	Parkhurst	50	PR: $17-$23
		Kenner	6	PR: $15-$30, larger size than above issue, identical sides
1961	Sports Cars	Topps	66	PR: $4-$7

1965	Spec Sheet	Donruss	66	PR: $6-$8
	# 49 Bobby Unser			PR: $12-$15
	#59 Connie Kalitta			PR: $12-$15
1965*	Hot Rods	Topps	66	PR: $10-$12
1969	Odd Rods	Donruss	44	PR: $6-$8
1970	Odder Odd Rods	Donruss	66	PR: $4-$6
1970	Dragstrips	Fleer	10	PR: $35
1970	Model Car Cards	Monogram	23	PR: $8-$12
1971	Drag Champs	Fleer	63	PR: $5-$10
1971	Odd Rod All Stars	Donruss	66	PR: $4-$6
1971	Stick Shift	Fleer	9 or 10	PR: $35
1972	Choppers & Hot Bikes	Donruss	66	PR: $2
1972	Super Cycles	Donruss	66	PR: $2
1972	Drag Nationals	Fleer	70	PR: $5-$11
1972	STP	Racing Pictorial	14	PR: $90-$400
1973	Race USA	Fleer	74	PR: $4-$8
1973	Fabulous Odd Rods	Donruss	66	PR: $6-$8
1973	Fantastic Odd Rods	Donruss Series I	66	PR: $6-$8, #1-66
1973	Fantastic Odd Rods	Donruss Series II	66	PR: $7-$10, #67-132
1973	Oddest Rods	Donruss	66	PR: $6-$8
1974	Kustom Kars I	Fleer	39	PR: $10
1975	Kustom Kars II	Fleer	49	PR: $10
1976	Crazy Cars	Wonder Bread	20	PR: $4
1977	Autos of 1977	Topps	99	PR: $1-$2
1970*	Gallery of Great Cars	B/A Gasoline	24	PR: $6-$8
1970*	Speedway	Sugar Daddy	25	PR: $16-$20

*Unsure of exact date, **Inserted into frankfurter packs, ***Speculation as to exact number

In late 1964 and early 1965, Donruss and Topps, both dominant manufacturers of baseball cards and chewing gum, decided to issue 66-card racing sets. The Topps set focused on the cars rather than the drivers and included everything from Bonneville racers to dragsters. The Donruss release, known as the Spec Sheet set, featured custom cars and ironically did not include the company's name. Only the wax packs used the company's name and logo. Information errors, fading, and print quality are some of the problems encountered with the Spec Set, although the car selection was an improvement over the Topps set. Both sets are significant to collectors and a nice look back at the early days of drag racing.

The Fleer drag racing sets produced in the early 1970s—"Drag Champs," "Drag Nationals," and "Race USA"—have shown some nice appreciation both in what they have meant to the hobby and in value. These sets document an important era in the sport and salute drivers such as Tommy Ivo, Gene Snow, Don Garlits, Tom Hoover, Chris Karamesines, and Don Prudhomme.

Both Indy Car and Formula One card sets have stalled in the market over the last twelve months. Expected appreciation in the value of certain releases just hasn't happened. Some analysts blame it on there being only seventeen Indy Car events, some of which are held out of the United States, causing the sport to suffer from the lack of consistent media exposure. NASCAR's overwhelming appeal is attributed to its American drivers, American cars, and oval tracks—in stark contrast to Indy Car.

A favorite with Indy Car collectors is the 1960 Parkhurst/Hawes Indy 500 set. This set focused on each winner of the Indianapolis 500

A 1995 Press Pass card featuring Kyle Petty

Since its release, the Maxx 1988 card set has acted as a market indicator, with many closely watching its increases or decreases in value

from 1911 to 1959. The set uses forty cards to depict forty-three races, because on three occasions the same driver used the same car to defend his title. The additional cards include non-Indy winners and associated events, traditions, or speedway landmarks. In late 1994 this set sold at an auction for $900.

In 1992, only three companies produced Winston Cup cards, yet a mere two years later over a dozen manufacturers had entered the field. To say the growth in racing cards is phenomenal, may indeed be an understatement. To put it in perspective, Kyle Petty already appears on over 300 cards.

Older card sets, such as the 1972 eleven-card STP set, although not responsible for the boom in card collecting, certainly has benefited from it, as the set can now command $2,500 in mint condition. Many attribute the boom to the success of Maxx's 1988 card set, the first major Winston Cup issue with a wide distribution. The overwhelming response to the first printing in Myrtle Beach, South Carolina led to a second in Charlotte, with several changes to the set. Since its release, the Maxx 1988 card set has acted as a market indicator, with many closely watching its increases or decreases in value. Maxx, which is the only company currently licensed by NASCAR, was the only manufacturer in the market until 1991.

Many of the new entries into the racing card market brought with them several successful trends that have worked well with other sports such as baseball and football. Inserts, premium cards, and announced production runs are not only common now, but expected by collectors. Action Packed released an interesting five-card Kyle Petty subset in conjunction with its 1994 Series II product. Using a unique marketing ploy, they affixed a genuine diamond to 1,000 of the Diamond in the Rough cards (#92). The cards were randomly inserted into packs and individually numbered. With inserts and premiums currently the rage in auto racing card collecting, it's hard to say what's next, but certainly interesting to watch.

1988 Maxx Myrtle Beach

❑ Complete Set (100)	$	500
❑ Complete Factory Set (100)	$	600
❑ Cover Card 10 (1A)	$	6
❑ Cover Card 100 (1B)	$	140
❑ CL (19/36/69/100)	$	14

*Unlisted Myrtle Beach Cards Same Price as Charlotte

❑ 10	Talladega Streaks	$	110
❑ 26	Phil Parsons w/o Marcia	$	110
❑ 43	Daytona International Speedway	$	18
❑ 47	Single File	$	16
❑ 59	1988 Begins	$	16
❑ 88	Ken Bouchard (Engaged)	$	10

1988 Maxx Charlotte

❑ Complete Set (100)	$	100
❑ Complete Factory Set (100)	$	150
❑ Common Card (1-100)	$	.75
❑ Common Driver (1-100)	$	1.25
❑ Cover Card 10 (1A)	$	.50
❑ Cover Card 100 (1B)	$	60
❑ CL (19/100)	$	.25
❑ Race Tracks (21/35/53/56)	$	1.25
❑ Race Tracks (73/77/86/91)	$	1.25
❑ Semistars	$	2

❑ 2	Richard Petty's Car	$	3
❑ 3	J. D. McDuffie	$	2.50
❑ 5	Davey Allison	$	14

❏ 7	B. Allison, Bonn, Bodine Cars	$	4
❏ 9	Atlanta International, Earnhardt's Car	$	4
❏ 10	Darrell Waltrip	$	4
❏ 13	Alabama Thunder, Earnhardt's Car	$	4
❏ 14	Rusty Wallace	$	7
❏ 17	The Winston, Earnhardt's Car	$	8
❏ 20	Neil Bonnett	$	5
❏ 25	Morgan Shepherd	$ 2.50	

❏ 26	Phil Parsons with Marcia	$ 2.25	
❏ 30	Bobby Allison	$	3
❏ 31	Richard Petty, Rudd Cars	$ 2.50	
❏ 33	Derrike Cope	$ 2.50	
❏ 36A	CL (Checklist) without Petty	$	10
❏ 36B	CL with Petty	$	1
❏ 38	Dale Earnhardt's Car Wrangler	$	9
❏ 40	Davey Allison ROY	$	20
❏ 41	Alan Kulwicki's Car	$	3
❏ 43	Richard Petty	$	8
❏ 46	Lake Speed	$ 2.50	
❏ 47	Daytona International Speedway	$	8
❏ 48	Mark Martin	$	6
❏ 49	D. Earnhardt, D. Allison Cars	$	5
❏ 50	Bill Elliott	$	7
❏ 54	Dale Earnhardt's Car Goodwrench	$	13
❏ 58	Alan Kulwicki	$	7
❏ 59	Brett Bodine	$ 2.50	
❏ 60	Richard Petty's Car	$	4
❏ 61	Dale Jarrett	$	3
❏ 62	R. Wallace, G. Bodine Cars	$	3
❏ 63	Terry Labonte	$	4
❏ 67	Geoff Bodine	$	4
❏ 69A	CL with 1988 Begins	$	10
❏ 69B	CL with Bodine	$	1
❏ 74	Ken Schrader	$	3
❏ 80	Sterling Marlin	$	4
❏ 82	Riverside International/R. Petty's Car	$ 2.50	
❏ 84	D. Earnhardt, R. Petty Cars	$ 4.50	
❏ 87	Dale Earnhardt Winston Cup Champion	$	80
❏ 88	Ken Bouchard (Married)	$ 2.25	
❏ 89	Davey Allison's Car	$	6
❏ 95	Ernie Irvan	$	5
❏ 98	Michael Waltrip	$ 2.50	

Phil Parsons

HOME: Denver, NC   BORN: 6/21/57
HT: 5'9"   WT: 165
FAMILY: Children-Kinsley Rae

STATISTICS:

YEAR	RACES	WON	TOP 5	TOP 10	POLES	$ WON
1983	5	0	0	0	0	$ 23,850
1984	23	0	0	3	0	90,700
1985	28	0	1	4	0	105,060
1986	17	0	1	5	0	84,680
1987	29	0	0	7	0	180,261
TOTALS	102	0	2	19	0	$484,551

Younger brother (by 16 years) of driver Benny Parsons... Phil had an excellent performance record driving Charlotte/Daytona Dash and Grand National series races... originally from Detroit, Michigan.

©1988 J.R. Maxx, Inc., Charlotte, N.C.

1989 Maxx Previews

❏ Complete Set (10)	$	30
❏ Common Card	$	2
❏ Cover Card (A)	$	10
❏ Cover Card T-Bird (B)	$	2
❏ Semistars	$ 2.50	

*Five Cards Per 1988 Maxx Combo

❏ NNO	Bill Elliott	$	4
❏ NNO	Mark Martin	$	3
❏ NNO	Richard Petty	$	3
❏ NNO	Rusty Wallace	$	4

1989 Maxx

❏ Complete Set (220)	$	310
❏ Complete Factory Set (220)	$	335
❏ Complete Tool Box Set (220)	$	385
❏ Complete Peak Set (100)	$	170
❏ Common Card (1-220)	$	1
❏ Common Driver (1-220)	$ 1.50	
❏ Semistars	$ 2.50	

❏ 2	Ernie Irvan	$	7
❏ 3	Dale Earnhardt	$	85
❏ 5A	Geoff Bodine ERROR (ERR)	$	12
❏ 5B	Geoff Bodine CORRECTED (COR)	$	10

❑ 6	Mark Martin	$	8
❑ 7	Alan Kulwicki	$	14
❑ 9	Bill Elliott	$	10
❑ 11	Terry Labonte	$	5
❑ 12	Bobby Allison	$	4
❑ 17	Darrell Waltrip	$	5
❑ 21	Neil Bonnett	$	7
❑ 25	Ken Schrader	$	4
❑ 26	Ricky Rudd	$	4
❑ 27	Rusty Wallace	$	10
❑ 28	Davey Allison	$	30
❑ 29	Dale Jarrett	$	4
❑ 33	Harry Gant	$	5
❑ 42	Kyle Petty	$	6
❑ 43	Richard Petty	$	16
❑ 50	Bill Elliott Winston Cup Champ	$	10
❑ 54	Rusty Wallace	$	10
❑ 60	Dale Earnhardt Pit Champs	$	12
❑ 66	Rick Mast	$	3
❑ 75	Morgan Shepherd	$	3
❑ 83	Lake Speed	$	3
❑ 94	Sterling Marlin	$	5
❑ 100	Bill Elliott FF (Fan's Favorite)	$	8
❑ 101	Richard Petty's Car YR (Year in Review)	$	4
❑ 102	Dale Earnhardt's Car YR	$	7
❑ 108	Dale Earnhardt's Car YR	$	7
❑ 113	Davey Allison's Car YR	$	5
❑ 114	Alan Kulwicki/R. Wall Cars YR	$	4
❑ 119	Davey Allison's Car YR	$	5
❑ 121	Dale Earnhardt's Car YR	$	7
❑ 124	Davey Allison's Car YR	$	5
❑ 135	Rob Moroso	$	10
❑ 140	Darrell Waltrip/Michael Waltrip	$	4
❑ 142	Neil Bonnett VL (Victory Lane)	$	2.50
❑ 143	Neil Bonnett VL	$	2.50
❑ 144	Dale Earnhardt VL	$	13
❑ 146	Bill Elliott VL	$	3
❑ 148	Dale Earnhardt VL	$	13
❑ 151	Bill Elliott VL	$	3
❑ 152	Rusty Wallace VL	$	3
❑ 154	Rusty Wallace VL	$	3
❑ 155	Bill Elliott VL	$	3
❑ 156	Bill Elliott VL	$	3
❑ 159	Davey Allison VL	$	6
❑ 160	Dale Earnhardt VL	$	13
❑ 161	Bill Elliott VL	$	3
❑ 162	Davey Allison VL	$	6
❑ 163	Bill Elliott VL	$	3
❑ 165	Rusty Wallace VL	$	3
❑ 166	Rusty Wallace VL	$	3
❑ 167	Rusty Wallace VL	$	3
❑ 168	Alan Kulwicki VL	$	4
❑ 169	Rusty Wallace VL	$	3
❑ 178	Kenny Wallace	$	4
❑ 180	Davey Allison/Bobby Allison	$	14
❑ 181	Richard Petty's Car C (Classics)	$	4
❑ 193	Richard Petty's Car C	$	4
❑ 202	Geoff Bodine/Brett Bodine	$	3
❑ 204	Steve Grissom	$	3.50
❑ 208	Jimmy Spencer	$	3
❑ 210	Rusty Wallace/Kenny Wallace	$	6
❑ 220	Richard Petty/Kyle Petty	$	16

1989 Maxx Stickers

❑ Complete Set (20)	$	45
❑ Common Sticker	$	3

*One per Pack

1989 Maxx Crisco

❑ Complete Set (25)	$	7
❑ Common Card (1-24)	$	.20
❑ Header Card (NNO)	$	.20
❑ Semistars	$	.40
❑ 4 Bill Elliott	$	.75
❑ 5 Rusty Wallace	$	1
❑ 6 Dale Earnhardt	$	3.50
❑ 10 Davey Allison	$	1
❑ 13 Alan Kulwicki	$	1
❑ 14 Neil Bonnett	$	.60
❑ 17 Richard Petty	$	.75

1990 Maxx

❑ Complete Set (200)	$	60
❑ Complete Factory Set White (200)	$	110
❑ Complete Factory Set Red/White (200)	$	70
❑ Complete Factory Set Red/Yellow (200)	$	60
❑ Complete Tin Glossy Set (200)	$	165
❑ Common Card (1-200)	$	.40
❑ Common Driver (1-200)	$	.60
❑ Semistars	$	1

*Glossy Cards 1.5x to 3x

❑ 1	Terry Labonte	$	2
❑ 2	Ernie Irvan	$	3
❑ 3	Dale Earnhardt	$	16
❑ 5	Ricky Rudd	$	1.50
❑ 6	Mark Martin	$	4
❑ 7	Alan Kulwicki	$	5
❑ 8A	Bobby Hillin ERR	$	9
❑ 8B	Bobby Hillin COR	$	2
❑ 9	Bill Elliott	$	4.50
❑ 11	Geoff Bodine	$	2
❑ 12	Bobby Allison	$	1.50
❑ 13A	Mickey Gibbs ERR	$	6
❑ 13B	Mickey Gibbs COR	$	2
❑ 14	A. J. Foyt	$	2
❑ 17	Darrell Waltrip	$	2
❑ 21	Neil Bonnett	$	3
❑ 22	Rob Moroso	$	4
❑ 25	Ken Schrader	$	1.50
❑ 27	Rusty Wallace	$	5
❑ 28A	Davey Allison ERR	$	20
❑ 28B	Davey Allison COR	$	10
❑ 29	Dale Jarrett	$	1.50
❑ 33	Harry Gant	$	1
❑ 39A	Kirk Shelmerdine ERR	$	6
❑ 39B	Kirk Shelmerdine COR	$	3
❑ 42	Kyle Petty	$	2
❑ 43	Richard Petty	$	4.50
❑ 66	Dick Trickle	$	1.25
❑ 69A	Checklist A ERR	$	4

❏ 69B	Checklist A COR	$ 2
❏ 70	J. D. McDuffie	$ 1.50
❏ 77A	Ben Hess ERR	$ 5
❏ 77B	Ben Hess COR	$ 1.25
❏ 81	Kenny Bernstein	$ 1.25
❏ 85A	Tim Morgan ERR	$ 3
❏ 85B	Larry McClure COR	$ 3
❏ 94	Sterling Marlin	$ 2
❏ 95	Kenny Wallace	$ 1.50
❏ 97A	Chuck Bown ERR	$ 10
❏ 97B	Chuck Bown COR	$ 1.50
❏ 100	Darrell Waltrip FF	$ 1.50
❏ 116	Dale Earnhardt AP	$ 7
❏ 118	Shawna Robinson	$ 2
❏ 137A	Bill Engle ERR	$ 6
❏ 137B	Bill Engle COR	$ 1.50
❏ 142	Steve Grissom	$ 1.25
❏ 150	Dick Trickle ROY	$ 1.25
❏ 151	Bobby Hamilton	$ 1.25
❏ 175	Davey Allison YR	$ 4
❏ 179	Dale Earnhardt YR	$ 7
❏ 182	Bill Elliott YR	$ 1.50
❏ 184	Bill Elliott YR	$ 1.50
❏ 190	Rusty Wallace YR	$ 2
❏ 198	Rusty Wallace YR	$ 2

1990 Maxx Holly Farms

❏ Complete Set (30)		$ 10
❏ Complete Factory Set (30)		$ 11
❏ Common Card (HF1-HF30)		$ .25
❏ Semistars		$ .50

❏ HF1	Dale Earnhardt	$ 3
❏ HF2	Bill Elliott	$ 1
❏ HF4	Rusty Wallace	$ 1.25
❏ HF6	Richard Petty	$ 1
❏ HF8	Mark Martin	$ 1
❏ HF9	Davey Allison	$ 1.50
❏ HF10	Neil Bonnett	$ .75
❏ HF11	Alan Kulwicki	$ 1
❏ HF23	Ernie Irvan	$ .60

1991 ARCA

❏ Complete Set (68)		$ 14
❏ Common Card (1-68)		$ .20
❏ Semistars		$ .50

1991 IROC

❏ Complete Set (12)		$ 430
❏ Common Card (1-12)		$ 27
❏ Semistars		$ 31

*Beware of Counterfeits

❏ 4	Mark Martin	$ 55
❏ 5	Bill Elliott	$ 50
❏ 6	Al Unser, Jr.	$ 40
❏ 10	Rusty Wallace	$ 65
❏ 12	Dale Earnhardt	$ 145

1991 Maxx

❏ Complete Set (240)		$ 10
❏ Complete Factory Set (240)		$ 12
❏ Complete Mail Order Set (308)		$ 20
❏ Common Card (1-240)		$ .05
❏ Common Driver (1-240)		$ .15
❏ Semistars		$ .25

❏ 2	Rusty Wallace	$ 1
❏ 3	Dale Earnhardt	$ 2.75
❏ 4	Ernie Irvan	$ .60
❏ 6	Mark Martin	$ .75
❏ 7	Alan Kulwicki	$ 1
❏ 9	Bill Elliott	$ .65
❏ 11	Geoff Bodine	$ .40
❏ 14	A. J. Foyt	$ .40
❏ 28	Davey Allison	$ 1.25
❏ 33	Harry Gant	$ .40
❏ 36	Neil Bonnett	$ .50
❏ 42	Kyle Petty	$ .40
❏ 43	Richard Petty	$ .70
❏ 50	Bill Elliott Pit Champs	$ .50
❏ 53	Bobby Labonte	$ .65
❏ 100	Rob Moroso ROY	$ 1
❏ 123	Ward Burton	$ .40
❏ 139	Joe Nemechek	$ .40
❏ 147	Robert Pressley	$ .40
❏ 173	Dale Earnhardt YR	$ 1.25
❏ 174	Dale Earnhardt YR	$ 1.25
❏ 175	Davey Allison YR	$ .50
❏ 178	Dale Earnhardt YR	$ 1.25
❏ 179	Dale Earnhardt YR	$ 1.25
❏ 180	Rusty Wallace YR	$ .50
❏ 182	Rusty Wallace YR	$ .50
❏ 184	Dale Earnhardt YR	$ 1.25
❏ 185	Dale Earnhardt YR	$ 1.25
❏ 187	Dale Earnhardt YR	$ 1.25
❏ 190	Ernie Irvan YR	$ .40
❏ 191	Dale Earnhardt YR	$ 1.25
❏ 192	Dale Earnhardt YR	$ 1.25
❏ 193	Bill Elliott YR	$ .50
❏ 196	Davey Allison YR	$ .50
❏ 197	Alan Kulwicki YR	$ .50
❏ 198	Dale Earnhardt YR	$ 1.25
❏ 200	Dale Earnhardt YR	$ 1.25
❏ 201	Jeff Burton	$ .40
❏ 203	Todd Bodine	$ .40
❏ 220	Dale Earnhardt AP (All-Pro)	$ 1.50

1991 Maxx Update

❏ Complete Set (48)		$ 7.50
❏ Common Card		$ .15
❏ Semistars		$ .30

*One Set per Mail Order Factory

❏ 3	Dale Earnhardt	$ 2.50
❏ 4	Ernie Irvan	$ .60
❏ 6	Mark Martin	$ .75
❏ 7	Alan Kulwicki	$ 1
❏ 9	Bill Elliott	$ .75
❏ 11	Geoff Bodine	$ .50
❏ 17	Darrell Waltrip	$ .50
❏ 42	Kyle Petty	$ .50
❏ 43	Richard Petty	$ .75

❏ 50	Bill Elliott Pit Champs	$	.60
❏ 53	Bobby Labonte	$	.55
❏ 100	Rob Moroso ROY (Rookie of the Year)	$	1
❏ 139	Joe Nemechek	$	.50
❏ 147	Robert Pressley	$	.50
❏ 200	Dale Earnhardt YR	$	1
❏ 220	Dale Earnhardt AP	$ 1.25	

1991 Maxx
The Winston Acrylics

❏ Complete Set (20)	$	9
❏ Common Card	$	.50
❏ Semistars	$	.75

*One Set Per Mail Order Factory

NNO	Davey Allison	$ 1.50	
NNO	Dale Earnhardt	$ 3.50	
NNO	Bill Elliott	$	1
NNO	Alan Kulwicki	$ 1.50	
NNO	Mark Martin	$ 1.25	
NNO	Rusty Wallace	$ 1.25	

1991 Maxx
Bill Elliott Team /Coors Melling

❏ Complete Elliott Set (40)	$	15
❏ Common Card	$	.50
❏ Bill Elliott Card	$ 1.35	
❏ Complete Coors/Melling Set (40)	$	15

*Coors/Melling Version: Same Price

1991 Maxx McDonald's

❏ Complete Set (31)	$	15
❏ Common Card (1-30)	$	.50
❏ Common Error (21/22/23/24)	$	.75
❏ Cover Card (NNO)	$	.50
❏ Semistars	$	1

*Errors Missing Blue Part of Logo

❏ 1A	Dale Earnhardt ERR	$	7
❏ 1B	Dale Earnhardt COR	$	4
❏ 2A	Mark Martin ERR	$ 2.50	
❏ 2B	Mark Martin COR	$ 1.50	
❏ 3A	Geoff Bodine ERR	$ 1.50	
❏ 3B	Geoff Bodine COR	$	1
❏ 4A	Bill Elliott ERR	$	3
❏ 4B	Bill Elliott COR	$	2
❏ 6	Rusty Wallace	$	2
❏ 8	Alan Kulwicki	$	2
❏ 9	Ernie Irvan	$ 1.50	
❏ 13	Davey Allison	$	3
❏ 26	Richard Petty	$	2
❏ 30	Dale Earnhardt/Martin/Elliott	$	3

1991 Maxx Motorsport

❏ Complete Set (40)	$	20
❏ Common Card (1-40)	$	.30
❏ Common Driver (1-40)	$	.60
❏ Semistars	$	1

❏ 1	Bill Elliott	$	3
❏ 2	Davey Allison	$	5
❏ 5	Mark Martin	$	2
❏ 7	Alan Kulwicki	$	3
❏ 28	Davey Allison's Car	$ 1.50	
❏ 30	Davey Allison's Car	$ 1.50	
❏ 35	Alan Kulwicki's Car	$ 1.25	

1991 Maxx Winston
20th Anniversary Foils

❏ Complete Set (21)	$	10
❏ Common Card	$	.50
❏ Richard Petty Cards	$	1
❏ Dale Earnhardt Cards	$	2

1991 Motorcraft Racing

❏ Complete Set (7)	$	10
❏ Common Card (1-7)	$ 1.50	

1991 Pro Set

❏ Complete Set (143)	$	15
❏ Common Card (1-143)	$	.05
❏ Common Driver (1-143)	$	.15
❏ Semistars	$	.25

❏ 5	Rusty Wallace	$	1
❏ 6	Rusty Wallace	$	1
❏ 13	Ernie Irvan	$	.60
❏ 14	Ernie Irvan	$	.60
❏ 18A	Rick Hendrick ERR	$	.50
❏ 18B	Rick Hendrick COR	$	.50
❏ 21	Mark Martin	$	.75
❏ 33	Geoff Bodine	$	.40
❏ 38A	Bobby Allison ERR	$	.60
❏ 38B	Bobby Allison COR	$	.60
❏ 54	Kyle Petty	$	.40
❏ 63	Harry Gant	$	.40
❏ 65	Richard Petty	$	.75
❏ 68	Richard Petty's Car	$	.50
❏ 74	Geoff Bodine	$	.40
❏ 87	Kyle Petty	$	.40
❏ 93	Alan Kulwicki	$	1
❏ 94	Alan Kulwicki's Car	$	.50
❏ 99	Mark Martin	$	.75
❏ 103	Ted Musgrave	$	.50
❏ 126	Geoff Bodine	$	.40
❏ 129	Harry Gant	$	.40
❏ 130	Richard Petty	$	.75
❏ 133	Alan Kulwicki	$	1
❏ 134	Alan Kulwicki Army Car	$ 1.25	
❏ 143A	Phil Parsons ERR	$	.50
❏ 143B	Phil Parsons COR	$	.50
❏ AU38	Bobby Allison AUTO (Autograph)	$	125
❏ NNO	Winston Cup HOLO (Hologram)/5000	$	125

1991 Pro Set Legends

❏ Complete Set (37)	$	5
❏ Common Card (L1-L37)	$	.20
❏ Semistars	$	.30

*Random Inserts in Packs

☐ L11A	Donnie Allison ERR	$ .40
☐ L11B	Donnie Allison COR	$ .40
☐ L24	Neil Bonnett	$ .75
☐ L31	Bobby Allison	$ .40

1991 Pro Set Petty Family

☐ Complete Set (50)		$ 4.50
☐ Common Card (1-50)		$ .10
☐ Richard Petty Cards		$ .40
☐ Kyle Petty (48)		$ .30

1991 STP Richard Petty

☐ Complete Set (10)		$ 15
☐ Common Card (1-10)		$ 1.70

1991 Traks

☐ Complete Set (200)		$ 16
☐ Complete Factory Set (200)		$ 18
☐ Common Card (1-200)		$ .05
☐ Common Driver (1-200)		$ .15
☐ Semistars		$ .25

☐ 1	Jeff Gordon	$ 6
☐ 2	Rusty Wallace	$ 1
☐ 3A	Dale Earnhardt ERR	$ 3
☐ 3B	Dale Earnhardt COR	$ 3
☐ 4	Ernie Irvan	$ .60
☐ 6	Mark Martin	$ .75
☐ 7	Alan Kulwicki	$ 1
☐ 10	Ernie Irvan with Car	$ .60
☐ 18	Mike Wallace	$ .40
☐ 26	Neil Bonnett	$ .60
☐ 27A	Mike Coyler ERR	$ .50
☐ 27B	Mike Coyler COR	$ .50
☐ 28	Davey Allison	$ 1.50
☐ 33	Harry Gant	$ .40
☐ 34	Todd Bodine	$ .50
☐ 42	Kyle Petty	$ .40
☐ 43	Richard Petty	$ .75
☐ 47	Kyle Petty	$ .40
☐ 50	Mark Martin	$ .75
☐ 55	Ted Musgrave with Car	$ .50
☐ 73	Alan Kulwicki's Car	$ .50
☐ 85	Richard Petty with Car	$ .75
☐ 87	Joe Nemechek	$ .50
☐ 103A	Dale Earnhardt ERR	$ 3
☐ 103B	Dale Earnhardt COR	$ 3
☐ 108	David Green	$ .40
☐ 112	Harry Gant	$ .40
☐ 124	Rusty Wallace	$ 1
☐ 125	Rob Moroso	$ .75
☐ 131A	Jim Phillips ERR	$ .30
☐ 131B	Jim Phillips COR	$ .30
☐ 133A	Winston Kelley ERR	$ .30
☐ 133B	Winston Kelley COR	$ .30
☐ 134A	Allen Bestwick ERR	$ .30
☐ 134B	Allen Bestwick COR	$ .30
☐ 135A	Dick Brooks ERR	$ .30
☐ 135B	Dick Brooks COR	$ .30
☐ 137A	Eli Gold ERR	$ .30
☐ 137B	Eli Gold COR	$ .30

☐ 156	Davey Allison	$ 1.50
☐ 172A	L. D. Ottinger ERR	$ .30
☐ 172B	L. D. Ottinger COR	$ .30
☐ 179	Rusty Wallace	$ 1
☐ 186A	Teresa Earnhardt ERR	$ .75
☐ 186B	Teresa Earnhardt COR	$ .75
☐ 189A	Tim Petty ERR	$ .30
☐ 189B	Tim Petty COR	$ .30
☐ 190A	Dale Earnhardt ERR	$ 3
☐ 190B	Dale Earnhardt COR	$ 3
☐ 200	Richard Petty The King	$ 1

1991 Traks Mello Yello Kyle Petty

☐ Complete Set (13)		$ 10
☐ Common Card (1-13)		$ 1

1991 Traks Mom-n-Pop's Biscuits Dale Earnhardt

☐ Complete Set (6)		$ 13
☐ Common Card (1-6)		$ 2.25

1991 Traks Mom-n-Pop's Ham Dale Earnhardt

☐ Complete Set (6)		$ 13
☐ Common Card (1-6)		$ 2.25

1991 Traks Richard Petty

☐ Complete Set (50)		$ 8
☐ Complete Factory Set (50)		$ 10
☐ Common Card (1-50)		$ .30

1991 Winner's Choice Ricky Craven

☐ Complete Set (30)		$ 20
☐ Common Card (1-30)		$ .75
☐ Ricky Craven Cards		$ 1
☐ 17	Richard Petty/Ricky Craven	$ 1.50

1992 ARCA

☐ Complete Set (110)		$ 18
☐ Common Card (1-110)		$ .25
☐ Semistars		$ .50

1992 Arena Joe Gibbs Racing

☐ Complete Set (12)		$ 9
☐ Common Card (1-10)		$ .65
☐ CL (NNO)		$ .65
☐ 1	Joe Gibbs	$ 1.25
☐ 2	Dale Jarrett	$ 1.75
☐ NNO	Dale Jarrett's Car HOLO	$ 2

1992 Dayco Series 1

☐ Complete Set (10)		$ 10
☐ Common Card (1-9)		$ .75
☐ Cover Card (NNO)		$ .75

❏ 1	Davey Allison	$ 2.50
❏ 2	Rusty Wallace	$ 2
❏ 4	Ernie Irvan	$ 1.50

1992 Food Lion
Richard Petty

❏ Complete Set (116)	$ 18
❏ Common Petty (1-116)	$ .30
❏ Cover Cards	$ .10
❏ Richard Petty HOLO	$ 300

1992 Hooters
Alan Kulwicki

❏ Complete Set (15)	$ 12
❏ Common Card (1-15)	$ 1

1992 Mac Tools
Winner's Cup

❏ Complete Set (21)	$ 16
❏ Common Card	$ .50
❏ Cover Card CL	$ .25
❏ Semistars	$ .75

❏ NNO	Davey Allison	$ 4
❏ NNO	Ernie Irvan	$ 1.50
❏ NNO	Mark Martin	$ 2
❏ NNO	Richard Petty	$ 1
❏ NNO	Rusty Wallace	$ 2.50

1992 Maxx Red

❏ Complete Set (300)	$ 12
❏ Complete Factory Set (304)	$ 14
❏ Common Card (1-300)	$ .05
❏ Common Driver (1-300)	$ .15
❏ Semistars	$ .25

*Four Vintage Cards per Factory Set

❏ 2	Rusty Wallace	$ 1
❏ 3	Dale Earnhardt	$ 2.50
❏ 4	Ernie Irvan	$ .50
❏ 6	Mark Martin	$ .65
❏ 7	Alan Kulwicki	$ 1
❏ 11	Bill Elliott	$ 1
❏ 19	Randy LaJoie	$ .30
❏ 28	Davey Allison	$ 1.25
❏ 29	Jeff Gordon	$ 3
❏ 31	Clifford Allison	$ 1
❏ 33	Harry Gant	$ .40
❏ 42	Kyle Petty	$ .40
❏ 43	Richard Petty	$ .65
❏ 50	Jeff Gordon ROY	$ 4
❏ 88	Ricky Craven	$ .50
❏ 100	Bill Elliott FF	$ .55
❏ 141	A. J. Foyt	$ .30
❏ 202	Rusty Wallace MM (Memorable Moment)	$ .50
❏ 203	Dale Earnhardt's Car MM	$ .60
❏ 222	Neil Bonnett	$ .50
❏ 231	Dale Earnhardt AP	$ 1.25
❏ 233	Mark Martin AP	$ .40
❏ 264	Ernie Irvan YR	$ .30

❏ 265	Dale Earnhardt YR	$ 1
❏ 269	Rusty Wallace	$ .50
❏ 271	Dale Earnhardt YR	$ 1
❏ 273	Davey Allison YR	$ .50
❏ 274	Davey Allison YR	$ .50
❏ 276	Davey Allison YR	$ .50
❏ 278	Davey Allison YR	$ .50
❏ 279	Bill Elliott YR	$ .50
❏ 280	Rusty Wallace YR	$ .50
❏ 281	Dale Earnhardt YR	$ 1
❏ 282	Ernie Irvan YR	$ .30
❏ 284	Alan Kulwicki YR	$ .50
❏ 289	Dale Earnhardt YR	$ 1
❏ 291	Davey Allison YR	$ .50
❏ 292	Davey Allison YR	$ .50
❏ 293	Mark Martin YR	$ .40
❏ 294	Dale Earnhardt YR	$ 1

1992 Maxx Update

❏ Complete Set (32)	$ 5
❏ Common Card	$ .15
❏ Common Driver (U1-U30)	$ .25
❏ Semistars	$ .30

❏ U5	Jerry Glanville	$ .20
❏ U6	Jeff Gordon	$ 3.25
❏ U11	Mark Martin	$ 1
❏ U19	Joe Gibbs	$ .30

1992 Maxx Black

❏ Complete Set (300)	$ 25
❏ Complete Factory Set (304)	$ 30
❏ Common Card (1-300)	$ .10
❏ Common Driver (1-300)	$ .25
❏ Semistars	$ .40

*Stars: 1.5x to 2x Red Card Hi
*Four Vintage Cards per Factory Set

1992 Maxx Black Update

❏ Complete Set (32)	$ 5
❏ Common Card	$ .15
❏ Common Driver (U1-U30)	$ .25
❏ Semistars	$ .30

*Stars: Same price as Red updates

1992 Maxx All-Pro Team

❏ Complete Set (50)	$ 5
❏ Common Card (1-50)	$ .10
❏ CL (NNO)	$ .10
❏ Semistars	$ .25
❏ 1	Dale Earnhardt	$ 2
❏ 2	Harry Gant	$ .50
❏ 3	Mark Martin	$ .75

1992 Maxx Craftsman

❏ Complete Set (8)	$ 12
❏ Common Card	$ 1.50
❏ Bill Elliott (NNO)	$ 2.50

1992 Maxx
Bobby Hamilton

☐ Complete Set (16) $ 3
☐ Common Card $ .25

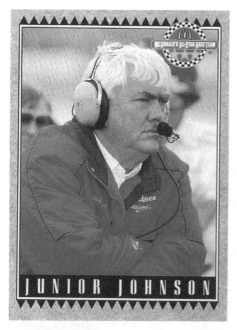

1992 Maxx McDonald's

☐ Complete Set (37)		$ 13
☐ Common Card (1-36)		$ .20
☐ Cover Card (NNO)		$ .20
☐ Semistars		$ .40
☐ 1	Dale Earnhardt, Bobby Allison, Elliott	$ 2
☐ 2	Dale Earnhardt	$ 3
☐ 3	Davey Allison	$ 1.50
☐ 4	Bill Elliott	$ 1
☐ 13	Ernie Irvan	$ .75
☐ 14	Mark Martin	$ .75
☐ 18	Rusty Wallace	$ 1
☐ 20	Alan Kulwicki	$ 1
☐ 30	Richard Petty	$ .75

1992 Maxx Motorsport

☐ Complete Set (50)		$ 25
☐ Common Card (1-50)		$ .50
☐ Common Driver (1-50)		$ .75
☐ Semistars		$ 1
☐ 1	Bill Elliott	$ 2
☐ 2	Davey Allison	$ 5
☐ 3	Alan Kulwicki	$ 2.50
☐ 5	Mark Martin	$ 1.50
☐ 36	Bill Elliott with Crew	$ 1.50
☐ 37	Davey Allison with Crew	$ 4
☐ 38	Alan Kulwicki with Crew	$ 2
☐ 40	Mark Martin with Crew	$ 1.25
☐ 50	Martin, Kulwicki, Allison, Elliott	$ 4

1992 Maxx Sam Bass

☐ Complete Set (11)		$ 11
☐ Common Card (1-11)		$ 1
☐ Semistars		$ 1
☐ 1	Richard Petty	$ 3
☐ 4	Tim Richmond	$ 1.50
☐ 6	Rob Moroso	$ 1.75
☐ 8	Bill Elliott	$ 2.75
☐ 10	Neil Bonnett	$ 2

1992 Maxx Texaco
Davey Allison

☐ Complete Set (20)		$ 8
☐ Common Card (1-20)		$ .30
☐ Davey Allison (1/10)		$ 2.50
☐ Auto. Cover Card		$ 140

1992 Maxx
The Winston

☐ Complete Set (50)		$ 16
☐ Common Card (1-50)		$ .20
☐ Semistars		$ .40
☐ 1	Davey Allison	$ 1.50
☐ 5	Bill Elliott	$ 1
☐ 6	Rusty Wallace	$ 1
☐ 7	Alan Kulwicki	$ 1
☐ 8	Ernie Irvan	$ .60
☐ 9	Richard Petty	$ .75
☐ 14	Dale Earnhardt	$ 2.50
☐ 17	Mark Martin	$ .75
☐ 21	Davey Allison's Car	$ .60
☐ 34	Dale Earnhardt's Car	$ 1
☐ 41	Davey Allison's Car	$ .60
☐ 42	Davey Allison Pole WIN	$ 1.50
☐ 48	Davey Allison/Kyle Petty Cars	$ .50
☐ 50	Davey Allison WIN	$ 1.50

1992 Pro Set

☐ Complete Set (248)		$ 15
☐ Common Card (1-248)		$ .05
☐ Common Driver (1-248)		$ .15
☐ Semistars		$ .25
☐ 1	Dale Earnhardt	$ 2.50
☐ 2	Alan Kulwicki	$ 1
☐ 20	Ernie Irvan with Crew	$ .50
☐ 30	Kyle Petty	$ .40
☐ 31	Ricky Craven	$ .50
☐ 32	Clifford Allison	$ .75
☐ 43	Richard Petty	$ .75
☐ 44	Kyle Petty	$ .40
☐ 45	Richard Petty	$ .75
☐ 49	Harry Gant	$ .40
☐ 59	Dale Earnhardt's Car	$ .75
☐ 60	Ernie Irvan	$ .60
☐ 64A	Dorsey Schroeder's Car ERR	$ .30
☐ 64B	Dorsey Schroeder's Car COR	$ .50
☐ 67A	Hut Stricklin Chevy	$ .30
☐ 67B	Hut Stricklin No Chevy	$ .50

❑ 71	Mark Martin	$	.75
❑ 95	Ernie Irvan	$	.60
❑ 96	Mark Martin	$	.75
❑ 99	Rusty Wallace	$	1
❑ 100	Alan Kulwicki	$	1
❑ 115	Rusty Wallace	$	1
❑ 128	Jeff Gordon	$ 3.50	
❑ 130A	Waddell Wilson ERR	$	.30
❑ 130B	Waddell Wilson COR	$	.40
❑ 161	Dale Earnhardt	$ 2.50	
❑ 164A	David Fuge ERR	$	.30
❑ 164B	David Fuge COR	$	.40
❑ 169A	Felix Sabates ERR	$	.30
❑ 169B	Felix Sabates COR	$	.40
❑ 182	Dale Earnhardt	$ 2.50	
❑ 183	Davey Allison	$ 1.25	
❑ 190	Harry Gant	$	.40
❑ 199	Neil Bonnett	$	.50
❑ 211	Davey Allison	$ 1.25	
❑ 215	Neil Bonnett/Baker/Joy ANN	$	.40
❑ 223	Davey Allison with Crew	$	1
❑ 224	Dale Earnhardt with Crew	$ 1.40	
❑ 229	Davey Allison's Car	$	.50
❑ 242	Mark Martin Busch Pole	$	.40
❑ 248A	Bud Moore ERR Paul	$	.30
❑ 248B	Bud Moore COR Walter	$	.40
❑ NNO	Earnhardt HOLO/5000 White	$ 225	
❑ NNO	Earnhardt HOLO/5000 Black	$ 160	

1992 Pro Set Legends

❑ Complete Set (32)		$	5
❑ Common Card (L1-L32)		$	.20
❑ Semistars		$	.30

*Random Inserts in Packs

❑ L4A	Dick Hutcherson ERR	$	.40
❑ L4B	Dick Hutcherson COR	$	.40
❑ L32	Bobby Allison	$	.50

1992 Pro Set Maxwell House

❑ Complete Set (30)		$	15
❑ Common Card (1-30)		$	.30
❑ Semistars		$	.60
❑ 10	Davey Allison	$	3
❑ 12	Ernie Irvan	$ 1.50	
❑ 13	Mark Martin	$ 1.75	
❑ 16	Rusty Wallace	$ 2.25	
❑ 18	Alan Kulwicki	$ 1.50	
❑ 25	Richard Petty	$ 1.50	

1992 Pro Set Rudy Farms

❑ Complete Set (20)		$	25
❑ Common Card (1-15)		$	1
❑ Common Legends (L1-L5)		$	.75
❑ Semistars		$ 1.50	
❑ 2	Davey Allison	$	5
❑ 4	Ernie Irvan	$ 2.50	
❑ 5	Mark Martin	$	3
❑ 9	Rusty Wallace	$ 3.50	

❑ 11	Alan Kulwicki	$	3
❑ 15	Richard Petty	$ 2.50	

1992 Pro Set Tic Tac Hut Stricklin

❑ Complete Set (6)	$	7
❑ Common Card (1-6)	$	.75
❑ Stricklin Cards (1/6)	$ 1.50	

1992 Slim Jim Bobby Labonte

❑ Complete Set (29)	$	30
❑ Common Card (1-29)	$	.75

1992 STP Daytona 500

❑ Complete Set (10)		$	12
❑ Common Card (1-10)		$	1
❑ 1	Richard Petty	$	2
❑ 2	Richard Petty in Car	$ 1.50	
❑ 8	Davey Allison	$	4
❑ 9	Richard Petty	$	2

1992 Traks

❑ Complete Set (200)		$	12
❑ Complete Factory Set (200)		$	15
❑ Common Card (1-200)		$	.05
❑ Common Driver (1-200)		$	.15
❑ Semistars		$	.25
❑ 2	Rusty Wallace	$	1
❑ 3	Dale Earnhardt	$ 2.50	
❑ 4	Ernie Irvan	$	.60
❑ 6	Mark Martin	$	.75
❑ 7	Alan Kulwicki	$	1
❑ 10	Ricky Craven	$	.50
❑ 15	Rusty Wallace/Mike/Kenny	$	.75
❑ 28	Davey Allison	$ 1.25	
❑ 33	Harry Gant	$	.40
❑ 38	Mark Martin	$	.75
❑ 42	Kyle Petty	$	.40
❑ 43	Richard Petty	$	.65
❑ 60	Dale Earnhardt in Pits	$	.75
❑ 69	Kyle Petty	$	.40
❑ 72	Rusty Wallace/E. Dickerson	$	.60
❑ 73	Alan Kulwicki	$	1
❑ 85	Richard Petty	$	.75
❑ 101	Jeff Gordon	$ 3.50	
❑ 103	Dale Earnhardt	$ 2.50	
❑ 104	Ernie Irvan	$	.60
❑ 114	Neil Bonnett	$	.50
❑ 124	Rusty Wallace	$	1
❑ 133	Harry Gant	$	.40
❑ 142	Kyle Petty	$	.40
❑ 156	Davey Allison	$ 1.50	
❑ 175	Dale Earnhardt with Crew	$ 1.25	
❑ 179	Rusty Wallace	$	1
❑ 190	Dale Earnhardt	$ 2.50	
❑ 193	Dale Earnhardt's Car CL	$	.50
❑ 200	Richard Petty with Lynda	$	.75

1992 Traks Autographs

❑ Complete Set (10)		$	500
❑ Common Autograph (A1-A9)		$	30
❑ Cover Card (NNO)		$	12
❑ Semistars		$	40

*Random Inserts in Packs
*Some Cards Available Unsigned

❑ A1	Dale Earnhardt/R. Petty	$	225
❑ A2	Rusty Wallace	$	80
❑ A4	Ernie Irvan	$	60
❑ A5	Ricky Rudd SP	$	50
❑ A7	Jeff Gordon	$	150

1992 Traks ASA

❑ Complete Set (51)		$	5
❑ Common Card (1-51)		$	.20
❑ CL (NNO)		$	.20
❑ Semistars		$	.25

❑ 13	Rusty Wallace with Car	$	1.25
❑ 36	Alan Kulwicki with Car	$	1
❑ 39	Davey Allison with Car	$	2.25
❑ 41	Mark Martin	$	1

1992 Traks Baby Ruth Jeff Gordon

❑ Complete Set (4)		$	12
❑ Common Card (1-4)		$	1.50
❑ Jeff Gordon (1/2)		$	4.50

1992 Traks Goody's

❑ Complete Set (25)		$	10
❑ Common Card (1-25)		$	.25
❑ Semistars		$	.40

❑ 9	Jeff Gordon	$	3
❑ 19	Dale Earnhardt	$	3
❑ 20	Ernie Irvan	$	1
❑ 21	Davey Allison	$	2
❑ 25	Richard Petty	$	1.25

1992 Traks Kodak Ernie Irvan

❑ Complete Set (25)		$	28
❑ Common Card (1-25)		$	.75
❑ Gold Cards (11/21)		$	1.50
❑ E. Irvan Cards (1A/6A/16A/25)		$	2.75
❑ E. Irvan Golds (1B/6B/16B)		$	4.25

1992 Traks Mom-n-Pop's Ham Dale Earnhardt

❑ Complete Set (6)		$	20
❑ Common Card (1-6)		$	4

1992 Traks Benny Parsons

❑ Complete Set (50)		$	8
❑ Common Card (1-50)		$	.20
❑ CL (49-50)		$	.20

1992 Traks Robert Pressley

❑ Complete Set (12)		$	8
❑ Common Card (1-12)		$	.60
❑ Robert Pressley Cards		$	1.50

1992 Traks Racing Machines

❑ Complete Set (100)		$	20
❑ Complete Factory Set (100)		$	25
❑ Common Card (1-100)		$	.15
❑ Semistars		$	.25

❑ 2	Rusty Wallace's Car	$	.75
❑ 3	Dale Earnhardt's Car	$	1.50
❑ 4	Ernie Irvan's Car	$	.50
❑ 6	Mark Martin's Car	$	.60
❑ 7	Alan Kulwicki in Pits	$	.75
❑ 9	D. Earnhardt/R. Rudd/Gant Cars	$	1
❑ 19	Richard Petty in Pits	$	.50
❑ 24	Rusty Wallace with Truck	$	1
❑ 28	Davey Allison's Car	$	1
❑ 34	D. Earnhardt/D. Allison Cars	$	1.50
❑ 40	Jeff Gordon/D. Allison Cars	$	1.50
❑ 42	Kyle Petty's Car	$	.40
❑ 43	Richard Petty's Car	$	.50
❑ 44	Dale Earnhardt Race Action	$	1.25
❑ 51	Alan Kulwicki's Car	$	.75
❑ 54	Dale Earnhardt in Pits	$	1.50
❑ 58	Rusty Wallace/R. Rudd Cars	$	.75
❑ 60	Harry Gant/Bobby Labonte Cars	$	.40
❑ 65	Davey Allison/M. Waltrip Cars	$	1
❑ 76	Mark Martin in Pits	$	.60
❑ 78	Rusty Wallace in Pits	$	.75
❑ 80	Richard Petty Action	$	.50
❑ 84	Dale Earnhardt Race Action	$	1.25
❑ 89	Dale Earnhardt in Pits	$	1.50
❑ 91	Dale Earnhardt/T. Houston Cars	$	1
❑ 93	Davey Allison/M. Shepherd Cars	$	1
❑ 95	Ernie Irvan in Pits	$	.50
❑ 99	Davey Allison's Car CL	$	.50
❑ 100	D. Earnhardt/R. Petty Cars CL	$	.40

1992 Traks Racing Machines Bonus

❑ Complete Set (20)		$	5
❑ Complete Factory Set (20)		$	5
❑ Common Card (1B-20B)		$	.05
❑ Common Driver (1B-20B)		$	.10
❑ Semistars		$	.20

*Two Cards per Pack
*One Bonus Set per Factory Set

❑ 3B	Dale Earnhardt's Car	$	.75
❑ 10B	Ricky Craven	$	.50
❑ 20B	Jeff Gordon Baby Boomer	$	2.50

1992 Traks Team Sets

❑ Complete Set (200)		$	40
❑ Complete Earnhardt (25)		$	8
❑ Complete D. Allison (25)		$	6
❑ Complete K. Petty (25)		$	5

❑ Complete M. Waltrip (25)		$	5
❑ Complete Irvan (25)		$	6
❑ Complete D. Waltrip (25)		$	5
❑ Complete Stricklin (25)		$	5
❑ Complete R. Petty (25)		$	6
❑ Common Card (1-200)		$	.30
❑ Common Driver (1-200)		$	.60
❑ 2	Dale Earnhardt	$	1
❑ 13	Dale Earnhardt/Childress	$	1
❑ 21	Dale Earnhardt with Smokey	$	1
❑ 23	Dale Earnhardt	$	1
❑ 26	Davey Allison	$	1
❑ 42	Davey Allison	$	1
❑ 44	Davey Allison	$	1
❑ 49	Davey Allison/McReyn/Yates	$	1
❑ 50	Davey Allison CL	$	.50
❑ 108	Ernie Irvan	$	.75
❑ 119	Ernie Irvan	$	.75
❑ 125	Ernie Irvan with Car	$	.75
❑ 176	Richard Petty	$	.75
❑ 184	Richard Petty with Crew	$	.75
❑ 185	Richard Petty with Crew	$	.75
❑ 200	Richard Petty King	$	.75

1992 Wheels
Kyle Petty

❑ Complete Set (14)		$	6
❑ Common Card (1-14)		$	.50
❑ Kyle Petty Cards		$	1

*Gold Cards: Same Price

1992 Wheels
Rusty Wallace

❑ Complete Set (14)		$	8
❑ Common Card (1-14)		$	.75
❑ Rusty Wallace Cards		$	1.25

*Gold Cards: Same Price

1992 Winner's Choice Busch

❑ Complete Set (150)		$	20
❑ Complete Factory Set (150)		$	22
❑ Common Card (1-150)		$	.10
❑ Common Driver (1-150)		$	.20
❑ Semistars		$	.50
❑ 2	Ricky Craven	$	1.25
❑ 3	Ricky Craven	$	1.25
❑ 64	Robert Pressley	$	1
❑ 68	Joe Nemechek	$	1
❑ 76	Jeff Gordon	$	5
❑ 77	Jeff Gordon's Car	$	2
❑ 78	Jeff Burton	$	1
❑ 98	Shawna Robinson	$	.75

1992 Winner's Choice Busch Autographs

❑ Complete Set (4)		$	190
❑ Common Autograph		$	40
❑ Semistars		$	55

1993 Action Packed

❑ Complete Set (207)		$	125
❑ Complete Series 1 Set (84)		$	70
❑ Complete Series 2 Set (84)		$	50
❑ Complete Series 3 Set (39)		$	15
❑ Common Card (1-84)		$	.60
❑ Common Card (85-168)		$	.40
❑ Common Card (169-207)		$	.20
❑ Common Driver (1-84)		$	1
❑ Common Driver (85-168)		$	.60
❑ Common Driver (169-207)		$	.30
❑ King Richard (50-54)		$	1.25
❑ King Richard BR (70-72/75-76)		$	1.25
❑ Back in Black (120-123)		$	2
❑ Back in Black BR (124-127)		$	2
❑ Rusty Wallace (191-197)		$	.75
❑ Semistars (1-84)		$	1.50
❑ Semistars (85-168)		$	1
❑ Semistars (169-207)		$	.50
❑ 1	Alan Kulwicki WIN (Winner Inserts, Winner)	$	10
❑ 5	Davey Allison WIN	$	6
❑ 6	Rusty Wallace WIN	$	2
❑ 8	Ernie Irvan WIN	$	1.50
❑ 9	Mark Martin WIN	$	1.75
❑ 10	Richard Petty BR (Braile)	$	2
❑ 21	Davey Allison PW (Pole Winners, Power)	$	6
❑ 22	Mark Martin PW	$	1.75
❑ 25	Ernie Irvan PW	$	1.50
❑ 26	Alan Kulwicki PW	$	5
❑ 28	Rusty Wallace PW	$	2
❑ 32	Jeff Gordon	$	8
❑ 34	Ernie Irvan	$	1.75
❑ 40	Alan Kulwicki T10 (Top 10)	$	5
❑ 43	Davey Allison T10	$	6
❑ 44	Mark Martin T10	$	1.75
❑ 61	Jeff Gordon YG (Young Guns)	$	5
❑ 63	Jeff Gordon/Wallace/Labonte YG	$	5
❑ 64	Alan Kulwicki	$	5
❑ 77	Mark Martin	$	2
❑ 78	Mark Martin	$	2
❑ 79	Davey Allison's Car	$	3
❑ 80	Davey Allison	$	6
❑ 81	Richard Petty	$	2
❑ 83	Rusty Wallace	$	2.50
❑ 85	Alan Kulwicki	$	2.50
❑ 86	Jeff Gordon	$	5
❑ 87	Jeff Gordon's Car	$	2
❑ 88	Dale Earnhardt	$	5
❑ 89	Dale Earnhardt's Car	$	2
❑ 92	Richard Petty D93 (Daytona 93)	$	1.25
❑ 93	Jeff Gordon D93	$	4
❑ 94	Dale Earnhardt D93	$	4
❑ 95	Dale Earnhardt D93	$	4
❑ 97	Davey Allison	$	3.50
❑ 98	Davey Allison's Car	$	1.50
❑ 107	Rusty Wallace	$	2
❑ 109	Mark Martin	$	1.50
❑ 128	Ernie Irvan	$	1.25
❑ 138	Dale Earnhardt PW	$	4
❑ 139	Dale Earnhardt WIN	$	4

❑ 140	Allison Family TA (The Allisons)	$	2
❑ 144	Davey Allison Family TA	$	2
❑ 146	Davey Allison/Clifford/Bobby TA	$	2
❑ 150	Jeff Gordon YG	$	4
❑ 153	Jeff Gordon YG	$	4
❑ 156	Jeff Gordon/Wallace/Labonte YG	$	4
❑ 160	Richard Petty/Kyle Petty FS	$	1
❑ 163	Rusty Wallace/Kenny Wallace B	$ 1.50	
❑ 171	Dale Earnhardt	$ 2.50	
❑ 173	Jeff Gordon	$ 2.50	
❑ 176	Mark Martin	$	.75
❑ 182	Ernie Irvan	$	.60
❑ 198	Dale Earnhardt WIN	$	2
❑ 199	Ernie Irvan WIN	$	.50
❑ 201	Ernie Irvan PS	$	.50
❑ 202	Dale Earnhardt WIN	$	2
❑ 205	Jeff Gordon PS	$	2
❑ 207	Dale Earnhardt WIN	$	2

1993 Action Packed
Davey Allison

❑ Complete Set (6)	$	8
❑ Common Card (DA1-DA6)	$ 1.50	
*Random Inserts in Series 3 Packs		

1993 Action Packed
Alan Kulwicki

❑ Complete Set (6)	$	8
❑ Common Card (AK1-AK6)	$ 1.50	
*Random Inserts in Series 3 Packs		

1993 Action Packed 24K Gold

❑ Complete Set (72)	$3500	
❑ Complete Series 1 (17)	$1500	
❑ Complete Series 2 (21)	$1000	
❑ Complete Series 3 (34)	$1000	
❑ Common Card (1G-17G)	$	35
❑ Common Card (18G-38G)	$	25
❑ Common Card (39G-72G)	$	22
❑ Young Guns (9G-12G)	$	60
❑ King Richard (13G-17G)	$	50
❑ Back in Black (18G-21G)	$	100
❑ Back in Black (22G-25G)	$	100
❑ Young Guns (26G-32G)	$	50
❑ Alan Kulwicki (39G-44G)	$	80
❑ Davey Allison (45G-50G)	$	80
❑ Semistars (1G-17G)	$	45
❑ Semistars (18G-32G)	$	30
❑ Semistars (33G-72G)	$	25

❑ 1G	Alan Kulwicki	$	200
❑ 4G	Davey Allison	$	200
❑ 5G	Mark Martin	$	60
❑ 10G	Jeff Gordon YG	$	125
❑ 12G	Jeff Gordon/Wallace/Labonte YG	$	125
❑ 26G	Jeff Gordon YG	$	100
❑ 29G	Jeff Gordon YG	$	100
❑ 32G	Jeff Gordon/Wallace/Labonte YG	$	100
❑ 35G	Richard Petty D93	$	50
❑ 36G	Jeff Gordon D93	$	100
❑ 37G	Dale Earnhardt D93	$	100
❑ 38G	Dale Earnhardt D93	$	100
❑ 53G	Dale Earnhardt D93	$	100
❑ 55G	Jeff Gordon	$	100
❑ 58G	Mark Martin	$	50
❑ 64G	Ernie Irvan	$	40

1993 Dayco Series 2
Rusty Wallace

❑ Complete Set (15)	$	10
❑ Common Card (11-25)	$	.75

1993 Finish Line

❑ Complete Set (180)	$	14
❑ Common Card (1-180)	$	.05
❑ Common Driver (1-180)	$	.10
❑ Semistars	$	.20

❑ 1	Alan Kulwicki	$	.75
❑ 5	Rusty Wallace	$	1
❑ 14	Jeff Gordon's Car	$	.75
❑ 37	Alan Kulwicki	$	.75
❑ 40	Ernie Irvan	$	.60
❑ 48	Davey Allison's Car	$	.60
❑ 61	Richard Petty	$	.75
❑ 66	Davey Allison	$ 1.25	
❑ 68	Ernie Irvan	$	.60
❑ 76	Alan Kulwicki	$	.75
❑ 83	Jeff Gordon	$ 2.50	
❑ 85	Richard Petty	$	.75
❑ 89	Davey Allison	$ 1.25	
❑ 110	Jeff Gordon	$ 2.50	
❑ 114	Richard Petty	$	.75
❑ 119	Neil Bonnett	$	.50
❑ 122	Rusty Wallace	$	1
❑ 133	Mark Martin	$	.75
❑ 164	Mark Martin	$	.75
❑ NNO	Alan Kulwicki MEM (Memorial)	$	6
❑ NNO	Davey Allison HOLO (Hologram)/5000	$	150

1993 Finish Line Silver

❑ Complete Set (180)	$	125
❑ Common Card (1-180)	$	.40
❑ Common Driver (1-180)	$	.60
❑ Semistars	$	1
*Stars 2.5x to 5x		
*One Per Foil Pack/Two Per Jumbo Pack		

1993 Finish Line
Davey Allison

❑ Complete Set (15)	$	16
❑ Common Card (1-15)	$ 1.50	
*One Per Jumbo Pack		

1993 Hi-Tech Tire Test

❑ Complete Set (10)	$	5
❑ Common Card (1-10)	$	.30
❑ Cover Card (10)	$	.30

❑ 1	Dale Earnhardt's Car	$ 1.25	
❑ 3	Davey Allison's Car	$	1

❏ 4	Rusty Wallace's Car	$	.75
❏ 5	Ernie Irvan's Car	$	.50
❏ 6	Mark Martin's Car	$	.60
❏ 9	Bill Elliott's Car	$	.75

1993 Maxwell House

❏ Complete Set (32)		$	20
❏ Complete Series 1 (16)		$	10
❏ Complete Series 2 (16)		$	10
❏ Common Card (1-15)		$	.50
❏ Common Card (16-30)		$	.50
❏ Cover Card (NNO)		$	.50
❏ Semistars		$	.75

❏ 2	Alan Kulwicki	$	1.25
❏ 3	Davey Allison	$	2
❏ 6	Mark Martin	$	1.25
❏ 9	Ernie Irvan	$	1
❏ 10	Rusty Wallace	$	1.50
❏ 15	Richard Petty	$	.75
❏ 17	Davey Allison/Bobby Allison	$	2
❏ 18	Richard Petty/Kyle Petty	$	.75
❏ 19	Rusty Wallace/Kenny Wallace	$	1
❏ 24	Jeff Gordon/Kenny Wallace/Bobby Labonte	$	3
❏ 25	Jeff Gordon	$	4

1993 Maxx

❏ Complete Set (300)		$	20
❏ Complete Factory Set (300)		$	22
❏ Common Card (1-300)		$	.05
❏ Common Driver (1-300)		$	.10
❏ Semistars		$	.20

❏ 2	Rusty Wallace	$	1
❏ 3	Dale Earnhardt	$	2.50
❏ 4	Ernie Irvan	$	.60
❏ 6	Mark Martin	$	.75
❏ 7	Alan Kulwicki	$	.75
❏ 11	Bill Elliott	$	1
❏ 24	Jeff Gordon	$	2.50
❏ 28	Davey Allison	$	1.25
❏ 43	Richard Petty	$	.75
❏ 46	Al Unser, Jr.	$	.60
❏ 56	Dale Earnhardt's Car	$	.75
❏ 94	Davey Allison/Elliott Cars MM (Memorable Moment)	$	.50
❏ 121	Davey Allison's Car	$	.60
❏ 131	Davey Allison Crash MM	$	.50
❏ 156	Richard Petty MM	$	.35
❏ 168	Jeff Gordon's Car	$	.75
❏ 190	Alan Kulwicki WC (Winston Cup) Champ	$	.75
❏ 193	Bill Elliott FF	$	.60
❏ 199	Davey Allison/R. Petty Cars MM	$	.50
❏ 219	Neil Bonnett	$	.50
❏ 220	Davey Allison MM	$	.50
❏ 245	Richard Petty MM	$	.35
❏ 264	Davey Allison YR	$	.60
❏ 265	Bill Elliott YR	$	.50
❏ 266	Bill Elliott YR	$	.50
❏ 267	Bill Elliott YR	$	.50
❏ 268	Bill Elliott YR	$	.50
❏ 269	Alan Kulwicki YR	$	.50

❏ 270	Davey Allison YR	$	.60
❏ 274	Dale Earnhardt YR	$	1
❏ 276	Ernie Irvan YR	$	.30
❏ 277	Alan Kulwicki YR	$	.50
❏ 278	Davey Allison YR	$	.60
❏ 279	Ernie Irvan YR	$	.30
❏ 281	Ernie Irvan YR	$	.30
❏ 286	Rusty Wallace YR	$	.50
❏ 290	Mark Martin YR	$	.40
❏ 292	Davey Allison YR	$	.60
❏ 293	Bill Elliott YR	$	.50
❏ 294	Alan Kulwicki MM	$	.50

1993 Maxx Baby Ruth Jeff Burton

❏ Complete Set (4)		$	8
❏ Common Card (1-4)		$	2

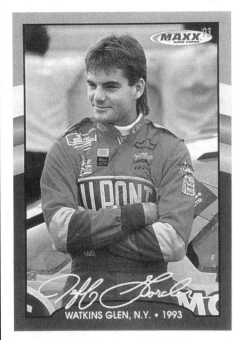

WATKINS GLEN, N.Y. • 1993

1993 Maxx Jeff Gordon

❏ Complete Set (20)		$	8
❏ Common Card (1-20)		$	.50
❏ Jeff Gordon (10)		$	1.50
❏ Jeff Gordon AUTO		$	200

1993 Maxx Motorsport

❏ Complete Set (50)		$	25
❏ Common Card (1-50)		$	.40
❏ Common Driver (1-50)		$	.75
❏ Semistars		$	1

❏ 6	Bill Elliott	$	2.50
❏ 13	Mark Martin	$	2
❏ 41	Davey Allison	$	4

❑ 42	Davey Allison's Car	$	1.50
❑ 43	Alan Kulwicki	$	2.50
❑ 47	Alan Kulwicki/Bill Elliott	$	2.50
❑ 49	Davey Allison's Car	$	1.50

1993 Maxx Premier Plus

❑ Complete Set (212)		$	80
❑ Complete Factory Set (212)		$	90
❑ Common Card (1-212)		$	.25
❑ Common Driver (1-212)		$	.50
❑ Semistars		$	.75

❑ 2	Rusty Wallace	$	3
❑ 3	Dale Earnhardt	$	6
❑ 4	Ernie Irvan	$	2
❑ 6	Mark Martin	$	2.50
❑ 7	Alan Kulwicki	$	3
❑ 11	Bill Elliott	$	3
❑ 24	Jeff Gordon	$	6
❑ 28	Davey Allison	$	4
❑ 29	Davey Allison/Bill Elliott MM	$	1.25
❑ 39	Jeff Gordon's Car	$	2.50
❑ 43	Richard Petty	$	2.50
❑ 46	Al Unser, Jr.	$	2
❑ 48	Richard Petty MM	$	1
❑ 56	Dale Earnhardt's Car	$	2.50
❑ 57	Davey Allison/Richard Petty MM	$	1.25
❑ 60	Davey Allison/Kyle Petty MM	$	1.25
❑ 62	Davey Allison Crash MM	$	2
❑ 74	Richard Petty MM	$	1
❑ 79	Davey Allison's Car	$	1.75
❑ 81	Alan Kulwicki MM	$	1.25
❑ 172	Alan Kulwicki WC Champ	$	2
❑ 175	Bill Elliott FF	$	1.75
❑ 179	Davey Allison YR	$	2
❑ 180	Bill Elliott YR	$	1.50
❑ 181	Bill Elliott YR	$	1.50
❑ 182	Bill Elliott YR	$	1.50
❑ 183	Bill Elliott YR	$	1.50
❑ 184	Alan Kulwicki YR	$	1.50
❑ 185	Davey Allison YR	$	2
❑ 186	Mark Martin YR	$	1.25
❑ 187	Davey Allison YR	$	2
❑ 189	Dale Earnhardt YR	$	3
❑ 191	Ernie Irvan YR	$	1
❑ 192	Alan Kulwicki YR	$	1.50
❑ 193	Davey Allison YR	$	2
❑ 194	Ernie Irvan YR	$	1
❑ 196	Ernie Irvan YR	$	1
❑ 201	Rusty Wallace YR	$	1.50
❑ 205	Mark Martin YR	$	1.25
❑ 207	Davey Allison YR	$	2
❑ 208	Bill Elliott YR	$	1.50
❑ NNO	Mascot Card	$	8
❑ NNO	Jeff Gordon/Bobby Labonte/K. Wallace	$	20

1993 Maxx Premier Series

❑ Complete Set (300)		$	45
❑ Common Card (1-300)		$	.10
❑ Common Driver (1-300)		$	.25
❑ Semistars		$	.40
*Stars 1.25x to 2x Green Card Collection			

1993 Maxx Retail Jumbos

❑ Complete Set (9)		$	30
❑ Common Card (1-9)		$	3
❑ Semistars		$	3.50

*One per Special Retail Pack

❑ 5	Mark Martin	$	4
❑ 7	Bill Elliott	$	5

1993 Maxx Texaco Davey Allison

❑ Complete Set (20)		$	10
❑ Common Card (1-20)		$	.40
❑ Davey Allison Cards		$	1
❑ Davey Allison AU/5000 (AU1)		$	175

1993 Maxx Winnebago Motorsports

❑ Complete Set (11)		$	20
❑ Common Card (1-10)		$	1
❑ Common Driver (1-10)		$	2
❑ CL (NNO)		$	1

❑ 2	J. Gordon/B. Labonte/Bickle/K. Wallace	$	8

1993 Maxx The Winston

❑ Complete Set (50)		$	20
❑ Common Card (1-50)		$	.20
❑ Semistars		$	.30

❑ 1	Dale Earnhardt	$	3
❑ 2	Mark Martin	$	1
❑ 3	Ernie Irvan	$	.75
❑ 8	Rusty Wallace	$	1.25
❑ 9	Davey Allison	$	2
❑ 14	Bill Elliott	$	1.25
❑ 21	Dale Earnhardt's Car	$	1.50
❑ 29	Davey Allison's Car	$	1
❑ 41	Ernie Irvan PW	$	.50
❑ 49	Dale Earnhardt's Car WIN	$	1.50
❑ 50	Dale Earnhardt VL	$	1.50
❑ 51	Dale Earnhardt Chromium	$	5

1993 Motorcraft Decade of Champions

❑ Complete Set (10)		$	8
❑ Common Card (NNO)		$	1
❑ Cover Card (NNO)		$	.50

1993 Motorcraft Manufacturer's Champion

❑ Complete Set (10)		$	8
❑ Common Card (1-8)		$	.50
❑ Cover Card (NNO)		$	.50
❑ Trophy Card (NNO)		$	.50
❑ Semistars		$	1

❑ 1	Davey Allison	$	3
❑ 3	Bill Elliott	$	2
❑ 5	Alan Kulwicki	$	2
❑ 7	Mark Martin	$	1.50

1993 Pepsi 400 Victory Lane

❏ Complete Set (5)		$	12
❏ Common Card (1-5)		$	1.25
❏ 1	Davey Allison	$	6
❏ 2	Ernie Irvan	$	3

1993 Press Pass Preview

❏ Complete Set (34)		$	9
❏ Common Card (1-34)		$	.20
❏ Common Driver (1-34)		$	.25
❏ Semistars		$	.30
❏ 1	Davey Allison Foil	$	1.50
❏ 8	Alan Kulwicki	$	1
❏ 10	Mark Martin	$	.75
❏ 15	Rusty Wallace	$	1
❏ 17	J. Gordon/K. Wallace/ B. Labonte	$	2.50
❏ 18A	Jeff Gordon Redemption Expired	$	2.50
❏ 18B	Jeff Gordon Foil	$	4
❏ 21	Alan Kulwicki	$	1
❏ 22	Rusty Wallace	$	1
❏ 26	Jeff Gordon's Car	$	1.25

1993 Traks

❏ Complete Set (200)		$	170
❏ Complete Reg. Set (150)		$	12
❏ Complete Silver Set (50)		$	160
❏ Common Card (1-150)		$	.05
❏ Common Card (151-200)		$	1.50
❏ Common Driver (1-150)		$	.10
❏ Common Driver (151-200)		$	2.50
❏ Semistars (1-150)		$	.20
❏ Semistars (151-200)		$	3.50

*Silver Random Inserts in Packs

❏ 2	Rusty Wallace WIN	$	.50
❏ 5	Neil Bonnett	$	.50
❏ 6	Mark Martin	$	.75
❏ 7	Alan Kulwicki	$	.75
❏ 24	Jeff Gordon's Car	$	.75
❏ 27	Alan Kulwicki Early Ride	$	.75
❏ 28	Davey Allison	$	1.25
❏ 39	Jeff Gordon	$	2.50
❏ 58	Rusty Wallace	$	1
❏ 67	Mark Martin	$	.75
❏ 69	Davey Allison/Yates	$	1
❏ 82	Alan Kulwicki First Win	$	.75
❏ 84	Al Unser, Jr.	$	.60
❏ 100	Davey Allison	$	1.25
❏ 127	Davey Allison	$	1.25
❏ 128	Davey Allison's Car	$	.60
❏ 142	Alan Kulwicki on Pole	$	.60
❏ 151	Jeff Gordon	$	25
❏ 161	Mark Martin	$	7
❏ 164	Rusty Wallace	$	8
❏ 178	Davey Allison/Bobby Allison	$	12
❏ 181	Rusty Wallace	$	8
❏ 190	Davey Allison	$	20
❏ 196	Alan Kulwicki MEM	$	14

❏ 197	Al Unser, Jr.	$	6
❏ 200	Davey Allison	$	20

1993 Traks First Run

❏ Complete Set (200)		$	900
❏ Complete Reg. Set (150)		$	30
❏ Complete Silver Set (50)		$	875
❏ Common Card (1-150)		$	.20
❏ Common Card (151-200)		$	10
❏ Common Driver (1-150)		$	.25
❏ Common Driver (151-200)		$	12
❏ Semistars (1-150)		$	.30
❏ Semistars (151-200)		$	13

*Stars (1-150): 1.5x to 3x
*Stars (151-200): 2x to 4x
*Random Inserts in Packs

❏ 151	Jeff Gordon	$	100
❏ 161	Mark Martin	$	30
❏ 164	Rusty Wallace	$	35
❏ 178	Davey Allison/Bobby Allison	$	40
❏ 181	Rusty Wallace	$	35
❏ 190	Davey Allison	$	65
❏ 196	Alan Kulwicki MEM	$	40
❏ 197	Al Unser, Jr.	$	30
❏ 200	Davey Allison	$	65

1993 Traks Kodak Ernie Irvan

❏ Complete Factory Set (6)		$	16
❏ Common Card (1-6)		$	2
❏ Ernie Irvan Cards (1/3/5)		$	4

1993 Traks Trivia

❏ Complete Set (50)		$	12
❏ Common Card (1-50)		$	.15
❏ Semistars		$	.30
❏ 1	Mark Martin	$	.50
❏ 2	Jeff Gordon	$	2
❏ 3	Rusty Wallace	$	.60
❏ 4	Davey Allison	$	1
❏ 6	Mark Martin	$	.50
❏ 9	Alan Kulwicki	$	.75
❏ 11	Rusty Wallace	$	.60
❏ 18	Davey Allison/Bobby Allison	$	1
❏ 19	Mark Martin	$	.50
❏ 23	Mark Martin	$	.50
❏ 24	Jeff Gordon	$	2
❏ 28	Davey Allison	$	1
❏ 29	Rusty Wallace	$	.60
❏ 32	Mark Martin	$	.50
❏ 34	Davey Allison with Crew	$	.75
❏ 35	Alan Kulwicki	$	.75
❏ 36	Jeff Gordon	$	2
❏ 37	Mark Martin	$	.50
❏ 39	Rusty Wallace	$	.60
❏ 40	Davey Allison/Jerry Glanville	$	.75
❏ 41	Mark Martin	$	.50
❏ 45	Jeff Gordon	$	2

1993 Wheels Mom-n-Pop's Dale Earnhardt

❏ Complete Set (6)		$	12
❏ Common Card (1-6)		$	2

1993 Wheels Rookie Thunder

❏ Complete Set (100)		$	10
❏ Common Card (1-100)		$	.05
❏ Common Driver (1-100)		$	.10
❏ Semistars		$	.20
❏ 2	Richard Petty	$	.30
❏ 25	Rusty Wallace	$	.50
❏ 27	Alan Kulwicki	$	.60
❏ 28	Davey Allison	$	.75
❏ 32	Jeff Gordon	$ 1.25	
❏ 37	Jeff Gordon	$ 1.25	
❏ 46	Rusty Wallace	$	.50
❏ 48	Alan Kulwicki	$	.60
❏ 49	Davey Allison	$	.75
❏ 50	Jeff Gordon	$ 1.25	
❏ 51	Jeff Gordon	$ 1.25	
❏ 56	Davey Allison	$	.75
❏ 57	Alan Kulwicki	$	.60
❏ 58	Alan Kulwicki	$	.60
❏ 59	Alan Kulwicki	$	.60
❏ 61	Richard Petty	$	.30
❏ 62	Jeff Gordon with Car	$	1
❏ 65	Rusty Wallace	$	.50
❏ 66	Rusty Wallace	$	.50
❏ 67	Rusty Wallace	$	.50
❏ 68	Rusty Wallace	$	.50
❏ 70	Jeff Gordon	$ 1.25	
❏ 71	Jeff Gordon	$ 1.25	
❏ 79	Richard Petty	$	.30
❏ 80	Richard Petty	$	.30
❏ 82	Jeff Gordon	$ 1.25	
❏ 84	Davey Allison	$	.75
❏ 85	Davey Allison	$	.75
❏ 86	Alan Kulwicki	$	.60
❏ 87	Rusty Wallace	$	.50
❏ 90	Rusty Wallace	$	.50
❏ 93	Jeff Gordon's Car	$	.50
❏ 96	Richard Petty	$	.30
❏ 97	Jeff Gordon	$ 1.25	
❏ 98	Jeff Gordon/K. Schrader	$ 1.25	
❏ 99	Richard Petty	$	.30
❏ 100	Davey Allison	$	.75

1993 Wheels Rookie Thunder Platinum

❏ Complete Set (100)		$	80
❏ Common Card (1-100)		$	.30
❏ Common Driver (1-100)		$	.50
❏ Semistars		$	.75

*Stars: 3x to 5x
*One per Foil Pack

1993 Wheels Rookie Thunder SPs

❏ Complete Set (7)		$	60
❏ Common Card (SP1-SP7)		$	6

*Random Inserts in Packs

❏ SP2	Davey Allison/Bobby Allison	$	15
❏ SP3	Davey Allison	$	15
❏ SP4	Alan Kulwicki	$	10
❏ SP5	Alan Kulwicki	$	10
❏ SP6	Richard Petty	$	8
❏ SP7	Richard Petty	$	8

1994 Action Packed

❏ Complete Set (209)		$	90
❏ Complete Series 1 (66)		$	25
❏ Complete Series 2 (72)		$	25
❏ Complete Series 3 (71)		$	40
❏ Common Card (1-66)		$	.25
❏ Common Card (67-138)		$	.25
❏ Common Card (139-209)		$	.40
❏ Common Driver (1-66)		$	.50
❏ Common Driver (67-138)		$	.50
❏ Common Driver (139-207)		$	.75
❏ Kyle Petty (92-97)		$	.60
❏ Neil Bonnett (98-102)		$	.75
❏ Ernie Irvan (194-198)		$	1
❏ Mark Martin (199-203)		$ 1.25	
❏ Semistars Series 1/2		$	.60
❏ Semistars Series 3		$	1
❏ Kyle Petty Diam/1000 (92D)		$	300
❏ 1	Dale Earnhardt	$ 3.50	
❏ 2	Rusty Wallace	$ 1.50	
❏ 3	Mark Martin	$ 1.25	
❏ 6	Ernie Irvan	$	1
❏ 8	Dale Earnhardt WC Champ	$	3
❏ 14	Jeff Gordon	$ 3.50	
❏ 29	Alan Kulwicki	$ 1.25	
❏ 30	Jeff Gordon ROY	$	3

DALE EARNHARDT
WINNER OF 6 1993 RACES

❏ 32	Dale Earnhardt WIN	$ 2.50	
❏ 33	Mark Martin WIN	$	.75
❏ 34	Ernie Irvan with Crew WIN	$	.60
❏ 40	Davey Allison WIN	$ 1.50	
❏ 41	Dale Earnhardt's Car	$ 1.25	
❏ 58	Ernie Irvan with Car	$	.60
❏ 67	Rusty Wallace	$ 1.50	
❏ 68	Dale Earnhardt	$ 3.50	
❏ 69	Mark Martin	$ 1.25	
❏ 73	Jeff Gordon	$ 3.50	
❏ 81	Ernie Irvan	$	1
❏ 93	Kyle Petty BR	$	.75
❏ 99	Dale Earnhardt/Neil Bonnett	$ 2.50	

❏ 103	Jeff Gordon DR	$ 2.50	
❏ 104	Dale Earnhardt DR	$ 2.50	
❏ 105	Ernie Irvan DR	$ .60	
❏ 126	Dale Earnhardt's Car	$ 1.25	
❏ 131	Jeff Gordon's Car	$ 1.25	
❏ 146	Jeff Gordon	$ 4	
❏ 148	Ernie Irvan	$ 1.50	
❏ 153	Mark Martin	$ 2	
❏ 178	Richard Petty	$ 1.25	
❏ 179	Dale Earnhardt WIN	$ 3	
❏ 180	Dale Earnhardt WIN	$ 3	
❏ 181	Ernie Irvan WIN	$ 1	
❏ 182	Ernie Irvan WIN	$ 1	
❏ 183	Rusty Wallace WIN	$ 1.25	
❏ 186	Rusty Wallace WIN	$ 1.25	
❏ 187	Dale Earnhardt WIN	$ 3	
❏ 188	Ernie Irvan WIN	$ 1	
❏ 189	Jeff Gordon WIN	$ 3	
❏ 190	Rusty Wallace WIN	$ 1.25	
❏ 191	Rusty Wallace WIN	$ 1.25	
❏ 192	Rusty Wallace WIN	$ 1.25	
❏ 204	Rusty Wallace/Kenny/Mike	$ 1.25	
❏ 206	Rusty Wallace WS	$ 1.25	
❏ 209	Jeff Gordon WS	$ 3	

1994 Action Packed Richard Childress Racing

❏ Complete Set (20)	$ 12	
❏ Common Card (1-20)	$ .40	
❏ Dale Earnhardt (3-4)	$ 1.50	
❏ Dale Earnhardt's Car (2/5-6)	$ .75	
❏ SP (18/20)	$ 3	

*Random Inserts in Series 3 Packs

1994 Action Packed 24K Gold

❏ Complete Set (59)	$2000	
❏ Complete Series 1 (20)	$ 700	
❏ Complete Series 2 (25)	$ 700	
❏ Complete Series 3 (14)	$ 700	
❏ Common Driver (1G-10G)	$ 30	
❏ Common Car (11G-20G)	$ 25	
❏ Common Driver (21G-45G)	$ 30	
❏ Common Driver (179G-193G)	$ 30	
❏ Semistars	$ 40	

*Random Inserts in Packs
*Gordon AUTO Not Included in Set Price

❏ 1G	Rusty Wallace	$ 60	
❏ 2G	Dale Earnhardt	$ 100	
❏ 3G	Mark Martin	$ 50	
❏ 4G	Ernie Irvan	$ 40	
❏ 10G	Davey Allison	$ 70	
❏ 11G	Dale Earnhardt's Car	$ 50	
❏ 21G	Rusty Wallace	$ 60	
❏ 22G	Dale Earnhardt	$ 100	
❏ 23G	Mark Martin	$ 50	
❏ 27G	Jeff Gordon	$ 100	
❏ 35G	Ernie Irvan	$ 40	
❏ 179G	Dale Earnhardt WIN	$ 80	
❏ 180G	Dale Earnhardt WIN	$ 80	
❏ 182G	Ernie Irvan WIN	$ 35	
❏ 183G	Rusty Wallace WIN	$ 50	
❏ 186G	Rusty Wallace WIN	$ 50	
❏ 187G	Dale Earnhardt WIN	$ 80	
❏ 188G	Ernie Irvan WIN	$ 35	
❏ 189G	Jeff Gordon WIN AUTO	$ 300	
❏ 190G	Rusty Wallace WIN	$ 50	
❏ 191G	Rusty Wallace WIN	$ 50	
❏ 192G	Rusty Wallace WIN	$ 50	

1994 Action Packed Champ and Challenger

❏ Complete Set (42)	$ 20	
❏ Complete Factory Set (42)	$ 25	
❏ Common Card (1-42)	$ .75	

1994 Action Packed Champ and Challenger 24K Gold

❏ Complete Set (12)	$ 600	
❏ Common Card	$ 55	

1994 ARCA

❏ Complete Set (100)	$ 20	
❏ Common Card (1-100)	$ .20	
❏ Semistars	$ .40	

1994 Dayco Series 3

❏ Complete Set (15)	$ 10	
❏ Common Card (26-40)	$ .75	

❏ 26	Neil Bonnett	$ 1.25	
❏ 27	Rusty Wallace	$ 2	

1994 Finish Line

❏ Complete Set (150)	$ 12	
❏ Common Card (1-150)	$ .05	
❏ Common Driver (1-150)	$ .10	
❏ Semistars	$ .20	

❏ 7	Mark Martin	$ .60	
❏ 10	Ernie Irvan	$ .50	
❏ 29	Rusty Wallace	$ .75	
❏ 31	Ernie Irvan	$ .50	
❏ 36	Jeff Gordon	$ 1.50	
❏ 57	Neil Bonnett	$ .40	
❏ 58	Richard Petty OWN	$ .50	
❏ 64	Richard Petty	$ .50	
❏ 74	Rusty Wallace	$ .75	
❏ 75	Jeff Gordon	$ 1.50	
❏ 85	Mark Martin	$ .60	
❏ 90	Rusty Wallace	$ .75	
❏ 123	Jeff Gordon's Car	$ .60	
❏ 126	Mark Martin	$ .60	
❏ NNO	Jeff Gordon ROY	$ 8	
❏ NNO	Hermie Sadler ROY	$ 4	
❏ NNO	Harry Gant Last Ride	$ 5	
❏ NNO	Sterling Marlin 5x7	$ 8	

1994 Finish Line Silver

❏ Complete Set (150)	$ 90	
❏ Common Card (1-150)	$ .45	
❏ Common Driver (1-150)	$ .85	

1994 Finish Line
Neil Bonnett

| ❏ Complete Set (5) | $ 9 |
| ❏ Common Card | $ 1.50 |
*Random Inserts in Retail Packs

1994 Finish Line Busch Grand National

❏ Complete Set (15)	$ 16
❏ Common Card (1-15)	$ 1
❏ Semistars	$ 1.75
*BGN Prefix on Card Numbers
*Random Inserts in Packs

1994 Finish Line Down Home

❏ Complete Set (10)	$ 30
❏ Common Card (1-10)	$ 3
❏ Semistars	$ 3.75
*Random Inserts in Packs

❏ 2	Ernie Irvan	$ 5.50
❏ 4	Mark Martin	$ 5.50
❏ 10	Rusty Wallace	$ 6.50

1994 Finish Line Gold Signature

| ❏ Complete Set (5) | $ 60 |
| ❏ Common Card (1-5) | $ 10 |
*Random Inserts in Hobby Packs

❏ NNO	Ernie Irvan	$ 14
❏ NNO	Mark Martin	$ 15
❏ NNO	Rusty Wallace	$ 17

1994 Finish Line New Stars on the Horizon

❏ Complete Set (8)	$ 12
❏ Common Card (1-8)	$ 1.50
❏ Semistars	$ 2
*Random Inserts in Packs

1994 Finish Line Victory Lane

❏ Complete Set (18)	$ 60
❏ Common Card (VL1-VL18)	$ 2.50
❏ Semistars	$ 3.50

*One per Jumbo Pack

❏ VL1	Davey Allison	$ 6
❏ VL3	Ernie Irvan	$ 3
❏ VL5	Mark Martin	$ 4
❏ VL9	Rusty Wallace	$ 6
❏ VL10	Rusty Wallace	$ 6
❏ VL14	Mark Martin	$ 5
❏ VL16	Davey Allison	$ 6
❏ VL18	Ernie Irvan	$ 3

1994 Finish Line Gold

| ❏ Complete Set (100) | $ 17 |

❏ Common Card (1-100)	$ .08
❏ Common Driver (1-100)	$ .15
❏ Semistars	$ .35
❏ 8	Ernie Irvan	$ .60
❏ 10	Rusty Wallace	$ 1
❏ 11	Jeff Gordon	$ 3
❏ 14	Mark Martin	$ .75
❏ 24	Rusty Wallace	$ 1
❏ 28	Jeff Gordon	$ 2
❏ 43	Ernie Irvan	$ .60
❏ 48	Mark Martin	$ .75
❏ 59	Rusty Wallace	$ 1
❏ 60	Jeff Gordon	$ 2.50
❏ 65	Jeff Gordon's Car	$ 2
❏ 68	Rusty Wallace	$ 1
❏ 72	Mark Martin	$ .75
❏ 80	Ernie Irvan	$ .60
❏ 81	Mark Martin	$ .75
❏ 83	Richard Petty	$ .60
❏ 88	Jeff Gordon	$ 3
❏ 93	Ernie Irvan	$ .60
❏ NNO	Ernie Irvan HOLO/3000	$ 90

1994 Finish Line Gold Autographs

❏ Complete Set (19)	$ 250
❏ Common Auto	$ 15
❏ Semistars	$ 20

*Random Inserts in Packs

| ❏ 80 | Ernie Irvan | $ 40 |
| ❏ 81 | Mark Martin | $ 40 |

1994 Finish Line Gold Calling Cards

| ❏ Complete Set (9) | $ 100 |
| ❏ Common Card | $ 9 |

*Random Inserts in Packs
*Pin Number Revealed: Half Value
*Phone Time Value 2.50
*Calling Cards Expire 12/31/95

❏ NNO	Jeff Gordon/3000	$ 28
❏ NNO	Ernie Irvan/3000	$ 10
❏ NNO	Mark Martin/3000	$ 10
❏ NNO	Rusty Wallace/3000	$ 10

1994 Finish Line Gold Teamwork

| ❏ Complete Set (10) | $ 50 |
| ❏ Common Card (TG1-TG10) | $ 5 |

*Random Inserts in Packs

❏ TG1	Rusty Wallace/Parrott	$ 8
❏ TG2	Mark Martin/Hmiel	$ 6
❏ TG6	Jeff Gordon/Evernham	$ 12
❏ TG7	Ernie Irvan/McReynolds	$ 6

1994 High Gear

❏ Complete Set (200)	$ 40
❏ Complete Series 1 (100)	$ 18
❏ Complete Series 2 (100)	$ 22

❑ Common Card (1-100)		$ .08
❑ Common Card (101-200)		$ .10
❑ Common Driver (1-100)		$ .15
❑ Common Driver (101-200)		$ .20
❑ Earnhardt Family (180-184)		$ .20
❑ Semistars (1-100)		$ .25
❑ Semistars (101-200)		$ .35

*Produced by Wheels

❑ 1	Dale Earnhardt		$ 3
❑ 2	Rusty Wallace		$ .75
❑ 3	Mark Martin		$ .60
❑ 5	Ernie Irvan		$ .50
❑ 24	Neil Bonnett		$ .40
❑ 28	Richard Petty		$ .50
❑ 71	Rusty Wallace DOY		$ .60
❑ 73	Jeff Gordon ROY		$ 4
❑ 76	Rusty Wallace WIN		$ .60
❑ 77	Davey Allison WIN		$ 1.25
❑ 79	Dale Earnhardt WIN		$ 2
❑ 80	Rusty Wallace WIN		$ .60
❑ 81	Rusty Wallace WIN		$ .60
❑ 83	Ernie Irvan WIN		$ .30
❑ 85	Dale Earnhardt WIN		$ 3
❑ 89	Mark Martin BC		$ .50
❑ 91	Rusty Wallace BC		$ .60
❑ 92	Dale Earnhardt BC		$ 2
❑ 95	Ernie Irvan BC		$ .30
❑ 97	Jeff Gordon BC		$ 4
❑ 100	Davey Allison/Alan Kulwicki Tribute		$ 1.50
❑ 101	Jeff Gordon		$ 4.50
❑ 106	Mark Martin		$ .75
❑ 128	Ernie Irvan		$ .60
❑ 168	Ernie Irvan		$ .60
❑ 175	Mark Martin		$ .75
❑ 186	Dale Earnhardt WIN		$ 2.50
❑ 187	Rusty Wallace WIN		$ .75
❑ 188	Dale Earnhardt WIN		$ 2.50
❑ 189	Mark Martin WIN		$ .60
❑ 190	Mark Martin WIN		$ .60
❑ 191	Mark Martin WIN		$ .60
❑ 192	Mark Martin WIN		$ .60
❑ 193	Rusty Wallace WIN		$ .75
❑ 194	Rusty Wallace WIN		$ .75
❑ 195	Ernie Irvan WIN		$ .50
❑ 196	Rusty Wallace WIN		$ .75
❑ 197	Ernie Irvan WIN		$ .50
❑ 198	Rusty Wallace WIN		$ .75
❑ 199	Mark Martin WIN		$ .60
❑ 200	Rusty Wallace WIN		$ .75
❑ MMS1	Mark Martin AUTO/1000		$ 130
❑ NNO	Jeff Gordon BC AUTO/1500		$ 175

1994 High Gear Gold

❑ Complete Set (200)		$ 300
❑ Complete Series 1 (100)		$ 150
❑ Complete Series 2 (100)		$ 150
❑ Common Card (1-100)		$ .50
❑ Common Card (101-200)		$ .60
❑ Common Driver (1-100)		$ 1
❑ Common Driver (101-200)		$ 1.25
❑ Earnhardt Family (180-184)		$ 1.25

❑ Semistars (1-100)		$ 1.50
❑ Semistars (101-200)		$ 2

*Unlisted Stars: 3x to 6x
*Random Inserts in Packs

❑ 1	Dale Earnhardt SP		$ 18
❑ 6	Geoff Bodine SP		$ 2
❑ 71	Rusty Wallace DOY SP		$ 8
❑ 81	Rusty Wallace WIN SP		$ 8
❑ 91	Rusty Wallace BC SP		$ 8

1994 High Gear Dominators

❑ Complete Set (7)		$ 315
❑ Complete Series 1 (3)		$ 144
❑ Complete Series 2 (3)		$ 135
❑ Common Card (D1-D4)		$ 32
❑ Common Card (D5-D7)		$ 22

*D1-D3 Inserts in Series 1 Hobby Boxes
*D4 Random Insert in Day One Boxes
*D5-D7 Inserts in Series 2 Boxes

❑ D1	Mark Martin/3000		$ 31
❑ D2	Rusty Wallace/3000		$ 36
❑ D3	Dale Earnhardt/3000		$ 72
❑ D4	Ernie Irvan/1750		$ 38
❑ D5	Jeff Gordon/1750		$ 75
❑ D6	Mark Martin/1750		$ 41

1994 High Gear Legends

❑ Complete Set (6)		$ 30
❑ Complete Series 1 (3)		$ 12
❑ Complete Series 2 (3)		$ 18
❑ Common Card (LS1-LS3)		$ 4
❑ Common Card (LS4-LS6)		$ 4

*Random Inserts in Packs

❑ LS4	Richard Petty		$ 10

1994 High Gear Mega Gold

❑ Complete Set (12)		$ 115
❑ Common Card (MG1-MG12)		$ 5
❑ Semistars		$ 7
❑ Dale Earnhardt 7 (MG1S)		$ 70

*Random Inserts in Series 2 Packs

❑ MG1	Dale Earnhardt		$ 30
❑ MG2	Ernie Irvan		$ 10
❑ MG3	Rusty Wallace		$ 14
❑ MG4	Mark Martin		$ 12
❑ MG5	Jeff Gordon		$ 35

1994 High Gear Rookie Shootout Autographs

❑ Complete Set (7)		$ 370
❑ Complete Series 1 (3)		$ 160
❑ Complete Series 2 (4)		$ 210
❑ Common AUTO/1500 (RS1-RS3)		$ 50
❑ Common AUTO/1000 (RS4-RS7)		$ 55

*Random Inserts in Packs

1994 High Gear Rookie Thunder Update

❑ Complete Set (5)	$	19
❑ Common Card (101-104)	$	2
❑ Update CL (NNO)	$	.50

*Platinum: 1.5x to 3x
*Two Cards and CL per Series 1 High Gear Box

❑ 102	Jeff Gordon	$	8
❑ 104	Dale Earnhardt	$	7

1994 High Gear Day One

❑ Complete Set (100)	$	32
❑ Common Card (101-200)	$	.15
❑ Common Driver (101-200)	$	.25
❑ Earnhardt Family (180-184)	$	.50
❑ Semistars	$	.40
❑ Complete Gold Set (100)	$	250

*Gold Cards: 5x to 8x
*Random Inserts in Packs

❑ 101	Jeff Gordon	$	7
❑ 106	Mark Martin	$	2
❑ 128	Ernie Irvan	$ 1.50	
❑ 168	Ernie Irvan	$ 1.50	
❑ 175	Mark Martin	$	2
❑ 186	Dale Earnhardt WIN	$	6
❑ 187	Rusty Wallace WIN	$	2
❑ 188	Dale Earnhardt WIN	$	6
❑ 189	Mark Martin WIN	$ 1.50	
❑ 190	Mark Martin WIN	$ 1.50	
❑ 191	Mark Martin WIN	$ 1.50	
❑ 192	Mark Martin WIN	$ 1.50	
❑ 193	Rusty Wallace WIN	$	2
❑ 194	Rusty Wallace WIN	$	2
❑ 195	Ernie Irvan WIN	$	1
❑ 196	Rusty Wallace WIN	$	2
❑ 197	Ernie Irvan WIN	$	1
❑ 198	Rusty Wallace WIN	$	2
❑ 199	Mark Martin WIN	$ 1.50	
❑ 200	Rusty Wallace WIN	$	2

1994 High Gear Power Pak Teams

❑ Complete Earnhardt (21)	$	20
❑ Complete Gant (34)	$	20
❑ Complete Wallace (41)	$	20
❑ Common Earnhardt Team (1-20)	$	.75
❑ Harry Gant (1/29)	$ 1.50	
❑ Common Wallace Team (1-40)	$	.75
❑ Rusty Wallace (2/34/35/37/38/39)	$ 1.50	
❑ CL (Earnhardt, Gant, Wallace)	$	1
❑ Complete Gold Earnhardt (21)	$	35
❑ Complete Gold Gant (34)	$	35
❑ Complete Gold Wallace (41)	$	35

*Gold Cards: 1.5x to 2x

1994 Hi-Tech Brickyard 400

❑ Complete Set (70)	$	9
❑ Common Card (1-70)	$	.05
❑ Common Driver (1-70)	$	.10
❑ Semistars	$	.20

❑ 9	Dale Earnhardt's Car	$ 1.25	
❑ 20	Jeff Gordon's Car	$ 1.25	
❑ 37	Rusty Wallace	$	.50
❑ 38	Dale Earnhardt	$ 1.50	
❑ 40	Mark Martin	$	.50
❑ 52	Jeff Gordon	$	2
❑ 69	Jeff Gordon	$	2

1994 Hi-Tech Brickyard 400 Richard Petty

❑ Complete Set (6)	$	8
❑ Common Card (1-6)	$	1
❑ Richard Petty (1/4)	$ 2.50	

*Random Inserts in Packs

1994 Maxx

❑ Complete Set (340)	$	33
❑ Complete Factory Set (244)	$	22
❑ Complete Series 1 (240)	$	16
❑ Complete Series 2 (100)	$	12
❑ Common Card (1-240)	$	.05
❑ Common Card (241-340)	$	.10
❑ Common Driver (1-240)	$	.10
❑ Common Driver (241-340)	$	.20
❑ Semistars (1-240)	$	.20
❑ Semistars (241-340)	$	.35

❑ 2	Rusty Wallace	$	1
❑ 3	Dale Earnhardt	$ 2.50	
❑ 6	Mark Martin	$	.75
❑ 7	Alan Kulwicki	$	.75
❑ 11	Bill Elliott	$	1
❑ 23	Dale Earnhardt's Car	$	.75
❑ 24	Jeff Gordon	$ 3.50	
❑ 28	Davey Allison	$ 1.25	
❑ 29	Ernie Irvan	$	.60
❑ 31	Neil Bonnett	$	.50
❑ 43	Richard Petty	$	.60
❑ 65	Jeff Gordon's Car	$ 1.75	
❑ 72	John Andretti	$	.30
❑ 201	Jeff Gordon WC ROY	$ 2.25	
❑ 202	Bill Elliott FF	$	.50
❑ 203	Davey Allison IROC Champ	$ 1.25	
❑ 208	Rusty Wallace YR	$	.50
❑ 209	Davey Allison YR	$	.60
❑ 211	Dale Earnhardt YR	$	1
❑ 212	Rusty Wallace YR	$	.50
❑ 213	Rusty Wallace YR	$	.50
❑ 214	Rusty Wallace YR	$	.50
❑ 215	Ernie Irvan YR	$	.30
❑ 218	Dale Earnhardt YR	$	1
❑ 219	Dale Earnhardt YR	$	1
❑ 222	Dale Earnhardt YR	$	1
❑ 223	Rusty Wallace YR	$	.50
❑ 224	Dale Earnhardt YR	$	1
❑ 225	Dale Earnhardt YR	$	1
❑ 226	Mark Martin YR	$	.40
❑ 227	Mark Martin YR	$	.40
❑ 228	Mark Martin YR	$	.40
❑ 229	Mark Martin YR	$	.40
❑ 230	Rusty Wallace YR	$	.50

❏ 231	Rusty Wallace YR	$ .50
❏ 232	Ernie Irvan YR	$ .30
❏ 233	Rusty Wallace YR	$ .50
❏ 234	Ernie Irvan YR	$ .30
❏ 235	Rusty Wallace YR	$ .50
❏ 236	Mark Martin YR	$ .40
❏ 237	Rusty Wallace YR	$ .50
❏ 238	Dale Earnhardt WC Champ	$ 1
❏ 241	Bill Elliott	$ 1.25
❏ 250	Ernie Irvan	$ .75
❏ 258	Mark Martin	$ 1
❏ 322	Rusty Wallace WS	$ 1
❏ 327	Jeff Gordon's Car WS	$ 1.25
❏ 328	Jeff Gordon WS	$ 3.50
❏ 335	Jeff Gordon/Wallace/Earnhardt	$ 3

1994 Maxx Autographs

❏ Complete Set (37)		$ 650
❏ Common AUTO		$ 12
❏ Semistars		$ 15

*Cards are Series 1, Series 2, and Rookie Class w/Seal
*Random Inserts in Series 2 and Medallion Packs

❏ 6	Mark Martin	$ 35
❏ 9	Bill Elliott '91 Maxx	$ 65
❏ 11	Bill Elliott '92 Maxx Red	$ 65
❏ 24	Jeff Gordon	$ 180
❏ 227	Mark Martin	$ 35

1994 Maxx Rookie Class of '94

❏ Complete Set (10)		$ 70
❏ Common Card (1-10)		$ 7
❏ Semistars		$ 8

*Random Inserts in Series 2 Packs

1994 Maxx Rookies of the Year

❏ Complete Set (16)		$ 120
❏ Common Card (1-16)		$ 5
❏ Semistars		$ 6

*Random Inserts in Series 1 Packs
*Four per Factory Set

❏ 3	Dale Earnhardt	$ 25
❏ 6	Rusty Wallace	$ 10
❏ 8	Alan Kulwicki	$ 10
❏ 9	Davey Allison	$ 12
❏ 16	Jeff Gordon	$ 35

1994 Maxx Medallion

❏ Complete Set (75)		$ 60
❏ Complete Reg. Set (55)		$ 12
❏ Complete Clear Set (20)		$ 45
❏ Common Card (1-55)		$ .20
❏ Common Card (56-75)		$ 2
❏ Semistars (1-55)		$ .35
❏ Semistars (56-75)		$ 2.50

*One Series 2 Clearchrome per Pack

❏ 1	Jeff Gordon's Car	$ 2.25
❏ 3	Bill Elliott	$ 1.25

❏ 4	Rusty Wallace	$ 1.25
❏ 33	Mark Martin	$ 1
❏ 53	Jeff Gordon BY	$ 3.50
❏ 56	Jeff Gordon	$ 12
❏ 61	Ernie Irvan	$ 3
❏ 64	Bill Elliott	$ 5
❏ 69	Rusty Wallace	$ 5
❏ 70	Mark Martin	$ 4
❏ 99SP	Dale Earnhardt 1988/99	$ 600

1994 Maxx Motorsport

❏ Complete Set (25)		$ 40
❏ Common Card (1-25)		$ 1.25
❏ Semistars		$ 2
❏ 1	Ernie Irvan	$ 5
❏ 2	Rusty Wallace	$ 7
❏ 3	Mark Martin	$ 6
❏ 4	Bill Elliott	$ 6

1994 Maxx Premier Plus

❏ Complete Set (200)		$ 70
❏ Complete Factory Set (206)		$ 85
❏ Common Card (1-200)		$ .20
❏ Common Driver (1-200)		$ .40
❏ Semistars		$ .75
❏ 2	Rusty Wallace	$ 2.50
❏ 3	Dale Earnhardt	$ 6
❏ 6	Mark Martin	$ 2
❏ 7	Alan Kulwicki	$ 2.50

❏ 9	Bill Elliott FF	$ 2
❏ 11	Bill Elliott	$ 2.50
❏ 13	Jeff Gordon's Car MM	$ 2.50

❑ 23	Dale Earnhardt's Car	$ 2.25
❑ 24	Jeff Gordon	$ 8
❑ 28	Davey Allison	$ 4
❑ 29	Ernie Irvan	$ 1.50
❑ 31	Davey Allison's Car MM	$ 1.50
❑ 43	Richard Petty	$ 2
❑ 46	Jeff Gordon WC ROY	$ 6
❑ 58	Davey Allison IROC Champ	$ 3.50
❑ 65	Jeff Gordon's Car	$ 3.25
❑ 69	Davey Allison's Car MM	$ 1.50
❑ 77	Neil Bonnett	$ 1.50
❑ 118	Rusty Wallace with Crew	$ 1.50
❑ 167	Rusty Wallace YR	$ 1.25

❑ 168	Davey Allison YR	$ 2.50
❑ 170	Dale Earnhardt YR	$ 3
❑ 171	Rusty Wallace YR	$ 1.25
❑ 172	Rusty Wallace YR	$ 1.25
❑ 173	Rusty Wallace YR	$ 1.25
❑ 174	Ernie Irvan YR	$ .75
❑ 177	Dale Earnhardt YR	$ 3
❑ 178	Dale Earnhardt YR	$ 3
❑ 181	Dale Earnhardt YR	$ 3
❑ 182	Rusty Wallace YR	$ 1.25
❑ 183	Dale Earnhardt YR	$ 3
❑ 184	Dale Earnhardt YR	$ 3
❑ 185	Mark Martin YR	$ 1
❑ 186	Mark Martin YR	$ 1
❑ 187	Mark Martin YR	$ 1
❑ 188	Mark Martin YR	$ 1
❑ 189	Rusty Wallace YR	$ 1.25
❑ 190	Rusty Wallace YR	$ 1.25
❑ 191	Ernie Irvan YR	$ .75
❑ 192	Rusty Wallace YR	$ 1.25
❑ 193	Ernie Irvan YR	$ .75

❑ 194	Rusty Wallace YR	$ 1.25
❑ 195	Mark Martin YR	$ 1
❑ 196	Rusty Wallace YR	$ 1.25

1994 Maxx Premier Plus
Alan Kulwicki

❑ Complete Set (14)	$ 60
❑ Common Card (1-14)	$ 5

*Random Inserts in Packs
*Six per Factory Set

1994 Maxx Premier Series

❑ Complete Set (300)	$ 57
❑ Complete Factory Set (308)	$ 67
❑ Common Card (1-300)	$ .15
❑ Common Driver (1-300)	$ .30
❑ Semistars	$ .50

❑ 2	Rusty Wallace	$ 2
❑ 3	Dale Earnhardt	$ 6
❑ 6	Mark Martin	$ 1.50
❑ 7	Alan Kulwicki	$ 2
❑ 11	Bill Elliott	$ 2
❑ 13	Jeff Gordon MM	$ 3.50
❑ 23	Dale Earnhardt's Car	$ 2
❑ 24	Jeff Gordon	$ 6
❑ 28	Davey Allison	$ 3
❑ 29	Ernie Irvan	$ 1.25
❑ 31	Neil Bonnett	$ 1
❑ 43	Richard Petty	$ 1.25
❑ 53	Davey Allison's Car MM	$ 1
❑ 65	Jeff Gordon's Car	$ 3
❑ 258	Rusty Wallace with Crew	$ 1.50
❑ 260	Jeff Gordon WC ROY	$ 5
❑ 261	Bill Elliott FF	$ 1.50
❑ 262	Davey Allison IROC Champ	$ 3
❑ 267	Rusty Wallace YR	$ 1
❑ 268	Davey Allison YR	$ 2
❑ 270	Dale Earnhardt YR	$ 2.50
❑ 271	Rusty Wallace YR	$ 1
❑ 272	Rusty Wallace YR	$ 1
❑ 273	Rusty Wallace YR	$ 1
❑ 274	Ernie Irvan YR	$ .60
❑ 277	Dale Earnhardt YR	$ 3.50
❑ 278	Dale Earnhardt YR	$ 3.50
❑ 281	Dale Earnhardt YR	$ 3.50
❑ 282	Rusty Wallace YR	$ 1
❑ 283	Dale Earnhardt YR	$ 3.50
❑ 284	Dale Earnhardt YR	$ 3.50
❑ 285	Mark Martin YR	$ .75
❑ 286	Mark Martin YR	$ .75
❑ 287	Mark Martin YR	$ .75
❑ 288	Mark Martin YR	$ .75
❑ 289	Rusty Wallace YR	$ 1
❑ 290	Rusty Wallace YR	$ 1
❑ 291	Ernie Irvan YR	$ .60
❑ 292	Rusty Wallace YR	$ 1
❑ 293	Ernie Irvan YR	$ .60
❑ 294	Rusty Wallace YR	$ 1
❑ 295	Mark Martin YR	$ .75
❑ 296	Rusty Wallace YR	$ 1

	297	Dale Earnhardt WC Champ	$ 5

1994 Maxx Premier Series Jumbos

Complete Set (12)	$ 23
Complete Series 1 (8)	$ 12
Complete Series 2 (4)	$ 10
Common Card (1-8)	$ 1.50
Common Card (9-12)	$ 2
Semistars (1-8)	$ 2

*Series 1 Set in Premier Factory Set
*Series 2 Set in Premier Binder

	6	Richard Petty	$ 2.50
	7	Alan Kulwicki	$ 2.50
	8	Jeff Gordon	$ 7
	11	Davey Allison	$ 4

1994 Maxx
The Select 25

Complete Set (25)	$ 61
Common Card (1-25)	$ 2
Semistars	$ 2.50

	1	Dale Earnhardt	$ 15
	2	Rusty Wallace	$ 6
	3	Mark Martin	$ 5
	6	Ernie Irvan	$ 4
	8	Bill Elliott	$ 5
	14	Jeff Gordon	$ 15

1994 Maxx Texaco
Ernie Irvan

Complete Set (50)	$ 16
Common Card (1-50)	$ .30
Ernie Irvan Cards	$ 1

1994 Optima XL

Complete Set (64)	$ 27
Common Card (1-64)	$ .15
Common Driver (1-64)	$ .30
Earnhardt Family (43-46)	$ .25
Semistars	$ .50

*Produced by Press Pass

	4	Dale Earnhardt	$ 4.50
	6	Jeff Gordon	$ 4.50
	8	Ernie Irvan	$ 1
	12	Mark Martin	$ 1.25
	22	Rusty Wallace	$ 1.50
	25	Ernie Irvan	$ 1
	26	Jeff Gordon	$ 4.50
	27	Mark Martin	$ 1.25
	30	Rusty Wallace	$ 1.50
	32	Ernie Irvan DD	$ .60
	35	Rusty Wallace DD	$ 1
	38	Jeff Gordon TC	$ 3
	41	Dale Earnhardt's Car TC	$ 2.25
	43A	Teresa Earnhardt	$ .75
	43B	Teresa Earnhardt with Dale	$ 100
	52	Ernie Irvan/Rusty Wallace/M. Martin WCS	$ 1

	56	Jeff Gordon WCS	$ 3
	62	Jeff Gordon NM	$ 3
	CC1	Jeff Gordon Chrome	$ 80
	CC2	Ernie Irvan Chrome	$ 50

1994 Optima XL Red Hot

Complete Set (64)	$ 160
Common Card (1-64)	$ 1.25
Common Driver (1-64)	$ 2
Earnhardt Family (43-46)	$ 1.75
Semistars	$ 3

*Unlisted Stars: 3x to 6x
*Random Inserts in Packs

	4	Dale Earnhardt	$ 16
	5	Jeff Gordon	$ 16
	8	Ernie Irvan	$ 5
	12	Mark Martin	$ 6
	22	Rusty Wallace	$ 8
	25	Ernie Irvan	$ 5
	26	Jeff Gordon	$ 16
	27	Mark Martin	$ 6
	30	Rusty Wallace	$ 8
	38	Jeff Gordon TC	$ 12
	41	Dale Earnhardt's Car TC	$ 6
	43A	Teresa Earnhardt	$ 5
	43B	Teresa Earnhardt with Dale	$ 100
	56	Jeff Gordon WCS	$ 12
	62	Jeff Gordon NM	$ 12

1994 Optima XL
Double Clutch

Complete Set (6)	$ 120
Common Card (DC1-DC6)	$ 15
Random Inserts in Packs	

	DC1	Dale Earnhardt	$ 60
	DC2	Ernie Irvan	$ 20
	DC5	Mark Martin	$ 22

1994 Pepsi 400
Victory Lane

Complete Set (6)	$ 8
Common Card (NNO)	$ 1.25
Cover Card (NNO)	$ .30

	NNO	A. J. Foyt	$ 1.50
	NNO	Richard Petty	$ 2.50

1994 Power Preview

Complete Set (31)	$ 4
Common Card (1-31)	$ .05
Prism Cars (19-30)	$ .20
Semistars	$ .30

	8	Rusty Wallace	$ .50
	12	Jeff Gordon	$ 1.50
	15	Mark Martin	$ .50
	22	Jeff Gordon's Car FOIL	$ 1
	31	Dale Earnhardt WC Champ	$ 1.25

1994 Power

❏ Complete Set (150)		$	15
❏ Common Card (1-150)		$	.05
❏ Common Driver (1-150)		$	.10
❏ Semistars		$	.20

*Prism Cars: 1x to 1.5x
*One per Special Retail Pack

❏ 2	Dale Earnhardt DB	$	2
❏ 3	Ernie Irvan DB	$	.30
❏ 5	Jeff Gordon DB	$	2.50
❏ 16	Dale Earnhardt PW(Pole Winners)	$	2
❏ 17	Rusty Wallace PW	$	.50
❏ 18	Ernie Irvan PW	$	.30
❏ 20	Mark Martin PW	$	.40
❏ 25	Davey Allison PW	$	1
❏ 38	Dale Earnhardt SL (Stat Leaders)	$	2
❏ 39	Rusty Wallace SL	$	.50
❏ 55	Mark Martin SL	$	.40
❏ 64	Richard Petty PO (Power Owners)	$	.40
❏ 89	Jeff Gordon	$	2.50
❏ 90	Jeff Gordon	$	2.50
❏ 95	Ernie Irvan	$	.40
❏ 110	Richard Petty	$	.50
❏ 122	Rusty Wallace	$	.75
❏ 123	Rusty Wallace	$	.75
❏ NNO	Dale Earnhardt HOLO/3500	$	115

1994 Power Gold

❏ Complete Set (150)		$	50
❏ Common Card (1-150)		$	.20
❏ Common Driver (1-150)		$	.35
❏ Semistars		$	.50

*Stars: 2x to 4x
*One per Foil Pack

1994 Press Pass

❏ Complete Set (150)		$	15
❏ Common Card (1-150)		$	.05
❏ Common Driver (1-150)		$	.10
❏ Harry Gant (145-146)		$	.20
❏ Semistars		$	.20

❏ 5	Dale Earnhardt	$	3
❏ 7	Jeff Gordon	$	3
❏ 11	Ernie Irvan	$	.50
❏ 17	Mark Martin	$	.60
❏ 28	Rusty Wallace	$	.75
❏ 31	Rusty Wallace/Kenny Wallace	$	.75
❏ 118	Rusty Wallace DOY	$	.75
❏ 121	Mark Martin TT	$	.60
❏ 123	Rusty Wallace TT	$	.75
❏ 124	Jeff Gordon ROY	$	3
❏ 127	Davey Allison HR (Heroes of Racing)	$	1
❏ 130	Alan Kulwicki HR	$	.60
❏ 141	Mark Martin ART (Art Card)	$	.60
❏ 144	Rusty Wallace ART	$	.75

1994 Press Pass Checkered Flags

❏ Complete Set (4)		$	20
❏ Common Card (CF1-CF4)		$	3

*Random Inserts in Packs

❏ CF1	Dale Earnhardt	$	8
❏ CF2	Ernie Irvan	$	3
❏ CF3	Mark Martin	$	4
❏ CF4	Rusty Wallace	$	5

1994 Press Pass Cup Chase

❏ Complete Set (30)		$	320
❏ Common Card (CC1-CC30)		$	5
❏ Semistars		$	6

*Random Inserts in Packs
*Cards were redeemable until 3/31/95

❏ CC5	Dale Earnhardt FIRST	$	130
❏ CC7	Jeff Gordon	$	30
❏ CC11	Ernie Irvan	$	10
❏ CC17	Mark Martin SECOND	$	18
❏ CC28	Rusty Wallace THIRD	$	25

1994 Press Pass Prospects

❏ Complete Set (5)		$	8
❏ Common Card (PP1-PP5)		$	1.50
❏ Semistars		$	2

*Random Inserts in Packs

1994 Press Pass Race Day

❏ Complete Set (12)		$	145
❏ Complete Series 1 (10)		$	90
❏ Complete Series 2 (2)		$	40
❏ Common Card (RD1-RD10)		$	6
❏ Semistars		$	8

*RD1-RD10 Random Inserts in Press Pass
*RD11/Cover Card Random Inserts in VIP

❏ RD1	Davey Allison	$	14
❏ RD3	Ernie Irvan	$	10
❏ RD7	Jeff Gordon	$	30
❏ RD9	Rusty Wallace	$	12
❏ RD10	Dale Earnhardt	$	25
❏ RD11	Sterling Marlin	$	20
❏ NNO	Cover Card	$	20

1994 Quality Care Glidden/Speed

❏ Complete Set (10)		$	5
❏ Common Card (1-10)		$	.40
❏ Cover Card (NNO)		$	.50

❏ NNO	Bob Glidden	$	.75
❏ NNO	Lake Speed	$	1

1994 SkyBox

❏ Complete Factory Set (27)		$	9
❏ Common Card (1-26)		$	.20
❏ Common Driver (1-26)		$	.40
❏ Semistars		$	.60

*One Brickyard Exchange Card per Factory Set
*Exchange Expiration Date 7/1/95

❏ 1	Dale Earnhardt	$	3
❏ 3	Ernie Irvan's Car	$	.75

		$	
❏ 4	Jeff Gordon's Car	$	3
❏ 9	Mark Martin's Car	$	1
❏ 12	Rusty Wallace's Car	$	1.25
❏ NNO	Brickyard Exchange/Dick Trickle	$	3
❏ NNO	Brickyard Exchange/Jeff Gordon	$	6

1994 Slim Jim
David Green

		$	
❏ Complete Set (18)		$	12
❏ Common Card (31-48)		$	.50
❏ David Green Cards		$	1

1994 Traks

		$	
❏ Complete Set (200)		$	25
❏ Complete Series 1 (100)		$	14
❏ Complete Series 2 (100)		$	12
❏ Common Card (1-100)		$	.05
❏ Common Card (101-200)		$	.05
❏ Common Driver (1-100)		$	.10
❏ Common Driver (101-200)		$	.10
❏ Semistars		$	.20
❏ 2	Rusty Wallace	$	.75
❏ 6	Mark Martin	$	.60
❏ 7	Alan Kulwicki	$	.60
❏ 10	Jeff Gordon's Car	$	1
❏ 19	Davey Allison	$	1
❏ 24	Jeff Gordon	$	3
❏ 25	Neil Bonnett CL	$	.30
❏ 28	Ernie Irvan	$	.50
❏ 29	Neil Bonnett	$	.40
❏ 36	Jeff Gordon	$	3
❏ 45	Ernie Irvan	$	.50
❏ 50	Neil Bonnett CL	$	.30
❏ 60	Mark Martin	$	.60
❏ 62	Rusty Wallace	$	.75
❏ 66	Ernie Irvan	$	.50
❏ 80	Rusty Wallace	$	.75
❏ 66	Ernie Irvan	$	.50
❏ 80	Rusty Wallace	$	.75
❏ 82	Mark Martin	$	.60
❏ 86	Jeff Gordon	$	2
❏ 91	Ernie Irvan	$	.50
❏ 101	Ernie Irvan	$	.50
❏ 102	Rusty Wallace	$	.75
❏ 106	Jeff Gordon	$	3
❏ 113	Mark Martin	$	.60
❏ 135	Ernie Irvan	$	.50
❏ 144	Mark Martin	$	.60
❏ 157	Rusty Wallace	$	.75
❏ 163	Ernie Irvan	$	.50
❏ 171	Jeff Gordon	$	3
❏ 176	Mark Martin	$	.60
❏ 193	Rusty Wallace	$	.75
❏ 198	Ernie Irvan	$	.50

1994 Traks First Run

		$	
❏ Complete Set (200)		$	60
❏ Complete Series 1 (100)		$	30
❏ Complete Series 2 (100)		$	30
❏ Common Card (1-100)		$	.20

		$	
❏ Common Card (101-200)		$	.20
❏ Common Driver (1-100)		$	.30
❏ Common Driver (101-200)		$	.30
❏ Semistars		$	.50
*Stars: 1.5x to 3x			
*Random Inserts in Packs			

1994 Traks Autographs

		$	
❏ Complete Set (13)		$	375
❏ Common Auto. (A1-A12)		$	25
❏ Cover Card (NNO)		$	6
❏ Semistars		$	30
*Random Inserts in Packs			
❏ A2	Jeff/Ward Burton	$	40
❏ A4	Jeff Gordon	$	110
❏ A6	Ernie Irvan	$	40
❏ A8	Mark Martin	$	40
❏ A12	Rusty Wallace	$	50

1994 Traks Winners

		$	
❏ Complete Set (25)		$	130
❏ Common Driver (W1-W25)		$	4
❏ Semistars		$	5
*Random Inserts in Series 2 Packs			
❏ W2	Rusty Wallace	$	10
❏ W3	Ernie Irvan	$	7
❏ W4	Ernie Irvan	$	7
❏ W6	Rusty Wallace	$	10
❏ W7	Ernie Irvan	$	7
❏ W8	Jeff Gordon	$	16
❏ W9	Rusty Wallace	$	10
❏ W14	Mark Martin	$	8
❏ W21	Jeff Gordon	$	16
❏ W22	Jeff Gordon	$	16
❏ W24	Rusty Wallace	$	10

1994 Traks Auto Value

		$	
❏ Complete Set (51)		$	10
❏ Common Card (1-51)		$	.25
❏ CL (NNO)		$	.15
❏ Semistars		$	.40
❏ 15	Neil Bonnett	$	.60
❏ 21	Rusty Wallace	$	1
❏ 25	Jeff Gordon	$	3
❏ 33	Mark Martin	$	.75
❏ 34	Alan Kulwicki	$	1
❏ 37	Davey Allison	$	1.50
❏ 43	Ernie Irvan	$	.60

1994 Traks
Hermie Sadler

		$	
❏ Complete Set (10)		$	5
❏ Common Card (1-10)		$	.60

1994 VIP

		$	
❏ Complete Set (100)		$	15
❏ Common Card (1-100)		$	.08

❑ Common Driver (1-100)		$	.15
❑ Semistars		$	.25

*Produced by Press Pass

❑ 10	Dale Earnhardt	$	2.50
❑ 12	Jeff Gordon	$	2.50
❑ 16	Ernie Irvan	$	.50
❑ 21	Mark Martin	$	.75
❑ 34	Rusty Wallace	$	1
❑ 38	Jeff Gordon with Car	$	2.50
❑ 42	Dale Earnhardt with Car	$	2.50
❑ 51	Ernie Irvan with Car	$	.50
❑ 53	Mark Martin with Car	$	.75
❑ 74	Jeff Gordon ART	$	2
❑ 75	Ernie Irvan ART	$	.50
❑ 78	Mark Martin ART	$	.75
❑ 81	Rusty Wallace ART	$	1

1994 VIP Driver's Choice

❑ Complete Set (9)		$	70
❑ Common Card (DC1-DC9)		$	5
Random Inserts in Packs			

❑ DC1	Dale Earnhardt	$	20
❑ DC2	Ernie Irvan	$	7
❑ DC5	Mark Martin	$	8
❑ DC9	Rusty Wallace	$	10

1994 VIP Exchange 24K

❑ Complete Set (7)		$	320
❑ Common Card (EC1-EC7)		$	20
❑ Exchange Cards Expired		$	4

*Random Inserts in Packs
*Exchange 24K Expiration Date 12/31/94

❑ EC1	Dale Earnhardt	$	110
❑ EC3	Jeff Gordon	$	125
❑ EC4	Ernie Irvan	$	30
❑ EC5	Mark Martin	$	35
❑ EC7	Rusty Wallace	$	40

1994 Wheels Harry Gant

❑ Complete Set (80)		$	10
❑ Common Card (1-80)		$	.10
❑ Common Gant (1-80)		$	.20
❑ Semistars		$	.30

❑ 66	Jeff Gordon	$	2.50
❑ 67	Ernie Irvan	$	1
❑ 73	Rusty Wallace	$	1
❑ 74	Mark Martin	$	.75
❑ HGS1	Harry Gant 4x6 AUTO/3300	$	35
❑ NNO	Harry Gant 4x6 HOLO/1000	$	40

1994 Wheels Harry Gant Gold

❑ Complete Set (80)		$	35
❑ Common Card (1-80)		$	.30
❑ Common Gant (1-80)		$	.50
❑ Semistars		$	1

*Stars: 2x
*One Per Pack

1994 Wheels Harry Gant Down on the Farm

❑ Complete Set (5)		$	25
❑ Common Card (SP1-SP5)		$	5
*Random Inserts in Packs			

1995 Action Packed

❑ Complete Set (78)		$	36
❑ Common Card (1-78)		$	.50
❑ Semistars		$	.75

❑ 7	Dale Earnhardt	$	4
❑ 8	Bill Elliott	$	1.25
❑ 9	Jeff Gordon	$	4
❑ 15	Mark Martin	$	1
❑ 23	Rusty Wallace	$	1.25

❑ 33	Dale Earnhardt PW	$	3
❑ 34	Bill Elliott PW	$	1
❑ 36	Jeff Gordon PW	$	3
❑ 38	Ernie Irvan PW	$	.75
❑ 40	Mark Martin PW	$	.75
❑ 46	Rusty Wallace PW	$	1
❑ 48	Dale Earnhardt WIN	$	3
❑ 49	Bill Elliott WIN	$	1
❑ 50	Jeff Gordon WIN	$	3
❑ 51	Ernie Irvan WIN	$	.75
❑ 55	Mark Martin WIN	$	.75
❑ 58	Rusty Wallace WIN	$	1
❑ 59	Dale Earnhardt WC Champ	$	3
❑ 60	Mark Martin T10	$	.75
❑ 61	Rusty Wallace T10	$	1

❏ 66	Jeff Gordon T10	$	3
❏ 68	Bill Elliott T10	$	1
❏ 69	Bill Elliott DD	$	1
❏ 70	Jeff Gordon DD	$	3
❏ 71	Ernie Irvan DD	$	.75
❏ 72	Mark Martin DD	$	.75
❏ 73	Richard Petty DD	$	.75
❏ 77	Rusty Wallace DD	$	1

1995 Action Packed Bill Elliott

❏ Complete Set (6)	$	6
❏ Common Elliott (BE1-BE6)	$	1
*Random Inserts in Packs		

1995 Action Packed 24K Gold

❏ Complete Set (10)	$	370
❏ Common Card (1G-10G)	$	25
❏ Semistars	$	30
*Random Inserts in Packs		
❏ 1G Bill Elliott	$	50

❏ 2G	Jeff Gordon	$	110
❏ 3G	Ernie Irvan	$	35
❏ 4G	Mark Martin	$	40
❏ 5G	Richard Petty	$	35
❏ 9G	Rusty Wallace	$	50

1995 Action Packed McDonald's Bill Elliott

❏ Complete Set (21)	$	20
❏ Complete Factory Set (21)	$	20
❏ Common Card (MC1-MC21)	$	1
❏ Autograph Certificate	$	70
*Random Inserts in Packs		

1995 Assets

❏ Complete Set (50)	$	29
❏ Common Card (1-50)	$	.30
❏ Semistars	$	.50

❏ 1	Dale Earnhardt	$	4
❏ 2	Rusty Wallace	$	1.50
❏ 3	Jeff Gordon	$	4.50
❏ 18	Ernie Irvan	$	.75
❏ 27	Mark Martin	$	1
❏ 29	Dale Earnhardt	$	4
❏ 30	Rusty Wallace	$	1.50
❏ 31	Jeff Gordon	$	4.50
❏ 38	Ernie Irvan	$	.75
❏ 41	Mark Martin	$	1
❏ 44	Dale Earnhardt	$	4
❏ 46	Dale Earnhardt's Car	$	1.50
❏ 49	Jeff Gordon's Car	$	1.50

1995 Assets Gold Signature

❏ Complete Set (50)	$	690
❏ Common Card (1-50)	$	4
❏ Semistars	$	6

*Gold Signature: 10x to 17x
*Random Inserts in Packs

❏ 1	Dale Earnhardt	$	65
❏ 2	Rusty Wallace	$	25
❏ 3	Jeff Gordon	$	70
❏ 18	Ernie Irvan	$	18
❏ 27	Mark Martin	$	20
❏ 29	Dale Earnhardt	$	65
❏ 30	Rusty Wallace	$	25
❏ 31	Jeff Gordon	$	70
❏ 38	Ernie Irvan	$	18
❏ 41	Mark Martin	$	20
❏ 44	Dale Earnhardt	$	65
❏ 46	Dale Earnhardt's Car	$	25
❏ 49	Jeff Gordon's Car	$	30

1995 Assets 1-Minute $2 Phone Cards

❏ Complete 1-Minute Set (20)	$	60
❏ Common 1-Minute Card (1-20)	$	2.50
❏ Semistars	$	3
❏ Complete 1-Minute Gold Signature Set (20)	$	300
*1-Minute Gold Signature: 5x		

*1-Minute Expiration Date: 12/31/95
❏ Complete $2 Phone Set (20) $ 140
*$2 Phone Cards: 2x
❏ $2 Phone Signature Set (20) $ 500
*$2 Phone Signature: 8x
* One Phone Card per Pack
* Pin Number Revealed: Half Value
* $2 Expiration Date: 5/1/96

❏ 4	Dale Earnhardt	$ 10
❏ 7	Ernie Irvan	$ 3.50
❏ 9	Jeff Gordon	$ 10
❏ 13	Mark Martin	$ 4
❏ 18	Rusty Wallace	$ 5

1995 Assets $5/$25 Phone Cards

❏ Complete $5 Set (10) $ 150
❏ Common $5 Card (1-10) $ 12
❏ Complete $25 Set (10) $ 600
*$25 Phone Cards: 3x
*Random Inserts in Packs
*Pin Number Revealed: Half Value
*Expiration Date: 5/1/96

❏ 2	Dale Earnhardt	$ 35
❏ 4	Jeff Gordon	$ 35
❏ 7	Mark Martin	$ 16
❏ 9	Rusty Wallace	$ 18

1995 Assets $100/$1000 Phone Cards

❏ Complete $100 Set (5) $ 750
❏ Common $100 Card (1-5) $ 150
❏ $1000 Phone Cards $1500

*Random Inserts in Packs
*Pin Number Revealed: .1x to .25x

❏ 1	Ricky Rudd	$ 150
❏ 2	Dale Earnhardt	$ 250
❏ 3	Jeff Gordon	$ 250
❏ 4	Mark Martin	$ 175
❏ 5	Rusty Wallace	$ 175

1995 Assets Coca-Cola Die Cuts

❏ Complete Set (10) $ 115
❏ Common Card (1-10) $ 6
❏ Semistars $ 8

*Random Inserts in Packs
*Expiration Date: 12/1/95

❏ 1	Dale Earnhardt	$ 25
❏ 2	Rusty Wallace	$ 10
❏ 3	Jeff Gordon	$ 30
❏ 4	Bobby Labonte WIN	$ 40
❏ 8	Mark Martin	$ 8

1995 Assets Images Previews

❏ Complete Set (5) $ 110
❏ Common Card (RI1-RI5) $ 10

*Random Inserts in Packs

❏ RI1	Dale Earnhardt	$ 40
❏ RI2	Al Unser, Jr.	$ 14
❏ RI4	Jeff Gordon	$ 50

1995 Finish Line

❏ Complete Set (120) $ 19
❏ Common Card (1-120) $ .04
❏ Common Driver (1-120) $ .08
❏ Semistars $ .20

*Produced by Classic

❏ 1	Dale Earnhardt	$ 2.50
❏ 2	Rusty Wallace	$ .75
❏ 6	Mark Martin	$ .60
❏ 24	Jeff Gordon	$ 3
❏ 28	Ernie Irvan	$ .40
❏ 34	Rusty Wallace	$ .75
❏ 43	Richard Petty	$ .40
❏ 51	Ernie Irvan	$ .40
❏ 53	Jeff Gordon	$ 3
❏ 54	Mark Martin	$ .60
❏ 67	Jeff Gordon with Crew	$ 2
❏ 70	Rusty Wallace	$ .75
❏ 79	Mark Martin	$ .60
❏ 89	Dale Earnhardt	$ 2.50
❏ 92	Ernie Irvan	$ .40
❏ 104	Richard Petty	$ .40
❏ 105	Jeff Gordon	$ 3
❏ 111	Dale Earnhardt	$ 2.50
❏ NNO	Dale Earnhardt AU/250 Blue	$ 500
❏ NNO	Dale Earnhardt AU/250 Red	$ 500

1995 Finish Line Printer's Proof

❏ Complete Set (120) $2030
❏ Common Card (1-120) $ 10
❏ Common Driver (1-120) $ 15
❏ Semistars $ 25

*Stars: 50x
*Random Inserts in Hobby Packs

❏ 1	Dale Earnhardt	$ 125
❏ 2	Rusty Wallace	$ 55
❏ 6	Mark Martin	$ 35
❏ 24	Jeff Gordon	$ 120
❏ 28	Ernie Irvan	$ 30
❏ 34	Rusty Wallace	$ 55
❏ 51	Ernie Irvan	$ 30
❏ 53	Jeff Gordon	$ 120
❏ 54	Mark Martin	$ 35
❏ 67	Jeff Gordon with Crew	$ 75
❏ 70	Rusty Wallace	$ 55
❏ 79	Mark Martin	$ 35
❏ 89	Dale Earnhardt	$ 125
❏ 92	Ernie Irvan	$ 30
❏ 105	Jeff Gordon	$ 120
❏ 111	Dale Earnhardt	$ 125

1995 Finish Line Silver

❏ Complete Set (120) $ 75
❏ Common Card (1-120) $ .25
❏ Common Driver $ .50

❏ Semistars	$	.75

Stars: 3x
*One per Pack

1995 Finish Line Dale Earnhardt

❏ Complete Set (10)	$	90
❏ Common Card (DE1-DE10)	$	9

*Random Inserts in Packs

1995 Finish Line Gold Signature

❏ Complete Set (16)	$	280
❏ Common Card (GS1-GS16)	$	10
❏ Semistars	$	12

*Random Inserts in Retail Packs

❏ GS1	Jeff Gordon/1995	$	75
❏ GS2	Rusty Wallace/1995	$	30
❏ GS3	Dale Earnhardt/1995	$	65
❏ GS6	Mark Martin/1995	$	25

1995 Finish Line Standout Cars

❏ Complete Set (10)	$	45
❏ Common Card (SC1-SC10)	$	2.50
❏ Semistars	$	3

*Random Insert in Hobby Packs

❏ SC1	Dale Earnhardt's Car	$	10
❏ SC2	Mark Martin's Car	$	4
❏ SC3	Rusty Wallace's Car	$	5
❏ SC7	Jeff Gordon's Car	$	15

1995 Finish Line Standout Drivers

❏ Complete Set (10)	$	58
❏ Common Card (SD1-SD10)	$	3
❏ Semistars	$	4

*Random Inserts in Retail Packs

❏ SD1	Dale Earnhardt	$	17
❏ SD2	Mark Martin	$	6
❏ SD3	Rusty Wallace	$	8
❏ SD7	Jeff Gordon	$	18

1995 Finish Line Coca-Cola 600

❏ Complete Set (50)	$	18
❏ Complete Factory Set (65)	$	30
❏ Common Card (1-50)	$	.20
❏ Semistars	$	.40

*Stars: .5x Assets Singles

1995 Finish Line Coca-Cola 600 Die Cuts

❏ Complete Set (5)	$	3.50
❏ Common Card (1-5)	$	.50

*One Set per Factory Set

❏ C1	Dale Earnhardt	$	1.50
❏ C2	Rusty Wallace	$	.75
❏ C3	Jeff Gordon	$	1.50
❏ C4	Dale Jarrett	$	.50

❏ C5	Mark Martin	$	.60

1995 Finish Line Coca-Cola 600 Winners

❏ Complete Set (10)	$	10
❏ Common Card (CC1-CC10)	$	.30
❏ Semistars	$	.50

*One Set per Factory Set

❏ CC2	Dale Earnhardt	$	2
❏ CC6	Rusty Wallace	$	1
❏ CC7	Davey Allison's Car	$	1
❏ CC8	Dale Earnhardt	$	2
❏ CC9	Dale Earnhardt	$	2
❏ CC10	Jeff Gordon	$	2

1995 Finish Line Super Trucks

❏ Complete Set (80)	$	14
❏ Common Card (1-80)	$	.10
❏ Common Driver (1-80)	$	.20
❏ Common WC Driver (1-80)	$	.50
❏ Semistars	$	.40
❏ Jeff Gordon (17)	$	2.50
❏ Complete Rainbow Set (80)	$	60

*Rainbow Cards: 3x
*Random Inserts in Packs

1995 Finish Line Super Trucks Calling Cards

❏ Complete Set (10)	$	60
❏ Common Card (1-10)	$	6
❏ Semistars	$	8

Phone Time Value: 3 Minutes
*Random Inserts in Packs
*Expiration Date: 12/31/96

1995 Finish Line Super Trucks Champion's Choice

❏ Complete Set (6)	$	10
❏ Common Card (CC1-CC6)	$	1
❏ Common WC Driver (CC1-CC6)	$	2.50
❏ Semistars	$	1.50

*Random Inserts in Packs

1995 Finish Line Super Trucks Super Signature Series

❏ Complete Set (10)	$	30
❏ Common Card (SS1-SS10)	$	2
❏ Common WC Driver (SS1-SS10)	$	5
❏ Semistars	$	3
❏ Jeff Gordon (SS1)	$	10

*Random Inserts in Packs

1995 Finish Line Super Trucks Winter Heat Hot Shoes

❏ Complete Set (4)	$	6
❏ Common Card (HS1-HS4)	$	1.50

*Random Inserts in Packs

1995 High Gear

❑ Complete Set (100)		$	17
❑ Common Card (1-100)		$	.05
❑ Common Driver (1-100)		$	.08
❑ Semistars		$	.15
❑ 1	Dale Earnhardt	$	2.50
❑ 2	Rusty Wallace	$	.75
❑ 3	Mark Martin	$	.60
❑ 6	Jeff Gordon	$	2
❑ 13	Bill Elliott	$	.75
❑ 18	Ernie Irvan	$	.40
❑ 63	Mark Martin SS	$	.30
❑ 71	Dale Earnhardt's Car	$	.75
❑ 78	Jeff Gordon's Car	$	.75
❑ 86	Dale Earnhardt RW	$	1.50
❑ 87	Rusty Wallace RW	$	.40
❑ 88	Mark Martin RW	$	.30
❑ 91	Jeff Gordon RW	$	1.50
❑ 92	Bill Elliott RW	$	.40
❑ 96	Ernie Irvan RW	$	.25
❑ 98	Jeff Gordon in Pits	$	.75
❑ 100	Bill Elliott FF	$	.40
❑ SKS1	Steve Kinser/1500	$	50
❑ TLS1	Terry Labonte/1500	$	75
❑ NNO	E-Race to Win Unscratched	$	6
❑ NNO	E-Race to Win Winner	$	50

1995 High Gear Gold

❑ Complete Set (100)		$	60
❑ Common Card (1-100)		$	.25
❑ Common Driver (1-100)		$	.50
❑ Semistars		$	.75
*Stars: 3x			
*One per Pack			

1995 High Gear Busch Clash

❑ Complete Set (16)		$	60
❑ Common Card (BC1-BC16)		$	3
❑ Semistars (BC1-BC16)		$	4
*Random Inserts in Packs			
❑ Complete Gold Set (16)		$	115
Gold Cards: 1.5x			
*Random Inserts in Packs			
❑ BC4	Bill Elliott	$	5
❑ BC5	Ernie Irvan	$	4
❑ BC6	Rusty Wallace	$	7
❑ BC7	Jeff Gordon	$	14
❑ BC8	Dale Earnhardt	$	14
❑ BC10	Mark Martin	$	6

1995 High Gear Dominators

❑ Complete Set (4)		$	145
❑ Common Card (D1-D4)		$	25
*D1 Random Insert in Day One			
*D2-D4 Inserts in Series 1 Boxes			
*Mini Dominators Same Price			
❑ Uncut 4 Card Sheet		$	120

*4 Card Sheet One per Case

❑ D1	Rusty Wallace/1750	$	30
❑ D3	Dale Earnhardt/1750	$	65

1995 High Gear Legends

❑ Complete Set (3)		$	12
❑ Common Card (L1-L3)		$	4
*Random Inserts in Packs			

1995 High Gear Day One

❑ Complete Set (100)		$	33
❑ Common Card (1-100)		$	.10
❑ Common Driver (1-100)		$	.20
❑ Semistars		$	.40
❑ 1	Dale Earnhardt	$	4
❑ 2	Rusty Wallace	$	1.50
❑ 3	Mark Martin	$	1.25
❑ 6	Jeff Gordon	$	5
❑ 13	Bill Elliott	$	1.75
❑ 18	Ernie Irvan	$	1
❑ 63	Mark Martin SS (Split Shift)	$	.75
❑ 71	Dale Earnhardt's Car	$	1.25
❑ 78	Jeff Gordon's Car	$	1.75
❑ 86	Dale Earnhardt RW (Race Winner)	$	2.50
❑ 87	Rusty Wallace RW	$	1
❑ 88	Mark Martin RW	$	.75
❑ 91	Jeff Gordon RW	$	3.50
❑ 92	Bill Elliott RW	$	1
❑ 96	Ernie Irvan RW	$	.60
❑ 98	Jeff Gordon in Pits	$	1.75
❑ 100	Bill Elliott FF (Fan's Favorite)	$	1

1995 High Gear Day One Gold

❑ Complete Set (100)		$	175
❑ Common Card (1-100)		$	.50
❑ Common Driver (1-100)		$	1
❑ Semistars		$	2
Stars: 5x			
*One per Pack			

1995 Hi-Tech Brickyard 400

❑ Complete Factory Set (100)		$	57
❑ Complete Set (90)		$	25
❑ Common Card (1-90)		$	.15
❑ Common Driver (1-90)		$	.30
❑ Semistars		$	.50
❑ Complete Wood Box (100)		$	225
*Wood Box Cards: 3x			
❑ 2	Dale Earnhardt's Car	$	1.75
❑ 3	Jeff Gordon's Car UWE 00	$	1.75
❑ 40	Jeff Gordon Race Action	$	2
❑ 41	Dale Earnhardt	$	3.50
❑ 53	Jeff Gordon	$	4
❑ 56	Dale Earnhardt	$	3.50
❑ 70	Mark Martin	$	1
❑ 77	Dale Earnhardt's Car	$	1.75
❑ 79	Ernie Irvan	$	1
❑ 72	Rusty Wallace	$	1.25

❑ 86	Ernie Irvan	$ 1
❑ 87	Dale Earnhardt	$ 3.50
❑ 88	Jeff Gordon	$ 4
❑ 89	Jeff Gordon's Car	$ 1.75
❑ NNO	Jeff Gordon Gold/10000	$ 10

1995 Hi-Tech Brickyard 400 Top Ten

❑ Complete Set (10)		$ 15
❑ Common Card (BY1-BY10)		$ .75

*One Set per Factory Set

❑ BY1	Jeff Gordon	$ 4.50
❑ BY3	Bill Elliott's Car	$ 1.25
❑ BY4	Rusty Wallace	$ 2
❑ BY5	Dale Earnhardt	$ 3.50

1995 Maxx

❑ Complete Set (180)		$ 27
❑ Common Card (1-180)		$ .05
❑ Common Driver (1-180)		$ .08
❑ Semistars		$ .20

❑ 2	Rusty Wallace	$ .75
❑ 3	Jeff Gordon's Car MM	$ 1
❑ 6	Mark Martin	$ .60
❑ 11	Bill Elliott	$ .75
❑ 13	Rusty Wallace VL	$ .40
❑ 24	Jeff Gordon	$ 3
❑ 28	Ernie Irvan	$ .50
❑ 38	Ernie Irvan VL	$ .25
❑ 43	Richard Petty	$ .50
❑ 46	Ernie Irvan VL	$ .25
❑ 60	Rusty Wallace VL	$ .40

❑ 68	Ernie Irvan VL	$ .25
❑ 72	Jeff Gordon VL	$ 2
❑ 80	Jeff Gordon VL	$ 2
❑ 83	Rusty Wallace VL	$ .40
❑ 87	Rusty Wallace VL	$ .40
❑ 89	Rusty Wallace VL	$ .40
❑ 105	Jeff Gordon VL	$ 2
❑ 109	Mark Martin VL	$ .30
❑ 115	Rusty Wallace VL	$ .40
❑ 119	Bill Elliott VL	$ .40
❑ 125	Mark Martin MM	$ .30
❑ 127	Rusty Wallace VL	$ .40
❑ 129	Rusty Wallace VL	$ .40
❑ 146	Mark Martin VL	$ .30
❑ 169	Jeff Gordon's Car	$ 1

1995 Maxx Chase the Champion

❑ Complete Set (1)	$ 10
❑ Common Card (1)	$ 10

*Random Insert in Packs
*First Card of a Ten Card Set

1995 Maxx License to Drive

❑ Complete Set (5)	$ 50
❑ Common Card (1-5)	$ 10
❑ Semistars	$ 12

*Random Inserts in Packs

1995 Maxx Over the Wall

❑ Complete Set (10)	$ 53
❑ Common Card (1-10)	$ 5
❑ Semistars	$ 6

*Random Inserts in Packs

❑ 1	Jeff Gordon in Pits	$ 15
❑ 8	Bill Elliott in Pits	$ 6

1995 Maxx Super Trucks

❑ Complete Set (5)	$ 30
❑ Common Card (1-5)	$ 6
❑ Semistars	$ 7

*Random Inserts in Packs

1995 Press Pass

❑ Complete Set (145)		$	20
❑ Common Card (1-145)		$	.05
❑ Common Driver (1-145)		$	.10
❑ Semistars		$	.20

❑ 9	Dale Earnhardt	$	2
❑ 10	Jeff Gordon	$	3
❑ 13	Ernie Irvan	$	.50
❑ 19	Mark Martin	$	.60
❑ 34	Rusty Wallace	$	.75
❑ 38	Jeff Gordon's Car	$	1.50
❑ 41	Dale Earnhardt's Car	$	1
❑ 66	Mark Martin	$	.60
❑ 102	Jeff Gordon ST (Small Town Sat. Night)	$	2
❑ 104	Mark Martin ST	$	.40
❑ 115	Dale Earnhardt's Car AW	$	.75
❑ 126	Richard Petty S (Sports Kings)	$	.50
❑ 129	Jeff Gordon PR (Personal Rides)	$	2
❑ 132	Richard Petty PR	$	.50
❑ 135	Rusty Wallace PR	$	.50
❑ 136	Jeff Gordon BT (Breaking Through)	$	2

1995 Press Pass Red Hot

❑ Complete Set (145)		$	150
❑ Common Card (1-145)		$	.50
❑ Common Driver (1-145)		$	1
❑ Semistars		$	2.50

*Stars: 7x
*Random Inserts in Packs

1995 Press Pass Checkered Flags

❑ Complete Set (8)		$	39
❑ Common Card (CF1-CF8)		$	3

*Random Inserts in Packs

❑ CF2	Dale Earnhardt	$	11
❑ CF3	Jeff Gordon	$	13
❑ CF4	Ernie Irvan	$	4
❑ CF6	Mark Martin	$	5
❑ CF8	Rusty Wallace	$	6

1995 Press Pass Cup Chase

❑ Complete Set (36)		$	260
❑ Common Card (1-36)		$	5
❑ Semistars		$	6

*Random Inserts in Packs

❑ 9	Dale Earnhardt	$	110
❑ 10	Jeff Gordon	$	110
❑ 13	Ernie Irvan	$	6
❑ 15	Bobby Labonte WIN	$	40
❑ 18	Sterling Marlin WIN	$	20
❑ 19	Mark Martin WIN	$	50
❑ 34	Rusty Wallace	$	35

1995 Press Pass Cup Chase Redemption

❑ Complete Set (5)		$	195
❑ Common Card (CCR1-CCR5)		$	22

*Prizes for Cup Chase Race Winners
*One per Case

❑ CCR1	Sterling Marlin	$	25
❑ CCR2	Dale Earnhardt	$	60
❑ CCR3	Jeff Gordon	$	60
❑ CCR4	Jeff Gordon	$	70
❑ CCR5	Rusty Wallace	$	35

1995 Press Pass Race Day

❑ Complete Set (12)		$	95
❑ Common Cards (RD1-RD12)		$	5
❑ Semistars		$	6

*Random Inserts in Packs

❑ RD1	Cover Card	$	8
❑ RD3	Dale Earnhardt	$	20
❑ RD4	Jeff Gordon	$	20
❑ RD5	Ernie Irvan	$	7
❑ RD9	Mark Martin	$	9
❑ RD12	Rusty Wallace	$	10

1995 Press Pass Premium

❑ Complete Set (36)		$	24
❑ Common Card (1-36)		$	.30
❑ Semistars		$	.50
❑ Complete Holofoil (36)		$	50

*Holofoil Cards: 2x
*One Holofoil per Pack

❑ Complete Red Hot (36)		$	300

*Red Hot Cards: 10x
*Random Inserts in Packs

❑ 1	Dale Earnhardt	$	5
❑ 2	Mark Martin	$	1.50
❑ 3	Rusty Wallace	$	2.50
❑ 8	Jeff Gordon	$	5
❑ 19	Ernie Irvan	$	1
❑ 20	Richard Petty	$	1
❑ 30	Mark Martin	$	1.50
❑ 31	Rusty Wallace	$	2.50
❑ 33	Jeff Gordon	$	5

1995 Press Pass Premium Phone Cards

❑ Complete Set (9)		$	115
❑ Common Card (PT1-PT9)		$	12
❑ Complete $50 Set (9)		$	650

*$50 Phone Cards: 6x

❑ 1995 Jeff Gordon Autograph			$2400

*Autographed $5 Cards: 2x to 3x
*Autographed $50 Cards: 1.5 Face Value
*Random Inserts in Packs
*$5 Expiration Date: 1/31/96

❑ PT2	Jeff Gordon	$	35
❑ PT6	Mark Martin	$	16

1995 Press Pass Premium Hot Pursuit

❑ Complete Set (9)		$	145
❑ Common Card (HP1-HP9)		$	10

❑ HP2	Dale Earnhardt	$	40
❑ HP3	Jeff Gordon	$	45
❑ HP5	Mark Martin	$	16
❑ HP9	Rusty Wallace	$	18

1995 Select

❑ Complete Set (150)		$	32
❑ Common Card (1-150)		$	.10
❑ Common Driver (1-150)		$	.20
❑ Semistars		$	.40

*Produced by Pinnacle

❑ 12	Jeff Gordon	$	5
❑ 15	Ernie Irvan	$	1
❑ 20	Mark Martin	$	1.25
❑ 34	Rusty Wallace	$	1.50
❑ 38	Jeff Gordon's Car	$	3
❑ 41	Dale Earnhardt's Car	$	2
❑ 66	Mark Martin	$	1.25
❑ 109	Richard Petty/Kyle Petty IB	$	.75
❑ 111	Rusty Wallace/Kenny/Mike IB	$	1
❑ 112	Davey Allison/Bobby Allison IB	$	1.50
❑ 118	Jeff Gordon YS (Young Stars)	$	3
❑ 129	Richard Petty/Mark Martin I	$	.75
❑ 134	Alan Kulwicki/Geoff Bodine I	$	.75
❑ 135	Ernie Irvan PS (Pole Sitters)	$	.60
❑ 140	Rusty Wallace PS	$	1
❑ 141	Jeff Gordon PS	$	3
❑ 143	Mark Martin PS	$	.75
❑ NNO	Jeff Gordon YS Jumbo	$	18
❑ NNO	Geoff Bodine Magic Motion	$	5

1995 Select Flat Out

❑ Complete Set (150)		$	200
❑ Common Card (1-150)		$	1
❑ Common Driver (1-150)		$	1.50
❑ Semistars		$	2.50

*Stars: 5x
*Random Inserts in Packs

1995 Select Dream Machines

❑ Complete Set (12)		$	280
❑ Common Card (DM1-DM12)		$	20
❑ Semistars		$	25

*Random Inserts in Packs

❑ DM2	Rusty Wallace's Car	$	35
❑ DM3	Mark Martin's Car	$	30
❑ DM8	Jeff Gordon's Car	$	75

1995 Select Skills

❑ Complete Set (18)		$	120
❑ Common Card (SS1-SS18)		$	6
❑ Semistars		$	8

*Random Inserts in Packs

❑ SS1	Rusty Wallace	$	16
❑ SS2	Mark Martin	$	12
❑ SS3	Jeff Gordon	$	35
❑ SS4	Ernie Irvan	$	10

1995 Traks

❑ Complete Set (75)		$	17
❑ Common Card (1-75)		$	.10
❑ Semistars		$	.15

❑ 4	Jeff Gordon	$	3
❑ 9	Ernie Irvan	$	.50

❑ 13	Rusty Wallace	$	.75
❑ 26	Jeff Gordon	$	3
❑ 27	Dale Earnhardt	$	2.50
❑ 30	Mark Martin	$	.60
❑ 46	Rusty Wallace	$	.75
❑ 48	Mark Martin	$	.60
❑ 52	Jeff Gordon	$	3
❑ 53	Mark Martin	$	.60
❑ 58	Jeff Gordon	$	3
❑ 59	Ernie Irvan	$	.50
❑ 62	Mark Martin	$	.60
❑ 66	Rusty Wallace	$	.75
❑ 68	Jeff Gordon	$	3
❑ 74	Ernie Irvan	$	.50
❑ 75	Rusty Wallace	$	.75
❑ NNO	Richard Petty AUTO	$	100

1995 Traks First Run

❑ Complete Set (75)		$	30
❑ Common Card (1-75)		$	.25
❑ Semistars		$	.40

*Stars: 1.5x
*One per Pack

1995 Traks Behind the Scenes

❑ Complete Set (25)		$	4
❑ Common Card (BTS1-BTS25)		$	.25

*Two per Pack

❑ Complete First Run (25)		$	35

*First Run Cards: 6x
*Random Inserts in Packs

1995 Traks Challengers

❑ Complete Set (15)		$	260
❑ Common Card (C1-C15)		$	10
❑ Semistars		$	12

*Random Inserts in Packs
*Expiration Date: 11/30/95

❑ C1	Jeff Gordon	$	100
❑ C6	Rusty Wallace	$	30
❑ C8	Mark Martin	$	40
❑ C13	Ricky Craven	$	25
❑ C14	Robert Pressley	$	25
❑ C15	Randy LaJoie	$	25

1995 Traks On The Rise

❑ Complete Set (20)		$	5
❑ Common Card (OTR1-OTR20)		$	.25
❑ Semistars		$	.40

*One per Pack

❑ Complete First Run (20)		$	40

*First Run Cards: 6x
*Random Inserts in Packs

1995 Traks Race Scapes

❑ Complete Set (10)		$	3
❑ Common Card (1-10)		$	.40

1995 Traks Racing Machines

❑ Complete Set (20)		$	170
❑ Common Card (RM1-RM20)		$	8
❑ Semistars		$	10

❑ RM7	Jeff Gordon	$ 40
❑ RM9	Mark Martin	$ 12
❑ RM10	Rusty Wallace	$ 15

1995 Traks Series Stars

❑ Complete Set (20)		$ 235
❑ Common Card (SS1-SS20)		$ 12
❑ Semistars		$ 14

*Random Inserts in Packs
*Pealed Cards: Same Value

❑ SS4	Rusty Wallace	$ 20
❑ SS5	Mark Martin	$ 17
❑ SS8	Jeff Gordon	$ 50
❑ SS11	Ernie Irvan	$ 14
❑ SS19	Dale Earnhardt	$ 36

1995 Upper Deck

❑ Complete Set (300)		$ 30
❑ Complete Series 1 (150)		$
❑ Common Card (1-150)		$ .10
❑ Common Driver (1-150)		$ .20
❑ Semistars		$ .40

❑ 1	Rusty Wallace	$ 1.50
❑ 2	Jeff Gordon	$ 5
❑ 3	Bill Elliott	$ 1.50
❑ 6	Ernie Irvan	$ 1
❑ 8	Mark Martin	$ 1.25
❑ 44	Rusty Wallace with Car	$ 1.25

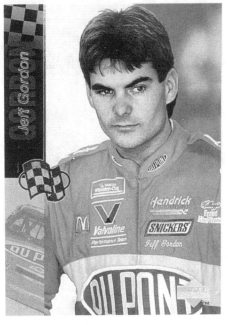

❑ 45	Jeff Gordon with Car	$ 3.50
❑ 46	Bill Elliott with Car	$ 1.25
❑ 49	Ernie Irvan with Car	$ .75

❑ 51	Mark Martin with Car	$ 1
❑ 70	Jeff Gordon's Car	$ 2.50
❑ 133	Michael Jordan CPC	$ 4
❑ 135	Joe Montana CPC	$ 1.25
❑ 136	Ken Griffey, Jr. CPC	$ 1.25
❑ 138	Jeff Gordon's Car	$ 1.50
❑ 149	Rusty Wallace CL	$ .40
❑ 150	Rusty Wallace CL	$ .40
❑ UD1	Sterling Marlin Salute	$ 25
❑ UD2	Jeff Gordon Salute	$ 70

1995 Upper Deck Gold Signature

❑ Complete Gold Signature Set (150)		$ 790
❑ Common Card (1-150)		$ 4
❑ Common Driver (1-150)		$ 8
❑ Semistars		$ 12

*Gold Signature Stars: 20x
*Gold Signature Random Inserts in Series 1 Packs

❑ 1	Rusty Wallace	$ 35
❑ 2	Jeff Gordon	$ 85
❑ 3	Bill Elliott	$ 35
❑ 6	Ernie Irvan	$ 20
❑ 8	Mark Martin	$ 25
❑ 44	Rusty Wallace with Car	$ 25
❑ 45	Jeff Gordon with Car	$ 70
❑ 46	Bill Elliott with Car	$ 25
❑ 49	Ernie Irvan with Car	$ 16
❑ 51	Mark Martin with Car	$ 20
❑ 70	Jeff Gordon's Car	$ 40
❑ 133	Michael Jordan CPC	$ 100
❑ 135	Joe Montana CPC	$ 60
❑ 136	Ken Griffey, Jr. CPC	$ 60
❑ 138	Jeff Gordon's Car	$ 40
❑ 149	Rusty Wallace CL	$ 15
❑ 150	Rusty Wallace CL	$ 15

1995 Upper Deck Silver Signature

❑ Complete Silver Signature Set (150)		$ 100
❑ Common Card (1-150)		$ .30
❑ Common Driver (1-150)		$ .60
❑ Semistars		$ 1.25

*Silver Signature Stars: 2.5x
*Silver Signature One per Hobby Pack
*Silver Signature Two per Retail Pack

1995 Upper Deck Oversized

| ❑ Complete Set (5) | | $ 30 |
| ❑ Common Card (1-5) | | $ 2.50 |

*One Set per Mail Redemption
*Random Inserts in Series 1 Boxes

❑ OS1	Rusty Wallace	$ 7
❑ OS3	Jeff Gordon	$ 16
❑ OS4	Mark Martin	$ 5
❑ OS5	Ernie Irvan	$ 4

1995 Upper Deck Predicator Race Winners

| ❑ Complete Set (10) | | $ 100 |
| ❑ Common Card (P1-P10) | | $ 6 |

❏ P1	Rusty Wallace WIN	$	23
❏ P2	Mark Martin WIN	$	20
❏ P4	Jeff Gordon WIN	$	32
❏ P8	Terry Labonte WIN	$	20
❏ P10	Long Shot WIN	$	20

1987 World of Outlaws

❏ Complete Set (52)		$	85
❏ Common Card (1-52)		$	.40
❏ Cover Card CL		$	.30
❏ Semistars		$	.75

*Cards are Skip Numbered

❏ 1A	Steve Kinser	$	8
❏ 1B	Steve Kinser	$	8
❏ 12	Sammy Swindell	$	2.50
❏ 37	Stevie Smith	$	2
❏ 42	Jeff Swindell	$	1.75
❏ 52	Jeff Gordon	$	60

1988 World of Outlaws

❏ Complete Set (48)		$	55
❏ Common Card (1-48)		$	.40
❏ Cover Card CL		$	.30
❏ Semistars		$	.75

*Cards are Skip Numbered

❏ 1	Steve Kinser	$	6
❏ 2	Sammy Swindell	$	2
❏ 54	Jeff Gordon	$	45
❏ NNO	Brent Kaeding	$	.75

1989 World of Outlaws

❏ Complete Set (32)		$	20
❏ Common Card (1-32)		$	.40
❏ Cover Card CL		$	.30
❏ Semistars		$	.60

❏ 2	Jeff Swindell	$	3
❏ 9	Doug Wolfgang	$	5
❏ 34	Steve Kinser	$	6

1989 World of Outlaws Postcards

❏ Complete Set (13)		$	8
❏ Common Card (1-13)		$	.60
❏ Semistars		$	1.25

❏ 8D	Doug Wolfgang	$	3
❏ 11X	Jeff Swindell	$	2

1990 World of Outlaws

❏ Complete Set (36)		$	20
❏ Common Card (1-36)		$	.30
❏ Cover Card CL		$	.30
❏ Semistars		$	.60

❏ 1	Steve Kinser	$	5
❏ 2	Doug Wolfgang	$	3
❏ 10	Sammy Swindell	$	5

1990 World of Outlaws Postcards

❏ Complete Set (10)		$	8
❏ Common Card (1-10)		$	.60
❏ Semistars		$	1.25

❏ 1	Sammy Swindell	$	2
❏ 8	Doug Wolfgang	$	2
❏ 11	Steve Kinser	$	3

1991 Kendall

❏ Complete Set (43)		$	8
❏ Common Driver (1-43)		$	.40
❏ Semistars		$	.75

1991 World of Outlaws

❏ Complete Set (114)		$	40
❏ Common Card (1-114)		$	.30
❏ Semistars		$	.75

❏ 2	Steve Kinser	$	4
❏ 11	Sammy Swindell	$	2
❏ 16	Doug Wolfgang	$	1.75
❏ 101	Steve Kinser with Car	$	2.50
❏ 107	Sammy Swindell with Car	$	4
❏ 112	Aaron Berryhill with Car SP	$	3
❏ 113	Frankie Kerr with Car SP	$	3
❏ 114	Jimmy Sills with Car SP	$	3

1991 World of Outlaws Most Wanted Inserts

❏ Complete Set (4)		$	15
❏ Common Card (1-4)		$	3

*Random Inserts in Packs

❏ 1	Stevie Smith	$	5
❏ 2	Danny Lasoski	$	5

1991 World of Outlaws Most Wanted

❏ Complete Set (5)		$	10
❏ Common Card (1-5)		$	1

❏ 4	Danny Lasoski	$	4
❏ 6	Bobby Davis, Jr.	$	2

1992 Racing Legends

❏ Complete Set (30)		$	12
❏ Common Card (1-30)		$	.30
❏ Semistars		$	.50

❏ 1	Steve Kinser with Car	$	2
❏ 2	Sammy Swindell with Car	$	.60
❏ 3	Sammy Swindell	$	.75

1992 World of Outlaws Most Wanted

❏ Complete Set (12)		$	10
❏ Common Card (1-12)		$	.75

❏ 1	Dave Blaney	$	1.25
❏ 2	Kenny Jacobs	$	1.25
❏ 4	Joe Gaerte	$	1.25
❏ 6	Tommie Estes, Jr.	$	1.25

1994 World of Outlaws

❏ Complete Set (50)	$	20
❏ Common Card (1-50)	$	.30
❏ Semistars	$	.60
❏ 2 Steve Kinser	$	2.50

1994 World of Outlaws Most Wanted

❏ Complete Set (12)	$	10
❏ Common Card (1-12)	$	.75
❏ 1 Steve Kinser	$	2.50
❏ 3 Mark Kinser	$	1.50

1965 Donruss Spec Sheet

❏ Complete Set (66)	$	200
❏ Common Card (1-66)	$	3.50

1965 Topps Hot Rods

❏ Complete Set (66)	$	325
❏ Gray Backs (1-66)	$	5
❏ White Backs (1-33/36/38/40/41/43)	$	5
❏ White Backs (50/58/59/60/61/63)	$	5
❏ Yellow Backs (1/2/5-8/10-13)	$	6
❏ Yellow Backs (16-18/20/22/24)	$	6
❏ Yellow Backs (26/28/29/31-33)	$	6

1970 Fleer Dragstrips

❏ Complete Set (10)	$	100
❏ Common Card	$	10
❏ Sticker Inserts	$	10

1971 Fleer AHRA Drag Champs

❏ Complete Set (63)	$	300
❏ Common Card	$	5
❏ Semistars	$	6
*American Version Unnumbered		
*American/Canadian Same Value		
❏ 18 Don Garlits	$	12
❏ 22 Funny Car Champs	$	10
❏ 24 Super Stock Champs	$	10
❏ 38 Ronnie Sox	$	7
❏ 54 Top Fuel Champs	$	10

1971 Fleer Stick Shift

❏ Complete Set (10)	$	100
❏ Common Card	$	10
❏ Sticker Inserts	$	10

1972 Fleer AHRA Drag Nationals

❏ Complete Set (70)	$	400
❏ Common Card (1-70)	$	6
❏ Semistars	$	8
*American/Canadian Same Value		
❏ 2 Don Garlits	$	12
❏ 27 Don Prudhomme	$	12

1973 Fleer AHRA Race USA

❏ Complete Set (74)	$	400
❏ Common Card (1-74)	$	6
❏ Semistars	$	8
❏ 4 Don Prudhomme	$	10
❏ 5 Don Prudhomme	$	10
❏ 6 Don Prudhomme	$	10
❏ 31 Don Garlits DOY	$	12
❏ 34 Ronnie Sox's Barracuda	$	9
❏ 35 Ronnie Sox's Barracuda	$	9
❏ 58 Don Garlits's Dragster	$	9
❏ 59 Don Garlits's Dragster	$	9
❏ 60 Don Garlits's Dragster	$	9

1989 Checkered Flag IHRA

❏ Complete Set (100)	$	25
❏ Common Card (1-100)	$	.30
❏ Semistars	$	.50

1989 MEGA Drag

❏ Complete Set (110)	$	225
❏ Common Card (1-110)	$	2.25
❏ Common Driver (1-110)	$	2.50
❏ Semistars	$	3
❏ 1 Darrell Gwynn	$	4
❏ 3 Eddie Hill	$	8
❏ 6 Joe Amato	$	4
❏ 12 Ed McCulloch	$	4
❏ 21 Shirley Muldowney	$	8
❏ 42 Scott Geoffrion	$	5
❏ 48 Darrell Alderman	$	5
❏ 108 Don Garlits	$	8

1990 Checkered Flag IHRA

❏ Complete Set (100)	$	25
❏ Common Card (1-100)	$	.30
❏ Semistars	$	.60

1991 Big Time Drag

❏ Complete Set (96)	$	25
❏ Common Card (1-96)	$	.30
❏ Cover Card (NNO)	$	.30
❏ Semistars	$	.50
❏ 1 Don Garlits with Car	$	1.25
❏ 2 Don Garlits with Car	$	1.25
❏ 3 Don Garlits's Car	$	.75

1991 Pro Set NHRA

❏ Complete Set (130)	$	12
❏ Common Card (1-130)	$	.10
❏ Common Driver (1-130)	$	.15
❏ Semistars	$	.25
❏ 6 Eddie Hill	$	1
❏ 8 Kenny Bernstein	$	1

❏ 10	Shirley Muldowney	$	1
❏ 13	Don Prudhomme	$	1
❏ 17	John Force	$	1.25
❏ 25	Scott Kalitta	$	.75

| ❏ 33 | Connie Kalitta | $ | .75 |
| ❏ 105 | Don Garlits | $ | 1 |

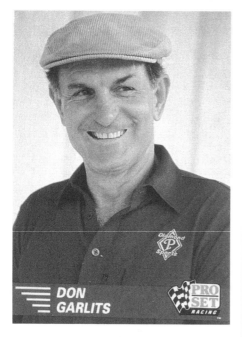

| ❏ 105AU | Don Garlits AUTO | $ | 50 |

1992 Pro Set NHRA

❏ Complete Set (200)	$	12
❏ Common Card (1-200)	$	.05
❏ Common Driver (1-200)	$	.10
❏ Semistars	$	.20

❏ 2	Kenny Bernstein	$	.50
❏ 3	Don Prudhomme	$	.50
❏ 5	Eddie Hill	$	.50
❏ 13	Scott Kalitta	$	.40
❏ 21	Connie Kalitta	$	.40
❏ 27	Shirley Muldowney	$	.50
❏ 30	Eddie Hill	$	.50
❏ 31	Don Prudhomme	$	.50
❏ 32	Kenny Bernstein	$	.50
❏ 35	John Force	$	.75
❏ 47	John Force	$	.75
❏ 102	Kenny Bernstein	$	.50
❏ 103	Don Prudhomme	$	.50
❏ 105	Eddie Hill	$	.50
❏ 117	John Force	$	.75

❏ 182	Don Garlits	$	.50
❏ NNO	Trophy HOLO White	$	200
❏ NNO	Trophy HOLO Black	$	200

1992 Pro Set Kenny Bernstein

❏ Complete Set (7)	$	8
❏ Common Card (1-6)	$	.75
❏ Kenny Bernstein Cards	$	1.50
❏ Cover Card (NNO)	$	.50

1993 Finish Line NHRA

❏ Complete Set (133)		$	12
❏ Common Card (1-133)		$	.05
❏ Common Driver (1-133)		$	.10
❏ Semistars		$	.20
❏ 10	Kenny Bernstein	$	.50
❏ 12	Kenny Bernstein	$	.50
❏ 22	Eddie Hill	$	.50
❏ 23	Eddie Hill	$	.50
❏ 36	Don Prudhomme	$	.50
❏ 53	John Force	$	.75
❏ 54	John Force	$	.75
❏ 131	Shirley Muldowney	$	.50

1993 Finish Line NHRA Autographs

❏ Complete Set (9)		$	200
❏ Common Autograph (1-9)		$	20
❏ Semistars		$	25
*Random Inserts in Packs			
❏ 3	Kenny Bernstein	$	35
❏ 5	John Force	$	35

1993 Finish Line NHRA Speedways

❏ Complete Set (17)		$	3
❏ Common Card (T1-T17)		$	.20
*Random Inserts in Packs			

1994 Action Packed NHRA

❏ Complete Set (42)		$	20
❏ Complete Factory Set (42)		$	22
❏ Common Card (1-42)		$	.50
❏ Semistars		$	.75
❏ 1	Eddie Hill	$ 1.50	
❏ 2	Scott Kalitta	$ 1.25	
❏ 3	Kenny Bernstein	$ 1.50	
❏ 21	John Force	$	2
❏ 32	Shirley Muldowney	$ 1.50	
❏ 34	Don Garlits	$ 1.50	

1994 Action Packed NHRA 24K Gold

❏ Complete Set (6)		$	200
❏ Common Card (31G-36G)		$	30
❏ 32G	Shirley Muldowney	$	50
❏ 34G	Don Garlits	$	50

1983 A&S Racing Indy

❏ Complete Set (51)		$	30
❏ Common Card (1-51)		$	.40
❏ CL (NNO)		$	.40
❏ Semistars		$	.75
❏ 1	Rick Mears	$	2
❏ 33	Mario Andretti	$	4
❏ 34	Bobby Rahal	$ 1.50	
❏ 43	Al Unser, Jr.	$	5
❏ 48	Al Unser	$	3

1984 A&S Racing Indy

❏ Complete Set (51)		$	30
❏ Common Card (1-51)		$	.40
❏ Semistars		$	.75
❏ 1	Al Unser	$	2
❏ 10	Rick Mears	$ 1.50	
❏ 16	Mario Andretti	$	3
❏ 36	Michael Andretti	$	4
❏ 47	Al Unser, Jr.	$	3

1985 A&S Racing Indy

❏ Complete Set (52)		$	30
❏ Common Card (1-52)		$	.40
❏ Semistars		$	.60
❏ 1	Mario Andretti	$ 2.50	
❏ 24	Al Unser, Jr.	$ 2.50	
❏ 25	Rick Mears	$	1
❏ 35	Al Unser	$ 1.75	
❏ 42	Michael Andretti	$ 2.50	
❏ 50	Mario Andretti/Michael Andretti	$ 1.50	
❏ 51	Al Unser, Jr./Al Unser	$ 1.50	

1986 A&S Racing Indy

❏ Complete Set (52)		$	30
❏ Common Card (1-52)		$	.40
❏ Semistars		$	.60
❏ 1	Al Unser	$ 1.50	
❏ 2	Mario Andretti	$ 2.25	
❏ 10	Al Unser, Jr.	$ 2.25	
❏ 43	Michael Andretti	$ 1.75	
❏ 45	Rick Mears	$	1

1987 A&S Racing Indy

❏ Complete Set (52)		$	25
❏ Common Card (1-52)		$	.40
❏ Semistars		$	.60
❏ 1	Mario Andretti/Carnegie	$ 1.50	
❏ 9	Al Unser	$ 1.50	
❏ 14	A. J. Foyt	$	2
❏ 18	Michael Andretti	$ 1.50	
❏ 20	Mario Andretti with Car	$ 1.50	
❏ 30	Al Unser, Jr.	$	2
❏ 39	Rick Mears	$	.75
❏ 45	Michael Andretti/Sullivan/Mears	$ 1.25	
❏ 48	Mario Andretti WIN	$ 1.50	

1991 All World Indy

❏ Complete Set (100)		$	4
❏ Complete Factory Set (100)		$	5
❏ Common Card (1-100)		$	.05
❏ Semistars		$	.10
❏ 1	Al Unser, Jr.	$	.40
❏ 4	John Andretti	$	.20
❏ 5	Mario Andretti	$	.40
❏ 25	Michael Andretti	$	.25
❏ 33	Michael Andretti/John Andretti	$	.20

❏ 35	Al Unser	$	.15
❏ 45	Al Unser, Jr. WIN	$	.25
❏ 66	Michael Andretti WIN	$	.25
❏ 75	Al Unser, Jr./Rahal	$	.25
❏ 96	Mario Andretti PPGC	$	.25
❏ 100	Al Unser, Jr. PPGC	$	.25

1991 CARMS Formula One

❏ Complete Set (105)	$	35
❏ Common Card (1-105)	$	.20
❏ Common Driver (1-105)	$	.30
❏ Semistars	$	.50

❏ 1	Ayrton Senna	$	8
❏ 2	Ayrton Senna's Car	$	2
❏ 3	Ayrton Senna	$	6
❏ 13	Nigel Mansell	$	3
❏ 15	Nigel Mansell	$	3
❏ 101	Mario Andretti	$	5

1991 Pro Tracs Formula One

❏ Complete Set (200)	$	10
❏ Common Card (1-200)	$	.05
❏ Common Driver (1-200)	$	.10
❏ Semistars	$	.20

❏ 1	Ayrton Senna	$	.75
❏ 9	Nigel Mansell	$	.50
❏ 106	Ayrton Senna	$	.75
❏ 107	Ayrton Senna in Car	$	.75
❏ 131	Nigel Mansell	$	.50
❏ 148	Ayrton Senna/Patrese/Berger	$	.75
❏ 151	Ayrton Senna	$	.75
❏ 165	Ayrton Senna/Nigel Mansell Cars	$	.75
❏ 166	Ayrton Senna	$	.75
❏ 172	Ayrton Senna/Berger	$	.75
❏ 180	Nigel Mansell	$	.50
❏ 193	Nigel Mansell/C. Chapman	$	.50

1992 All World Indy

❏ Complete Set (100)	$	4
❏ Complete Factory Set (100)	$	5
❏ Common Card (1-100)	$	.05
❏ Semistars	$	.15

❏ 1	Michael Andretti	$	.25
❏ 21	Al Unser, Jr.	$	.25
❏ 25	Mario Andretti	$	.25
❏ 46	Michael Andretti	$	.25
❏ 49	Andretti Family	$	.20
❏ 50	Andretti Trifecta	$	.20
❏ 51	Norman Schwartzkopf	$	.25
❏ 70	Mario Andretti	$	.25
❏ 79	Michael Andretti	$	.25
❏ 84	Al Unser, Jr.	$	.25

1992 Collect-a-Card
Andretti Racing

❏ Complete Set (101)	$	6
❏ Common Card (1-100)	$	.10
❏ Hologram (NNO)	$	1

1992 Grid Formula One

❏ Complete Set (200)	$	11
❏ Complete Factory Set (200)	$	12
❏ Common Card (1-200)	$	.05
❏ Common Driver (1-200)	$	.10
❏ Ayrton Senna's Car	$	.30
❏ Semistars	$	.15

❏ 34	Ayrton Senna	$	.50
❏ 38	Nigel Mansell	$	.30
❏ 41	Damon Hill	$	.30
❏ 51	Michael Shumacher	$	.75
❏ 67	Ayrton Senna	$	.50
❏ 71	Nigel Mansell	$	.30
❏ 74	Damon Hill	$	.30
❏ 84	Michael Schumacher	$	.75
❏ 100	Ayrton Senna/Prost/Piquet	$	.30
❏ 101	Ayrton Senna WIN	$	.30
❏ 102	Ayrton Senna/Berger/Lehto	$	.30
❏ 103	Ayrton Senna/Mansell/Alesi	$	.30
❏ 105	Ayrton Senna/Patrese/Mansell	$	.30
❏ 106	Ayrton Senna/Mansell/Prost	$	.30
❏ 109	Ayrton Senna/Mansell/Patrese	$	.30
❏ 110	Ayrton Senna WIN	$	.30
❏ 111	Ayrton Senna/Mansell/Prost	$	.30
❏ 114	Ayrton Senna/Berger/Patrese	$	.30
❏ 115	Ayrton Senna WIN	$	.30
❏ 162	Al Unser, Jr.	$	.30
❏ 186	Ayrton Senna	$	.50
❏ 188	Ayrton Senna	$	.50

1992 Hi-Tech
Mario Andretti

❏ Complete Factory Set (51)	$	20
❏ Common Card (1-51)	$	.50

1993 Hi-Tech Indy

❏ Complete Set (81)	$	10
❏ Common Card (1-81)	$	.15
❏ Semistars	$	.25

❏ 3	Mario Andretti	$	.75
❏ 6	Michael Andretti	$	.40
❏ 12	Al Unser, Jr.	$	.75
❏ 34	Al Unser, Jr. Indy Champ	$	.75
❏ 36	Al Unser, Jr.	$	.75
❏ 48	Michael Andretti	$	.40
❏ 58	Mario Andretti	$	.75
❏ 70	Mario Andretti/Guerrero/Chee	$	.50

1993 Hi-Tech Indy Checkered Flag Finishers

❏ Complete Set (12)	$	30
❏ Common Card (SP1-SP12)	$	2
❏ Semistars	$	3
*Random Inserts in Packs		

❏ SP1	Al Unser, Jr.	$	8
❏ SP3	Al Unser	$	5
❏ SP9	A. J. Foyt	$	4

1993 Maxx Williams Racing

❑ Complete Set (100)		$	18
❑ Common Card (1-100)		$	.20
❑ Semistars		$	.30
❑ 1	Nigel Mansell	$	.75
❑ 4	Damon Hill	$	.50
❑ 15	Mario Andretti	$	2
❑ 35	Jackie Stewart/Alan Jones	$	1
❑ 49	Nigel Mansell	$	.75
❑ 50	Nigel Mansell	$	.75
❑ 62	Nigel Mansell	$	.75
❑ 67	Nigel Mansell	$	.75

1994 Hi-Tech Indy

❑ Complete Set (52)		$	8
❑ Common Card (1-52)		$	.15
❑ Semistars		$	.25
❑ 4	Nigel Mansell	$	.40
❑ 6	Mario Andretti	$	.75
❑ 9	Al Unser, Jr.	$	.75
❑ 40	Luyendyk/Andretti/Boesel	$	.40

1994 Hi-Tech Indy Champ Driver

❑ Complete Set (37)		$	15
❑ Common Card (CD1-CD37)		$	.50
❑ Semistars		$	.75
*Random Inserts in Packs			
❑ CD3	Mario Andretti	$ 2.50	
❑ CD4	Michael Andretti	$ 2.50	
❑ CD14	A. J. Foyt	$ 1.50	
❑ CD35	Al Unser, Jr.	$	3

1994 Hi-Tech
A. J. Foyt

❑ Complete Set (6)	$	5
❑ Common Card (AJ1-AJ6)	$	1
*Random Inserts in Packs		

1994 Hi-Tech
Rick Mears

❑ Complete Set (6)	$	5
❑ Common Card (RM1-RM6)	$	1
*Random Inserts in Packs		

1995 SkyBox Indy

❑ Complete Set (108)		$	23
❑ Common Card (1-108)		$	.25
*Random Inserts in Packs			
❑ 12	Mario Andretti Pole Run	$	.50
❑ 13	Jacques Villeneuve RQ (Rookie Qualifer)	$	1
❑ 14	Al Unser, Jr. with Crew	$	1
❑ 19	Al Unser, Jr. in Car	$	1
❑ 22	Jacques Villeneuve in Car	$	1
❑ 23	Michael Andretti in Car	$	.50
❑ 27	Mario Andretti in Car	$	.50
❑ 52	Al Unser, Jr. MVP	$	1
❑ 62	Jacques Villeneuve in Car	$	1
❑ 70	Al Unser, Jr. in Car	$	1
❑ 71	Al Unser, Jr. WIN	$	1
❑ 72	Al Unser, Jr. WIN	$	1
❑ 73	Al Unser, Jr.	$ 1.50	
❑ 74	Jacques Villeneuve	$ 1.50	
❑ 77	Robbie Gordon	$	.65
❑ 78	Michael Andretti in Car	$	.50
❑ 104	Mario Andretti in Car	$	.50
❑ 106	Al Unser, Jr. with Car	$	1
❑ 107	Mario Andretti	$	.50
❑ 108	Al Unser, Jr.	$	1
❑ NNO	Al Unser, Jr. Champion	$	4

1995 SkyBox Indy
Heir to Indy

❑ Complete Set (6)	$	38
❑ Common Card (1-6)	$	6
❑ Semistars	$	8
*Random Inserts in Packs		
❑ 6	Jacques Villeneuve	$	13

1995 SkyBox Indy
Past Indy Champs

❑ Complete Set (18)	$	40
❑ Common Card (1-18)	$ 2.50	
❑ Semistars	$ 3.50	
*Random Inserts in Packs		
❑ 1	Al Unser, Jr.	$	8
❑ 13	Mario Andretti	$	5

Prototype Cards

Note: * = Significant collector interest in last 12 months

Year/Set	Manufacturer	Value	
1989			
Don Garlits Museum	Racing Legends	$ 22	
1990			
Mario Andretti	Action Packed	$ 240	
Rick Mears	Action Packed	$ 220	
Emerson Fittipaldi	Action Packed	$ 220	
Pancho Carter	Action Packed	$ 220	
1991			
"Tiger" Tom Piston	If It's Racing	$ 11	
Bill Elliott	Maxx	$ 100	*
3 Card Set – Winston Cup	Pro Set	$ 9	
Curtis Turner	Racing Legends	$ 12	
Curtis Turner Car	Racing Legends	$ 12	
Curtis Turner, Jr.	Racing Legends	$ 12	
Rob Moroso – Victory Lane	Gold Card	$ 11	
Rob Moroso – On Track	Gold Card	$ 11	
Harry Gant	C & M Productions	$ 12	
Harry Gant	Redline	$ 17	
Rob Moroso	Redline	$ 16	
Ken Schrader	Redline	$ 17	
Cale Yarborough	Redline	$ 17	
Alabama Gang (Red)	Sports Legends	$ 11	
Alabama Gang (Yellow)	Sports Legends	$ 6	
Herb Thomas	Sports Legends	$ 11	
Rob Moroso	Sports Legends	$ 6	
Alan Kulwicki	Sports Legends	$ 12	
Rusty Wallace	Sports Legends	$ 6	
Harry Hyde	Sports Legends	$ 6	
Phil Parsons	Sports Legends	$ 6	
Dale Jarrett	Sports Legends	$ 6	
Cale Yarborough	Sports Legends	$ 6	
Hut Stricklin	Sports Legends	$ 6	
Ernie Irvan	Traks	$ 22	
Mark Martin	Traks	$ 22	
Kyle Petty	Traks	$ 22	
The King – Richard Petty	Traks	$ 22	
The Racers Edge – Petty	Traks	$ 22	
Lee/Richard Petty – 1972	Traks	$ 31	
Wendell Scott	T.G. Racing	$ 13	
Tiny Lund	T.G. Racing	$ 13	
1992			
David Pearson	T.G. Racing	$ 16	
Cotton's Ride – Owens	T.G. Racing	$ 16	
Charlie Golzbach	T.G. Racing	$ 16	
Larry Frank	T.G. Racing	$ 16	
Kyle Petty	Traks	$ 22	
Goodwrench Chevy	Traks	$ 25	*
Rusty Wallace	Traks	$ 22	
Harry Gant	Traks	$ 21	
Benny Parsons	Traks	$ 21	
Richard Petty – QVC	Traks	$ 17	
Western Auto Team	Traks	$ 16	

Kodak Team	Traks	$	16
Raybestos Team	Traks	$	16
STP Team	Traks	$	17
Richard Petty – White Plastic	Gold Card	$	21
Richard Petty – Black Plastic	Gold Card	$	21
Kyle Petty – Plastic	Gold Card	$	27
Bill Elliott – Black	Maxx	$	55
Bill Elliott – Red	Maxx	$	55
3 Card Winston Cup Set	Pro Set	$	9
Harry Gant – Silver Hologram	Wheels	$	6
Harry Gant – Platinum	Wheels	$	11
Harry Gant – Gold	Wheels	$	11
Ricky Craven	Winner's Choice	$	14
Shawna Robinson	Winner's Choice	$	18
Joe Bessey	Winner's Choice	$	15
Mike Rowe	Winner's Choice	$	13
Joe Nemechek	Winner's Choice	$	20
Valvoline Pit Crew	Traks	$	9
Goodwrench Transporter – QVC	Traks	$	18 *
Goodwrench Transporter	Traks	$	12
Country Time Transporter	Traks	$	9
Alan Kulwicki – R. Machine	Traks	$	20
#101-Mello Yello	Action Packed	$	20
#102-Kyle Petty	Action Packed	$	20
#103-Mello Yello	Action Packed	$	20
Petty – "Royal Finish" – Bass Painting	Richmond Promotion – Edition: 143	$	260
Car #68 Country Time	Motorsports Model Cards	$	6
Car #43 STP – AM Series	Motorsports Model Cards	$	6
Car #11 Budweiser – AM Series	Motorsports Model Cards	$	6
Car #88 Gatorade – AM Series	Motorsports Model Cards	$	6
Car #28 Texaco – AM series	Motorsports Model Cards	$	6
Pennzoil Hauler – DieCards	Motorsports Model Cards	$	6
#1 Jimmy Cox – Bikers of Racing Scene	Eagle Productions	$	5
#2 Richard Childress – (BORS)	Eagle Productions	$	7
#3 Harry Gant – Bikers of Racing Scene	Eagle Productions	$	8
#4 Michael Waltrip – (BORS)	Eagle Productions	$	5
#5 The King – (BORS)	Eagle Productions	$	8

1993

Alliance Racing – Pearson-Metal	Card Dynamics – Edition: 99	$	80
Alliance Racing – Pressley-Metal	Card Dynamics – Edition: 99	$	80
Alliance #59-Metal	Card Dynamics – Edition: 99	$	80
Bill Elliott – Green Border	Maxx	$	16
Bill Elliott – Premium	Maxx	$	16
Bill Elliott – Premium Plus	Maxx	$	27
#BA1 Bobby Allison	Action Packed	$	43
#DE1 Dale Earnhardt	Action Packed	$	70 *
#JG1 Jeff Gordon	Action Packed	$	70 *
#DJ1 Dale Jarrett	Action Packed	$	43
#AK1 Alan Kulwicki	Action Packed	$	55
Promotional Sheet	Finish Line	$	16
4 Card Set	Finish Line	$	65
Budweiser Ford (Hologram)	Turn I	$	80
Bill Elliott (Hologram)	Turn I	$	80
#KP1 Kyle Petty	Action Packed	$	11
#KP2 Kyle Petty	Action Packed	$	11
#AK/DA Kulwicki & D. Allison	Action Packed	$	22
#RP1 Richard Petty	Action Packed	$	12
#RP2 Richard Petty	Action Packed	$	12
#RP3 Richard Petty	Action Packed	$	12
#RP4 Richard Petty	Action Packed	$	12
#RP5 Richard Petty	Action Packed	$	12
#RP 6 Richard Petty	Action Packed	$	12

Kulwicki & D. Allison – Gold	Action Packed	$	138
Rusty Wallace	Traks	$	16
Jeff Gordon	Traks	$	17
#P1 Richard Petty	Wheels	$	11
#P2 Jeff Gordon	Wheels	$	20 *
#P3 Kenny Wallace	Wheels	$	11
#P4 Bobby Labonte	Wheels	$	14 *
#P5 Davey Allison	Wheels	$	15
Rusty Wallace – Indy Tire Test	Hi-Tech	$	11
D. Allison – Indy Tire Test	Hi-Tech	$	12
#1 Chad Little	If It's Paper	$	3
#2 Schedule	If It's Paper	$	3

1994

#KP1 Kyle Petty	Action Packed	$	11
#KP2 Kyle Petty	Action Packed	$	11
#2R941 Dale Earnhardt	Action Packed	$	20 *
#2R942 Jeff Gordon	Action Packed	$	20 *
#2R943 Kyle Petty	Action Packed	$	11
#2R944 Dale Jarrett	Action Packed	$	17
#2R945 Miller Ford	Action Packed	$	17
Harry Gant	Finish Line	$	8.50
Rusty Wallace	Finish Line	$	9
Mark Martin	Finish Line	$	9
8 x 10 Card	Finish Line	$	11
Mark Martin – Series I	Traks	$	9
Havoline Racing – Series II	Traks	$	9
Promo Sheet	Press Pass	$	7
Harry Gant	Press Pass VIP	$	10
Harry Gant – Gold Signature	Press Pass VIP	$	160
Ernie Irvan	Press Pass VIP	$	12
Du Pont Chevy	Press Pass VIP	$	20 *
Rusty Wallace	Press Pass VIP	$	13
Mark Martin – Club Member	Press Pass VIP	$	11
Geoff Bodine – Club Member	Press Pass VIP	$	11
Bill Elliott – Sample	Maxx	$	10
Jeff Gordon – Sample	Maxx	$	14 *
Bill Elliott – Promo-Club Maxx	Maxx	$	17
Bill Elliott – Chromium	Maxx	$	22
Jeff Gordon	Power by Pro Set	$	12 *
B. Hillin – Tuff Stuff Show Promo	Power by Pro Set	$	16
J. Donlavey – Tuff Stuff Show Promo	Power by Pro Set	$	16
DB1 Dale Earnhardt	Power by Pro Set	$	13 *
PW1 Ernie Irvan	Power by Pro Set	$	8
#P1 Jeff Gordon	Wheels High Gear	$	20 *
#P2 Rusty Wallace	Wheels High Gear	$	9
#P3 Kyle Petty	Wheels High Gear	$	8
#1 Richard Petty	Hi-Tech	$	6.50
#2 Jeff Gordon	Hi-Tech	$	8.50
#3 Kyle Petty	Hi-Tech	$	6.50
Jeff Gordon	Finish Line Gold	$	12 *
Terry Labonte	Finish Line Gold	$	8
Ernie Irvan	SkyBox	$	25 *
#1 Kyle Petty	Press Pass Optima	$	7
#2 Rusty Wallace – Driver/Owner	Press Pass Optima	$	16
#2 Rusty Wallace	Press Pass Optima	$	8
#3 Jeff Gordon	Press Pass Optima	$	12 *
"A Fond Farewell"	Wheels	$	5
Jeff Gordon – Farewell Tour	Wheels	$	8
"Harley Harry" – Farewell Tour	Wheels	$	5
"Bandit on the Loose" – Farewell Tour	Wheels	$	5
KS1 Kirk Shelmerdine	Schelmerdine Collection	$	6 *

1995

#PR1 Rusty Wallace	Upper Deck Race Cards	$ 7.50	
#RW1 Rusty Wallace	Upper Deck Race Cards	$ 7	
P1 Mark Martin – Brickyard 400	Hi-Tech Race Cards	$ 10	
P2 Ernie Irvan – Brickyard 400	Hi-Tech Race Cards	$ 10	
P3 Dale Earnhardt – Brickyard 400	Hi-Tech Race Cards	$ 13	
Terry Labonte	Press Pass Cards	$ 5.50	
Kyle Petty	Press Pass Cards	$ 5	
Jeff Gordon	Press Pass Cards	$ 10	*
8 x 10 Card – Clear	Finish Line Cards	$ 22	
RP1 Dale Earnhardt	Finish Line Cards	$ 17	
HP1 Dale Earnhardt	Finish Line Cards	$ 17	
P1 Rusty Wallace	Wheels	$ 11	
P2 Jeff Gordon – High Gear	Wheels	$ 14	*
P3 Mark Martin – High Gear	Wheels	$ 11	
BTS1 Steve Hmiel	Traks Race Cards	$ 9	
OTR 14 Jeff Burton	Traks Race Cards	$ 9	
26 Jeff Gordon	Traks Race Cards	$ 14	*
'95 Winston Cup Preview	Traks Race Cards – Edition: 2,000	$ 20	
"Every Second Counts" – Gordon	Maxx Race Cards	$ 8	*
#12 Jeff Gordon	Select Race Cards	$ 14	*
#1 Kyle Petty	Press Pass Race Cards	$ 8	
Dale Earnhardt $1,000 Phone Card	Assets Race Cards	$ 28	*
Jeff Burton – Premier Series	Maxx Race Cards	$ 8	
#2 Bobby Labonte – Gold Foil '95 VIP	Press Pass Race Cards	$ 6	
#2 Bobby Labonte – Red Foil '95 VIP	Press Pass Race Cards	$ 16	

Additional Auto Racing Sets

Note: * = Significant collector interest in last 12 months.

Year/Set/(# cards in Set)	Manufacturer	Value	
1983			
UNO Racing (30)	UNO Playing Cards	$ 260	
1986			
Sportstar Photographics (13)	Sportstar	$ 900	*
1989			
Masters of Racing (152)	T.G. Racing	$ 185	
1990			
AC-Delco (7)	AC-Delco	$ 80	*
Holly Farms (30)	Maxx Race Cards	$ 32	
Masters of Racing, White Gold (110)	T.G. Racing	$ 32	
1991			
AC Proven Winners (10)	AC-Delco	$ 73	
Bill Elliott Team (40)	Maxx Race Cards	$ 30	
Bobby Allison (30)	Sports Legends	$ 16	
Coo Coo Marlin (30)	Racing Legends	$ 27	
David Pearson (6)	T.G. Racing	$ 50	
Donnie Allison	Sports Legends	$ 16	
Fireball Roberts I & II (42)	RSS Motorsports	$ 30	
Ford Motorsports (40)	Maxx Race Cards	$ 27	
Geoff Bodine (30)	Racing Legends	$ 16	
Handsome Harry (15)	CM Products	$ 10	
Harry Hyde (30)	Sports Legends	$ 15	

Herb Thomas (30)	Sports Legends	$	15
Homecoming at Hickory (12)	Hickory Speedway	$	11
Hut Stricklin (30)	Sports Legends	$	15
IROC (12)	Dodge	$	530
Junior Johnson (30)	Racing Legends	$	55
Motorsports Model Cards (90)	Motorsports Model Cards	$	20
Motorsports Model Premier (90)	Motorsports Model Cards	$	50
Ned Jarrett (30)	Sports Legends	$	15
Neil Bonnett (30)	Sports Legends	$	21
Pioneers of Racing (107)	Galfield Press	$	200 *
Racing For Kids (18-3 sheets)	Maxx Race Cards	$	50
Ricky Craven (30)	Winner's Choice	$	20
Rob Moroso (30)	Gold Card	$	18
Rob Moroso (30)	Sports Legends	$	15
Sterling Marlin (30)	Racing Legends	$	30
STP 20th Anniversary (10)	STP	$	36
Texas World Speedway (10)	Texas Speedway	$	6
"Tiger" Tom Pistone (15)	If It's Racing	$	5
Tiny Lund (55)	T.G. Racing	$	13
Wendell Scott (6)	T.G. Racing	$	20

1992

AC Proven Winners (8)	AC Racing	$	16
AC Racing (8)	AC Racing	$	31
Alan Kulwicki (30)	Sports Legends	$	18
Bikers of Racing Scene (34)	Eagle Promotions	$	10
Buck Baker (30)	Sports Legends	$	14.50
Cale Yarborough (30)	Redline Racing	$	15
Cale Yarborough (30)	Sports Legends	$	14
Country Star Racing (14)	Traks Race Cards	$	8
Chuck Bown (15)	Limited Editions	$	8
Curtis Turner (20)	Racing Legends	$	22
Dale Jarrett (30)	Sports Legends	$	15
Ford Motorsports (50)	Maxx Race Cards	$	25
GM Goodwrench Team (25)	Traks Race Cards	$	18.50
Harry Gant (33)	Racing Legends	$	27
Harry Gant (30)	Redline Racing	$	16
Harry Gant (6)	Sunbelt	$	5
Jack Ingram (20)	Racing Legends	$	22
Jimmy Hensley (15)	Limited Editions	$	7.50
Kellogg's-Back of Box (4)	Kellogg's	$	5
Ken Schrader (30)	Redline Racing	$	15
Kenny Wallace (15)	Limited Editions	$	8
Kodak Team (25)	Traks Team	$	9
McDonald's Race Team (4)	Maxx Race Cards	$	6
Mello Yello Team (25)	Traks Race Cards	$	7.50
Michigan Engine Bearings (12)	McCord Gaskets	$	11
MotorArt Calendar (12)	T.G. Racing	$	13
Motorcraft Racing (10)	Motorcraft Racing	$	26
Motorsports Model DieCards (54)	Motorsports Model Cards	$	15
Motorsports Model AM Series (90)	Motorsports Model Cards	$	22
NASCAR Manufacturers Champ. (10)	Ford Motorsports	$	11
Pennzoil Team (25)	Traks Race Cards	$	8
Phil Parsons (30)	Sports Legends	$	15
Preferred Collector, Traks Club (20)	Traks Race Cards	$	33
Race Car Haulers – Drivers (30)	RSS Motorsports	$	11
Raybestos Team (25)	Traks Race Cards	$	8
Rob Moroso (30)	Redline Racing	$	16.50
Ron Hornaday (4)	Big League Cards	$	6.50
Roy & Ray Hendricks (5)	Tenn. Racing	$	7
Sears Craftsman (8)	Maxx Race Cards	$	24
Sparky's Racing (10)	TMC	$	12
STP Team (25)	Traks Race Cards	$	9

Texaco Team (25)	Traks Race Cards	$ 16.50
Tommy Houston (15)	Limited Editions	$ 7
Western Auto Team (25)	Traks Race Cards	$ 9
Wendell Scott (30)	Sports Legends	$ 13
Winners Choice (150)	Winners Choice Cards	$ 27.50
Yesterday's Heroes (48)	Track Pack	$ 26

1993

Alliance Racing (12)	Traks Race Cards	$ 15
Allison Family (3)	Action Packed. Edition:5,000	$ 90
Case Knives (13)	Maxx Race Cards	$ 38
Finish Line Commemorative Sheets with binder – (30)	Finish Line Race Cards	$ 65
Ford '92 Manf. Champion (10)	Ford	$ 18
Ford Motorsports (50)	Maxx Race Cards	$ 25
Fred Lorenzen (16)	Sports Legends	$ 16
Jeff Gordon (15)	Limited Editions Race Cards	$ 14
Jerry Glanville (15)	Limited Edition Race Cards	$ 4
Kellogg's Terry Labonte (4)	Kellogg's	$ 5
Kodak (24)	Kodak	$ 32.0
Stove Top Stuffing Series I (3)	Stove Top	$ 6.50
Stove Top Stuffing Series II (3)	Stove Top	$ 5.50
Traks Trivia (50)	Traks Race Cards	$ 16.50
Winnebago Motorsports (11)	Maxx Race Cards	$ 22

1994

Bayer Racing (5)	Advanced Images	$ 5.50
Brickyard 400 in Tin (w/23k Gordon)(101)	Hi-Tech Race Cards	$ 70
Brickyard 400 in Wood Box (101)	Hi-Tech Race Cards	$ 165
Daytona Pepsi 400 (5)	Pepsi	$ 19
Earnhardt Power Pak Team Set (20)	Wheels Race Cards	$ 32
Earnhardt Power Pak Team – Gold (20)	Wheels Race Cards	$ 50
Ernie Irvan Fan Club (5)	Advanced Images	$ 10
Ford Motorsports 3.5" x 5" (25)	Maxx Race Cards	$ 38
Jeff Gordon Rookie of the Year (20)	Maxx Race Cards	$ 20 *
Lipton Tea (4)	Lipton	$ 5
MW Windows (5)	MW Windows	$ 25
Quality Care Racing (10)	Motorcraft Racing	$ 10
Sam Bass Acrylics	Maxx Club, Edition: 6000	$ 57
Smokin' Joe's (13)	Action Packed Race Cards	$ 23
The Winston Select 24K Gold	Action Packed Race Cards	$ 110
US Air Racing (5)	Advanced Images	$ 6
Wallace Power Pak Team (40)	Wheels Race Cards	$ 28
Wallace Power Pak Team – Gold (40)	Wheels Race Cards	$ 47.50

1995

McDonald's – Elliott (21)	Action Packed Race Cards	$ 12.50
Tide – Rudd (10)	Proctor & Gamble	$ 11.50
Valvoline "100 Years …" – Tin	Traks Race Cards	$ 21
Speed Street Coca-Cola 600 (65)	Finish Line Race Cards	$ 21
Sun Drop Earnhardt (3)	Action Packed Race Cards	$ 18

Auto Racing Autographs

Auto Racing Autograph Guide

Sig.- Usually refers to the signature on a card or albumn page, or possibly cut from a letter or document

SP- Signed photograph, color or black and white

* Deceased

Driver	Sig.	SP
Agajanian, J. C. *	$ 25	$ 45
Aitken, Johnny *	$ 34	$ 65
Alesi, Jean	$ 5	$ 8
Allen, Loy, Jr.	$ 4	$ 8
Allison, Bobby	$ 8	$ 16
Allison, Davey *	$ 18	$ 75
Allison, Donnie	$ 5	$ 10
Allison, James A. *	$ 25	$ 50
Amato, Joe	$ 6	$ 10
Anderson, Gil *	$ 40	$ 70
Anderson, Shelly	$ 4	$ 8
Andretti, John	$ 5	$ 10
Andretti, Mario	$ 10	$ 20

Mario Andretti

Driver	Sig.	SP
Andretti, Michael	$ 8	$ 15
Arfons, Art	$ 10	$ 20
Austin, Pat	$ 4	$ 8
Baker, Buck	$ 5	$ 10
Baker, Buddy	$ 5	$ 11
Baker, Cannonball *	$ 30	$ 60
Banks, Henry	$ 6	$ 12
Bernstein, Kenny	$ 6	$ 10
Berger, Gerhard	$ 5	$ 10
Bergere, Cliff *	$ 35	$ 70
Bettenhausen, Gary	$ 10	$ 20
Bettenhausen, Tony *	$ 40	$ 90
Bigelow, Tim	$ 10	$ 20
Bignotti, George	$ 10	$ 20
Bodine, Brett	$ 5	$ 10
Bodine, Geoff	$ 6	$ 11
Bodine, Todd	$ 4	$ 8
Boesel, Raul	$ 5	$ 10
Bonnett, Neil	$ 10	$ 45
Boutsen, Thiery	$ 5	$ 8
Boyer, Joe *	$ 25	$ 50
Brabham, Jack	$ 6	$ 12
Brabham, Geoff	$ 5	$ 8
Brayton, Scott	$ 5	$ 10
Breedlove, Craig	$ 14	$ 25
Browner, Clint *	$ 25	$ 50
Bruce-Brown, David *	$ 25	$ 50
Burman, Bob *	$ 28	$ 60
Burton, Jeff	$ 4	$ 8
Burton, Ward	$ 4	$ 8
Bryan, Jimmy *	$ 25	$ 50
Campbell, Malcolm Sir *	$ 70	$ 165
Capelli, Ivan	$ 5	$ 8
Carter, Pancho	$ 8	$ 17
Chase, Mike	$ 4	$ 8
Cheever, Eddie	$ 5	$ 8
Chenowethe, Dean *	$ 20	$ 55
Chevrolet, Gaston *	$ 300	$ 625
Chevrolet, Louis *	$ 800	$1,750
Christie, Walter *	$ 25	$ 50
Clark, Jimmy *	$ 55	$ 140
Cloutier, Joe *	$ 25	$ 50
Cogan, Kevin	$ 8	$ 17
Cooper, Earl *	$ 45	$ 95
Cope, Derrike	$ 5	$ 8
Craven, Ricky	$ 5	$ 8
Crawford, Jim	$ 5	$ 8
Crossfield, Scott	$ 8	$ 15
Cummings, Bill *	$ 28	$ 55
Curtis, Glenn	$ 210	$ 550
Daly, Derek	$ 5	$ 8
Davis, Floyd	$ 20	$ 45
Dawson, Joe *	$ 20	$ 45
De Palma, Ralph *	$ 55	$ 140
De Paolo, Peter *	$ 70	$ 145
Dingley, Bert *	$ 30	$ 60

Dale Earnhardt

Driver	Sig.	SP
Donohue, Mark *	$ 55	$ 110
Drake, Darrell *	$ 25	$ 50
Duesenberg, Augie *	$ 125	$ 300
Duesenberg, Fred *	$ 150	$ 350
Dunn, Mike	$ 4	$ 8
Durant, Cliff *	$ 40	$ 80
Earnhardt, Dale	$ 10	$ 40
Edenburn, Eddie *	$ 25	$ 50
Elliott, Bill	$ 10	$ 20
Fabi, Teo	$ 5	$ 10
Fangio, Juan-Manuel *	$ 60	$ 140
Fengler, Harlan *	$ 35	$ 70
Firestone, Dennis	$ 5	$ 8
Firestone, Harvey, Jr. *	$ 125	$ 300
Fisher, Carl *	$ 35	$ 70
Fittipaldi, Emerson	$ 10	$ 25
Flock, Tim	$ 5	$ 12
Ford, Henry *	$1,000	$2,600
Foyt, A. J.	$ 10	$ 22
Frame, Fred *	$ 25	$ 50
France, Bill, Sr.	$ 5	$ 10
Gant, Harry	$ 6	$ 11
Garlits, Don	$ 5	$ 15
Garza, Josele	$ 8	$ 16
Gilmore, Earl *	$ 35	$ 65
Goodyear, Scott	$ 5	$ 8
Goosen, Leo *	$ 30	$ 55
Gordon, Jeff	$ 10	$ 30

Driver	Sig.	SP
Goux, Jules *	$ 25	$ 50
Grant, Harry *	$ 25	$ 50
Grissom, Steve	$ 5	$ 8
Guerrero, Roberto	$ 5	$ 10
Guthrie, Janet	$ 5	$ 10
Gurney, Dan	$ 10	$ 20
Hall, Dean	$ 5	$ 8
Hamilton, Bobby	$ 5	$ 8
Hanks, Sam *	$ 20	$ 40
Harroun, Ray *	$ 100	$ 190
Hartz, Harry *	$ 30	$ 55
Hearne, Eddie *	$ 25	$ 50
Henning, Harry *	$ 30	$ 55
Hepburn, Ralph *	$ 22	$ 50
Hill, Graham *	$ 45	$ 90
Hill, Phil	$ 5	$ 15
Hillin, Bobby	$ 5	$ 8
Horn, Ted *	$ 20	$ 40
Hulman, Tony *	$ 85	$ 165
Hurtubise, Jim	$ 8	$ 16
Irvan, Ernie	$ 6	$ 10
Jarrett, Dale	$ 5	$ 10
Jarrett, Ned	$ 10	$ 18
Johncock, Gordon	$ 7	$ 15

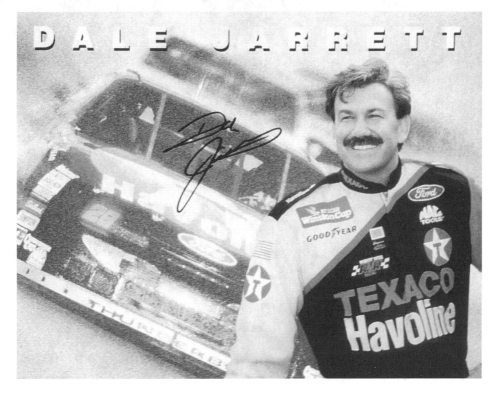

Dale Jarrett autographed handout

Parnelli Jones autographed photo

Driver	Sig.	SP
Johnson, Junior	$ 10	$ 20
Johnson, Tommy, Jr.	$ 4	$ 8
Jones, Parnelli	$ 6	$ 15
Kalitta, Connie	$ 4	$ 8
Kalitta, Scott	$ 6	$ 10

Driver	Sig.	SP
Keech, Ray *	$ 25	$ 50
Kinser, Steve	$ 4	$ 8
Krisiloff, Steve	$ 8	$ 16
Kulwicki, Alan *	$ 18	$ 75
Kurtis, Frank *	$ 40	$ 75
Labonte, Bobby	$ 5	$ 8
Labonte, Terry	$ 7	$ 15
LaJoie, Randy	$ 5	$ 8
Leonard, Joe	$ 5	$ 10
Lewis, Randy	$ 4	$ 8
Lockhart, Frank *	$ 20	$ 40
Lorenzen, Fred	$ 5	$ 10
Luyendyk, Arie	$ 10	$ 20
Mahler, John	$ 8	$ 15
Mansell, Nigel	$ 8	$ 15
Marcenac, Jean *	$ 30	$ 55
Marcis, Dave	$ 4	$ 8
Marlin, Sterling	$ 5	$ 8
Marshall, Mike	$ 4	$ 8
Martin, Mark	$ 8	$ 18
Mast, Rick	$ 4	$ 8
Mayfield, Jeremy	$ 4	$ 8
Mays, Rex *	$ 140	$ 275
McClenathan, Cory	$ 4	$ 8
McCluskey, Roger	$ 8	$ 18
McGrath, Jack *	$ 30	$ 55
McLaren, Bruce *	$ 40	$ 80
Mears, Rick	$ 35	$ 75

Stirling Moss autographed postcard

Driver	Sig.	SP
Meyer, Louis	$ 25	$ 50
Miller, Harry *	$ 35	$ 70
Milton, Tommy *	$ 30	$ 60
Moore, Lou *	$ 25	$ 50
Moss, Stirling	$ 20	$ 40
Muldowney, Shirley	$ 6	$ 18
Mulford, Ralph *	$ 35	$ 70
Muncy, Bill *	$ 25	$ 60
Murphy, Jimmy *	$ 25	$ 55
Musgrave, Ted	$ 5	$ 8
Myers, T. E. *	$ 40	$ 80
Nannini, Alessandro	$ 5	$ 8
Nemechek, Joe	$ 4	$ 8
Noble, Richard	$ 7	$ 14
Nolon, Dennis	$ 5	$ 12
Oldfield, Barney *	$ 165	$ 350
Ongais, Danny	$ 5	$ 10
Palmroth, Tero	$ 5	$ 8
Parsons, Benny	$ 10	$ 20
Parsons, Johnny *	$ 22	$ 45
Parsons, Phil	$ 5	$ 8
Patrese, Riccardo	$ 5	$ 10
Pearson, David	$ 10	$ 20
Penske, Roger	$ 8	$ 15
Petillo, Kelly	$ 50	$ 90

Autographed Joe Nemechek handout

Kyle Petty

Driver	Sig.	SP
Petty, Kyle	$ 8	$ 16
Petty, Lee	$ 15	$ 60
Petty, Richard	$ 10	$ 25
Pillsbury, Art *	$ 25	$ 50
Piquet, Nelson	$ 5	$ 11
Pressley, Robert	$ 4	$ 8
Prost, Alain	$ 5	$ 11
Prudhomme, Don	$ 5	$ 12
Pruett, Scott	$ 5	$ 8
Rahal, Bobby	$ 10	$ 25
Rathmann, Jim	$ 15	$ 30
Resta, Dario *	$ 40	$ 80
Reutemann, Carlos	$ 5	$ 10
Revson, Peter	$ 45	$ 90
Richmond, Tim	$ 5	$ 10
Rickenbacker, Eddie *	$ 100	$ 200
Ricker, Chester	$ 25	$ 50
Roberts, Floyd *	$ 55	$ 140
Roberts, Kenny	$ 5	$ 10
Robertson, George *	$ 25	$ 50
Rose, Mauri *	$ 100	$ 200
Ruby, Lloyd	$ 15	$ 35
Rudd, Ricky	$ 5	$ 10
Rutherford, Johnny	$ 5	$ 12
Ruttman, Troy	$ 10	$ 18
Sacks, Greg	$ 4	$ 8

Ricky Rudd handout

Morgan Shepherd autographed handout

Al Unser

Bobby Unser

Driver	Sig.	SP
Scheckter, Jody	$ 5	$ 10
Schrader, Ken	$ 5	$ 8
Senna, Ayrton*	$ 15	$ 45
Shaw, Wilbur *	$ 240	$ 575
Shelby, Carroll	$ 5	$ 12
Shepherd, Morgan	$ 5	$ 8
Simon, Dick	$ 5	$ 10
Sneva, Tom	$ 10	$ 20
Snyder, George	$ 10	$ 22
Snyder, Johnny *	$ 28	$ 60
Souders, George	$ 50	$ 95
Sparks, Art *	$ 25	$ 50
Speed, Lake	$ 4	$ 8
Spencer, Jimmy	$ 4	$ 8
St. James, Lyn	$ 6	$ 12
Stevens, Myron *	$ 25	$ 55
Stewart, Jackie	$ 10	$ 25

Driver	Sig.	SP
Strong, Lewis *	$ 28	$ 60
Sullivan, Danny	$ 8	$ 18
Theys, Dider	$ 5	$ 8
Thomas, Rene	$ 40	$ 90

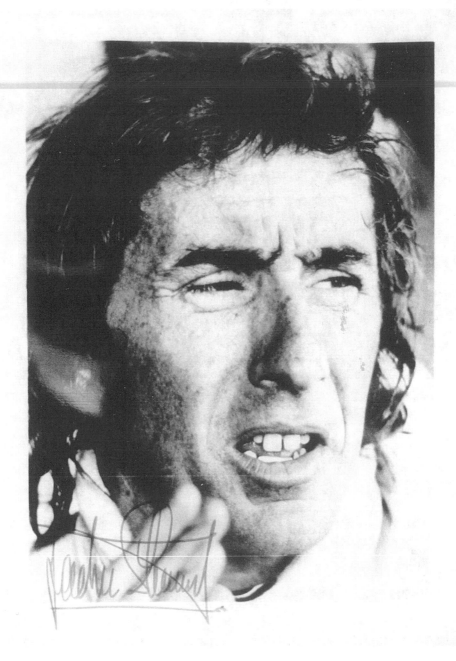

Jackie Stewart autographed photo

Rusty Wallace autographed handout

Dale Earnhardt autograph

Driver	Sig.	SP
Thompson, Mickey *	$ 55	$ 110
Trickle, Dick	$ 5	$ 8
Turner, Roscoe	$ 45	$ 100
Unser, Al	$ 10	$ 20
Unser, Al, Jr.	$ 10	$ 20
Unser, Bobby	$ 10	$ 20
Vanderbilt, William *	$ 50	$ 140
Vukovich, Bill *	$ 165	$ 390
Wagner, Fred *	$ 45	$ 90
Wallace, Kenny	$ 4	$ 8
Wallace, Mike	$ 4	$ 8
Wallace, Rusty	$ 10	$ 25
Waltrip, Darrell	$ 8	$ 16
Waltrip, Michael	$ 6	$ 15
Ward, Rodger	$ 20	$ 50
Watson, A. J.	$ 5	$ 10
Welch, Lew *	$ 25	$ 50
Wilcox, Howard *	$ 30	$ 55
Winfield, Ed *	$ 25	$ 60
Wood, Gar *	$ 25	$ 50
Yarborough, Cale	$ 8	$ 16
Yarborough, Lee Roy	$ 8	$ 16
Yunick, Smokey	$ 5	$ 10

Whereas so many other sports, such as baseball and football, rely on media revenue to offset costs, auto racing relies on corporate sponsorship. This relationship deems it necessary for drivers to maintain a certain public image representative of that sponsor and their products or services. These corporations depend upon the fans attending racing events so they can justify the millions of dollars being spent on their sponsorship. Every driver racing at a top professional level realizes the importance of fans and knows their support is worth taking a few moments out of his schedule to sign autographs. This is why you see a driver such as Mark Martin spending time after a victory at Watkins Glen to sign autographs.

A sign for an autograph session during the New York State Fair

Sources for Obtaining Autographs

There are many ways to obtain auto racing autographs. Many collectors begin by mailing requests directly to the driver (if they have a home address), to his race team or fan club, or to the various motorsports Halls of Fame, who will often forward the letter to the driver.

The Indianapolis 500 Hall of Fame and Museum is one such institution that doesn't mind forwarding fan mail to former winners or current participants as long as it's not within a month of the race. Race preparation is often hectic and may lead to an overlooked or lost letter.

Writing to a driver's race team can also be productive, as they will often see to it that the driver receives the request. If you are unsure of a driver's team you can contact NASCAR, Indy Car, or NHRA for current information. These organizations can also provide you with a list of public relations contacts. For example, you can contact Ken Schrader through Hendrick Motorsports of Harrisburg, NC, or through Muhleman Marketing of Charlotte, NC. Also keep in mind that some teams handle more than one driver. Hendrick Motorsports not only represented Ken Schrader in 1995, but also Jeff Gordon and Terry Labonte.

Most professional level drivers have fan clubs, which are additional contact sources. Although these clubs vary in membership privileges, many are good sources for obtaining autographed material. An excellent example of what fan club membership can provide you with is Ricky Craven's Fan Club. For a single $10.00 membership, you receive a personalized autographed color photo, an 8 x 10 Membership certificate, a quarterly fan club newsletter, a wallet size membership card, a pocket size schedule, a bumper sticker, and a KODIAK #41 hat.

Occasionally, driver home addresses appear in celebrity guides or autograph publications. For example, Al Unser's address at 7625 Cluteal NW, Albuquerque, NM 87121, appeared in the June 1995 issue of Autograph Collector magazine. Listed driver home addresses can be fruitless, though, because people move often, sometimes leaving no forwarding address or short forwarding orders. Don't be afraid to contact other collectors or dealers, many of which specialize in current celebrity addresses.

Corporate sponsorship often requires that drivers make numerous public appearances. From car dealerships to auto shows, drivers know their sponsor wants them to be recognized with their products or services. If you live near a city that has an annual racing event, pay close attention to local advertising, as drivers will make personal appearances while they are in an area for the race. While en route to Watkins Glen in 1995, Dale Earnhardt made an appearance in Syracuse, New York, at a local Chevrolet dealer. One hour before his scheduled appearance, 1,400 people were in line. One fan had begun waiting at 5:00 p.m. the previous day. Knowing how valuable his public is, Dale Earnhardt stayed as long as possible to sign anything and everything he could at no charge.

Dale Earnhardt at a press conference before an appearance at a Chevrolet dealership in Syracuse, New York

NASCAR fans of all ages wait hours for a single signature of their favorite driver

Racetracks are obvious sources for obtaining autographs. Many of these facilities offer access to the paddock or garage areas. This is where the cars are prepared for the event. Drivers commonly wander into these areas, so placing yourself strategically between the pit, the paddock, and a driver's transporter will certainly increase your chances of getting an autograph.

Most racing events begin on Thursday with practice rounds. The relaxed environment and smaller crowds on Thursday and Friday make these days more opportune to signature acquisition. While it is true that both Saturday and Sunday can provide a collector with opportunities, they are often diminished by the larger crowds.

Fan access to the pits or paddock is restricted in NASCAR Winston Cup racing. Track size often prohibits access to these areas to all but essential personnel. Aware of this, drivers generally make an effort to sign through fences, at garage entrances, or even at a designated area in the infield. Many collectors are familiar with "Autograph Alley" at Pocono International Raceway in Long Pond, Pennsylvania. This small area between the garages and the pits has holes in the fence and a small grandstand to accommodate collectors waiting for their favorite driver to walk by.

The PPG Indy Car series differs from NASCAR and allows access to paddocks and garages. With the exception of the Indianapolis 500, fans can purchase paddock passes (under $50), depending upon the venue. While the cars are being prepared you can wonder through the open spaces with hopes of running into someone worth adding to your collection. This is especially exciting to fans, as numerous celebrities are associated with Indy Car teams and drivers. Mid-Ohio, Laguna Seca, and Pennsylvania International Raceway are three track favorites among auto racing collectors.

The Indianapolis 500 is a unique event, not only to the sport, but also to collectors. It's easy to imagine why autograph acquisition can be limited, as over 350,000 attend the event and upwards of 150,000 can show up for a weekday practice. Garage passes are available (under $100) and are good for every day except race day. Although this will give you access to the area, practice for the event can last for a month, requiring an extraordinary amount of a collector's time.

The highest driver accessibility of all the circuits is the National Hot Rod Association (NHRA). Most of these drivers spend significant time honoring autograph requests. Paddock and staging areas are typically available for fans for under $40. Most autograph fans huddle outside transporters where drivers typically sign between rounds.

Fan access can vary from track to track, so when you are ordering your tickets, ask about the available credentials. Analyzing the advantages and disadvantages of each form of obtaining racing auto-

Rusty Wallace autographed photo (Photo courtesy of Miller Genuine Draft Racing Team)

graphs can make you a more efficient collector. If you know a driver responds with an authentic signature via mail, you may want to focus on the more difficult drivers to acquire.

Autographed Racing Card Inserts

Not particularly cost effective and certainly not predictable, autographed racing card inserts are another method of acquiring signatures. There is a great deal of excitement involved when you are searching through packs of auto racing trading cards, hoping to find an autographed insert. As a collector area of specialization, however, it is restricted to those few who have less concern for cost and greater interest in production or availability. Of all the sports trading cards, auto racing autographed inserts and premiums seem to have the greatest collector appeal.

The result of this marketing approach, which gained significant momentum in 1992, has lured many trading card collectors into the field of autographs. What began as a buying incentive from card manufacturers has now created a whole new hobby niche of collectors.

While many trading card dealers continue to complain about new card issues, they praise the increased use of autographed inserts. Most auto racing collectors welcome the change, saying it has increased their interest in the hobby.

If value is any indication of collector interest, just look at the appreciation over the last twelve months in the 1992 Traks Autograph complete set of ten. Many price guides have it on an annual appreciation rate of ten to fifteen percent, with the Earnhardt/Petty (A1) combination card well above the $200 level.

1995 Winston Cup Champion Jeff Gordon autographs a Racing Champion's die cast box

A Trend Toward Auto Racing's Use of an Autopen

The popularity of some of the drivers, particularly on the NASCAR circuit, has led to the use of automatic writing devices to answer autograph requests. The Autopen and other new technologies duplicate a driver's signature, making it difficult for a novice collector to determine its authenticity. Although these devices create examples that don't have to superimpose exactly one hundred percent, many often do. Sending out multiple requests or more than one item to be signed can provide you with enough examples for comparison. A quick glance under a magnifying glass can often provide an improved look at the strokes in a signature. If they appear unnatural or have strange accumulations of ink, you may have an inauthentic signature. A recent response to a mail request of mine for an autograph of Jeff Gordon turned out to be a mechanical signature. A knowledge of these devices and a nice selection of Gordon in-person signatures for comparison made it extremely easy for me to make my determination.

Postcards, Press Kits, and Paper Collectibles

Postcards, press kits, and other forms of paper-based collectibles are often overlooked by auto racing collectors; yet, they can be one of the most intriguing areas of collecting. Prior to the growth in trading cards, many drivers often handed out postcards (4" x 6") or giant sheets (11" x 17"). Typically these promotional items featured a color or black and white photograph of the driver and his car on the front side and text detailing the driver, sponsor, and car on the back. Similar to trading cards, these handouts were updated every year.

During the 1970s, oil companies became notorious for producing these handouts in massive quantities for distribution to drivers, dealers, customers, track owners, and race promoters.

Postcards, which date back to the beginning of auto racing, became one of the most popular mediums for promotion. The Indianapolis Motor Speedway was issuing postcards before World War II

A look inside a 1995 Ricky Craven press kit

Bobby Unser postcard

Arie Luyendyk handout

and Daytona International Speedway followed the lead when it opened in 1959. As the popularity of this form grew, so did the variations and price. No longer were postcards given away; they became a strong revenue base for track souvenir stands.

Individual drivers also produced postcards, which were found to be particularly useful in responding to autograph requests. For example, if you requested an autograph from Bobby Unser in 1980, he would respond by mailing you an autographed 6" x 8" color postcard. The postcard featured Unser and his car in a color photo montage on the front and a very simple back containing text primarily associated with copyright. If you wrote to Stirling Moss requesting an autograph in 1981, he typically responded with a nice letter and a 3-6/8" x 5-6/8" black and white postcard, which, like the note, was signed.

In the late 1950s, drag racing was the first racing form to up-size its handouts. Many sponsors opted for 8" x 10" black and white photographs or handouts. This was prompted by the increased access to pit areas. Corporations wanted greater exposure to potential customers and the smaller postcard size wasn't enough.

The natural evolution for these handouts included color photography and eventually the increased use of graphics. The first color handout is often attributed to Eddie Hill's Double Dragon gas dragster. This piece measured 6" x 9" and unlike similar pieces, didn't have a postcard format on its reverse side. Eventually, other manufacturers and even sanctioning bodies, such as NHRA, began to recognize this form of marketing, as well as its sales potential, and began to issue their own.

Increased driver popularity and the emergence of "Funny Cars" during the 1960s spurred the production of postcards and handouts. Consumers loved it, as the free items were often handed to drivers for an autograph.

A Quaker State sponsored Scott Brayton handout

By the 1970s, oil companies such as Quaker State, Wynns, and Witco expanded the idea by producing handouts of each of the drivers they sponsored. Pennzoil produced 150 different handouts in 1974. Its "Superstar" title series featured drivers from all forms of auto racing.

Model makers Revell and Crager followed suit by producing their own sets. While Revell opted for a smaller size, the Crager 5-Second Club handouts were extremely popular with both race fans

USAir/Jasper racing handout

Ted Musgrave handout

Handouts featuring Teo Fabi and Kenny Bernstein

and collectors. The Crager set commemorated the first sixteen drivers to break the six-second barrier on a quarter-mile track.

By the 1980s, virtually every driver in every form of auto racing had individual handouts to give to his fans. Although exact production numbers are not known, it's fair to assume that popular drivers, such as Richard Petty, had large quantities of handouts produced. Surprisingly, many of these handouts prior to 1985 are not easily found, because unless they were autographed they were not often kept.

Handouts currently produced typically use thin cardboard stock at a size of 8" x 10" or 8-1/2" x 11". The front is often a full color photo or photo montage of the driver and his car, while the back utilizes a single color ink, usually black, and often includes a photograph. For example, a typically used Jeff Gordon handout (8" x 10") for 1995 follows the format previously mentioned, with the reverse containing biographical information and career highlights. Stated at the bottom of the reverse side of the Gordon handout is, "COMPLIMENTARY – NOT FOR SALE." Dale Jarrett's primary handout for 1995 is larger (8-1/2" x 11") and has no photograph on the back, but does utilize four different colors of ink. Printed near the bottom of Jarrett's card on the reverse side is, " THIS CARD IS FREE, COMPLIMENTS OF TEXACO/HAVOLINE."

Like trading cards, a postcard or handout's condition is also paramount to its value. Since these items have always been free, both fans and collectors have paid little attention to their condition. This is why the older vintage items are so very hard to find. Postcards have benefited from the strong base of collectors for this form, while the contrary has been true for handouts. The popularity of autograph collecting has helped handouts, as this form is typically used for that purpose. Once a handout is autographed it is less likely to end up in the trash.

Unfortunately for handout and postcard collectors, there is no comprehensive listing of issues with values. The market for handouts is still in its infancy and it is difficult to gauge its eventual popularity, but postcards have a stronger and more mature market base, making it easier to gauge an issue's value.

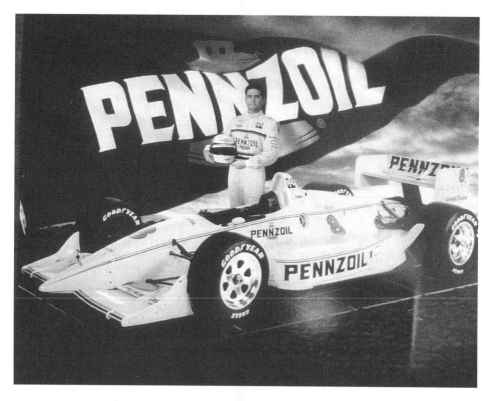

A Bobby Unser postcard

Although handouts have always been free, assembling a collection that includes, for example, a Dale Earnhardt handout of each year that he has won the Winston Cup Championship, is not going to be an easy task. This might be one of the few cases in memorabilia collecting in which it is easier to find the form autographed than unautographed.

Schedules are also produced individually, or may be printed on the reverse side of a handout. Woods Brothers Racing in 1995 did both. The schedule was printed on the back of their handout and on a 2-2/8" x 3-1/2" folded piece. Schedules, which are also typically free, have been a popular form of collectible in other sports such as baseball, but have yet to draw significant collector interest in auto racing.

Press/Media Kits

Overlooked currently by most auto racing collectors, press kits/media kits have yet to find their niche in the collectibles market. Although these kits are not or can not be sold, they are certainly worth holding on to. These kits are sought after and collected in other sports, especially boxing, and it is only a matter of time before they establish a strong demand in the auto racing collectibles market. Most of these information packages are assembled by the racing teams or sponsors and made available to the media assigned to report on a specific race. The primary function of the information package is to provide reporters and journalists with the necessary information to accurately and efficiently report on a driver or race. For members of the media, a thorough press kit means improved, accurate, and simplified reporting. There is no need to dig out the record books for statistics or waste time chasing down drivers for easy answers to often redundant questions. For the racing team, a comprehensive and accurate information kit usually means increased pre-race media coverage, greater sponsor exposure, and accurate reporting.

Sponsorship means everything to auto racing, so the greater the media exposure the better. This stresses the importance of a strong media kit, especially for a lesser known driver. Former and current NASCAR Winston Cup champions typically have comprehensive and extensive media kits. A common media/press kit is 9" x 12" with dual inside pockets for the storage of press releases. These press releases update the media on current developments with the racing teams and are typically stapled 8-1/2" x 11" letterhead sheets. These releases vary in their significance and are updated or removed from the kit at the appropriate time. Often included in a press kit is a black and white sheet of photographs (8" x 10") for media use, a handout, and even a media guide. The photographs typically include single shots of the driver, car owner, crew chief, and car. For example, GM Goodwrench Service Racing follows the typical press kit format listed previously, but includes die-cut pockets featuring Dale Earn-

The cover of the Mike Wallace Heilig-Meyers Racing '95 press kit

The Meineke Racing Team press kit

hardt and Rick Childress on one side and the crew alongside the car on the other. A 68-page 1995 media guide (4" x 7") is often included along with a handout, photographs (contact sheet), and current press releases.

Kellogg's Racing utilizes the same approach for press kits, but staples a 27-page insert into the folder to complete their media kit. This excellent black and white insert contains everything you would ever want to know about Terry Labonte, Hendrick Motorsports, and the Kellogg's company. There is even a page dedicated to collectors' cereal boxes.

The Miller Genuine Draft Team Penske approach to its media guide is a 68-page plastic spiral bound booklet with a pocket inside the front cover. This comprehensive booklet details the racing team and the career of Rusty Wallace. The cover features an outstanding illustration of Rusty Wallace and his car in a moonlit setting.

After reading through a racing press kit or media guide it is easy to understand why they might appeal to both fans and collectors. Most of these information packages have attractive covers

The cover of Kellogg's Racing press kit. Within the packet is a page dedicated to collector's cereal boxes.

or designs and are loaded with statistics— career records, track-by-track results, and biographical data.

Since these information packages are available primarily to members of the media, their distribution is limited. Most collectors will have to trade for them if they become available in the market or try to acquire dated material from members of the media. For unbound or unattached kits, it is difficult for collectors to determine if the package is complete. If any pieces are missing in a press kit, it is most often the black and white photographs. Upon the photographs' use by the media, they are seldom returned to the kit; instead, they are documented and inserted into a photographic file. Another barrier to collecting the kits is that some are simply photocopies and easy to reproduce. As a beginning collector you are probably better off acquiring only attached or bound information kits such as the 1995 Kellogg's Racing Team media kit.

These information packages are an integral part of the history of auto racing and as such are valuable to historians and researchers. It will be interesting to monitor whether they find a niche in the collectibles market.

The cover of the Texaco/Havoline Racing press kit

Sample Media Kit Contents – 1995 Kellogg's Racing Media Kit

Attractive die-cut color two pocket folder (9" x 12").
Twenty-eight-page black and white, two-sided media kit insert, attached by three staples to center of folder.

Pages 1-2	Introduction to Racing Team
Pages 3-4	Quick Facts – Terry Labonte
Pages 5-6	Quick Quotes – Terry Labonte
Page 7	Quick Facts – Gary Dehart
Page 8	Quick Quotes – Gary Dehart, Rick Hendrick
Page 9	Quick Facts – Rick Hendrick
Page 10	Team Statistics – Hendrick Motorsports
Page 11	Team Roster/Pit Crew Diagram
Page 12	Quick Facts – Jimmy Johnson, Jeff Andrews, Eddie Dickerson
Page 13	#5 Hendrick Chevrolet Career History
Page 14	#5 Hendrick Chevrolet Team Victories
Page 15	1994 Highlights/#5 Kellogg's Team
Page 16	1994 Results – Terry Labonte
Page 17	Quick Facts – The Kellogg's Company
Page 18	Collectors' Boxes – The Kellogg's Company
Page 19	Career Statistics – Terry Labonte
Page 20	Career Totals – Terry Labonte
Pages 21-25	Track Statistics
Page 26	Career Busch Series Statistics – Terry Labonte
Page 27	1995 NASCAR Winston Cup Series Schedule

Assorted Racing Collectibles

Selected entries and checklists, some with value guide

Auto Racing Arms

❏ Morgan Shepherd   Engraved 24 kt. gold and nickel Remington collectible $1,300
shotgun with a limited edition of 200, with presentation
case and optional show case

Auto Racing Artwork

Jeanne Barnes & Associates

Driver	Edition	Price
❏ Ernie Irvan	$ 750	$ 125
❏ Rusty Wallace	$ 750	$ 125
❏ Alan Kulwicki	$ 707	$ 107
❏ Darrell Waltrip	$ 700	$ 95
❏ 7 & 7 Gold	$ 2,000	$ 200

Auto Racing Collector Bottles – Signature Series

Fan Fuelers – 32 oz. Motor Sports Drink Bottles

❏ Derrike Cope	$6	❏ Mark Martin	$6
❏ Bill Elliott	$6	❏ Kyle Petty	$6
❏ Harry Gant	$6	❏ Ken Schrader	$6
❏ Jeff Gordon	$6	❏ Morgan Shepherd	$6
❏ Ernie Irvan	$6	❏ Kenny Wallace	$6
❏ Dale Jarrett	$6	❏ Rusty Wallace	$6
❏ Bobby Labonte	$6	❏ Darrell Waltrip	$6
❏ Terry Labonte	$6	❏ Michael Waltrip	$6
❏ Sterling Marlin	$6	❏ Winston Cup Series	$6

Auto Racing Cards – Non-Paper Based – selected entries with value guide

Highland Mint

Driver		Edition	Price
❏ Earnhardt, Dale	❏ Gold	500	$800
	❏ Silver	1,000	$325
	❏ Bronze	5,000	$100

☐ Gordon, Jeff	☐ Silver	1,000	$250
	☐ Bronze	5,000	$ 70
☐ Irvan, Ernie	☐ Silver	1,000	$215
	☐ Bronze	5,000	$ 50
☐ Martin, Mark	☐ Silver	250	$245
	☐ Bronze	1,500	$ 70
☐ Wallace, Rusty	☐ Silver	1,000	$240
	☐ Bronze	5,000	$ 60

Auto Racing Cereal Boxes – checklist

Official Cereals of NASCAR

Kellogg's Corn Flakes

- ☐ 1991   No. 41 yellow car
- ☐ 1992   Richard Petty
- ☐ 1992   No. 41 yellow car, head shots of Greg Sacks and Harry Hyde
- ☐ 1993   No. 14 painted yellow car
- ☐ 1994   Terry Labonte with cereal bowl
- ☐ 1994   No. 5 car bursting through box
- ☐ 1994   No. 5 crew during pit stop
- ☐ 1994   Dale Earnhardt with No. 3 car
- ☐ 1995   Dale Earnhardt – both single-pack and dual-pack boxes
- ☐ 1995   Terry Labonte, Darrell Waltrip, and Monte Carlo
- ☐ 1995   Three-box collector series featuring Terry Labonte:
- ☐ Victory lane shot of Labonte
- ☐ Finish line shot of No. 5 Hendrick Motorsports Chevrolet Monte Carlo
- ☐ Corny – cereal spokescharacter in race uniform

Kellogg's Frosted Mini-Wheats

- ☐ 1994   Jeff Gordon with cereal bowl
- ☐ 1994   Sam Bass artwork of Jeff Gordon
- ☐ 1995   "The Kid & The Champ" – Gordon, Earnhardt
- ☐ 1995   Jeff Gordon – Indianapolis Victory Lane photograph, also Frosted Mini-Wheats (Bite-Size)
- ☐ 1995   Jeff Gordon head shot with No. 24 car crossing finish line

Kellogg's Frosted Flakes

- ☐ 1995   Tony the Tiger in racing uniform
- ☐ 1995   Bill Elliott with Tony the Tiger I
- ☐ 1995   Bill Elliott with Tony the Tiger II

Kellogg's Raisin Bran

- ☐ 1993   Terry Labonte on back
- ☐ 1995   "The Waltrips"

Official Toaster Pastries of NASCAR

Kellogg's Pop Tarts

- ☐ 1995   Terry Labonte – card on back (all seven flavors)

Official Breakfast Bars of NASCAR

(To be announced)

The front and back panels of a box of Kellogg's Frosted Mini-Wheats featuring "The Kid & The Champ"

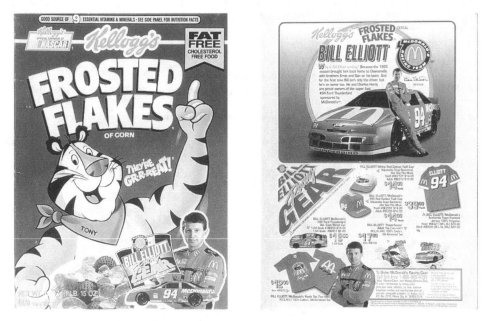

The front and back panels of Kellogg's Frosted Flakes advertising Bill Elliott racing gear. Beginning with the '95 season, McDonald's became Bill's and the Elliott/Hardy racing team's sponsor of the #94 Ford Thunderbird.

Official Frozen Waffles of NASCAR

(To be announced)

Note: 1995 is the first year any of the boxes were distributed nationally

Auto Racing Comics – selected entries with value guide

All-Time Sports

    ❑ 4 Auto Racing (c) $ 120

Crown Comics – Golfing/McCombs Publications, Winter 1944

    ❑ 7 JFa, AF, MB (c) Race Car (c) $ 165

A cover of the No. 18 "Revenge at Riverside" comic from the Charlton Comics Grand Prix series

Grand Prix – Charlton Comics

    ❑ 16-31

Hot Rod Comics – Fawcett Publications, 1952

❑ N# BP, BP (c) F: Clint Curtis $ 150
❑ 2 BP, BP (c) Safety Come in First $ 85
❑ 3 BP, BP (c) The Racing Game $ 45
❑ 4 BP, BP (c) Bonneville National Championships $ 45
❑ 5 BP, BP (c) $ 45
❑ 6 BP, BP (c) Race to Death, 2/53 $ 45
❑ 7 $ 40

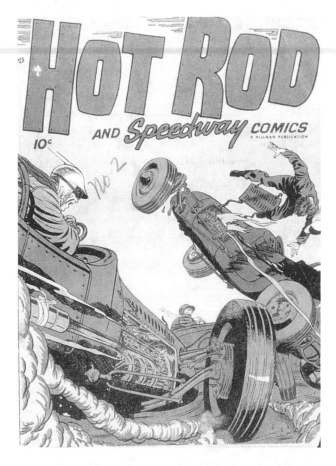

The No. 2 cover from the Hot Rod and Speedway Comics series published by Hillman

Hot Rod & Speedway – Hillman Periodicals, Feb.-March 1953

❑ 1 $ 120
❑ 2 $ 85
❑ 3-5 $ 45

Hot Rod King – Ziff-Davis, Fall 1982

❑ 1 $ 140

Hot Rod Racers – Charlton Comics, December 1964

❑ 1	$ 125
❑ 2-5	$ 18
❑ 6-15, July 1967	$ 12
❑ 16-31 (became Grand Prix – see above listing under Grand Prix)	

Hot Rods & Racing Cars – Motormag/Charlton, November 1951

❑ 1	$ 120
❑ 2	$ 65
❑ 3	$ 55
❑ 4-10	$ 45
❑ 11-20	$ 35
❑ 21-40	$ 30
❑ 41-50	$ 25
❑ 51-70	$ 20
❑ 71-100	$ 15
❑ 101-120	$ 11

Jack Armstrong – Parents' Institute, November 1947

❑ 9 Mystery of the Midgets	$ 40

Legends of NASCAR – Vortex Comics

❑ 1 HT, Bill Elliott ($1.50 cover price) 15,000 copies	$ 60
❑ 1a ($2.00 cover price) 45,000 copies	$ 14
❑ 1b (third printing) 80,000	$ 7
❑ 2 Richard Petty	$ 6
❑ 2a hologram (c) error	$ 12

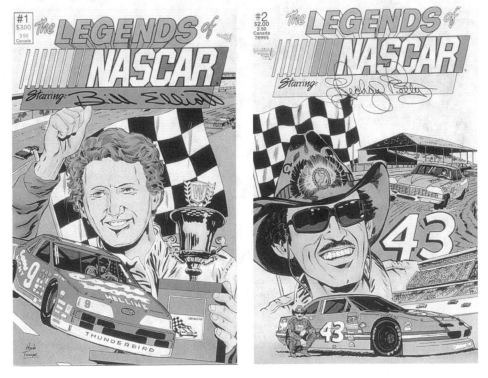

Bill Elliot and Richard Petty "Legends of NASCAR" by Vortex Comics

Richard Petty "Legends of NASCAR" comic with hologram, by Vortex Comics

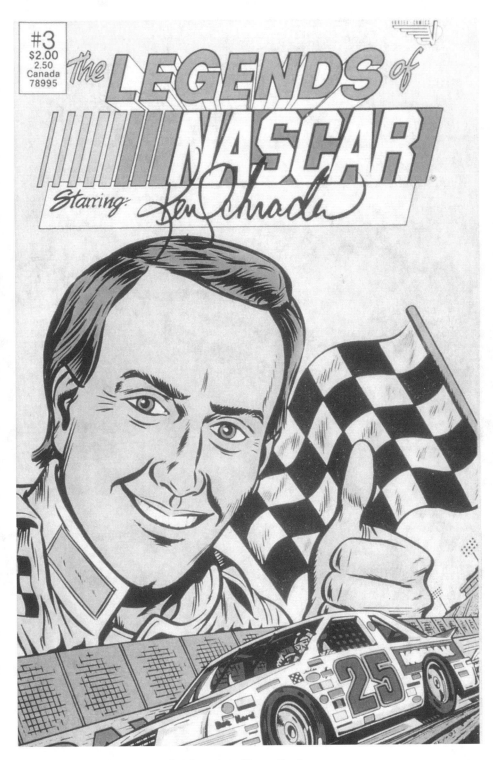

Ken Schrader "Legends of NASCAR" comic by Vortex Comics

251

Bobby Allison "Legends of NASCAR" comic by Vortex Comics

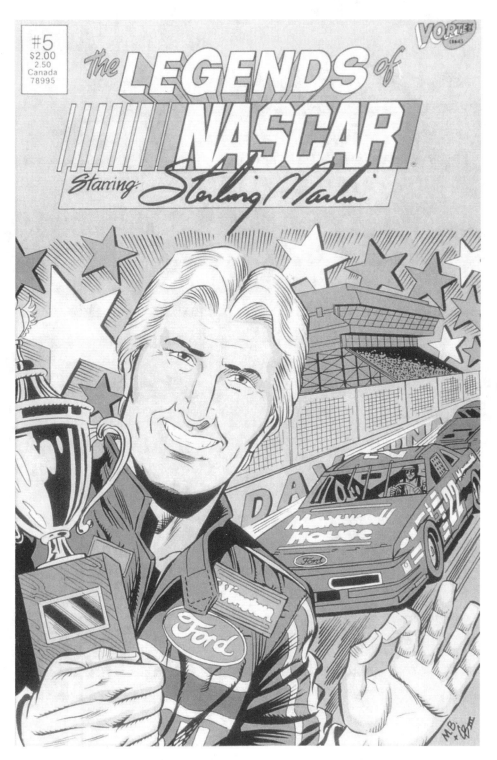

Sterling Marlin "Legends of NASCAR" comic by Vortex Comics

Benny Parsons "Legends of NASCAR" comic by Vortex Comics

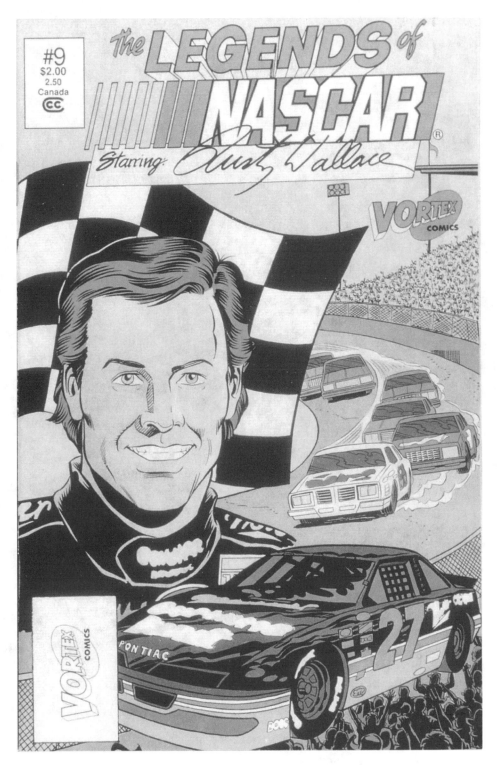

Rusty Wallace "Legends of NASCAR" comic by Vortex Comics

255

Talladega Superspeedway "Legends of NASCAR" Comic by Vortex Comics

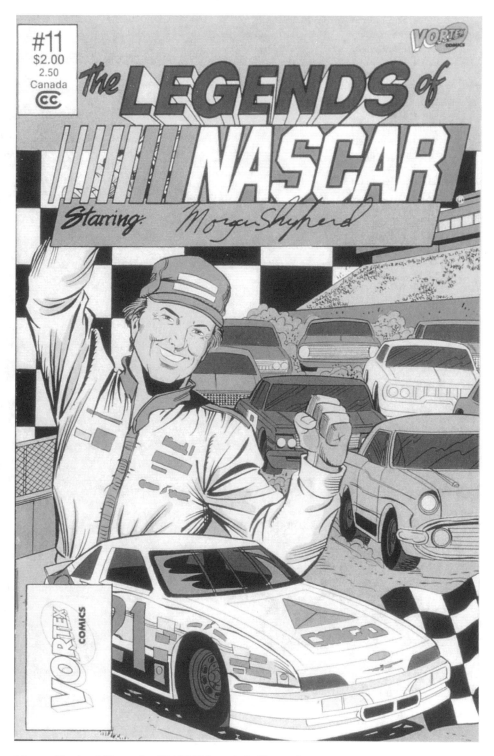

Morgan Shepherd "Legends of NASCAR" comic by Vortex Comics

❏ 2b hologram (c) corrected	$ 10
❏ 3 Ken Schrader	$ 4.50
❏ 3a hologram (c)	$ 6
❏ 4 Bob Allison	$ 10
❏ 4a hologram (c)	$ 15
❏ 5 Sterling Marlin	$ 4
❏ 5a hologram (c)	$ 6.50
❏ 6 Bill Elliott	$ 15
❏ 6a hologram (c)	$ 10
❏ 7 Junior Johnson	$ 4
❏ 7a hologram (c)	$ 5
❏ 8 Benny Parsons	$ 3
❏ 8a hologram (c)	$ 5
❏ 9 Rusty Wallace	$ 5
❏ 9a hologram (c)	$ 7
❏ 10 Talladega	$ 3
❏ 10a hologram (c)	$ 5
❏ 11 Morgan Shepherd	$ 6
❏ 11a hologram (c)	$ 5
❏ 12 Richard Petty Salute	$ 5
❏ 12a hologram (c)	$ 5
❏ 13 Harry Gant	$ 3
❏ 13a hologram (c)	$ 5

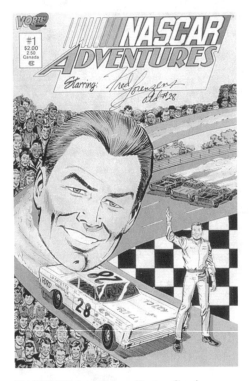

Fred Lorenzen "NASCAR Adventures" comic by Vortex Comics

NASCAR Adventures – Vortex Comics

❏ 1 Fred Lorenzen	$ 2
❏ 2 Richard Petty	$ 2
❏ 5 Ernie Irvan	$ 2
❏ 7 Mark Martin	$ 2

Richard Petty "NASCAR Adventures" comic by Vortex Comics

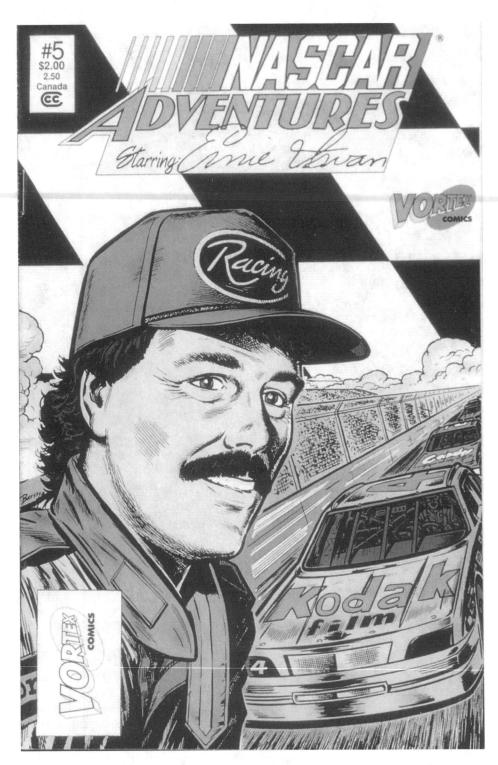

Ernie Irvan "NASCAR Adventures" comic by Vortex Comics

Mark Martin "NASCAR Adventures" comic by Vortex Comics

Supersnipe Comics – Formerly: Army & Navy Comics

    ❑ 4-6 Race Car Driver $ 90

True Comics – Parents' Magazine Press, April 1941

    ❑ 21 Car Racing $ 75
    ❑ 60 Car Racing $ 35

Auto Racing Cutlery – selected entries with value guide

Case Cutlery

Driver	Pattern	Production #	Title	Value
Allison, Bobby	Trapper	1000	1988 Daytona Winner	$165
	Coke	1200	The Legend	$250
	Coke	600	The Legend	$300
Allison, Davey	Trapper	2000	Rookie of the Year	$275
	Coke	1000	1992 Hardcharger	$665
	Trapper	2000	Hardcharger Trapper	$140
	Trapper	2000	Tribute to Davey	$140
	Trap/Bowie	500	Mint Set	$775
Baker, Buddy	Trapper	1200	First to Break 200 mph	$100
Bodine, Geoff	Trapper	1000	1986 Daytona Winner	$125
Bonnett, Neil	Trapper	1000	Alabama Gang	$300
Earnhardt, Dale	Trapper	2000	Winston Cup Champ '80, '86, '87	$145
	Trapper	2000	Winston Cup Champ '86, '87	$165
	Trapper	1500	Winston Cup Champ '90	$200
	Trapper	1000	Top Gun	$350
	Trapper	1500	RCR Enterprises	$200
	Trapper	2000	1991 Winston Cup Champion	$220
	Hunter	1500	Five Times (Marble Top)	$275
	Trap/Bowie	1000	Five Knives with Bowie	$1,000
	Trapper	1000	Three-Time Winston Winner	$250
	Trap/Kodiak	750	Seven-Knife Wall Set	$1,550
	Coke	1500	Six-Time Champ	$385
Elliott, Bill	Coke	1500	Two Knives – Bill and Jr.	$440
	Trapper	600	Awesome Bill	$950
	Trapper	1200	Winston Million	$500
	Trapper	3500	Winston Cup Champ 1988	$225
	Coke	1000	Driver of the Year	$400
	Coke	1500	10 Million Dollar Bill	$450
	Coke	300	10 Million Mint	$440
Gant, Harry	Trapper	1000	Handsome Harry	$220
	Trapper	250	Harry #33	$220
	Trapper	250	Harry #7 – Busch Grand National	$220
	Trapper	333	Farewell Tour 1994	$220
Gordon, Jeff	Trapper	100	Rookie of the Year	$250
Hamilton, Bobby	Trapper	168	Rookie of the Year	$220
Jarrett, Dale	Coke Stag	1000	Crunch Car	$210
Johnson, Junior	Trapper	1000	Ford	$125
	Trapper	2000	Last American Hero	$135
Kulwicki, Alan	Trapper	1000	1992 Winston Cup Champ	$220
	Trapper	1000	Tribute to Alan	$220
	Gold Bowie	250	Tribute to Alan	$650
Lorenzen, Fred	Trapper	500	1960 Golden Boy	$135
Marlin, Sterling	Trapper	500	Two-Time Winston Cup Champion	$110
Martin, Mark	Trapper	1000	Rising Star	$220

Driver	Pattern	Production #	Title	Value
McDuffie, J. D.	Bull Dog	350	Last Great Independent	$700
Myers, Bill	Trapper	500	1955 National Champion	$110
Myers, Bobby	Trapper	500	NC State Champion	$110
Pearson, David	Trapper	1200	1960 Rookie of the Year	$95
Petty, Richard	Sod Buster	Unknown	Richard Petty	$1,350
	G/D Barlow	Unknown	Richard Petty	$1,350
	Coke	1000	The King (Red Bone)	$900
	Coke	1000	The King (Blue Bone)	$900
	Coke	32	The King	$1,650
	Coke	2000	Tribute to the Legend	$450
Petty, Kyle	Buffalo	600	King of the Rock	$275
Petty, Lee	Trapper	2000	Stock Car Legend	$100
	Hunter	500	Stock Car Legend	$200
Pettys	3 Styles	1500	The Legend	$850
Pressley, Robert	Trapper	59	Future Champion	$1,000
Roberts, Fireball	Trapper	1000	Purple Pontiac	$110
Scott, Wendell	Trapper	250	Wendell Scott	$145
Shepherd, Morgan	Trapper	Unsure	Morgan Shepherd/Wood Brothers	$70
Wallace, Rusty	Coke	1000	1989 Winston Cup Champion	$275
	Trapper	300	Rusty's Back	$175
Waltrip, Darrell	Trapper	2000	Top Money Winner 1988	$155
	Coke	1000	Three-Time Winston Cup Champion	$260
Yarborough, Cale	Trapper	2000	Tribute to a Legend	$125
Asst. Drivers	Lockback	N/A	Packed with Maxx Card	$23
	Lockback	N/A	Kulwicki and D. Allison Knives w/Card	$35
Winston Set	Assorted	1500	20th Anniversary Set with Chest	$6,000

Hen/Rooster Cutlery

Driver	Pattern	Production #	Title	Value
Earnhardt, Dale	Trapper	2000	Winston Cup Champ '86, '87	$100
Petty, Lee	Trapper	2000	Stock Car Legend	$100
Yarborough, Cale	Trapper	2000	Tribute to a Legend	$100

Gerber Cutlery

	Pattern	Production #	Title	Value
Mac Tool Set	Lockback	1000	3 Knives – Earnhardt, Gant, and R. Petty	$400

Schrade Cutlery

	Pattern	Production #	Title	Value
Gant, Harry	Lockback	N/A	Harry Gant	$40

Frost Cutlery

Theme: "7 & 7" "The Merger of Two Racing Champions"

Item #	Description	Issue	Retail
SET-PE	Two Case 52100 Trappers, 12" x 16"	1,000	$666.67
CASE-PE	14" overall Bowie w/walnut display	1,000	$733.33
FC-PE	Two piece knives w/display box	2,500	$149.95
17-645FW/PE	Frostwood Bowie w/walnut display	5,000	$149.95
17-155PE	Single 17-155SS knife w/gift box	N/A	$38.95
D-KPE	4" closed lockback knife	N/A	$40.95

Theme: "The Intimidator Rolls a 7"

Item #	Description	Issue	Retail
CASE-DE/7T	14" overall Case Bowie knife w/display	1,000	$733.33
17-645FW/7T	11-1/2" overall Frostwood Bowie w/stand	2,500	$140.35
FC-DE 94	Set of (FC105SS/FC152SS) knives w/display box	2,500	$140.35
17-155RCR	3-3/4" knife w/display box – RCR 1994 WCC	N/A	$35.95
D-KO3/7T	4" knife w/display box – Earnhardt 7-Time Champion	N/A	$38.95
D-KRCR/94	4" knife w/display box – RCR 1994 WCC	N/A	$39.95
17-155DE/7T	3-3/4" knife w/display box – Earnhardt 7-Time Champ.	N/A	$35.95

This figurine from Salvino Sports Legends features Richard Petty

Auto Racing Figurines and Statues – selected entries with value guide

Endurance LTD – Checklist

- ❑ Clark, Jimmy
- ❑ Hill, Graham
- ❑ Mansell, Nigel
- ❑ Schumacher, Michael
- ❑ Senna, Ayrton

Racing Champions – 1991

- ❑ Cope, Derrike$6
- ❑ Elliott, Bill$10
- ❑ Hamilton, Bobby$6
- ❑ Marlin, Sterling$8
- ❑ Petty, Richard$15
- ❑ Schrader, Kenny$7

Ricker Pewter Statues

Driver	Ed. Size	Value
❑ Mario Andretti	500	$ 900
❑ Rick Mears	500	$ 450
❑ Don Garlits	650	$ 500

Salvino Sports Legends

Driver	#Issued	Value
❑ Foyt, A. J.	1,500 – Hand-signed	$ 275
❑ Petty, Richard	2,000 – Hand-signed	$ 300
	❑ 300 – Hand-signed Special Edition	$ 500
	❑ "Farewell," 2,500	$ 300
	❑ 8" Cold-Cast Pewter, 2,500	$ 110
❑ Waltrip, Darrell	1,500 – Hand-signed	$ 275

S.A.M. Bobbing Head Dolls

❑ Elliott, Bill	Issue: 5,000, 8"	$ 40

Sports Impressions

❑ Gordon, Jeff	Autographed, 975	$ 170
❑ Jarrett, Dale	Autographed, 975	$ 140
❑ Petty, Kyle	Autographed, 975	$ 15
❑ Wallace, Rusty	Autographed, 975	$ 155
❑ Waltrip, Darrell	Autographed, 975	$ 140

Auto Racing Games – selected entries with value guide

❑ A & P Motor Car Relay Race, Coast to Coast, Leg 4, (1930s), A & P cereal box	$55
❑ APBA Saddle Racing Game (APBA 1974)	$55
❑ Auto Race (D&M Co. 1920s)	$85
❑ Auto Race (Milton Bradley, 1920s)	$85
❑ Auto Race (Milton Bradley, 1930s) Radio Series	$140
❑ Auto Race (Gotham Steel, 1930s) metal	$145
❑ Auto Race Game (Milton Bradley, 1925)	$450
❑ Auto Race Knapp Electro Game with air, includes other sports (Knapp, 1929)	$185
❑ Brownie Auto Race (Jeanette Toy & Novelty, 1920s)	$165
❑ Cannonball Run (Cadaco, 1981) movie adaptation	$17

❑ Car Race & Game Hunt (Wilder, 1920s)	$140
❑ Champion Road Race (Champion Spark Plugs premium, 1934)	$140
❑ Circle Racer Board Game (1988)	$12
❑ Combination Four Games, Auto Race, Army & Navy, and Game Hunt (Wilder, 1920s)	$140
❑ Combination Board, Road Race and Air Race (Wilder, 1928)	$225
❑ Cross Country Racer (1940s) windup cars	$115
❑ Create-A-Race, Track Images – can be used as a game, Charlotte Motor Speedway	$25
❑ Daytona 500 Race Game (Milton Bradley, 1989)	$25
❑ Empire Auto Races (Empire, 1950s)	$35
❑ Famous 500 Mile Race Game (1988)	$15
❑ Flip It, Auto Race & Transcontinental Tour, (Deluxe Game Co., 1920s)	$85
❑ Formula One (Parker Brothers, 1963)	$60
❑ Formula One (Parker Brothers, 1964)	$55
❑ Formula One (Parker Brothers, 1968)	$40
❑ Game of Automobile Race (McLoughlin Bros., 1904) scarce	$1450
❑ Game of Auto Race (Orotech Co., 1920s)	$220
❑ Game of Midget Speedway (Whitman Publishing Company, 1942)	$70
❑ Game of Speed King (Russell, 1922)	$165
❑ Game of Stock Car Speedway (Johnstone, 1965)	$85
❑ Grande Auto Race (Atkins & Company, 1920s)	$165
❑ Harry Gant Stockcar Racing Game, Checkered Flag Racing Game, includes two die cast cars	N/A
❑ Hot Rod (Harett-Gilmar, 1953)	$35
❑ Hot Rod (Donald L. Cranmer, 1954)	$55
❑ Hot Wheels Game (Whitman, 1982)	$20
❑ Hot Wheels Wipe-Out Game (Mattel, 1968)	$30
❑ Huggin' The Rail (Selchow & Righter, 1948)	$90
❑ Indianapolis 500 Mile Race Game (Shaw, 1938) photos, cards, large board	$550
❑ Indianapolis 500 75th Running Race Game (International Games Inc., 1991)	$20
❑ Indy Car (S. Alden, 1993)	$45
❑ International Automobile Race (Parker Brothers, 1903/1904) scarce	$1350
❑ International Grand Prix (Cadaco, 1975)	$45
❑ Junior Motor Race (1930s) Peter Pan Series	$45
❑ Le Mans (Avalon Hill, 1961)	$40
❑ Midget Auto Race (Cracker Jack Company, 1930s)	$30
❑ Midget Auto Race (Samuel Lowe, 1941)	$35
❑ Moon Mullins Automobile Race (Milton Bradley, 1920s)	$140
❑ Mongoose & Snake Drag Race Set – reissue of 1970 Hot Wheels Game, 25,000	$28
❑ Motor Race (Wolverine Supply & Manufacturing Company, 1922)	$140
❑ Motor Race Game (1920s), metal cars, German-made	$100
❑ NASCAR Daytona 500 (Milton Bradley, 1990)	$20
❑ Pole Position (Parker Brothers, 1983)	$20
❑ Raceway (B & B Toy Manufacturing Company, 1950s)	$35
❑ Race for the Cup, Auto Racing (Milton Bradley, 1910s)	$110
❑ Race-O-Rama (Built-Rite, 1960) four race games	$40
❑ Racing Cars (Ace Playing Cards) made in West Germany	$15
❑ Road Race Game (1930s) made in the United Kingdom	$80
❑ Roll-O Motor Speedway (Supply Sales Company, 1922)	$55
❑ Six Day Race (Holtmann, 1986) made in Germany	$40
❑ Spedem Auto Race (All-Fair, 1922)	$275
❑ Spedem Junior Auto Race Game (All-Fair, 1929)	$190
❑ Speed Card Game (Pepus, 1946) made in the United Kingdom	$30
❑ Speed Circuit (3M, 1971)	$30
❑ Speedway, Big Bopper Game (Ideal, 1961)	$45
❑ Speedway Motor Race (J. Smarkola, 1925)	$85
❑ Speedway Motor Race (Smith, Line & French, 1920s)	$165
❑ Sto-Auto Race (Stough Company, 1920s) metal board	$55

❏ Stock Car Race (Gardner, 1950s)		$85
❏ Stock Car Racing Game (Whitman, 1956)		$30
❏ The Stock Car Racing Game (Ribbit Toy Company, 1981) Petty & Yarborough		$40
❏ Straightaway (Seichow & Righter, 1961)		$55
❏ Super Speedway Strategies – The Racing Game (1993)		N/A
❏ 300 Mile Race (Warren Built-Rite, 1955)		$85
❏ Thunder Road (Milton Bradley, 1986)		$25
❏ Tudor Electric Sports Car Race (Tudor, 1959)		$35
❏ USAC Auto Racing (Avalon Hill-Sports Illustrated, 1980) with race cards		$115
❏ Vallco Pro Drag Racing Game (Zyla, 1975)		$20
❏ Vanderbilt Cup Race Game (Bowers & Hard, 1910)		$715

Auto Racing Magazines/Publications – selected entries with value guide

Racing Pictorial

Year/Issue	Cover	Value
❏ 1959	USAC Emblem, six race cars	$240
❏ 1960-61	Indianapolis and Daytona photographs	$ 60
❏ 1961	(Color) Indy and Daytona photographs	$ 80
❏ 1961-62	Annual – A. J. Foyt and Ned Jarrett	$ 60
❏ 1962	(Color) Rodger Ward and NASCAR photos	$ 80
❏ 1962-63	Annual – Ward, Penske, and Jones	$ 60
❏ 1963	(Color) eight NASCAR and four Indy photos	$ 60
❏ 1963-64	Annual – four Indy and three NASCAR drivers	$ 56
❏ 1964	(Color) 1. A. J. Foyt, 2. NASCAR	$ 55
❏ 1964-65	Annual – 1. Jones and Ward, 2. Petty, Foyt	$ 55
❏ 1965	Summer – 1. Langhorne Crash, 2. NASCAR	$ 45
❏ 1965	Fall – 1. Foyt, Unser, 2. Johnson and Nelson	$ 45
❏ 1965-66	Annual – Clark and Chapman	$ 55
❏ 1966	Spring – Hurtubise, Petty, 2. Petty, Ruby	$ 55
❏ 1966	Summer – Indy 500 photographs	$ 45
❏ 1966	Fall – Andretti, Derringer	$ 45
❏ 1966-67	Annual – 1. Andretti, 2. Pearson, Nelson	$ 45
❏ 1967	Spring – seven Daytona 500 photographs	$ 40
❏ 1967	Summer – A. J. Foyt	$ 40
❏ 1967	Fall – Donohue, Hulme	$ 45
❏ 1967-68	Annual – Petty, Hulme	$ 45
❏ 1968	Spring – five Daytona photographs	$ 45
❏ 1968	Summer – five Indy 500 and Daytona photographs	$ 40
❏ 1968	Fall – Can-Am photos, Foyt, Andretti	$ 40
❏ 1968-69	Annual	$ 45
❏ 1969	Spring – six Daytona photos, Unser	$ 40
❏ 1969	Summer – Andretti	$ 40
❏ 1969	Fall – seven Andretti photographs	$ 40
❏ 1969-70	Annual – Issac and Yarborough	$ 40
❏ 1970	Spring – nine Daytona 500 photographs	$ 45
❏ 1970	Summer – Unser	$ 35
❏ 1970	Fall – Motschenbacher Can-Am driver	$ 27
❏ 1970-71	Annual – Issac, McCluskey	$ 22
❏ 1971	Spring – Unser	$ 30
❏ 1971	Summer – Indy 500 start, Daytona	$ 22
❏ 1971	Fall – Robson, Stewart	$ 27
❏ 1971-72	Annual – Daytona photographs	$ 40
❏ 1972	Spring – Foyt	$ 33
❏ 1972	Summer – NASCAR/Michigan, Indy start	$ 26
❏ 1972	Fall – SCCA and USAC cars	$ 26
❏ 1972-73	Annual – Foyt	$ 33
❏ 1973	Spring – Petty winning at Daytona	$ 28
❏ 1973	Summer – NASCAR/Michigan, Johncock	$ 30

Year/Issue	Cover	Value
❑ 1973	Fall – Bobby and Donny Allison, Donohue	$ 28
❑ 1973-74	Annual – NC Speedway, McCluskey	$ 27
❑ 1974	Spring – Petty, Unser, Daytona	$ 28
❑ 1974	Summer – NASCAR/Atlanta, Indy start	$ 23
❑ 1974	Fall – Hoosier 100 Dirt Car Race	$ 22
❑ 1974-75	Annual – Cale Yarborough	$ 22
❑ 1975	Spring – Foyt at Ontario, Daytona	$ 23
❑ 1975	Summer – Richard Petty, Daytona	$ 28
❑ 1975	Fall – Hoosier 100 start, Petty at Daytona	$ 25
❑ 1975-76	Annual – Richard Petty	$ 40
❑ 1976	Spring – Daytona and Indy starts	$ 27
❑ 1976	Summer – Yarborough, Rutherford	$ 27
❑ 1976	Fall – Pearson, Foyt	$ 27
❑ 1976-77	Annual – Johncock, Yarborough	$ 23
❑ 1977	Spring – Indy start, Foyt	$ 30
❑ 1977	Summer – Foyt	$ 30
❑ 1977	Fall – Sneva, Johncock	$ 30
❑ 1977-78	Annual – Yarborough	$ 35
❑ 1978	Spring – Foyt	$ 30
❑ 1978	Summer – Unser, Yarborough	$ 30
❑ 1978	Fall – Foyt	$ 30
❑ 1978-79	Annual – Andretti	$ 30
❑ 1979	Spring – Foyt	$ 25
❑ 1979	Summer – Mears	$ 25
❑ 1979	Fall – Unser	$ 30
❑ 1979-80	Annual – Foyt at Daytona, Petty	$ 35
❑ 1980	Spring – Rutherford	$ 25
❑ 1980	Summer – Rutherford, Yarborough	$ 25
❑ 1980	Fall – Bettenhausen dirt car champion	$ 25
❑ 1980-81	Annual – Dale Earnhardt	$ 50
❑ 1981	Spring – Rutherford	$ 25
❑ 1981	Summer – Foyt	$ 25
❑ 1981	Fall – Rice dirt car champion	$ 22
❑ 1981-82	Annual – Darrell Waltrip	$ 27
❑ 1982	Spring – Mears	$ 16
❑ 1982	Summer – Johncock	$ 16
❑ 1982-83	Annual – Darrell Waltrip	$ 26
❑ 1983	Spring – Johncock	$ 18
❑ 1983	Summer – Sneva	$ 15
❑ 1983-84	Annual – Bobby Allison	$ 25
❑ 1984	Spring – M. Andretti	$ 17
❑ 1985	Spring – M. Andretti	$ 17
❑ 1986	Spring – Michael Andretti	$ 17
❑ 1986	Final Issue – Bobby Rahal	$ 21

Sports Illustrated

Date	Cover	Value Range – Mint Condition
❑ 9/13/54	Jim Kimberly	$ 22
❑ 3/26/56	Jim Kimberly	$ 12
❑ 5/28/56	Bob Sweikert	$ 12
❑ 3/25/57	Carroll Shelby	$ 17
❑ 5/26/58	Pat O'Connor	$ 9
❑ 3/16/59	Phil Hill	$ 9
❑ 5/25/59	Indy 500 Cars	$ 9
❑ 10/19/59	Auto Racing	$ 9
❑ 11/16/59	Daytona 500	$ 9

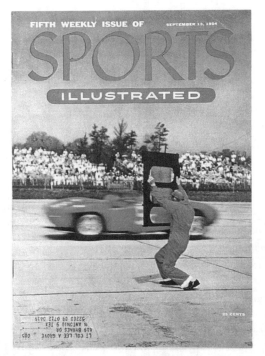

This September 13, 1954, issue of Sports Illustrated *is now worth $22*

Date	Cover	Value Range – Mint Condition
❑ 10/31/60	Jack Brabham	$ 9
❑ 5/29/61	Indy 500 Driver	$ 11
❑ 3/26/62	Ricardo Rodriguez	$ 14
❑ 5/27/63	Dan Gurney	$ 10
❑ 6/1/64	A. J. Foyt	$ 14
❑ 5/31/65	Lloyd Ruby	$ 9
❑ 5/30/66	John Boyd	$ 9
❑ 5/1/67	Jim Hall	$ 11
❑ 5/29/67	Indy 500	$ 11
❑ 2/26/68	Curtis Turner	$ 9
❑ 51/3/68	Graham Hill	$ 11
❑ 6/8/70	Al Unser	$ 11
❑ 6/7/71	Al Unser/Pete Revson	$ 11
❑ 9/6/71	Jackie Stewart	$ 8
❑ 2/28/72	A. J. Foyt	$ 10
❑ 6/5/72	Mark Donohue	$ 11
❑ 12/24/73	Jackie Stewart	$ 12
❑ 6/3/74	Johnny Rutherford	$ 11
❑ 5/19/75	A. J. Foyt	$ 9
❑ 2/28/77	Cale Yarborough	$ 8
❑ 6/5/78	Al Unser	$ 8
❑ 6/2/80	Johnny Rutherford	$ 8
❑ 5/25/81	A. J. Foyt	$ 9
❑ 6/3/85	Danny Sullivan	$ 7
❑ 9/9/85	NASCAR's Bill Elliott	$ 9
❑ 7/24/95	America's Hottest Sport	$ 4

Auto Racing Medallions – selected entries with value guide

Mint Collectibles of Racing

❏ 1	Sterling Marlin	$35
❏ 2	Ken Schrader	$35
❏ 3	Bill Elliott	$35
❏ 4	Harry Gant	$35
❏ 5	Alan Kulwicki	$40

Environment

	Edition	Price
❏ Brickyard 400 Collectors Set – silver	5,000	$ 90
❏ Brickyard 400 Collectors Set – 24 kt. gold select	100	$ 140
❏ Jeff Gordon silver medallion	15,000	$ 35
❏ Jeff Gordon 24 kt. gold select medallion w/gift box	5,000	$ 55
❏ 1995 Brickyard 400 silver medallion	10,000	$ 35
❏ 1995 Brickyard 400 24 kt. gold medallion w/gift box	500	$ 55
❏ Indy 500 Collectors Set – silver	195	$ 90
❏ Indy 500 Collectors Set – 24 kt. gold	95	$ 140
❏ Indy 500 Event medallion – silver	1,995	$ 35
❏ Indy 500 Event medallion – 24 kt. gold	500	$ 55
❏ Indy 500 Pace Car medallion – silver	1,995	$ 35
❏ Indy 500 Pace Car medallion – 24 kt. gold	500	$ 55
❏ Dale Earnhardt medallion – silver	15,000	$ 35
❏ Dale Earnhardt medallion – 24 kt. gold	5,000	$ 55
❏ Richard Petty medallion – silver	5,000	$ 35
❏ Richard Petty medallion – 24 kt. gold	500	$ 55
❏ Mark Martin medallion – silver	5,000	$ 35
❏ Mark Martin medallion – 24 kt. gold	500	$ 55

Sports Silver – 1 oz. .999 fine silver

❏ Morgan Shepherd	$30
❏ Davey Allison	$30
❏ Jeff Gordon	$30
❏ Richard Petty	$30
❏ Kyle Petty	$30
❏ Mark Martin	$30
❏ Terry Labonte	$30
❏ Sterling Marlin	$30
❏ Michael Waltrip	$30
❏ Bill Elliott	$30
❏ Ken Schrader	$30
❏ Bobby Hamilton	$30
❏ Harry Gant	$30
❏ Rusty Wallace	$30
❏ Dale Earnhardt	$30

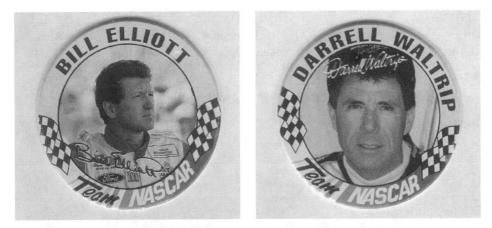

Bill Elliott and Darrell Waltrip are featured on these Team NASCAR original race caps

Auto Racing Milk Caps

❏ Mark Martin – Set of six Reese's Milk Caps $ N/A

Auto Racing Porcelain/Ceramic Plates – selected entries with value guide

The Hamilton Collection/Sports Impressions

Driver	Description	Retail
❏ Bill Elliott	6-1/2" diameter, 23 kt. gold border	$ 29.50
❏ Jeff Gordon	6-1/2" diameter, 23 kt. gold border	$ 29.50
❏ Dale Earnhardt	6-1/2" diameter, 23 kt. gold border	$ 29.50

This gold-bordered collector plate from Sports Impressions features driver Bill Elliott

Neat Ideas

Driver	Description	Retail
❑ Alan Kulwicki	7-1/2" ebony with 24 kt. gold trim – 10,000	$ 50.00
❑ Davey Allison	7-1/2" ebony with 24 kt. gold trim – 5,000	$ 50.00

Auto Racing Programs – selected entries with value guide

Daytona 500

❑ 1959	Lee Petty	Oldsmobile	$ 235
❑ 1960	Junior Johnson	Chevrolet	$ 125
❑ 1961	Marvin Panch	Pontiac	$ 100
❑ 1962	Fireball Roberts	Pontiac	$ 100
❑ 1963	Tiny Lund	Ford	$ 75
❑ 1964	Richard Petty	Plymouth	$ 250
❑ 1965	Fred Lorenzen	Ford	$ 35
❑ 1966	Richard Petty	Plymouth	$ 100
❑ 1967	Mario Andretti	Ford	$ 40
❑ 1968	Cale Yarborough	Mercury	$ 20
❑ 1969	L. R. Yarborough	Ford	$ 20
❑ 1970	Pete Hamilton	Plymouth	$ 20
❑ 1971	Richard Petty	Plymouth	$ 45
❑ 1972	A. J. Foyt	Mercury	$ 32
❑ 1973	Richard Petty	Plymouth	$ 35
❑ 1974	Richard Petty	Plymouth	$ 35
❑ 1975	Benny Parsons	Chevrolet	$ 20
❑ 1976	David Pearson	Mercury	$ 15
❑ 1977	Cale Yarborough	Chevrolet	$ 18
❑ 1978	Bobby Allison	Ford	$ 24
❑ 1979	Richard Petty	Oldsmobile	$ 30
❑ 1980	Buddy Baker	Oldsmobile	$ 15
❑ 1981	Richard Petty	Buick	$ 25
❑ 1982	Bobby Allison	Buick	$ 18
❑ 1983	Cale Yarborough	Pontiac	$ 16
❑ 1984	Cale Yarborough	Chevrolet	$ 15
❑ 1985	Bill Elliott	Ford	$ 20
❑ 1986	Geoff Bodine	Chevrolet	$ 15
❑ 1987	Bill Elliott	Ford	$ 18
❑ 1988	Bobby Allison	Buick	$ 15
❑ 1989	Darrell Waltrip	Chevrolet	$ 15
❑ 1990	Derrike Cope	Chevrolet	$ 13
❑ 1991	Ernie Irvan	Chevrolet	$ 16
❑ 1992	Davey Allison	Ford	$ 15
❑ 1993	Dale Jarrett	Chevrolet	$ 12
❑ 1994	Sterling Marlin	Chevrolet	$ 10

Auto Racing Thermometers – selected entries with value guide

T-Series Racing Plaques Inc.

❑ Jeff Gordon	$20	❑ Jimmy Hensley	$20
❑ Sterling Marlin (Raybestos)	$20	❑ Sterling Marlin (Maxwell House)	$20
❑ Bobby Labonte	$20	❑ Bobby Hamilton	$20
❑ Rusty Wallace	$20	❑ Richard Petty	$30
❑ Bill Elliott, 1992	$20	❑ Bill Elliott, 1993	$20
❑ Darrell Waltrip	$20	❑ Harry Gant, 1993 Lumina	$20

❑ Harry Gant, 1992 Oldsmobile	$20	❑ Geoff Bodine	$20
❑ Morgan Shepherd	$20	❑ Ken Schrader	$20
❑ Derrike Cope, Purolator	$20		

Auto Racing Tickets – selected entries with value guide

Daytona 500

❑ 1959	Lee Petty	Oldsmobile	$ 165
❑ 1960	Junior Johnson	Chevrolet	$ 85
❑ 1961	Marvin Panch	Pontiac	$ 40
❑ 1962	Fireball Roberts	Pontiac	$ 40
❑ 1963	Tiny Lund	Ford	$ 35
❑ 1964	Richard Petty	Plymouth	$ 150
❑ 1965	Fred Lorenzen	Ford	$ 25
❑ 1966	Richard Petty	Plymouth	$ 65
❑ 1967	Mario Andretti	Ford	$ 30
❑ 1968	Cale Yarborough	Mercury	$ 15
❑ 1969	L. R. Yarborough	Ford	$ 15
❑ 1970	Pete Hamilton	Plymouth	$ 15
❑ 1971	Richard Petty	Plymouth	$ 30
❑ 1972	A. J. Foyt	Mercury	$ 20
❑ 1973	Richard Petty	Plymouth	$ 17
❑ 1974	Richard Petty	Plymouth	$ 17
❑ 1975	Benny Parsons	Chevrolet	$ 10
❑ 1976	David Pearson	Mercury	$ 10
❑ 1977	Cale Yarborough	Chevrolet	$ 10
❑ 1978	Bobby Allison	Ford	$ 13
❑ 1979	Richard Petty	Oldsmobile	$ 12
❑ 1980	Buddy Baker	Oldsmobile	$ 10
❑ 1981	Richard Petty	Buick	$ 12
❑ 1982	Bobby Allison	Buick	$ 10
❑ 1983	Cale Yarborough	Pontiac	$ 10
❑ 1984	Cale Yarborough	Chevrolet	$ 10
❑ 1985	Bill Elliott	Ford	$ 15
❑ 1986	Geoff Bodine	Chevrolet	$ 10
❑ 1987	Bill Elliott	Ford	$ 12
❑ 1988	Bobby Allison	Buick	$ 10
❑ 1989	Darrell Waltrip	Chevrolet	$ 12
❑ 1990	Derrike Cope	Chevrolet	$ 9
❑ 1991	Ernie Irvan	Chevrolet	$ 11
❑ 1992	Davey Allison	Ford	$ 15
❑ 1993	Dale Jarrett	Chevrolet	$ 9
❑ 1994	Sterling Marlin	Chevrolet	$ 9

Brickyard 400

❑ 1994	Jeff Gordon	Chevrolet	$ 22
❑ 1995	Dale Earnhardt	Chevrolet	$ 20

Auto Racing Tools – selected entries with value guide

Channellock, Inc.

❑ Limited Edition Collection of four Signature Series tongue $160
and groove pliers with display case – 2,500 sets

Auto Racing Toy Cars – selected entries with value guide

Racing Toys – excluding "Hot-Rod"

Manufacturer	Description	Value Range
Arcade	Auto Racer, cast iron, 7-3/4" long, 1926	$200-$375
	Racer, driver's head & number highlighted with gold bronze, cast iron, 8" long, 1936	
	Racer, white rubber tires, cast iron, 5-3/4" long, 1936	$50-$100
Auburn	Race Car, rubber, 6" long, 1930s	$15-$30
	Race Car, red rubber, 6" long	$40-$85
	Race Car with goggled driver, rubber, 10" long	$50-$100
	Racer, rubber	$20-$40
	Racer, red vinyl with white plastic tires	$25-$50
Barclay	Race Car, white tires, 4" long	$25-$55
Best Toy & Novelty Factory	Racer (BEV1) "85," 4" long, rubber tires	$12-$25
	Racer (BEV11) "97," 4-1/2" long, Bluebird record car	$12-$25
C.A.W. Novelty Company	CWV8 Racer, #31, 3-5/8", sm. fin, plastic wheels – Indy Car style	$20-$35
	CWV10 Racer, #38, 3-3/8" closed cockpit – coupe, rounded back	$20-$35
	CWV11 Racer, #39, 3", transparent windshield, two-man	$20-$35
	CWV12 Three-piece auto set – midget coupe, midget racer, and Austin Bantam. Midget coupe, no #, 2-1/16"; Racer, no #, 2-1/8"	$55-$70
Champion	Racer, with two riders, 5-1/2" long	$130-$275
	Racer, detachable driver, 6" long, cast iron	$110-$200
	Racer, 9" long	$165-$325
Chein	Racer, #8, 20" long, spare tire mounted on rear, red with yellow trim	$750-$1700
	Racer No. 3, 6-1/2", windup	$125-$270
	Racer "52"	$65-$130

Manufacturer	Description	Value Range
Corgi/Playcraft Toys	Corgi 159 Patrick Eagle Indy Car	$50
(Prices are for mint item in box)	Corgi 161 Santa Pod Commuter Dragster	$50
	Corgi 162 Quartermaster Dragster	$45
	Corgi 164 Wild Honey Dragster	$45
	Corgi 166 Ford Mustang Organ Grinder Drag Funny Car	$45
	Corgi 167 U.S. Racing Buggy	$25
Corgi (Includes value range pricing)	Ferrari Daytona, 5" apple green body, black tow hook, red-yellow-silver black Daytona #5 & other racing decals, amber windows, headlights, black plastic interior, base, 4-spoke chrome wheels	$14-$35
	Ferrari Daytona, 4-3/4" long, white body with red roof & trunk, black interior, 2 working doors, amber windows & headlights, #81 & other decals	$14-$35
	Ferrari Daytona & Racing Car, blue/yellow Ferrari and Surtees on yellow trailer	$12-$30
	Ferrari Daytona JCB, 4-3/4" long, orange body with #33, Corgi and other decals, chrome spoked wheels	$16-$40
	Ferrari Racing Car, 3-5/8" long, red body, chrome plastic engine, roll bar & dash, driver, silver cast base and exhaust, Ferrari and #36 decals	$24-$60
Craftoy	Craftoy Racer, #81, 4-1/2", Miller Indy Car, "Made in USA"	$15-$25
	Craftoy Racer, #100, 4-1/4", Indy Car style, removable hood	$15-$25
	Craftoy Racer, no #, 3-3/4", Indy Car style, w/driver, slanted front	$15-$25
Hubley	Race Car #22, cast iron, 7 1-2" long	$40-$85
	Race Car #2241, 7" long, 1930s	$50-$100
	Racer, white rubber wheels, cast iron, 7" long	$200-$400
	Racer, cast iron, 10-3/4" long, 1931	$75-$250
	Racer, nickel-plated driver, cast iron, 4-3/4" long, 1960s	$75-$150
	Racer, red with black wheels, silver grille and driver, 7-1/2" long	$35-$75

Manufacturer	Description	Value Range
	Racer #12, die cast, prewar	$60-$125
	Racer #629, 7" long, 1939	$50-$135
Kansas Toy & Novelty Company	KTV14 Indy Racer, #14 or no #, 3-1/8", driver, boattail, multiple versions	$10-$15
	KTV22 Racer, #26, 4", "Bearcat," driver	$40-$80
	KTV25 Racer, #33, 3", "Bearcat," smaller version of KTV22	$30-$75
	KTV32 Stock Car, #41, metal disk wheels	$25-$45
	KTV35 Racer, #46, 2-7/8", Golden Arrow Record car, driver, large tail fin	$15-$30
	KTV57 Racer, no #, 1", solid cast	$20-$40
	KTTV63 Racer, #76, 4-1/4", Auburn speedster, driver, distinct large oval fin	$25-$45
	KTTV69 Racer, #81, 4-3/8", Miller, wood hubs and rubber wheels	$25-$45
	KTTV71 Indy Racer, #83, 4-5/8", driver, large rounded tail, wood hubs and rubber wheels	$25-$45
Kingsbury	Kingsbury Bluebird Racer	$850-$2200
	Kingsbury Golden Arrow Racer, 20", futuristic, large tail fin, windup	$600-$1300
	Kingsbury Sunbeam Racer, 19", sheet metal, rubber tires	$550-$1200
Marx	Giant King Racer, dark blue, tin windup, 12-1/4" long, 1928	$250-$725
	King Racer, yellow body, red trim, tin windup, 8-1/2" long, 1925	$375-$750
	King Racer, yellow with black outlines, 8-1/2" long, 1925	$250-$575
	Race 'N Road Speedway, HO scale racing set, 1950s	$60-$125
	Racer #3, miniature car, tin windup, 5" long	$75-$195
	Racer #4, miniature car, tin windup, 5" long	$75-$195
	Racer #5, miniature car, tin windup, 5" long, 1948	$75-$195
	Racer #7, miniature car, tin windup, 5" long, 1948	$75-$195

Manufacturer	Description	Value Range
	Racer #12, tin litho, windup, 16" long, 1942	$225-$625
	Racer #61, miniature car, tin windup, 4-3/4" long, 1930	$75-$195
	Racing Car, 2-man team, tin litho, windup, 12" long, 1940	$125-$425
	Racing Car, plastic driver, tin windup, 27" long, 1950	$100-$450
Matchbox	No. 8 Wildcat Dragster, 1971	$18
(Prices are for mint item in box)	No. 19 Lotus Racing Car, 1965	$18
	No. 29 Racing Mini, clear windows, 5-spoke wide wheels, 2-1/4" long, 1970	$18
	No. 52 BRM Racing Car, 1965	$20
	No. 62 Rat Rod Dragster, 1971	$15
	No. 64 Slingshot Dragster, 1971	$18
	No. 73 Ferrari F1 Racing Car, light & dark red body, plastic driver, white & yellow "73" decal on sides, 2-5/8" long, 1962	$35
Mattel's Hot Wheels	NASCAR Stocker, No. 3927, white, NASCAR/Mountain Dew base, 1983	$125-$165
	Pepsi Challenger, No. 2023, yellow Funny Car, 1982	$15-$20
	Race Ace, No. 2620, white, 1986	$20-$30
	Racer Rig, No. 6194, red/white, 1971	$100-$375
	Racing Team Van, yellow, Scene Machine, 1981	$50-$60
	Snake Dragster, No. 5951, white in a two pack, 1971	$65
	Snake Funny Car, No. 6409, assorted, 1970	$60-$300
Nylint Tool and Manufacturing	Nylint No. 5900 Race Team, 21" long	$125-$250
	Nylint No. 7800 Race Team set	$125-$250
Renwal	No. 58 "Speed King" Racing Car, 6-3/8" long	$35-$75
	No. 61 Racer, 4-3/16"	$10-$15
	No. 88 Racer, 4-3/8" long	$35-$100

Manufacturer	Description	Value Range
	No. 107 Speed King Friction Motor Racer, 10-1/4" long, with driver	$45-$150
	No. 150 Racer, 3-1/4" long	$12-$15
	No. 173 Speedway Racer, 9-1/2" long, with driver	$25-$60
	No. 207 Racer, with no motor	$100-$200
	No. 216 Champion Racer, 10-3/8", closed, siren	$100-$200
	No. 220 Take-Apart Racer, 10-1/2" long	$100-$200
	No. 243 Racer, 9-1/2", with driver	$100-$200
	No. 2061 Racer, same as No. 61, plus simulated chrome trim	$45-$100
	No. 2088 Racer, same as No. 88, plus simulated chrome trim	$70-$145
	No. 8001 Ferrari Racer, metal, 9-1/4", motorized	$125-$225
	No. 8002 Maserati Racer, metal, 9-1/4", motorized	$125-$225
	No. 8009 Racer, metal, 7"	$50-$80
Saunders	Saunders Race Car windup	$40-$80
	Saunders Race Car	$20-$35
	Saunders Stock Car Racer, 8", removable hood	$75-$200
Schuco	Grand Prix Racer 1070, 6"	$100-$200
	Micro Racer 101, 3-1/2", Porsche style	$100-$200
	Micro Racer 102, 3-1/2", Indy style	$100-$200
	Micro Racer 104, 3-1/2", Indy style	$100-$200
	Micro Racer 1036, 4-1/2"	$110-$220
	Micro Racer 1040, 4"	$110-$220
	Micro Racer 1041, 4"	$110-$220
	Micro Racer 1042, 4"	$110-$220
	Micro Racer 1043, 4"	$110-$220
	Studio Racer 1050, 5-1/2", includes tools	$125-$250
Sun Rubber	SR01 Open Racer, two drivers, 4-3/8", No. 505	$25-$40

Manufacturer	Description	Value Range
	SR02 Open Racer, 6-1/2", full rear fenders, No.1000	$35-$60
	SR03 Open Racer, boattail, 6-3/4", No. 12012	$30-$45
Thimble Drome	(Roy Cox) Champion Racer	$225-$450
	Racer	$165-$300
	Racer No. 25	$200-$375
	Racer with Engine	$300-$575
Thomas Toys	No. 132 Truck & Racer, 4"	$20-$40
	T-141 same as No. 132	$15-$30
	No. 160 International Racer, 5", with or without driver	$20-$45
	No. 212 Plated Two-Tone Racer with driver, 5", same as No. 160 except top half is specially plated	$60-$175
	No. 360 Indianapolis Speed Race, two racers with drivers, spring action	$90-$165
Tommy Toy	TTV27 Racer, futuristic design, torpedo tail	$20-$35
	TTV28 Racer, smaller than TTV27, rounded tail	$15-$25

Auto Racing Watches – selected entries with value guide

Driving Signature Series/Sun Time/Sun-Glo

Released in three styles: Men's Floater, Women's Floater, and Sun-Glo. Not all drivers available in all three styles. Retail: $65

- ❑ 7 & 7 (Petty/Earnhardt) – 3 styles
- ❑ Alan Kulwicki – 1 style
- ❑ Bill Elliott – 3 styles
- ❑ Bobby Labonte – 1 style
- ❑ Davey Allison – 1 style
- ❑ Dale Earnhardt – 3 styles
- ❑ Dale Jarrett – 1 style
- ❑ Darrell Waltrip – 3 styles
- ❑ Ernie Irvan – 2 styles
- ❑ Jeff Gordon – 3 styles
- ❑ #28 Car – 1 style
- ❑ Kyle Petty – 1 style
- ❑ Ken Schrader – 1 style
- ❑ Mark Martin – 3 styles
- ❑ Morgan Shepherd – 1 style
- ❑ Michael Waltrip – 1 style
- ❑ Ricky Craven – 1 style
- ❑ Richard Petty – 3 styles
- ❑ Rusty Wallace – 3 styles
- ❑ Terry Labonte – 1 style
- ❑ Winston Cup – 2 styles

Souvenirs

Souvenirs or Collectibles

The explosion in auto racing licensing and merchandising has made it difficult for fans and collectors to separate souvenirs from collectibles. A souvenir is something that causes a person to remember, thus it is a remembrance or memento. A collectible is an object that is collected by fanciers, people who have a special liking or interest. Collectibles become part of collections, which are accumulations of objects gathered for study, comparison, and exhibition. Souvenirs are mementos that are not collected, gathered, studied, compared, or exhibited. Souvenirs are not purchased with hopes of monetary appreciation, but only for the item's intrinsic value.

How an item is produced and marketed is a good indicator of whether the manufacturer intends it to be a collectible or a souvenir. Souvenirs are mass marketed to a large target audience and produced to meet demand. Collectibles are selectively marketed with limited production and are typical-

The Racing Images Motorsports Apparel & Souvenirs trailer

The cover of the PPG Indy Car Championship Apparel catalog

Covers of the Hooters souvenir catalog and handout, and the official "Geoff Bodine 1995 Apparel and Accessories" catalog

ly not reproduced to meet an increase in demand. Souvenirs have little regard for packaging, whereas collectibles make packaging a paramount marketing concern.

With the sale of licensed racing products now topping $400 million, it easy to understand why the marketing of auto racing is of considerable concern to the sport. Over five million people attended Winston Cup races in 1995, up from just over three million in 1990. The increased attendance has led to a ravenous demand for souvenirs and collectibles associated with the sport. Loyalty between the participants and their fans is unparalleled by any other sport. Fans flock to traveling souvenir trailers, buying nearly everything associated with their favorite driver, with racing apparel by far the most popular souvenir.

Both the drivers and organizations such as NASCAR, through NASCAR Properties, Inc., have taken a personal interest in souvenirs and memorabilia. In spring of 1995, Dale Earnhardt, who by some estimates netted $5 million in souvenir sales alone in 1994, even purchased Sports Image, Inc., the major distributor of his souvenirs. NASCAR is also bringing merchandising back underneath its wing in 1996. NASCAR Properties Inc. should top one hundred licensees alone in 1996, with products being sold in chain stores such as Kmart and Wal-Mart.

Racing teams such as Hendrick Motorsports and Jack Roush have also shown significant interest in souvenirs. From adding gift shops to their race shops or opening up separate souvenir shops, most have acknowledged the boom in racing memorabilia.

A Key Concern

The growth in the industry has also led to problems, as the collectibles market has witnessed the manufacture and distribution of unauthorized and counterfeit merchandise. This phenomenon is not unique to racing, as it has affected other sports as well. The growth in the baseball collectibles market during the 1980s saw a similar plague infect its domain, with consumer education eventually being acknowledged as the solution.

It is recommended that buyers purchase merchandise from reputable dealers whose association with the sport has been acknowledged

283

A cardboard "Sun-drop" Dale Earnhardt promotion

A look inside "The Family Channel" souvenir trailer

Collectors must remember that counterfeit and unauthorized merchandise not only is cheating the driver, but the consumer as well. These items have virtually no value from a collectible perspective and consumers should do everything they possibly can to avoid purchasing them.

Counterfeit products are exact duplicates of an original fully licensed product, and unauthorized items are products produced without the proper legal consent of the represented parties. Purchasing merchandise from reputable dealers whose association with the sport has been acknowledged is a recommended path for all collectors.

As expected, the most popular drivers are the primary targets of illegitimate products. Drivers such as Dale Earnhardt, Jeff Gordon, Rusty Wallace, Bill Elliott, Ernie Irvan, and Darrell Waltrip have to protect themselves by licensing nearly every conceivable trademark imaginable. Many drivers even own and operate their own souvenir trailers or souvenir sources. For example, Bill Elliott fans can contact the Elliott Museum and Souvenir Centre, P.O. Box 435, Dawsonville, GA 30534 or call 706-265-1565 to get the "Bill Elliott Souvenir Catalog." Sources such as these can assure both fans and collectors that they are getting legitimate products.

Once a consumer purchases a licensed authentic collectible or souvenir they can familiarize themselves with the proper disclaimers and tags. Paper-based products are also a source of counterfeiting, so collectors should question unclear visual images, color discrepancies, uneven borders, unfamiliar type, and different paper stock. Comparing items to known legitimate products is recommended. Subscribing to hobby periodicals that cover such issues is a must for all collectors.

Souvenir Sources

NASCAR

(DSD) = Driver's Souvenir Dealer
(SSD) = Sponsor's Souvenir Dealer
(CSD) = Car's Souvenir Dealer

#1   Rick Mast
        (DSD) First Racing Souvenirs
        Rt. 6 Box 224A
        Lexington, VA 24450
        540-463-4855

285

#2   Rusty Wallace
          (DSD, SSD, CSD) Motorsports Int. Corp.
          12650 U.S. Highway 12
          Brooklyn, MI 49230-9068
          800-922-9040

#3   Dale Earnhardt
          (DSD) Sports Image, Inc.
          5301 West W.T. Harris Blvd.
          Charlotte, NC 28269
          800-342-7612

          (CSD) RCR Museum and Welcome Center
          Industrial Drive, Bldg. #2
          Welcome, NC 27374
          800-476-3389

#4   Sterling Marlin
          (DSD, SSD, CSD) Greens Racing Souvenirs Inc.
          1727 Seymour Dr., P.O. Box 791
          South Boston, VA 24592
          800-572-8477

#5   Terry Labonte
          (DSD) Motorsports Traditions
          2835 Armentrout Dr.
          Concord, NC 28025
          704-376-2741

          (SSD) Garner & Nevins
          1300 Parkwood Circle, Suite 300
          Atlanta, GA 30339
          800-241-7449

          (CSD) Hendrick Motorsports
          4400 Papa Joe Hendrick Blvd.
          Harrisburg, NC 28075
          704-455-3400

#6   Mark Martin
          (DSD, SSD, CSD) Sports Design
          6000 Victory Lane
          Harrisburg, NC 28075
          704-455-1001

#7   Geoff Bodine
          (DSD, SSD, CSD) G.E.B. Inc.
          2605 Greengate Drive
          Greensboro, NC 27406
          910-373-0190

#8   Jeff Burton
          (DSD, SSD, CSD) Ketta Allen
          2240 Highway 49 N.
          Harrisburg, NC 28075
          800-STA-VOLA

#9   Lake Speed
          (DSD) Hormel Foods
          One Hormel Pl.
          Austin, MN 55912-3680
          800-LUV-SPAM

#10 Ricky Rudd
(SSD) Osterman API
1670 Indian Wood Circle
P.O. Box 8806
Maumee, OH 43537-8806
800-274-0274 ext. 430

#11 Brett Bodine
(DSD, SSD, CSD) Motorsports Traditions
2835 Armentrout Dr.
Concord, NC 28025
800-528-2777

#12 Derrike Cope
(DSD) Image Works, Inc.
1455 Ellsworth Industrial Blvd.
Atlanta, GA 30318
800-241-1052

(SSD) AJD Hat Brands
3301 Castlewood Rd.
Richmond, VA 23234
800-233-8514

(CSD) Wincraft, Inc
1124 West Fifth Ave.
Winona, MN 55987-7009
507-454-5510

#15 Dick Trickle
(DSD, SSD, CSD) Lon Johansen/Sports Ventures, Inc.
1061 Rembrandt Dr.
Concord, NC 28027
704-788-9010

#16 Ted Musgrave
(DSD, SSD, CSD) Sports Design
6000 Victory Lane
Harrisburg, NC 28075
704-455-1001

#17 Darrell Waltrip
(DSD, SSD, CSD) Motorsports Traditions
2835 Armentrout Dr.
Concord, NC 28025
800-528-2777

#18 Bobby Labonte
(DSD, SSD, CSD) Motorsports Traditions
2835 Armentrout Dr.
Concord, NC 28025
800-528-2777

#19 Loy Allen, Jr.
(DSD) Adair Wallace, c/o Healthsource
400 Aerial Ctr. Pkwy
Morrisville, NC 27560
800-849-9300 ext. 7756

#21 Morgan Shepherd
    (SSD) Osterman API
    1670 Indian Wood Circle
    P.O. Box 633
    Maumee, OH 43537-3587
    800-738-3587

#22 Ward Burton
    (SSD, CSD) The Source Int., Inc.
    P.O. Box 1788
    Kernersville, NC 27285
    800-358-4608

#23 Jimmy Spencer
    (DSD, SSD, CSD) Motorsports Traditions
    2835 Armentrout Dr.
    Concord, NC 28025
    800-528-2777

#24 Jeff Gordon
    (DSD, SSD, CSD) Motorsports Traditions
    2835 Armentrout Dr.
    Concord, NC 28025
    800-528-2777

#25 Ken Schrader
    (DSD) Hendrick Motorsports, Museum & Gift Shop,
    P.O. Box 9
    Harrisburg, NC 28075
    704-455-3400

#26 Hut Stricklin
    (DSD) King Racing
    103 Center Lane
    Huntersville, NC 28078
    704-875-8543

#27 Elton Sawyer
    (DSD) Super Sports Merchandisers
    1125 Fred Drive
    Morrow, GA 30260
    404-961-2231

#28 Dale Jarrett
    (DSD, SSD, CSD) Robert Yates Promotions, Inc.
    8298 Summit Ave.
    Charlotte, NC 28208
    800-618-0683

#30 Michael Waltrip
    (DSD, SSD, CSD) Motorsports Traditions
    2835 Armentrout Dr.
    Concord, NC 28025
    800-528-2777

#31 Greg Sacks
    (DSD) A. G. Dillard Motorsports
    1028 River Road
    Charlottesville, VA 22901
    800-645-1946

#33 Robert Pressley
(DSD, SSD, CSD) SCM Marketing
4198 N. Cherry St.
Winston-Salem, NC 27015
800-548-2384

#41 Ricky Craven
(DSD) Motorsports Traditions
2835 Armentrout Dr.
Concord, NC 28025
800-528-2777

#42 Kyle Petty
(DSD, SSD) W.W. Enterprises
3886 Elm Street, #B
Grove City, OH 43123
614-875-6949

#43 Bobby Hamilton
(DSD) Carolina Souvenirs, Inc.
5465 Morehead Rd.
Harrisburg, NC 28075
704-455-5843

(SSD, CSD) Richard Petty Museum
311 Branson Mill Rd.
Randleman, NC 27317
910-498-3745

#71 Dave Marcis
(DSD) Marcis Auto Racing
P.O. Box 645
Skyland, NC 28776
704-684-7170

#75 Todd Bodine
(DSD, SSD, CSD) Carolina Souvenirs, Inc.
5465 Morehead Rd.
Harrisburg, NC 28075
704-455-5843

#77 Bobby Hillin
(SSD, CSD) NASCAR Shop/Check 'N' Out Racing,
2107 Amity Hill Road
Statesville, NC 28677
704-878-6800

#81 Kenny Wallace
(DSD, SSD) Race Scan
3300 Browns Mill Road, Suite B-1
Johnson City, TN 37604
800-441-2841

#87 Joe Nemechek
(DSD) Sports Ventures/Lon Johansen
P.O. Box 445
Concord, NC 28026
704-788-9010

(SSD) Alcone Sims O'Brien/Keith Kesler
15 Whatney
Irvine, CA 92718
714-770-4400

(CSD) Peachstate Motorsports
P.O. Box 1537
Winder, GA 30680
404-307-1042

#90 Mike Wallace
(DSD) RCB Enterprises, Inc
224 Rolling Hill Road, Suite 9A
Mooresville, NC 28115
800-223-7223

#94 Bill Elliott
(DSD, SSD, CSD) Kudzu-Tommy Allison
P.O. Box 2516
Phenix City, AL 36868
800-723-5656

#98 Jeremy Mayfield
(DSD, SSD, CSD) KGA, Inc.
6960 Hilldale Court
Indianapolis, IN 46250
800-780-4048

Die Cast Companies

Action
Action Performance Racing Collectables Club of America
2401 West First Street
Tempe, AZ 85281

Ertl
P.O. Box 500
Dept. 776B
Dyersville, IA 52040

Peachstate/GMP
37 Polite Road
Winder, GA 30680

Raceway Replicas
P.O. Box 874
Naperville, IL 60566-0874

Racing Champions
800 Roosevelt Road
Building C, Suite 320
Glen Ellyn, IL 60137

Revell
8601 Waukegan
Morton Grove, IL 60053

White Rose/Matchbox
P.O. Box 2701
York, PA 17450

Trading Card Companies

Classic
1951 Old Cuthbert Road
Cherry Hill, NJ 08034

Finish Line
P.O. Box 271268
Tampa, FL 33688-1287

Hi-Tech Cards
1244 Hamilton St.
Allentown, PA 18102

Maxx Race Cards
P.O. Box 410648
Charlotte, NC 28241

Pinnacle Brands Inc.
and Action Packed
924 Avenue J East
Grand Prairie, TX 75050

Press Pass
14800 Quorum Dr.
Suite 420
Dallas, TX 75240

SkyBox International
300 North Duke street
Durham, NC 27702

Traks
P.O. Box 973
Fairburn, GA 30213

Upper Deck
5909 Sea Otter Place
Carlsbad, CA 92008

Wheels Race Cards
1368 Mocksville Marketplace
Mocksville, NC 27028

Other

Chevrolet Motor Company
Sports Image, Inc.
5301 West W.T. Harris
Charlotte, NC 28269
704-599-8100

Ford Motor Company
Ford World Catalog
P.O. Box 19787
Birmingham, AL 35219
800-444-4503

Goodyear Tire & Rubber
Goodyear Racing
10450 Holmes Road
Kansas City, MO 64131
800-655-5556

Hoosier Racing Tire
Hoosier Racing Tire Apparel
65465 US 31
Lakeville, IN 46536
219-784-3152

Mopar Sportswear
P.O. Box 360445
Cleveland, OH 44136
800-348-4696

Motorsports By Mail
2845 Armentrout Dr.
Concord, NC 28025
800-338-6016

NASCAR
NASCAR Catalog
P.O. Box 19807
Birmingham, AL 35219-0807
800-987-0606

PPG Industries, Inc.
Automotive Products
19699 Progress Drive
Strongsville, OH 44136
800-675-4PPG

Pontiac Motor Division
CCA, Inc.
31535 Southfield Road
Beverly Hills, MI 48025
800-638-0462

TNN/Motorsports
Merchandise Catalog
2806 Opryland Drive
Nashville, TN 37214
615-226-8568

Winston
Winston Cup Catalog
Motorsports by Mail
2845 Armentrout Drive
Concord, NC 28025
800-338-6016

Winston Cup Wives
Auxiliary – Waxx Clothes Line Speedsters
2004 Pitts School Road
Concord, NC 28027
800-643-4047

Fan and Collector Clubs

Joining your favorite driver's fan club is an ideal way of keeping up with his career. Whether these clubs are managed by family, friends, or a corporate organization, most do an outstanding job of keeping fans updated on the events surrounding their subject.

Although the membership dues and benefits vary, many include autographs, cards, photos, stickers, patches, key chains, newsletters, and other souvenirs depicting the driver. For example, when you join the Rusty Wallace Fan Club ($15.00 annual membership fee) you receive the following items: membership card, postcard photo, decals, certificate, newsletter (three per year), 8" x 10" color photo, contest (one per year), souvenirs and discounts, plus an opportunity to attend fan club meetings (two per year), which Rusty will attend.

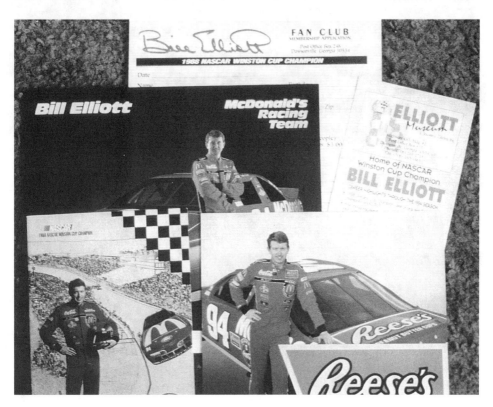

Handouts and information from the Bill Elliott Fan Club

Here is a sampling of what you receive as an official member of the Ted Musgrave Fan Club

Items received from the Ernie Irvan Fan Club

Drivers such as Bill Elliott, with a fan club that exceeds 12,000 members, employ full-time employees to manage the club and respond to the needs of his fans. Unlike so many other sports, motor racing recognizes the fans as the key to its success. Some of these clubs, like that of Richard Petty, have grown so large that they have an advisor for each state where there is a track, as well as regional directors. The Richard Petty Fan Club, which began in 1974, is the oldest active fan organization in NASCAR.

Corporate sponsors and racing teams have even taken note of the increased fan interest in these types of clubs. Roush Racing, for example, employs someone to handle Ted Musgrave's Fan Club. The club works as a vehicle of communication between the driver and his fans, while giving the racing team a tool to sell their products.

Memorabilia manufacturers have also seen the advantages of a club format. Many use it as a marketing vehicle by producing newsletters and prototype products and offering special discounts. In all cases, however, it is the racing fan and collector who benefit by these great clubs!

Collector Clubs

Action Packed Racing Club
P.O. Box 493
Itasca, IL 60143-0493

Finish Line's The Racing Club
P.O. Box 271808
Tampa, FL 33688-1808

Hi-Tech's Fast Lane Club
867 Clare Lane
York, PA 14702

Maxx Race Card's Club Maxx
P.O. Box 220281
Charlotte, NC 28222

Press Pass VIP Club
P.O. Box 871689
Dallas, TX 75287-1689

Traks' Inside Traks Club
P.O. Box 973
Fairburn, GA 30213

Wheels Racing Fan Club
1368 Mocksville Marketplace
Mocksville, NC 27028

Action Performance Racing
Collectables Club of America
2401 W. First St.
Tempe, AZ 85281

Racing Champions
Collector's Club
P.O. Box 198771
Nashville, TN 37219

Fan Clubs

NASCAR

Loy Allen Fan Club
P.O. Box 19461
Greensboro, NC 27419-9461

Bobby Allison Racing
6616 Walmsley Blvd.
Richmond, VA 23224

Davey Allison Fan Club
1421 13th Terrace
Pleasant Grove, AL 35127

John Andretti Fan Club
P.O. Box 59244
Indianapolis, IN 46259

Troy Beebe Fan Club
P.O. Box 10976
Bakersfield, CA 93389-0976

Joe Bessey Motorsports
P.O. Box 525
Scarborough, ME 04070-0525

Rich Bickle Fan Club
236 Highway 49S
Concord, NC 28025

Scott Bloomquist
Route 8, Box 2035
Rogersville, TN 37857

Brett Bodine Fan Club
1224 Starwood Drive
Charlotte, NC 28215

Geoff Bodine Fan Club
P.O. Box 377
Suffield, CT 06078-0377

Todd Bodine Fan Club
P.O. Box 257
Southmont, NC 27351

Neil Bonnett Fan Club
7081 N. Omar Road
Tucson, AZ 85741

Chuck Bown Fan Club
P.O. Box 63
Asheboro, NC 27204

Jeff Burton Fan Club
P.O. Box 339
Harrisburg, NC 28075

Ward Burton Fan Club
Route 4, Box 10
Scottsburg, VA 34558

Rick Carelli Fan Club
7300 N. Broadway
Denver, CO 80221

Derrike Cope Fan Club
P.O. Box 1542
Cornelius, NC 28031

Mike Cope Fan Club
14431 60th St.
N. Clearwater, FL 34620

Delma Cowart Fan Club
P.O. Box 264
Highland City, FL 33846

Ricky Craven Fan Club
743 Clough Mill Road
Pembroke, NH 03275

Bobby Dotter Fan Club
Rt. 8, Box 530-P
Mooresville, NC 28115

Dale Earnhardt Fan Club
P.O. Box 1250
Concord, NC 28115

Bill Elliott Fan Club
P.O. Box 248
Dawsonville, GA 30534

Harry Gant Fan Club
Rt. 3 Box 587
Taylorsville, NC 28681

Jeff Gordon Fan Club
P.O. Box 515
Williams, AZ 86046-0515

David Green Fan Club
T/S Communications
P.O. Box 8
Griffith, IN 46319

Steve Grissom Fan Club
P.O. Box 1788
Kernersville, NC 27285

Bobby Hamilton Fan Club
2601-A Bluefield Ave.
Nashville, TN 37214

Bobby Hillin Fan Club
135 Longfield Drive
Mooresville, NC 28115

Will Hobgood Fan Club
106 Beachwood Drive
West Columbia, SC 29170

Tommy Houston Fan Club
P.O. Box 5250
Conover, NC 28613

Ernie Irvan Fan Club
80 Lowe Avenue
Concord, NC 28027

Dale Jarrett Fan Club
724 Scott Drive
Fredericksburg, VA 22405

Bob Keselowski Fan Club
P.O. Box 214897
Auburn Hills, MI 48326

Alan Kulwicki Memorial Club
P.O. Box 1624
Mooresville, NC 28115

Bobby Labonte Fan Club
P.O. Box 358
Trinity, NC 27370

Terry Labonte Fan Club
P.O. Box 4617
Archdale, NC 27263

Randy LaJoie Fan Club
P.O. Box 3478
Westport, CT 06880

Tracy Leslie Fan Club
Parker Racing Inc.
8530 Cliff Cameron Drive
Charlotte, NC 28269

Chad Little Fan Club
P.O. Box 562323
Charlotte, NC 28256

Sterling Marlin Fan Club
1116 W. 7th St., Suite 62
Columbia, TN 38401

Mark Martin Fan Club
P.O. Box 68
Ash Flat, AR 72513

Rick Mast Racing
Rt.6, Box 224A
Lexington, VA 24450

Jimmy Means Fan Club
P.O. Box 90
Hackettstown, NJ 07840

Teddy Musgrave Fan Club
P.O. Box 1089
Liberty, NC 27298

Joe Nemechek
NEMCO Motorsports
P.O. Box 1131
Mooresville, NC 28115

Larry Pearson
The Source International
P.O. Box 1788
Kernersville, NC 27285

Tom Peck Fan Club
P.O. Box 249
McConnellsburg, PA 17233

Kyle Petty
(no organized fan club)
CFS Services
135 Longfield Dr.
Mooresville, NC 28115

Richard Petty Fan Club
1028 East 22nd St.
Kannapolis, NC 28083

Jeff Purvis Racing Club
P.O. Box 765
Clarksville, TN 37155-0765

Shawna Robinson
Creative Marketing Group Inc.
P.O. Box 999
Harrisburg, NC 28075

Ricky Rudd Fan Club
P.O. Box 7586
Richmond, VA 23231

Hermie Saddler Fan Club
P.O. Box 871
Emporia, VA 28847

Elton Sawyer/Patty Moise
P.O. Box 1901
Midlothian, VA 23112

Ken Schrader Fan Club
P.O. Box 599
Licking, MO 65542

Dennis Seltzer Alliance Race
Team Fan Club
P.O. Box 883
Arden, NC 28704

Morgan Shepherd Fan Club
P.O. Box 1456
Stow, OH 44224-0456

Lake Speed Fan Club
P.O. Box 499
Danville, WV 25053

Jimmy Spencer Fan Club
P.O. Box 1626
Mooresville, NC 28115

Hut Stricklin Fan Club
P.O. Box 1018
Calera, AL 35040

T. W. Taylor
22909 Airpark Dr.
Petersburg, VA 23803

Dick Trickle Fan Club
8520 Arbor Lane
Wisconsin Rapids, WI 54494

Bill Venturini Fan Club
7621 Texas Trail
Boca Raton, FL 33487

Kenny Wallace Fan Club
P.O. Box 3050
Concord, NC 28025

Rusty Wallace Fan Club
P.O. Box 1616
Manchester, MO 63011

Darrell Waltrip
P.O. Box 855
Franklin, TN 37065

Michael Waltrip Fan Club
100 Arlington Place
Franklin, TN 37064

Rick Wilson Fan Club
P.O. Box 304
Mulberry, FL 33860

Indy Car

Andretti Fan Club
3310 Airport Rd.
Allentown, PA 18103

Gary Bettenhausen
4 Old Norwich Rd.
Quaker Hill, CT 06375

Robbie Buhl Fan Club
P.O. Box 780
Clarkston, MI 48347

Emerson Fittipaldi Fan Club
1524 Camino Sierra Vista
Santa Fe, NM 87501

A. J. Foyt Fan Club
509 N. Wood Drive
Richmond, IN 47374

Robbie Gordon Fan Club
P.O.Box 3453
Dana Point, CA 92629

Roberto Guerrero
P.O. Box 381
Clay, KY 42404

Arie Luyendyk Fan Club
P.O. Box 3004
Cuyahoga Falls, OH 44223

Scott Pruett Fan Club
P.O. Box 7243
Citrus Heights, CA 95621

Johnny Rutherford
716 Brighton Blvd.
Zanesville, OH 34701

Danny Sullivan Fan Club
1614 East Cliff Road
Burnsville, MN 55337

Al Unser, Jr. Fan Club
P.O. Box 24227
Indianapolis, IN 46224

NHRA

Darrell Alderman
P.O. Box 71007
Madison Heights, MI 48071

Joe Amato Racing
P.O. Box 404
Pittston, PA 18640

Shelly Anderson
1240 S. Cucamonga Ave.
Ontario, CA 91761

Walt Austin Racing
5110 184th St. East
Tacoma, WA 98446

Gary Bolger
Creasy Family Racing
3632 Washington
Lansing, IL 60438

Gordie Bonin
Smokin' Joe's Racing
P.O. Box 484
Winston-Salem, NC 27102

Michael Botherton Racing
1317 Summertime Trails
Lewisville, TX 75067

Jim Epler
310 NW 89th Circle
Vancouver, WA 98665

Eddie and Ercie Hill
4923 Lake Park Drive
Wichita Falls, TX 76302

John Force Racing
Castrol GTX
23253 E. LaPalma Ave.
Yorba Linda, CA 92687

Don Garlits
13700 SW 16th Ave.
Ocala, FL 32676

Darrell Gwynn
4850 Southwest 52nd. St.
Davie, FL 33314

Jim Head
Smokin' Joe's Racing
P.O. Box 484
Winston-Salem, NC 27102

Al Hofman
Western Auto/Slick 50
P.O. Box 346
Umatilla, FL 32784

Hoover Racing
207 Lowry Ave. North
Minneapolis, MN 55411

Tommy Johnson, Jr.
P.O. Box 1226
Ottumwa, IA 52501

Connie and Scott Kalitta
American International
Airways
804 Willow Run Airport
Ypsilanti, MI 48198

Bruce Larson
Kendall Swamp Rat
P.O. Box 71
Dauphin, PA 17018

Cory McClenathan
1194 Knollwood Circle
Anaheim, CA 92801

Ed McCulloch
44840 Viejo Dr.
Hemet, CA 92544

Rance McDaniel
4481 W. Chennault
Fresno, CA 93722

Shirley Muldowney
P.O. Box 8723
Northridge, CA 91327-8723

Kenji Okazaki
Jim Dunn Racing
840 Kallin Ave.
Long Beach, CA 90815

Mark Oswald
237-B N. Hollywood Rd.
Houma, LA 70364

Mark Pawuk
P.O. Box 535
Richfield, OH 44256-8416

Cruz Pedregon Fan Club
P.O. Box 52
Moorpark, CA 93020-0052

Don Prudhomme
19428 Londelius St.
Northridge, CA 91324

Dean Skuza
Skuza Motorsports
650 Ken Mar Industrial Parkway
Broadview Heights, OH 44147

Bob Vandergriff, Jr.
845 McFarland Rd.
Alpharetta, GA 30201

Del Worsham
P.O. Box 2486
Seal Beach, CA 90740

Jim Yates Racing
4740 Eisenhower Ave.
Alexandria, VA 22304

Source Notes

The following organizations and individuals will be referred to as "The List of Contributors" in individual chapter listings:

Public Affairs Department - Ford Motor Company - Ford Quality Care Racing - Dick Trickle, Team Lowe's Racing - Sports Marketing Enterprises - Denise W. Michaux - Brett Bodine - Junior Johnson, Exide Batteries Racing Team- Exide Motorsports - Geoff Bodine, Pennzoil Racing - Bahari' Racing - Michael Waltrip - Cohn & Wolf - Drew Brown, Ernie Irvan Fan Club - Selena King, Alumax Indy Car Race Team - Alumax Alluminum - Rick Shaffer- Stefan Johansson - Tony Bettenhausen, Ricky Craven Fan Club, Du Pont Motorsports - Performance PR Plus - Kimberly O'Brien - Jeff Gordon - Rick Hendrick, Hardee's Racing - Bob Boyles - Greg Sacks, Troy Beebe, The Ertl Company Inc. - Robert W. Eager, Mattel Inc. - Diane L. Kapantzos, Bobby Labonte Fan Club, Cruz Pedregon Motorsports - McDonald's Racing Team - Cruz Pedregon - Cory McClenathan - Jim Yates, Gene M. Snow Enterprises Inc. - Gene Snow, STP Products Inc. - Bobby Hamilton - Richard Petty, Skoal Racing - U.S. Tobacco Motorsports - Jay Wells - Rick Mast, Pennzoil Racing - Hall Racing - Jim Hall - Gil de Ferran, Diamond Ridge Motorsports - Peggy Schrock - Meineke Racing Team - Steve Grissom, Indy Car, Jasper Motorsports - Bobby Hillin, Camp & Associates Inc. - Larry M. Camp - Interstate Batteries Motorsports - Bobby Labonte, Simpson Products, Pioneer Drag Racing Team - Tom Hoover, Maxx Race Cards - Jill Santuccio, Cotter Communications - David Hart - Western Auto Racing - Shelly Anderson, King Sports Inc. - Kirk Weeks - Quaker State Racing - Hut Stricklin - Kenny Bernstein, Smokin' Joe's Racing - Rob Goodman - Jim Head - Gordie Bonin, Hormel Foods - Spam Racing - Lake Speed, National Sprint Car Hall of Fame - Thomas J. Schmeh, Roush Racing - Stephanie Smith - Ted Musgrave, Entertainment Marketing Corp. - Tide Racing - Ricky Rudd, D-R Racing Enterprises - Anna Marie Malfitana - Tim Fedewa, Motorsports Hall of Fame - Barbara Flis, Sabco Racing - Jon Sands - Kyle Petty, Kmart Texaco Havoline Racing - Newman/Haas Racing - Michael Knight - Michael Andretti - Paul Tracy, Rahal Hogan - Bobby Rahal - Raul Boesel, Kodak Film Racing - Sterling Marlin, Stavola Brothers Racing - Ketta Allen - Jeff Burton, Forsythe Racing - Thomas Soltis - Teo Fabi, Don Garlits Museum of Drag Racing, Hooters Racing, Creasy Family Racing - Gary Bolger, Fred Lorenzen - Autodreamers, International Motorsports Hall of Fame - Don Naman, PPG Indy Car World Series - Carol M. Wilkins, Phoenix Network - Kenny Koretsky, Muhleman Marketing Inc. - Bob Hice - Ricky Craven, Project Indy - Andreas Leberle - Hubert Stromberger, Team Menard - Andy Card - Arie Luyendyk - Scott Brayton, Galles Racing - Adrian Fernandez, Elliott Museum and Souvenir Centre Inc. - Cindy K. Elliott, Indy Regency Racing Eurosport - Lesley Incandela, American International Motorsports - Tammy Oberhofer - Connie Kalitta - Scott Kalitta, Kellogg Company - Jennie Donohue - Kellogg's Racing - Terry Labonte - Rick Hendrick, Miller Brewing Company - Marc Abel - Rusty Wallace, Hooters Racing - Jill Horton - Elton Sawyer, Al Hofmann, Dale Earnhardt Fan Club, Chesrown Racing, Inc - Cathy Carelli - Rick Carelli, Bobby Allison Motorsports Team, Inc. - Derrike Cope, NHRA, Valvoline Racing - Joe Amato Racing - Donna Bresnahan, Elliott Hardy Promotions - Bill Elliott, Keystone Marketing Co - Gigi D'Antonio - Tommy Houston - Mike Wallace, The Source International Inc. - Teddi Smith - Ward Burton, Dover Downs, Mid-Ohio Sports Car Course - Michelle Gajoch, Portland International Raceway, The Milwaukee Mile - Dave Austin, Bristol International Raceway, Grand Prix of Cleveland - Denny Young - IMG Motorsports, New Hampshire International Speedway - Lorraine Faford, Molson Indy - Jerry Priddle - Edelman Houston Group, Charlotte Motorsports Inc - Charlotte Motor Speedway - Eddie Gossage, Atlanta Motor Speedway, Sears Point Raceway, North Carolina Motor Speedway, Toyota Grand Prix of Long Beach and Anheuser-Busch, Inc.

Introduction

Quotations used by permission from: Stavola Brothers Racing Team, Newman/Haas Racing, Camp & Associates, Inc. - Interstate Batteries Motorsports, Tide Racing Team, Smokin' Joe's Racing, Skoal Racing, Bahari' Racing, Kellogg's Racing, STP Products Inc., MBNA Motorsports, Muhlman Marketing, Inc. - Kodiak Racing Team, Joe Gibbs Racing - McDonald's Racing Team, Rahal Hogan, Miller Genuine Draft Team Penske, Sabco Racing, Du Pont Refinish Motorsports. Source: 1995 media guides and press kits.

Chapter One

Information provided by "The List of Contributors," with special appreciation given to the following organizations: NHRA, NASCAR, and Indy Car.

Chapter Two

Information provided by "The List of Contributors," with special appreciation given to the following organization: Indy Car.

Chapter Three

Information provided by "The List of Contributors," with special appreciation given to the following organization: NASCAR.

Chapter Four

Information provided by "The List of Contributors," with special appreciation given to the following organization: Indy Car.

Chapter Five

Information provided by "The List of Contributors," with special appreciation given to the following organization: NASCAR.

Chapter Six

Information provided by Action - Action Performance Racing Collectables Club of America, Ertl, Mattell, Peachstate/GMP, Raceway Relics, Racing Champions, Revell, and White Rose/Matchbox. Additional cross-references: *AutoWeek, Beckett Racing Monthly, Collector's World of Racing, Die-Cast Digest, INDY CAR Racing Magazine, Kovels Sports Collectibles, Racing Collectibles, Sports Collectors Digest, Stock Car Racing, The Official NASCAR 95 Preview and Press Guide, Toy Collector and Price Guide, Winston Cup Illustrated*, and *Winston Cup Scene*. Also a special thank you to Dan's Dugout in Watkins Glen, NY and 7th Inning Stretch in North Syracuse, NY.

Chapter Seven

Information courtesy of AMT, Monogram, MPC, Jo Han, and Revell. Additional cross-references: *Collector's World of Racing, Die-Cast Digest, INDY CAR Racing Magazine, Kovels Sports Collectibles, Racing Collectibles, Sports Collectors Digest, Stock Car Racing, Toy Collector and Price Guide* and *Scale Auto Enthusiast*.

Chapter Eight

Information provided by Classic, Finish Line, Hi-Tech Cards, Maxx Race Cards, Pinnacle Brands Inc., Press Pass, SkyBox, Traks, Upper Deck, and Wheels Race Cards. Additional cross-references: *AutoWeek, Beckett Racing Monthly, Collector's World of Racing, Die-Cast Digest, INDY CAR Racing Magazine, Kovels Sports Collectibles, Racing Collectibles, Sports Collectors Digest, Stock Car Racing, The Official NASCAR 95 Preview and Press Guide, Toy Collector and Price Guide, Winston Cup Illustrated*, and *Winston Cup Scene*.

Chapter Nine

Information provided by International Motorsports Hall of Fame, Motorsports Hall of Fame of America, and NASCAR, Indy Car, and NHRA. Special appreciation to AMG and East Syracuse Chevrolet for their cooperation. Additional cross-references: *Autograph Collector*, *Sports Collectors Digest*.

Chapter Ten

Information provided by "The List of Contributors." Additional cross-references: *AutoWeek*, *Beckett Racing Monthly*, *Collector's World of Racing*, *Die-Cast Digest*, *INDY CAR Racing Magazine*, *Kovels Sports Collectibles*, *Racing Collectibles*, *Sports Collectors Digest*, *Stock Car Racing*, *The Official NASCAR 95 Preview and Press Guide*, *Toy Collector and Price Guide*, *Winston Cup Illustrated*, and *Winston Cup Scene*.

Chapter Eleven

Information provided by Kellogg's Racing and NASCAR. Cross-references include: *Comic Collector*, *Malloy's Sports Collectibles Value Guide*, *Collecting Toy Cars & Trucks*, *AutoWeek*, *Beckett Racing Monthly*, *Collector's World of Racing*, *Die-Cast Digest*, *INDY CAR Racing Magazine*, *Kovels Sports Collectibles*, *Racing Collectibles*, *Sports Collectors Digest*, *Stock Car Racing*, *The Official NASCAR 95 Preview and Press Guide*, *Toy Collector and Price Guide*, *Winston Cup Illustrated*, and *Winston Cup Scene*.

Chapter Thirteen

It is the duty and responsibility of every auto racing collector to purchase only those items licensed by the appropriate sanctioning body, racing team, or driver. The list of names presented in this section is not an endorsement or all inclusive. Licensing terms and conditions vary due to a number of factors, including sponsor changes. Information provided by "The List of Contributors." Additional cross-references: *AutoWeek*, *Beckett Racing Monthly*, *Collector's World of Racing*, *Die-Cast Digest*, *INDY CAR Racing Magazine*, *Kovels Sports Collectibles*, *Racing Collectibles*, *Sports Collectors Digest*, *Stock Car Racing*, *The Official NASCAR 95 Preview and Press Guide*, *Toy Collector and Price Guide*, *Winston Cup Illustrated*, and *Winston Cup Scene*.

Chapter Fourteen

Information provided by "The List of Contributors." Additional cross-references: *AutoWeek*, *Beckett Racing Monthly*, *Collector's World of Racing*, *Die-Cast Digest*, *INDY CAR Racing Magazine*, *Kovels Sports Collectibles*, *Racing Collectibles*, *Sports Collectors Digest*, *Stock Car Racing*, *The Official NASCAR 95 Preview and Press Guide*, *Toy Collector and Price Guide*, *Winston Cup Illustrated*, and *Winston Cup Scene*.

Selected Bibliography and Recommended Reading

Craft, John. *The Anatomy and Development of the Stock Car*. Osceola, WI: Motorbooks International Publishers and Wholesalers, 1993.

Gunnell, John, editor. *Race Car Flashback*. Iola, WI: Krause Publications, 1994.

Mansell, Nigel and Jeremy Shaw. *Indy Car Racing*. Osceola, WI: Motorbooks International Publishers and Wholesalers, 1993.

Malloy, Roderick A. *Malloy's Sports Collectibles Value Guide*. Radnor, PA: Wallace-Homestead Book Company, 1993.

O'Brien, Richard. *Collecting Toy Cars and Trucks*. Florence, AL: Books Americana, Inc., 1994.

Perkins, Chris. *Indy Car*. London, England: Osprey/Reed Consumer Books, Inc., 1993.

Prothero, Steve and Phil Regli. *Collectors' Guide to Sports Illustrated*. Las Vegas: P&R Publications, 1994.

Sports Illustrated. Sports Almanac and Record Book. New York: Bishop Books/Time Inc., annual.

The 1995 Information Please Sports Almanac. New York: Houghton Mifflin Company, 1995.

The World Almanac. Mahwah, NJ: Funk & Wagnalls Corporation, 1995.

Periodicals

Autograph Collector. P.O. Box 55328, Stockton, CA 95205.

AutoWeek. 1400 Woodbridge, Detroit, MI 48207-3187.

Beckett Racing Monthly. Beckett Publications, 15850 Dallas Parkway, Dallas, TX 75248.

Collector's World of Racing. Na-Tex Publishing, Inc., 5700 Hwy. 29, South Harrisburg, NC 28075.

Die-Cast Digest. Die-Cast Digest, Inc., 4920 Raccoon Valley Road, Knoxville, TN 37938.

Drag Racing. Rosecrans Corporation, 16752 Burke Lane, Huntington Beach, CA 92647.

INDY CAR Racing Magazine. ICR Publications, Inc., 617 S. 94th St., Milwaukee, WI 53214.

Kovels Sports Collectibles. Antiques Inc., 30799 Pinetree Rd., Suite 127, Pepper Pike, OH 44124.

Racing Collectibles. SportStars, Inc., P.O. Box 607785, Orlando, FL 32860-7785.

Sports Collectors Digest. Krause Publications, 700 East State Street, Iola, WI 54990-0001.

Sports Illustrated. Time Inc., Time & Life Building, Rockefeller Center, New York, NY 10020.

Stock Car Racing. 47 S. Main St., Ipswich, MA 01938.

The Official NASCAR 95 Preview and Press Guide. UMI Publications, Inc., 1135 N. *Tryon Street,* Charlotte, NC 28230.

Trading Cards. Krause Publications, 700 East State Street, Iola, WI 54990-0001.

Toy Shop. Krause Publications, 700 East State Street, Iola, WI 54990-0001.

Winston Cup Illustrated. Griggs Publishing Co., Inc., P.O. Box 500, Concord, NC 28026.

Winston Cup Scene. 128 S. Tryon St., Suite 2275, Charlotte, NC 28202

About the Author

Mark Allen Baker has been an avid collector of sports memorabilia since the mid 1960s. As a collector of racing memorabilia, Baker has taken his expertise to the airwaves on numerous national radio shows and to the pages of many prominent publications. Baker is the author of *All-Sport Autograph Guide, Complete Guide to Boxing Collectibles, Team Baseballs—The Complete Guide to Autographed Team Baseballs,* and *SCD Baseball Autograph Handbook.*

Captions for Back Cover Photographs:

Top: Ray Harroun piloted this Marmon Wasp to victory in the first Indianapolis 500 in 1911. He averaged almost 75 mph in the race, which took over 6 1/2 hours to complete. Harroun relied on a rear view mirror instead of a riding mechanic to monitor traffic. (Courtesy of IMS Museum)

Middle: Tom Hoover has been a drag racer for over 30 years and is always a threat to win on the NHRA Funny Car circuit. Here "Showtime" Hoover performs a burnout during the 1994 NHRA season. (Courtesy Tom Hoover Racing)

Bottom: The late country and western singer Marty Robbins dabbled in NASCAR racing using Mopar products to challenge Petty, Pearson and Yarborough.